Disc[illegible]

Spain

Contents

Throughout this book, we use these icons to highlight special recommendations:

The Best...
Lists for everything from bars to wildlife – to make sure you don't miss out

Don't Miss
A must-see – don't go home until you've been there

Local experts reveal their top picks and secret highlights

Detour
Special places a little off the beaten track

If you like...
Lesser-known alternatives to world-famous attractions

These icons help you quickly identify reviews in the text and on the map:

Sights

Eating

Drinking

Sleeping

Information

This edition written and researched by

Stuart Butler

Anthony Ham, Anna Kaminski, John Noble, Miles Roddis

Bren[illegible] [illegible]ington

Barcelona

Catalonia & Eastern Spain

Camino de Santiago & Basque Spain

Madrid & Around

Seville & Andalucía's Hill Towns

Granada & Andalucía's South Coast

Contents

Plan Your Trip

On the Road

Contents

On the Road

In Focus

Survival Guide

This Is Spain

From soulful flamenco and daring architecture, to delicious food and avant-garde cities, Spain could be Europe's most exotic country. Wherever you venture you'll discover a beguiling land with a mix of stirring and often curious traditions, live-for-the-moment hedonism and a willingness to embrace the future with a relentlessly adventurous spirit.

Spain's dynamic cities are temples to all that's modern and cool. Madrid, Barcelona, Valencia and Seville have become bywords for that peculiarly Spanish talent for living the good life, at full volume and all night long. At the same time, most cities promise a daytime feast of more sedate but nonetheless exceptional sites, from world-class art galleries and graceful Islamic-era monuments to *barrios* (neighbourhoods) overflowing with medieval charm, and zany Gaudí flights of fancy.

Spaniards have turned eating and drinking into an art form. From the culinary flamboyance of *pintxos* (Basque tapas) in San Sebastián to steaming seafood-infused paella served under the Valencian sunshine, Spanish food has an enviable reputation. In fact, if you really want to experience the best of Spain the way to do it is not to rush through an endless succession of tourist sights, but rather to slow the pace down and make eating the centrepiece of your day.

Spain has obvious appeal. However, some visitors feel as though visiting the country is akin to standing outside a riotous party with your nose pressed up against the glass. Spain is perhaps the best-known, least-understood country in Europe, but it's also one of the most welcoming and accessible. By taking part in the central pillars of Spanish life – like flamenco and eating customs – a trip to Spain can be a party, where having a good time is almost guaranteed.

> “Spain is a beguiling mix of stirring and often curious traditions.”

Flamenco at the Feria de Abril (p43), Seville

Spain

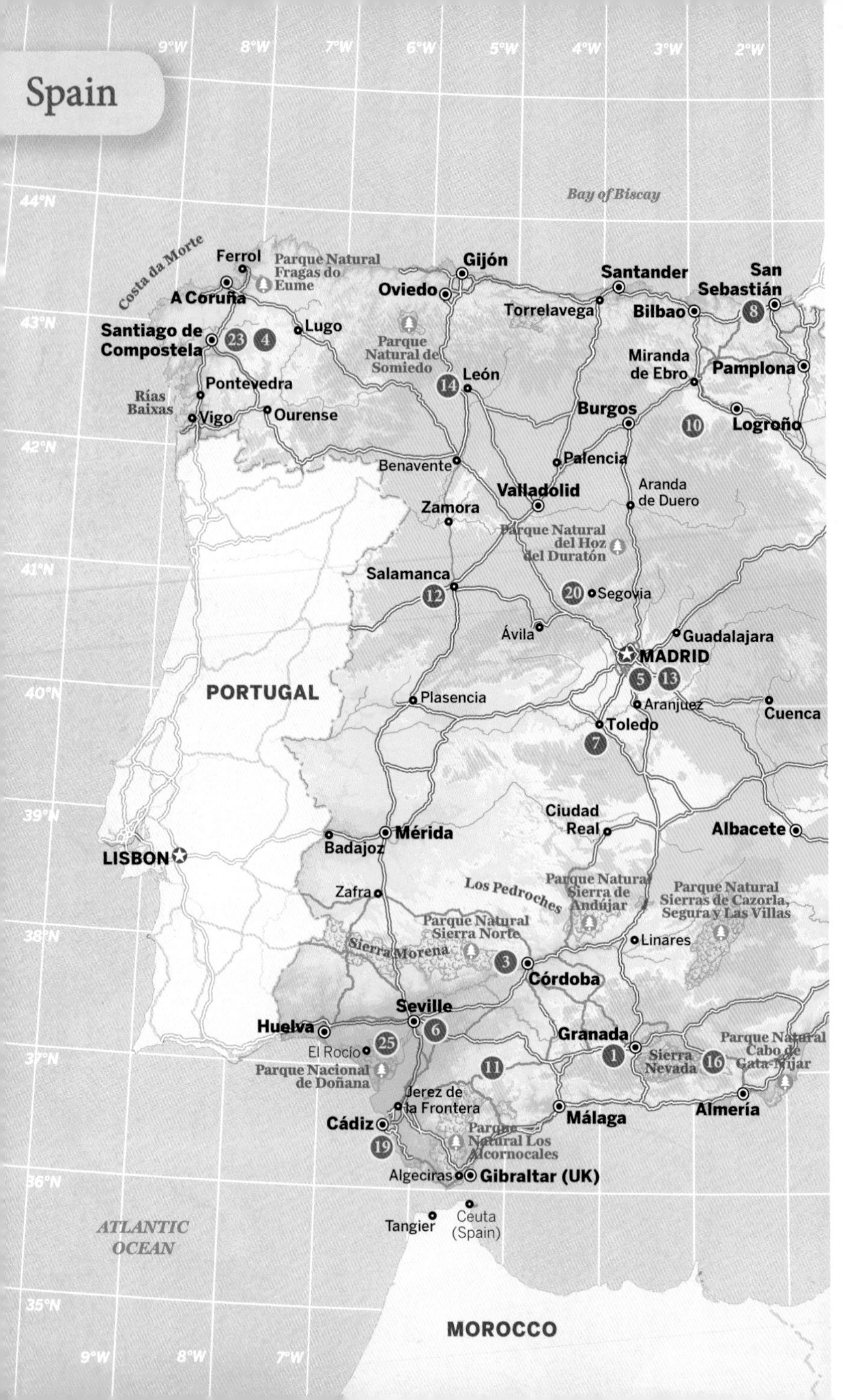

9°W
8°W
7°W
6°W
5°W
4°W
3°W
2°W
44°N
43°N
42°N
41°N
40°N
39°N
38°N
37°N
36°N
35°N
Bay of Biscay
Costa da Morte
Ferrol
A Coruña
Parque Natural Fragas do Eume
Gijón
Oviedo
Santander
Torrelavega
Bilbao
San Sebastián
Santiago de Compostela
Lugo
Parque Natural de Somiedo
León
Miranda de Ebro
Pamplona
Pontevedra
Rías Baixas
Vigo
Ourense
Burgos
Logroño
Palencia
Benavente
Valladolid
Aranda de Duero
Zamora
Parque Natural del Hoz del Duratón
Salamanca
Segovia
Ávila
Guadalajara
MADRID
PORTUGAL
Plasencia
Aranjuez
Cuenca
Toledo
Ciudad Real
Albacete
Mérida
Badajoz
LISBON
Zafra
Los Pedroches
Parque Natural Sierra de Andújar
Parque Natural Sierras de Cazorla, Segura y Las Villas
Parque Natural Sierra Norte
Sierra Morena
Linares
Córdoba
Seville
Huelva
Granada
El Rocío
Parque Nacional de Doñana
Sierra Nevada
Parque Natural Cabo de Gata-Níjar
Jerez de la Frontera
Málaga
Almería
Cádiz
Parque Natural Los Alcornocales
Algeciras
Gibraltar (UK)
Tangier
Ceuta (Spain)
ATLANTIC OCEAN
MOROCCO
1
3
4
5
6
7
8
10
11
12
13
14
16
19
20
23
25

25 Top Experiences

1. Alhambra
2. La Sagrada Família
3. Mezquita
4. Camino de Santiago
5. Madrid Nightlife
6. Easter, Seville
7. Toledo
8. Pintxos, San Sebastían
9. Ciudad de las Artes y las Ciencias
10. La Rioja Wine Country
11. Flamenco, Andalucía
12. Renaissance Salamanca
13. Madrid's Golden Art Triangle
14. León Catedral
15. Paradors
16. Sierra Nevada & Las Alpujarras
17. Hiking the Pyrenees
18. Jamón
19. Cádiz
20. Segovia
21. Michelin-Starred Restaurants
22. Costa Brava
23. Santiago de Compostela
24. Las Fallas
25. El Rocío & the Parque Nacional de Doñana

25 Spain's Top Experiences

Alhambra

The palace complex of Granada's Alhambra (p304) is close to architectural perfection. It is perhaps the most refined example of Islamic art anywhere in the world, not to mention the most enduring symbol of 800 years of Moorish rule in what was known as Al-Andalus. From afar, the Alhambra's red fortress towers dominate the Granada skyline, set against a backdrop of the Sierra Nevada's snowcapped peaks. Up close, the Alhambra's perfectly proportioned Generalife gardens complement the exquisite detail of the Palacio Nazaríes. Put simply, this is Spain's most beautiful monument.

1

SYLVAIN SONNET/GETTY IMAGES ©

2

La Sagrada Família

The Modernista brainchild of Antoni Gaudí remains a work in progress more than 80 years after its creator's death. Fanciful and profound, inspired by nature and barely restrained by a Gothic style, Barcelona's quirky temple (p76) soars skyward with a playful majesty. The improbable angles and departures from architectural convention will have you shaking your head in disbelief, but the detail of the decorative flourishes are worth studying for hours.

Mezquita

A church that became a mosque before reverting to a church, Córdoba's Mezquita (p270) charts the evolution of western and Islamic architecture over a 1000-year trajectory. Its most innovative features include some early horseshoe arches, an intricate mihrab, and a veritable forest of 856 columns, many of them recycled from Roman ruins. The sheer scale of the Mezquita reflects Córdoba's erstwhile power as the most cultured city in 10th-century Europe. It was also inspiration for even greater buildings to come, most notably in Seville and Granada.

3

The Best... Post-Islamic Architectural Wonders

LA SAGRADA FAMÍLIA, BARCELONA
Gaudí's masterpiece and icon of Barcelona in all its Modernista splendour. (p76)

MUSEO GUGGENHEIM, BILBAO
The astonishing Frank Gehry–designed symbol of the new Bilbao. (p153)

CIUDAD DE LAS ARTES Y LAS CIENCIAS, VALENCIA
Valencia's showpiece avant-garde complex by world-renowned local architect Santiago Calatrava. (p128)

BAEZA, ANDALUCÍA
Andalucía's finest Renaissance collection, tucked away in little-visited Jaén province. (p322)

The Best... Nightlife

MADRID
Nights that never seem to end, with bars, clubs and great live music. (p214)

VALENCIA
Nights in the old quarter of Barrio del Carmen are famous throughout Spain. (p130)

SITGES
Where Barcelona comes to let its hair down; a huge gay scene and unforgettable Carnaval. (p107)

SALAMANCA
Feel-good nights beneath floodlit Renaissance buildings. (p233)

©MICHI B./GETTY IMAGES ©

Camino de Santiago

Every year, tens of thousands of pilgrims and walkers with all manner of motivations set out to walk across northern Spain. Their destination, Santiago de Compostela (p174), is a place of untold significance for Christians, but the appeal of this epic walk goes far beyond the religious. With numerous routes across the north, there is no finer way to get under Spain's skin and experience the pleasures and caprices of its natural world. Even completing one small stage will leave you with a lifetime of impressions.

INGOLF POMPE/GETTY IMAGES ©

Madrid Nightlife

Madrid is not the only European city with nightlife, but few can match its intensity. As Ernest Hemingway said, 'Nobody goes to bed in Madrid until they have killed the night'. There are wall-to-wall bars, small clubs, live venues and mega-clubs beloved by A-list celebrities across the city, with unimaginable variety. But it's in Huertas, Malasaña, Chueca and La Latina that you'll really understand what we're talking about (p214). Revellers on Calle de la Cava Baja, La Latina

The Best... Islamic Splendour

ALHAMBRA, GRANADA
The priceless jewel in Andalucía's crown and the symbol of Al-Andalus. (p304)

MEZQUITA, CÓRDOBA
Perfection and harmony in this glorious early-Islamic mosque. (p270)

ALCÁZAR, SEVILLE
Pleasure palace with exquisite architecture and gardens. (p254)

ALJAFERÍA, ZARAGOZA
A rare, glittering outpost of Al-Andalus in the north. (p119)

6 Easter in Seville

Return to Spain's medieval Christian roots and join Seville's masses for the dramatic Easter celebration of Semana Santa (p43).Elaborate *pasos* (figures) of Christ and the Virgin Mary are paraded around the city to the emotive acclaim of the populace; the most prestigious procession is the *madrugada* (early hours) of Good Friday. It's an unforgettable experience, an exotic and utterly compelling fusion of pageantry, solemnity and deep religious faith. There are processions across Spain, but none on the scale of Seville.

Penitents parade during Semana Santa in Seville

RELIGIOUS IMAGES/UIG/GETTY IMAGES ©

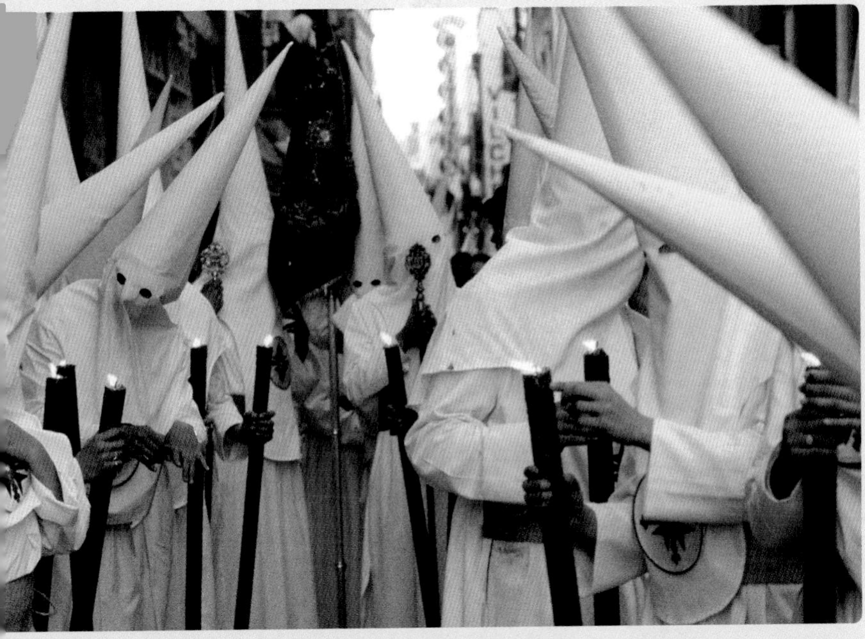

GUILLERMO FLORES/GETTY IMAGES ©

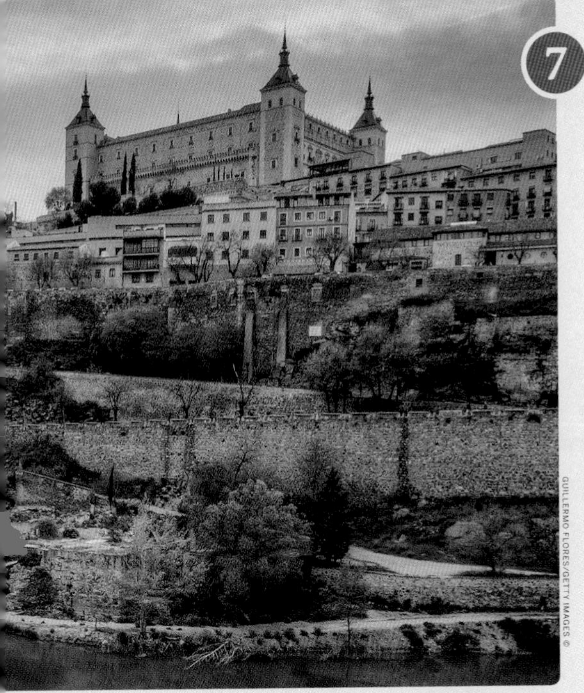

7 Three Cultures in Toledo

Symbolic home to Spain's Catholic Church and the army, the medieval core of Toledo (p224) is an extraordinary piece of world heritage. Known as 'the city of the three cultures' (where Muslims, Jews and Christians once rubbed shoulders), it remains a fascinating labyrinth today with former mosques, synagogues and churches; the latter are still very much in use and the cathedral is one of Spain's most imposing. Given Toledo's proximity to Madrid, the city can get overrun with day-trippers. Stay overnight – that's when Toledo really comes into its own. Alcázar, Toledo

Pintxos in San Sebastián

8

Chefs here have turned bar snacks into an art form. Sometimes called 'high cuisine in miniature', *pintxos* (Basque tapas) are piles of flavour often mounted on a slice of baguette. As you step into any bar in central San Sebastián (p160), the choice lined up along the counter will leave first-time visitors gasping. In short, this is Spain's most memorable eating experience.

9

Ciudad de las Artes y las Ciencias

Created by Santiago Calatrava, one of the nation's star architects, the City of Arts and Sciences (p128) in Valencia has helped transform Spain's third-largest city into one of the country's most vibrant. A daring and visually stunning piece of contemporary architecture, the complex includes a state-of-the-art theatre (Palau de les Arts Reina Sofía), grand aquarium (Oceanogràfic), planetarium (Hemisfèric) and science museum (Museo de las Ciencias Príncipe Felipe). Palau de les Arts Reina Sofía (left) and the Hemisfèric light up the Valencia skyline

La Rioja Wine Country

La Rioja (p162) is the sort of place where you could spend weeks meandering along quiet roads in search of the finest drop. Bodegas offering wine-tastings and picturesque villages that shelter excellent wine museums are the mainstay in this region. The Frank Gehry–designed Hotel Marqués de Riscal (p164), close to Elciego, has been likened to Bilbao's Guggenheim in architectural scale and ambition, and has become the elite centre for wine tourism in the region.

10

The Best... Places for Spanish Food

OLD TOWN, SAN SEBASTIÁN
Spain's culinary capital, with more Michelin stars than Paris. (p159)

BARCELONA
Home of Catalonia's legendary cuisine, blending the traditional with the innovative. (p85)

LA LATINA, MADRID
The best tapas from around Spain in one medieval, inner-city neighbourhood. (p205)

VALENCIA
The birthplace of paella and still the place to find the most authentic version. (p129)

SEVILLE
Andalucía's tapas obsession, heart and soul. (p261)

Flamenco in Andalucía

Who needs rock 'n' roll? Like all great anguished music, flamenco has the power to lift you out of the doldrums and stir your soul. It's as if by sharing in the pain of innumerable generations you open a door to a secret world of musical ghosts and ancient Andalucian spirits. On the other side of the coin, flamenco culture can also be surprisingly jolly and tongue-in-cheek. There's only one proviso: you have to hear it live, preferably in its Seville-Jerez-Cádiz heartland.

11

The Best... Most Authentic Flamenco

PEÑA LA PERLA, CÁDIZ
Upbeat *alegrías* performed by equally upbeat local residents. (p287)

CASA DE LA MEMORIA DE AL-ANDALUS, SEVILLE
The most intimate of the many nightly flamenco shows. (p264)

EL LAGÁ TIO PARRILLA, JEREZ
In true Jerez fashion, shows end with a rousing, fast-paced *bulería*. (p277)

PEÑA DE LA PLATERÍA, GRANADA
Highly ornamental *granainas* in Spain's oldest *peña* (club). (p305)

CORRAL DE LA MORERÍA, MADRID
The capital's best flamenco can be heard here. (p217)

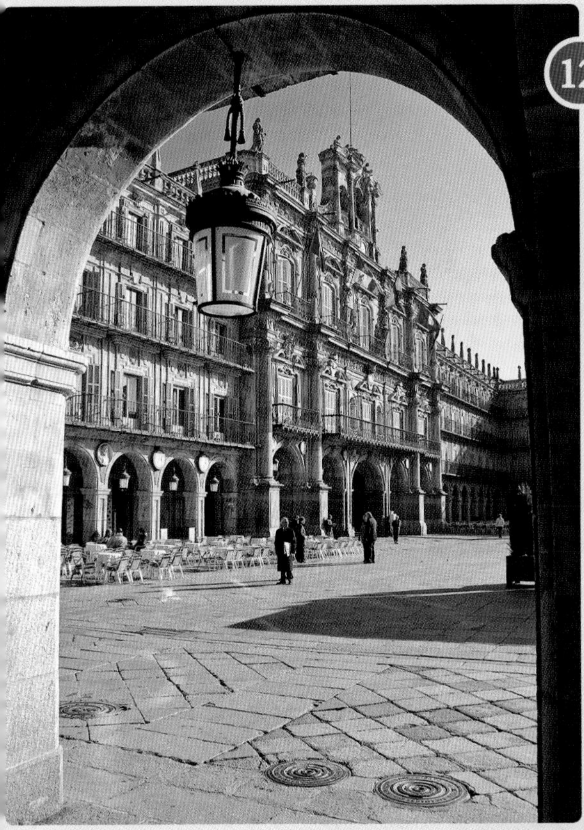

12 Renaissance Salamanca

Luminous when floodlit, the elegant central square of Salamanca, the Plaza Mayor (p234), is possibly the most attractive in all of Spain. It is just one of many highlights in a city whose architectural splendour has few peers. Salamanca is home to one of Europe's oldest and most prestigious universities, so student revelry also lights up the nights. It's this combination of grandeur and energy that makes so many people call Salamanca their favourite city in Spain. Plaza Mayor

13 Madrid's Golden Art Triangle

Madrid may lack architectural landmarks, but it more than compensates with an extraordinary collection of art galleries. Housing works by Goya, Velázquez, El Greco and masters from across Europe, the showpiece is the Museo del Prado (p206), but also within a short stroll are the Centro de Arte Reina Sofía (p200), showcasing Picasso's *Guernica,* plus works by Dalí and Miró, and the Museo Thyssen-Bornemisza (p201), which carries all the big names spanning centuries. Centro de Arte Reina Sofía, by architects José Luis Iñiguez de Onzoño, Antonio Vázquez de Castro and Ian Ritchie

JEAN-PIERRE LESCOURRET/GETTY IMAGES ©

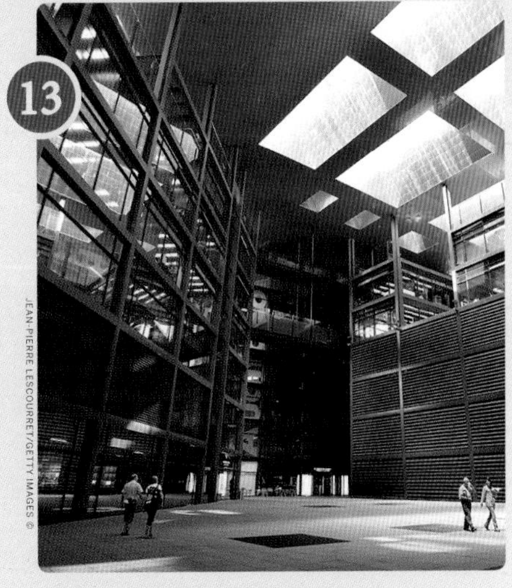

14

León Catedral

With its soaring towers, flying buttresses and an interior that will simply take your breath away, León's fabulous cathedral (p171) is truly one of the Gothic masterpieces of Spain. Add to this a large student population who flood the streets with night-time revelry, an attractive old quarter and a flurry of other sights and monuments and it becomes clear that León is, above all else, a fantastic place to experience everyday life in the heart and soul of Spain.

DAVID C TOMLINSON/GETTY IMAGES ©

15

Staying in a Beautiful Parador

Sleeping like a king has never been easier than in Spain's state-run chain of *paradores* – often palatial, always supremely comfortable former castles, palaces, monasteries and convents. Ranking among Europe's most atmospheric sleeping experiences, many are sited on prime real estate (like inside the grounds of Granada's Alhambra) and prices are more reasonable than you might imagine, especially if you book online and far in advance.

Sierra Nevada & Las Alpujarras

Dominated by the Mulhacén (3479m), mainland Spain's highest peak, the Sierra Nevada makes a stunning backdrop to the city of Granada. Skiing in winter and hiking in summer can be mixed with exploration of the fascinating villages of Las Alpujarras (p319), arguably Andalucía's most engaging collection of *pueblos blancos* (white villages). One of the last outposts of Moorish settlement in Spain, the hamlets of Las Alpujarras resemble North Africa, set oasis-like amid the woodlands and deep ravines for which the region is renowned. Village of Pampaneira (p320), Sierra Nevada

16

The Best... Village Escapes

LAS ALPUJARRAS
The villages of these valleys are an organic blend of man-made and natural beauty. (p319)

AÍNSA
Medieval stone village in the Pyrenean foothills. (p124)

ARCOS DE LA FRONTERA
The poster child for Andalucía's white hill villages. (p271)

EL ROCÍO
A guns-at-noon atmosphere, a spectacular festival and a wild hinterland. (p285)

The Best...
Areas for Hiking

SIERRA NEVADA
Extraordinary scenery and wildlife, and mainland Spain's highest terrain. (p319)

PARC NACIONAL DE ORDESA Y MONTE PERDIDO
Where the Pyrenees truly take your breath away. (p123)

PICOS DE EUROPA
Magnificent mountain scenery and wild bears. (p173)

LAS ALPUJARRAS
Rural Andalucía at its best amid gorgeous valleys. (p319)

Hiking the Pyrenees

Spain is a walker's destination of exceptional variety, but we reckon the Pyrenees offer the most special hiking country. The Parque Nacional de Ordesa y Monte Perdido (p123) is one of the high points (pun intended) of the Pyrenees. Centred on Monte Perdido (3348m), it offers plenty of opportunities for tough excursions along great rock walls and glacial cirques, accompanied by the occasional chamois. Even better, there are limits on the number of people allowed in the park at any one time.

Left: Flowers blooming in the Pyrenees; Above: Hiking around Huesca

Sample the Best Jamón

18

Jamón (cured ham) is Spain's culinary constant and one of the few things that unite the country. If there is a national dish, this is it, more so even than paella. Nearly every bar and restaurant in Spain has at least one *jamón* on the go at any one time, strapped into a cradle-like frame called a *jamonera*. Wafer-thin slices of the best *jamón* (known as *jamón ibérico de bellota,* although there are many different kinds) is simplicity itself and our idea of Spanish culinary heaven.

WALTER BIBIKOW/GETTY IMAGES ©

Hanging out in Cádiz

19

Cádiz (p284) has a laid-back, live for the present feel. Locals party the sweltering summer nights away in the old town squares and waterfront bars, while Carnaval celebrations are renowned throughout the country for their fun and fervour. The city itself has charm as well – fascinating historical monuments, snaking whitewashed lanes, panoramic viewpoints and a cathedral square as beautiful as any in Spain.

View from Torre Tavira towards the Catedral (p284), Cádiz

Segovia

One of the most beautiful medium-sized towns in Spain, Segovia has the usual glittering array of Castilian churches and a fine location, strung out along a ridge against a backdrop of often snowcapped mountains. But two buildings of legend set Segovia apart. Its multiturreted Alcázar (p237) provided the inspiration for Walt Disney's castle confection, while a gigantic but elegant Roman aqueduct (p236) of granite blocks (held together by not a drop of mortar) has stood the test of time in the heart of town for almost 2000 years. Alcázar, Segovia

20

The Best... Art Galleries

MUSEO DEL PRADO, MADRID
World-class gallery with Goya, Velázquez and the pick of European masters. (p206)

CENTRO DE ARTE REINA SOFÍA, MADRID
Stunning contemporary art gallery including Dalí, Miró and Picasso's *Guernica*. (p200)

MUSEO PICASSO MÁLAGA
More than 200 Picasso works in a stunningly converted palace in the city of his birth. (p309)

TEATRE-MUSEU DALÍ, FIGUERES
Salvador Dalí's weird-and-wonderful legacy that's so much more than a museum. (p117)

21 A Galaxy of Michelin Stars

Spanish cuisine is quite simply fantastic. Few countries on Earth can offer such diversity, such innovative chefs and a general public who are so passionate about eating. You can eat phenomonally well almost anywhere, but at least once in your trip book a table (you'll need to do this quite some time in advance) at one of Spain's multi-Michelin-star gastronomic temples – some of which are considered among the best restaurants in the world.

22 Costa Brava

Easily accessible by air and land from the rest of Europe, and filled with villages and beaches of the kind that spawned northern Europe's summer obsession with the Spanish coast, the Costa Brava in Catalonia is one of our favourite corners of the Mediterranean. Beyond this, however, the spirit of Salvador Dalí lends personality and studied eccentricity to the Costa Brava experience, from his one-time home in Port Lligat (p115) near Cadaqués to Dalí-centric sites in Figueres (p116) and Castell de Púbol (p118). Calella de Palafrugell (p115), Costa Brava

Santiago de Compostela

As the reputed final resting place of St James, one of the 12 Apostles, Santiago de Compostela (p174) in Galicia in Spain's far northwest resonates with the sacred like nowhere else in the country. Its splendid cathedral (p178) is the suitably extravagant objective of pilgrims traversing the Camino de Santiago across northern Spain. Look beyond the cathedral and you'll find a smattering of other gilt-edged monuments and an eating culture that is Galicia in a nutshell.

Catedral de Santiago de Compostela

23

The Best... Beaches

COSTA BRAVA
Cliffs, coves, forests and a turquoise sea combine to make pure oceanic poetry. (p114)

COSTA DA MORTE, GALICIA
Wild and windswept Atlantic shore with beautiful villages. (p180)

PLAYA DE LA CONCHA, SAN SEBASTIÁN
Arguably the most perfect city beach in Europe. (p155)

CABO DE GATO
The Mediterranean before the tourist invasion. (p323)

TARIFA & THE COSTA DE LA LUZ
World-class windsurfing and miles of near-pristine beaches. (p313)

Las Fallas

Spain's noisiest festival is also one of its most spectacular. Taking place every March in Valencia, Las Fallas (p130) is an explosive fiesta of fireworks, music and bonfires that light up the sky for almost a week. But this is more than just noise. A festival with deep cultural roots and great inventiveness, Las Fallas sees each Valencia neighbourhood try to outdo the others in elaborate wood and papier-mâché sculptures that go up in flames in an extraordinary climax.

24

The Best... Fiestas

LAS FALLAS, VALENCIA
Possibly the country's noisiest festival, Las Fallas is an explosion of fireworks and burning effigies. (p130)

FERIA DE ABRIL, SEVILLE
Eating, drinking, dressing up (both you and your horse) and lots and lots of flamenco. (p43)

LOS SANFERMINES, PAMPLONA
Run, very fast, away from a pack of marauding bulls. (p167)

CARNAVAL, ANDALUCÍA
Cádiz puts on its fancy dress clothes for the most riotous Carnaval celebration in Spain. (p42)

25

El Rocío & the Parque Nacional de Doñana

With sandy streets and a bejewelled church, hoof prints, hitching posts and hat-clad honchos, El Rocío is like something out of a Clint Eastwood film. You might be forgiven for thinking you'd found the most exotic place in Spain, but that honour goes instead to the Parque Nacional de Doñana (p285) surrounding El Rocío. Here, flocks of flamingos tinge the skies pink, herds of deer and boar flit between the trees and the Iberian lynx, the world's rarest big cat, slinks ever closer to extinction.

Spain's Top Itineraries

Barcelona & Around Eastern Highlights

5 DAYS

Spain's most exciting city delivers on all fronts. Once you're done with Barcelona, this itinerary whips you through Roman Spain in Tarragona, Islamic marvels in Zaragoza and ends with Girona's huddle of ancient streets.

1 Barcelona (p51)

In a couple of rushed days you can just about tick off the main sites in Barcelona. Start your explorations of the city at **La Sagrada Família**, Gaudí's unfinished masterpiece. See more of his Modernista madness at the nearby **Casa Batiló**, **La Pedrera** and the **Parc Güell**. On day two explore the medieval maze of the **Barri Gòtic** and Barcelona's most famous street, **La Rambla**. If time permits make a dash to the zany collection of art hanging in the **Museu Picasso**.

BARCELONA ➔ TARRAGONA

🚗 **1¼ hrs** Along AP7 🚌 **1½ hrs** Around 16 per day

2 Tarragona (p108)

Lorded over by a dominating **Cathedral**, Tarragona is often bypassed by tourists, but its tangle of medieval streets hide more than just a house of God. At the bottom of the old town stand reminders of Roman Tarragona: a breathtaking **Amfiteatre Romà**, the fascinating **Pretori i Circ Romans** and **Fòrum Romà**, and the ever-rewarding **Museu Nacional Arqueològic de Tarragona**.

TARRAGONA ➔ ZARAGOZA

🚗 **2½ hrs** Along AP2 🚌 **1¼ hrs** Numerous per day

3 Zaragoza (p118)

One of the most interesting yet overlooked cities in Spain, Zaragoza has a lot going for it. Wonderful Islamic palaces – tick, heavy hitting Christian shrines – tick, remarkable Roman ruins – tick, glut of great museums – tick, superb restaurants – tick. You visiting it on this tour – oh yes!

ZARAGOZA ➔ GIRONA

🚗 **3½ hrs** Along the AP2 & AP7 🚌 **3¼ hrs** Two per day via Barcelona

4 Girona (p111)

The wobbly medieval streets of Girona are filled with gems, including the billowing baroque facade of the **Cathedral**, a fascinating **Jewish quarter**, some beautiful gardens and delicious places to eat.

Basílica de Nuestra Señora del Pilar (p118), Zaragoza
HUGHES HERVÉ/GETTY IMAGES ©

Barcelona to Granada
The Big Hitters

Even in five days, you can get a taste of what makes Spain special. Spend a couple of days in Barcelona, take a high-speed train to Madrid for one night, then a train or car, via magnificent Toledo, to Granada for two more nights.

1 Barcelona (p51)

There's no better introduction to Spain than strolling along **La Rambla**, then branching out into the 15th-century **Barri Gòtic** with its fine monuments, lovely plazas and medieval streetscape. You could pause in the **Museu Picasso**, but make sure you leave time for the city's astonishing collection of works left by Antoni Gaudí: **La Sagrada Família** is one of Spain's most extraordinary buildings, followed closely by **Casa Batlló**, **La Pedrera** and **Park Güell**.

BARCELONA ➔ MADRID

Six hours Along the A2 via Zaragoza **Three hours** From Barcelona's Estació Sants to Madrid's Puerta de Atocha.

2 Madrid (p196)

With just a day in the Spanish capital, head for the **Museo del Prado** with its masterpieces by Velázquez, Goya and a host of European masters, followed by a visit to the nearby **Centro de Arte Reina Sofía**. For some quiet down time, immerse yourself in the oasis that is the **Parque del Buen Retiro**. After dark skip from bar to bar in **La Latina**, a *barrio* famous for its delicious tapas varieties.

MADRID ➔ TOLEDO

One hour Along AP41 **30 min** From Madrid's Puerta de Atocha

3 Toledo (p224)

The Rome of Spain, the labyrinth of narrow streets and plazas of Toledo are crammed with Christian, Jewish and Islamic monuments. Check out the dominating **Catedral de Toledo**, the **Sinagoga del Tránsito** and the **Mezquita del Cristo de la Luz**.

TOLEDO ➔ GRANADA

4¼ hrs Along the A4 and A44 **5½ hrs** via Madrid

4 Granada (p300)

Explore the **Albayzín**, Granada's one-time Islamic quarter with its whitewashed tangle of laneways. Also don't miss the gilded **La Capilla Real**, the city's extravagant Christian counterpoint to the dominant Islamic splendour. For food, Granada has some of Spain's most generous tapas and there are excellent places for flamenco. But it's the **Alhambra**, arguably Spain's most beautiful collection of buildings, that you came so far to see.

Tapas bar, Madrid

10 DAYS

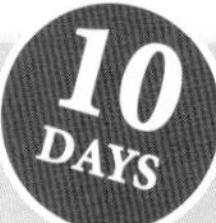

Madrid to Santiago de Compostela
Spain's Beguiling North

If your holiday extends to 10 days, you can (with your own wheels) range through Spain's Castilian heartland, visit San Sebastián, then follow the stunning northern coast to Galicia. Your starting point is the nation's capital, Madrid.

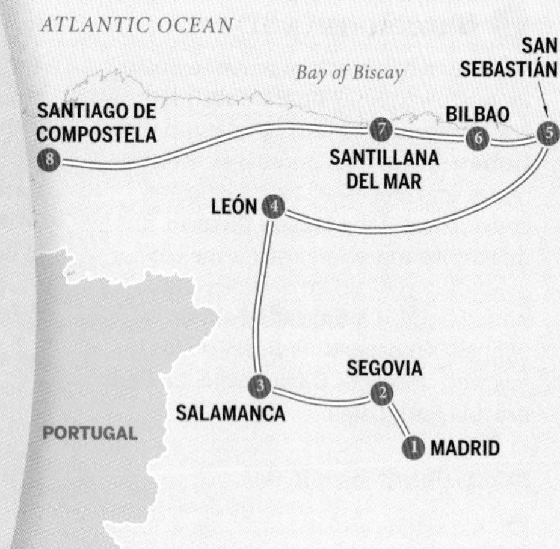

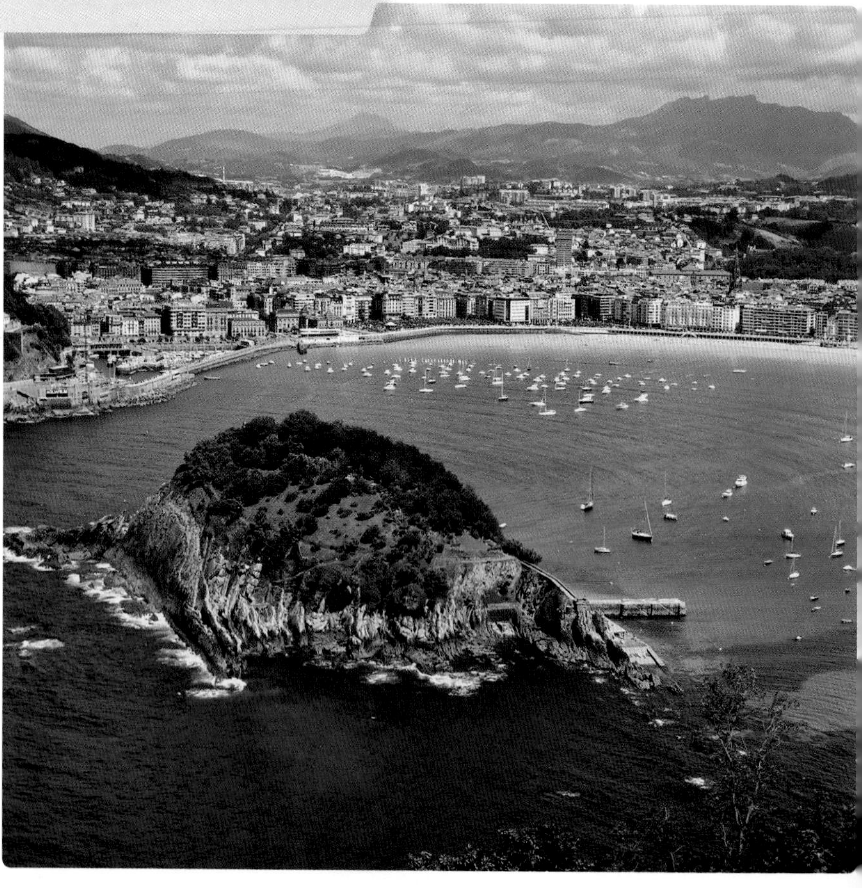

❶ Madrid (p196)

Whip about the main sights, taking in the breathtaking art of the **Museo Thyssen-Bornemisza** and then continuing on to the **Museo del Prado**, one of the world's most renowned art galleries. Have an evening drink at **Plaza de Santa Ana**, followed by a tapas crawl around the bars of **La Latina**.

MADRID ➔ SEGOVIA

One hour Along the A6 and AP 61 **30 min** From Madrid's Chamartín station.

❷ Segovia (p236)

One of Spain's most engaging inland towns, Segovia has a splendid Roman-era **aqueduct** and the whimsical **Alcázar**. In between are delightful streets, fine restaurants, sweeping views and architectural highlights.

SEGOVIA ➔ SALAMANCA

Two hours Along the AP6 and AP51 **2¾ hours** Two buses daily.

❸ Salamanca (p233)

Salamanca's exceptional architecture finds glorious expression in the **Plaza Mayor**, arguably Spain's most beautiful square. The city is at its floodlit best at night, with irresistible energy flowing through the streets.

SALAMANCA ➔ LEÓN

2½ hours Along the A66 and the N630.

❹ León (p171)

Nothing can prepare you for the first time you step inside Leon's **cathedral**, where masses of stained-glass windows bathe the interior in ethereal light. The **Real Basílica de San Isidro** is also splendid, as is the charming old quarter, **Barrio Húmedo**.

Playa de la Concha (p155), San Sebastián
ANGUS OBORN/GETTY IMAGES ©

LEÓN ➔ SAN SEBASTIÁN

Four hours On the A231 and AP1 **Five hours**

❺ San Sebastián (p155)

Graceful architecture and the postcard-perfect **Playa de la Concha** are a stunning combination best viewed from atop **Monte Igueldo**. San Sebastián is also known for its mind-blowing tapas and Michelin-starred restaurants, such as **Arzak**.

SAN SEBASTIÁN ➔ BILBAO

One hour Along AP8

❻ Bilbao (p148)

Best known for the **Museo Guggenheim**, Bilbao has plenty more to offer, including the excellent **Museo de Bellas Artes**, the **Euskal Museoa**, fine riverside walks and superb food.

BILBAO ➔ SANTILLANA DEL MAR

1½ hours Along the A8

❼ Santillana del Mar (p162)

All along the coast of Cantabria and Asturias, isolated coves conceal picturesque fishing villages, but if you can linger in just one place, pass the night in **Santillana del Mar**, a timeless village with an idyllic setting.

SANTILLANA DEL MAR ➔ SANTIAGO DE COMPOSTELA

Five hours On the E70 or **six hours** on the A6

❽ Santiago de Compostela (p174)

Santiago de Compostela is a suitably epic last stop on your journey through northern Spain. Its **cathedral** is the city's soaring centrepiece, but the city radiating out from here is a microcosm of urban Spain.

Seville to Valencia
Andalucía & the Mediterranean

Ten days in Spain just about enables you to see the best of Andalucía, including magnificent cities and hilltop villages, as well as get a taste of the Spanish Mediterranean. You'll need a car for Andalucía. Consider flying from Granada to Valencia to save a long slog behind the wheel.

1 Seville (p254)

Seville is Andalucía in a nutshell. The **Barrio de Santa Cruz** is all dressed in white, there are exquisite Islamic monuments such as the **Alcázar**, and the **cathedral** and **Giralda** are superb. Throw in some of Spain's best tapas and a thriving flamenco scene, and you'll find two days here is barely enough.

SEVILLE ➔ ARCOS DE LA FRONTERA

One hour Along the AP4 and A382 **Two hours** Two per day.

2 Arcos de la Frontera (p271)

You've seen the pictures of brilliantly white villages clinging precariously to an Andalucian hilltop. There are many candidates throughout the region, but none surpasses Arcos de la Frontera. Breathtaking from a distance and enchanting within, this is one place where the reality is every bit as beautiful as you imagined.

ARCOS DE LA FRONTERA ➔ RONDA

One hour Along the A384 and A374 **Two hours** Three per day

3 Ronda (p281)

Clifftop Ronda is another dreamy Andalucian *pueblo blanco* (white village). The views from the **Puente Nuevo** are exceptional, but turn around to explore the town and you'll unearth Arab-era baths, fine churches, Spain's most beautiful bullring and ancient walls.

RONDA ➔ CÓRDOBA

2¾ hours Along the A45 **Two hours**

Puente Nuevo, Ronda

4 Córdoba (p266)

One of the most celebrated landmarks of world Islamic architecture, Córdoba's **Mezquita** should not be missed; its forest of striped horseshoe arches are aesthetic harmony wrought in stone. The **Judería**, gardens of the **Alcázar** and **Arab baths** are other highlights, as are Córdoba's restaurants and festivals.

CÓRDOBA ➔ GRANADA

2¼ hours Along the A45 and A92 **Four hours** Change in Bobadilla

5 Granada (p300)

If Córdoba represents Andalucía's early glories, Granada is its glittering highpoint. The **Alhambra**, arguably the most important cultural site in Spain, is blessed with the **Palacio Nazaríes** and **Generalife** gardens. There are fine views of the Alhambra and the Sierra Nevada from across the valley in the **Albayzín**.

GRANADA ➔ VALENCIA

Five hours Along the A7 **Seven hours**

6 Valencia (p125)

Valencia has many strings to its bow. Its most eye-catching attraction is the futuristic **Ciudad de las Artes y las Ciencias**, but the **Cathedral**, **La Lonja** and beachside restaurants will more than fill your day here. The night belongs to the historic **Barrio del Carmen**.

Barcelona to Cádiz
The Best of Spain

Two weeks will allow you to race around the main urban highlights of the country, taking in a little bit of everything from Barcelona style and tapas on the seashore in San Sebastián, to Madrid art galleries and flamenco in Seville. You can cover this route by car or train but be prepared for a couple of fairly long days of travel.

❶ Barcelona (p51)

Two days is the absolute minimum time to tick off the highlights of Barcelona. You should make a beeline straight for Gaudí's extraordinary **La Sagrada Família**, but also leave time for **Park Güell** as well as the **Museu Picasso**, the **Barri Gòtic** and the mouth-watering range of restaurants and bars.

BARCELONA ➜ PARC NACIONAL DE ORDESA Y MONTE PERDIDO

Four hours along the A2 and A22 to Torla

❷ Parc Nacional de Ordesa y Monte Perdido (p123)

The magnificent Pyrenees mountains, which stand like soldiers between Spain and France, are full of beautiful, flower-filled valleys and bleak, rocky peaks and escarpments, but if we had to pick just one place in which to break the journey between Barcelona and San Sebastián it would be the **Parc Nacional de Ordesa y Monte Perdido**. You should plan on a minimum of at least two nights in and around the park.

PARC NACIONAL DE ORDESA Y MONTE PERDIDO ➜ SAN SEBASTIÁN

3½ hours Along the N240 and A15

❸ San Sebastián (p155)

San Sebastián offers one of the finest urban beaches in Europe, a hedonistic summer lifestyle and is, according to some of the world's top chefs, the culinary capital of the planet.

SAN SEBASTIÁN ➜ SEGOVIA

4½ hours Along the E5 via Burgos **4¾ hours**

❹ Segovia (p236)

Segovia might have the castle Sleeping Beauty dreamt about, as well as a Roman aqueduct that must have been created by someone who could dream big, but this Unesco-protected city remains somewhat off the standard Spanish tourist circuit, which makes a stop here all the more rewarding.

SEGOVIA ➜ MADRID

1¼ hours Along the AP6 **30 minutes to two hours** Arrives at Madrid Puerta de Atocha station.

Cathedral (p237), Segovia
CRAIG PERSHOUSE/GETTYIMAGES ©

5 Madrid (p196)

The capital of Spain has art galleries and museums to rival any European capital and a nightlife scene that the rest of the world can only stand back and stare at in awe. You should allow at least two days for Madrid.

MADRID ➔ GRANADA

🚗 **4¼ hours** Along the A15 🚌 **4½ hours** Departs Madrid Chamartín station

6 Granada (p300)

The pinnacle of Islamic architecture in Europe is to be found in the beautiful city of Granada. The **Alhambra** might well be the most sublime sight in Spain but Granada is a city with more than one trick up its sleeve. The cobblestone streets of the **Albayzín**, or old town, are straight out of North Africa and the city's teashops and boutiques will keep you enthralled for hours. If time allows, tack on an extra couple of days for the nearby **Sierra Nevada** mountains and the snow-drop villages of **Las Alpujarras**.

GRANADA ➔ SEVILLE

🚗 **2¾ hours** Along the A92 🚌 **Three hours**

7 Seville (p254)

Put simply, Seville puts the exotic into Spain. This passionate city is the home of the soul-ripping sound of flamenco, the sombre and spectacular **Semana Santa** processions, the glory and gore of bull-fighting, and the jolly relief of the **Feria de Abril**. The divine **Alcázar** and near-perfect **Giralda** point to the majesty of Seville's Moorish past and the enormous **cathedral** will simply blow you away.

SEVILLE ➔ CÁDIZ

🚗 **1½ hours** Along the AP4 🚌 **Two hours**

8 Cádiz (p284)

Surrounded on three sides by water, Cádiz's lovely buildings have a languid waterfront atmosphere, while its tightly packed white-walled streets pulse with life. Highlights include the **cathedral** with stunning views from its tower and signposts to what may be Europe's oldest continuously inhabited city.

Spain Month by Month

Top Events

- **Semana Santa (Holy Week)**, usually March or April
- **Las Fallas**, March
- **Bienal de Flamenco**, September
- **Carnaval**, February or March
- **Feria de Abril**, April

January

Three Kings

The Día de los Reyes Magos (Three Kings' Day), or simply Reyes, on 6 January, is the most important day on a Spanish kid's calendar. The evening before, three local politicians dress up as the three wise men and lead a sweet-distributing frenzy of Cabalgata de Reyes through the centre of most towns.

February

Life's a Carnaval

Riotously fun Carnaval, ending on the Tuesday 47 days before Easter Sunday, involves fancy-dress parades and festivities. It's wildest in Cádiz, Sitges and Ciudad Rodrigo.

Return to the Middle Ages

In one of Spain's coldest corners, Teruel's inhabitants don their medieval finery and step back to the Middle Ages with markets, food stalls and a re-enactment of a local lovers' legend during the Fiesta Medieval.

Contemporary Art Fair

One of Europe's biggest celebrations of contemporary art, Madrid's Feria Internacional de Arte Contemporánea (Arco) draws gallery reps and exhibitors from all over the world. It's a thrilling counterpoint to the old masters on display year-round in galleries across the capital.

March

Las Fallas

The extraordinary festival of Las Fallas consists of several days of all-night dancing and drinking, first-class fireworks and processions

April Feria de Abril

from 15 to 19 March. Its principal stage is Valencia city and the festivities culminate in the ritual burning of effigies in the streets.

April

Semana Santa (Holy Week)

Easter (the dates change each year) entails parades of *pasos* (holy figures), hooded penitents and huge crowds. It's extravagantly celebrated in Seville, as well as Málaga, Córdoba, Toledo and Ávila.

Moros y Cristianos (Moors & Christians)

Colourful parades and mock battles between Christian and Muslim 'armies' in Alcoy, near Alicante, in late April make this one of the most spectacular of many such festivities staged in the Valencia and Alicante provinces.

Feria de Abril (April Fair)

This week-long party, held in Seville in the second half of April, is the biggest of Andalucía's fairs. *Sevillanos* ride around on horseback and in elaborate horse-drawn carriages by day and, dressed up in their traditional finery, dance late into the night.

May

Feria del Caballo (Horse Fair)

A colourful equestrian fair in Andalucía's horse capital, Jerez de la Frontera, the Feria del Caballo is one of Andalucía's most festive and extravagant fiestas. It features parades, horse shows, bullfights and plenty of music and dance.

Córdoba's Courtyards Open Up

Scores of beautiful private courtyards are opened to the public for two weeks in Córdoba for the Concurso de Patios Cordobeses. It's a rare chance to see an otherwise-hidden side of Córdoba, strewn with flowers and freshly painted.

Fiesta de San Isidro

Madrid's major fiesta celebrates the city's patron saint with bullfights, parades, concerts and more. Locals dress up in traditional costumes and some of the events, such as the bullfighting season, last for a month.

June

Romería del Rocío

Focused on Pentecost weekend, the seventh after Easter, this festive pilgrimage is made by up to one million people to the shrine of the Virgin in El Rocío. This is Andalucía's Catholic tradition at its most curious and compelling.

Feast of Corpus Christi

On the Thursday in the ninth week after Easter (sometimes May, sometimes June), religious processions and celebrations take place in Toledo and other cities.

Bonfires & Fireworks

Midsummer bonfires, fireworks and roaming giants and other figures feature on the eve of the Fiesta de San Juan (24 June; Dia de Sant Joan), notably along the Mediterranean coast, including in Barcelona.

Electronica Festival

Performers and spectators come from all over the world for Sónar, Barcelona's two-day celebration of electronic music and said to be Europe's biggest festival of its kind. Dates vary each year.

Wine Battle

On 29 June Haro, one of the premier wine towns of La Rioja, enjoys the Batalla del Vino, squirting wine all over the place in one of Spain's messiest playfights, pausing only to drink the good stuff.

July

Festival Internacional de Guitarra

Córdoba's contribution to Spain's impressive calendar of musical events, this fine international guitar festival ranges from flamenco and classical to rock, blues and beyond. Headline performances take place in the Alcázar gardens at night.

Running of the Bulls

The Fiesta de San Fermín (Sanfermines) is the week-long nonstop festival and party in Pamplona with the daily *encierro* (running of the bulls) as its centrepiece. Similar, smaller-scale events occur elsewhere through the summer.

Día de la Virgen del Carmen

Around 16 July in most coastal towns, particularly in some parts of Andalucía, the image of the patron of fisherfolk is carried into the sea or paraded on a flotilla of small boats.

Feast of St James

The Día de Santiago marks the day of Spain's national saint and is spectacularly celebrated in Galicia at Santiago de Compostela. With so many pilgrims in town, it's the city's most festive two weeks of the year.

August

La Tomatina

Buñol's massive tomato-throwing festival, held in late August, must be one of the messiest get-togethers in the country. Thousands of people launch about 100 tonnes of tomatoes at one another in just an hour or so!

September

Bienal de Flamenco

There are flamenco festivals all over Spain throughout the year, but this is the most prestigious of them all. Held in Seville in even-numbered years (and Málaga every other year) it draws the biggest names in the genre.

Feria de Pedro Romero

The honouring of Pedro Romero, one of the legends of bullfighting, is a good excuse for the people of Ronda to host weeks of partying. Highlights include a flamenco festival, an unusual program of bullfighting and much all-night partying.

La Rioja's Grape Harvest

Logroño celebrates the feast day of St Matthew (Fiesta de San Mateo) and the year's

grape harvest. There are grape-crushing ceremonies and endless opportunities to sample the fruit of the vine in liquid form.

Barcelona's Big Party

Barcelona's Festes de la Mercè marks the end of summer with four days of parades, concerts, theatre, fire running and more. Barcelona's always fun, but this is a whole new level.

San Sebastián Film Festival

It may not be Cannes, but San Sebastián's annual, two-week celebration of film is one of the most prestigious dates on Europe's film-festival circuit. It's held in the second half of the month and has been gathering plaudits since 1957.

Romans & Carthaginians

In the second half of the month, locals dress up to re-enact ancient battles during the festival of Carthagineses y Romanos in Cartagena. It's among the more original mock battles staged around Spain.

October

Día de Nuestra Señora del Pilar

In Zaragoza on 12 October, the faithful mix with hedonists to celebrate this festival dedicated to Our Lady of the Pillar. The pillar in question is in the cathedral, but much of the fun happens in the bars nearby.

Fiesta de Santa Teresa

The patron saint of Ávila is honoured with 10 days of processions, concerts and fireworks around her feast day.

November

Festival Jazz Madrid

One of two annual jazz festivals in the capital (the other is in the spring), this increasingly prestigious festival plays out in the famous jazz clubs and larger theatres across the city.

Far left: April Moros y Cristianos
Left: August La Tomatina

What's New

For this new edition of Discover Spain, our authors have hunted down the fresh, the transformed, the hot and the happening. These are some of our favourites. For up-to-the-minute recommendations, see lonelyplanet.com/spain.

1 **BARCELONA REINVENTED**
Bullfighting's gone, master chef Ferran Adrià has opened a new restaurant, Gaudí's Palau Güell has reopened after two decades, there's new museums, and new cultural hubs from La Ribera to El Raval...What can we say? It's Barcelona (p51).

2 **MUSEO DEL PRADO, MADRID**
Not only does the Prado now open seven days a week, but it's also unveiled a near-perfect copy of the Mona Lisa that came from the studio of Leonardo da Vinci. (p206)

3 **SANTIAGO'S GUGGENHEIM**
Cidade da Cultura de Galicia is Galicia's grand answer to Bilbao's Guggenheim. Inaugurated in 2011, it will eventually include major performance and exhibition spaces and the Library and Archive of Galicia. (p177)

4 **METROPOL PARASOL, SEVILLE**
Seville's giant 'flying waffle' has injected a dose of modernism into the city's traditional urban core. It's sparking predictable controversy, and the jury's still out on its architectural merits. (p255)

5 **MUSEO CARMEN THYSSEN, MÁLAGA**
Andalucía's emerging art capital has just added a new string to its bow in this showcase of 19th-century Spanish and Andalucian art. (p310)

6 **A BULL MUSEUM**
Pamplona's Running of the Bulls now has a museum worthy of the fiesta's fame. The new Museo del Encierro has a 3D re-creation of the run and child-friendly exhibits. (p166)

7 **TOLEDO'S ALCÁZAR**
We'd been waiting for years for them to reopen Toledo's Alcázar, one of inland Spain's most iconic buildings, and it was worth the wait. It's home to Spain's best military museum and the architecture is something special. (p225)

Get Inspired

 Books

- **The Ornament of the World** (2003) A fascinating look at Andalucía's Islamic centuries.
- **Ghosts of Spain** (2007) Giles Tremlett's take on contemporary Spain and its tumultuous past.
- **Getting to Mañana** (2004) Miranda Innes's terrific take on starting a new life in an Andalucian farmhouse.
- **A Late Dinner** (2007) Paul Richardson's beautifully written journey through Spanish food.
- **A Handbook for Travellers** (1845) Richard Ford's sometimes irascible, always enlightening window on 19th-century Spain.
- **Sacred Sierra: A Year on a Spanish Mountain** (2009) Jason Webster's excellent alternative to the expat-renovates-a-Spanish-farmhouse genre.

 Films

- **Broken Embraces** (2009) Pedro Almodóvar's film noir-inspired movie.
- **Mar Adentro** (2004) Alejandro Amenábar's touching movie filmed in Galicia.
- **Jamón Jamón** (1992) Launched the careers of Javier Bardem and Penélope Cruz.

Music

- **Paco de Lucía Antología** (1995) Collected works by Spain's most celebrated flamenco guitarist.
- **Lagrimas Negras** (2003) Bebo Valdés and Diego El Cigala in stunning flamenco-Cuban fusion.
- **Sueña La Alhambra** (2005) Enrique Morente, one of flamenco's most enduring and creative voices.
- **La Luna en el Río** (2003) Carmen Linares, flamenco's foremost female voice in the second half of the 20th century.

Websites

- **Lonely Planet** (www.lonelyplanet.com) Country information, build your own itinerary and the Thorn Tree Forum.
- **Paradores** (www.parador.es) Start planning that special night in Spain.
- **Vayafiestas.com** (www.vayafiestas.com) Spanish-only site with month-by-month info on fiestas around the country.
- **Spain Travel Guide** (www.spanishfiestas.com) Detailed tourist information for most Spanish regions.

Short on time?

This list will give you an instant insight into the country.

Read *The New Spaniards* (2006) The updated version of John Hooper's classic portrait of contemporary Spain.

Watch *Todo sobre mi madre* (All About My Mother; 1999) Considered by many to be Almodóvar's masterpiece.

Listen *Una leyenda flamenca* (1993) Camarón de la Isla, flamenco's late, all-time singing legend.

Log on *Welcome to Spain* (www.spain.info) Useful official tourist office site.

Windmills, Consuegra (p238)

Need to Know

Currency
Euro (€)

Language
Spanish *(castellano)*. Also Catalan, Basque and Galician.

ATMs
Widely available.

Credit Cards
Visa and Mastercard are widely accepted; American Express is less common.

Visas
Generally not required for stays up to 90 days; some nationalities need a Schengen visa.

Mobile Phones
Local SIM cards widely available and can be used in European and Australian mobile phones.

Wi-Fi
Widely available in hotels as well as many coffee shops and other public spaces.

Internet
Most large towns have one or two internet cafes.

Driving
Drive on the right; steering wheel is on the left side of the car.

Tipping
Small change, more if you wish.

When to Go

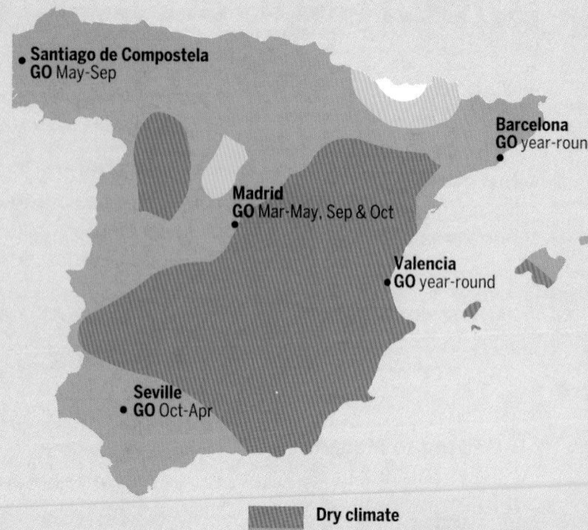

High Season (Jun–Aug, Easter)

- Accommodation books out and prices increase by up to 50%.
- Low season in some inland places.
- Expect warm, dry, sunny weather; more humid in coastal areas.

Shoulder (Mar–May, Sep & Oct)

- A good time to travel with mild, clear weather and fewer crowds.
- Local festivals can send prices soaring.

Low Season (Nov–Feb)

- Cold in central Spain; rain in the north and northwest.
- Mild temperatures in Andalucía and the Mediterranean Coast.
- This is high season in ski resorts.

Advance Planning

- **One month before** Reserve your entry ticket to Granada's Alhambra and book any long-distance train journeys. Reserve high season accommodation.
- **Two weeks before** Book cookery courses in San Sebastián, Barcelona or elsewhere.
- **One week before** Book tour of Parque Nacional de Doñana. Reserve low season accommodation.

Your Daily Budget

Budget less than €75

- Dorm beds: €17 to €22
- Doubles in *hostales:* €55 to €65 (more in Madrid & Barcelona)
- Supermarkets and lunch *menú del día*
- Use museum and gallery 'free admission' afternoons

Midrange €75–175

- Room in midrange hotel: €65 to €140
- Lunch and/or dinner in local restaurant
- Car rental: from €25 per day

Top End over €175

- Room in top-end hotel: €140 and up (€200 in Madrid and Barcelona)
- Fine dining for lunch and dinner
- Regularly stay in *paradores*

Exchange Rates

Australia	A$1	€0.80
Canada	C$1	€0.77
Japan	¥100	€.90
New Zealand	NZ$1	€0.64
UK	UK£1	€1.23
US	US$1	€0.76

For current exchange rates see www.xe.com.

What to Bring

- **Passport or EU ID Card** You'll need it to enter the country and for credit card transactions.
- **Money belt** Petty theft is a small but significant risk in some cities and tourist areas.
- **Travel insurance**
- **National and/or International Driving Licence** Essential if you plan to rent a car.

Arriving in Spain

- **Aeroport del Prat, Barcelona**

Buses €5.65; every six to 15 minutes from 6.10am to 1.05am; 30 to 40 minutes to the centre.

Trains €3.60; from 5.42am to 11.38pm; 35 minutes to the centre.

Taxis €25 to €30; 30 minutes to the centre.

- **Barajas airport, Madrid**

Metro & buses €4.50; every five to 10 minutes from 6.05am to 2am; 30 to 40 minutes to the centre.

Taxis €25 to €35; 20 minutes to the centre.

Getting Around Spain

- **Air** Numerous internal flights, including with low-cost companies; some flights require a change in Madrid or Barcelona.
- **Bus** Private companies cover the whole country, more cheaply and more slowly than trains, often going where the rails don't.
- **Train** Extensive and extremely modern network with the high-speed AVE trains connecting Madrid with many cities in around two hours.

Accommodation

- **Hostales** Budget accommodation, often with private bathroom.
- **Hotels** Wide range of midrange and top-end hotels.
- **Paradores** State-run hotels, usually in sumptuously converted historic buildings.
- **Casas Rurales** Charming and usually family-run rural accommodation.

Be Forewarned

- **Museums** Most major museums close on Mondays.
- **Restaurants** Most restaurants open from 1.30pm to 4pm and from 9pm to 11.30pm.
- **Shops** Many smaller shops close from 2pm to 5pm.

Barcelona

Barcelona is a mix of sunny Mediterranean charm and European urban style. From Gothic to Gaudí, the city bursts with art and architecture; Catalan cooking is among the country's best; summer sunseekers fill the beaches in and beyond the city; and the bars and clubs heave year-round.

From its origins as a middle-ranking Roman town, of which vestiges can be seen today, Barcelona became a medieval trade juggernaut. Its old centre constitutes one of the greatest concentrations of Gothic architecture in Europe. Beyond this core are some of the world's more bizarre buildings: surreal spectacles capped by Antoni Gaudí's church, La Sagrada Família.

Barcelona has been breaking ground in art, architecture and style since the late 19th century. From Picasso and Miró to the modern wonders of today, the racing heart of Barcelona has barely skipped a beat. Equally busy are the city's avant-garde chefs, who compete with old-time classics for the gourmet's attention.

Gaudí's Casa Batlló (p73)

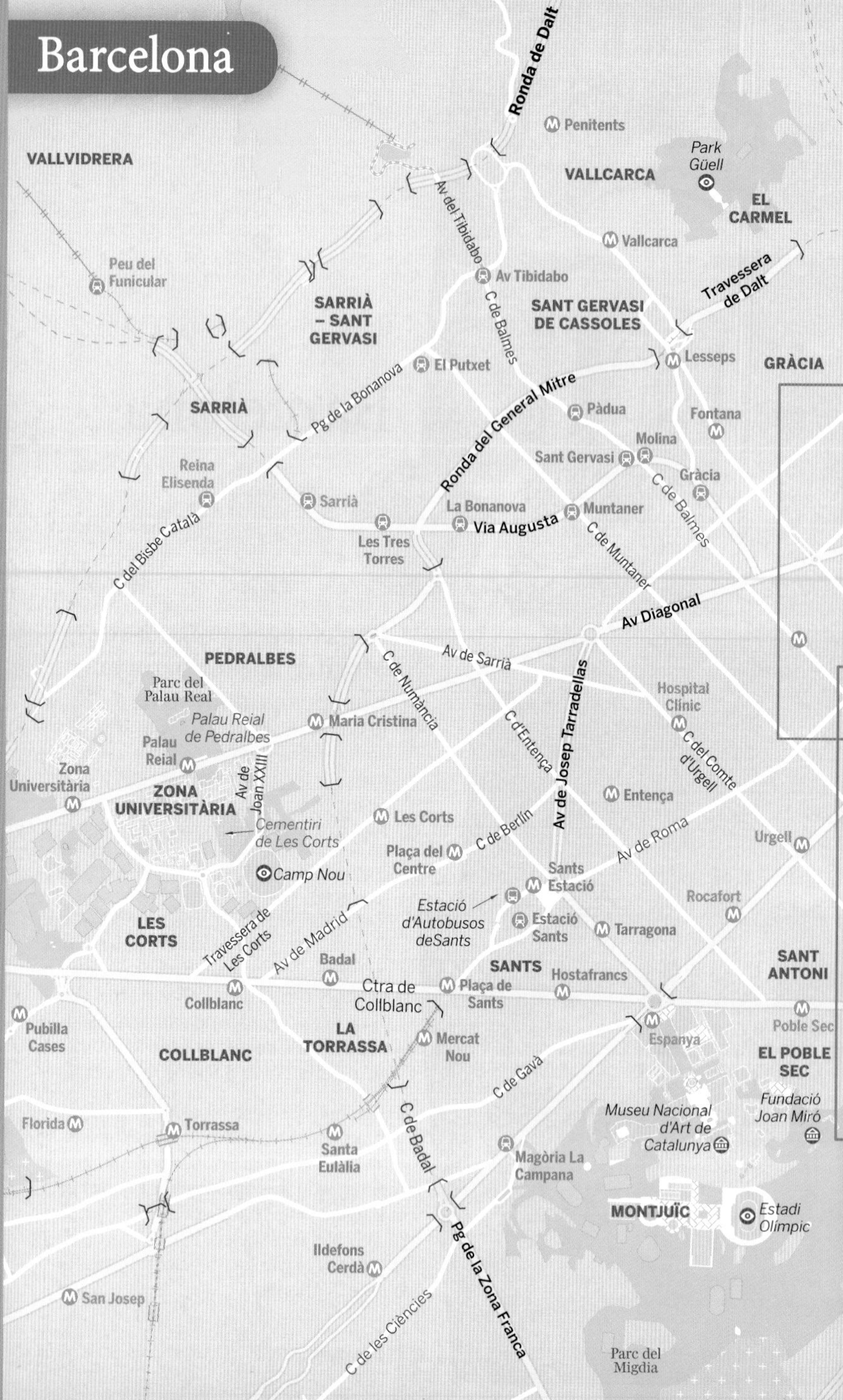
Barcelona
Ronda de Dalt
Penitents
VALLVIDRERA
VALLCARCA
Park Güell
EL CARMEL
Av del Tibidabo
Vallcarca
Peu del Funicular
Av Tibidabo
SARRIÀ – SANT GERVASI
SANT GERVASI DE CASSOLES
Travessera de Dalt
C de Balmes
Lesseps
GRÀCIA
El Putxet
Pg de la Bonanova
Ronda del General Mitre
Pàdua
Fontana
SARRIÀ
Molina
Sant Gervasi
Reina Elisenda
Gràcia
Sarrià
La Bonanova
Muntaner
Via Augusta
Les Tres Torres
C de Muntaner
C del Bisbe Català
Av Diagonal
PEDRALBES
Av de Sarrià
C de Numància
Parc del Palau Real
Hospital Clínic
Palau Reial de Pedralbes
Maria Cristina
C d'Entença
Palau Reial
Av de Joan XXIII
C del Comte d'Urgell
Zona Universitària
ZONA UNIVERSITÀRIA
Av de Josep Tarradellas
Entença
Les Corts
Cementiri de Les Corts
C de Berlín
Av de Roma
Urgell
Plaça del Centre
Camp Nou
Sants Estació
Estació d'Autobusos deSants
Rocafort
LES CORTS
Travessera de Les Corts
Av de Madrid
Estació Sants
Tarragona
SANTS
SANT ANTONI
Badal
Hostafrancs
Ctra de Collblanc
Plaça de Sants
Collblanc
Pubilla Cases
LA TORRASSA
Mercat Nou
Espanya
Poble Sec
COLLBLANC
EL POBLE SEC
C de Gavà
Fundació Joan Miró
Museu Nacional d'Art de Catalunya
C de Badal
Florida
Torrassa
Santa Eulàlia
Magòria La Campana
MONTJUÏC
Estadi Olímpic
Pg de la Zona Franca
Ildefons Cerdà
San Josep
C de les Ciències
Parc del Migdia

Sagrera
C de Felip II
Besòs
Sant Martí
Besòs Mar
Navas
C d'Aragó
EL GUINARDÓ
Guinardó
C de Sant Antoni Maria Claret
Camp de l'Arpa
C de las Navas Tolosa
Bac de Roda
Gran Via de les Corts Catalanes
C de Pere IV
Hospital de la Santa Creu i de Sant Pau
Alfons X
CAMP DE L'ARPA
EL CLOT
LA VERNEDA
Hospital de Sant Pau
C de Pi i Margall
Travessera de Gràcia
Clot
SANT MARTÍ
C de Bac de Roda
LA DRETA DE L'EIXAMPLE
Selva de Mar
Encants
C de Padilla
C d'Aragó
Av Diagonal
EL POBLENOU
Joanic
Glòries
Torre Agbar
Poblenou
Pg de Calvell
C de Sardenya
Pg de Sant Joan
C de Còrsega
Av Diagonal
Monumental
Av Meridiana
C dels Almogàvers
Llacuna
Platja de la Nova Mar Bella
Cementiri de l'Est
Marina
Bogatell
L'EIXAMPLE
EL FORT PIENC
Platja del Bogatell
Arc de Triomf
C de la Marina
See Central Barcelona Map (p66)
VILA OLÍMPICA
Platja de la Nova Icària
See L'Eixample Map (p74)
Ciutadella Vila Olímpica
Port Olímpic
MEDITERRANEAN SEA
BARRI GÒTIC
EL RAVAL
Platja de la Barceloneta
Ronda de Sant Antoni
CIUTAT VELLA
LA BARCELONETA
Platja de Sant Sebastià
Marina
Platja de Sant Miquel
PORT VELL
Port Vell
Castell de Montjuïc
Estació del Port
Ronda del Litoral
0 1 km
0 0.5 miles
1 La Sagrada Família
2 Eat Like a Local
3 Gaudí's Barcelona
4 La Rambla
5 Barri Gòtic
6 Nouveau Catalan Cuisine
7 Museu Picasso

Barcelona Highlights

1

La Sagrada Família

The Sagrada Família (p76) is Antoni Gaudí's masterpiece, which he worked on for 43 years. It's a slender structure where everything is devoted to geometric perfection and sacred symbolism. It's also a work-in-progress spanning the generations but never losing Gaudí's modernity, originality and architectural synthesis of natural forms.

Need to Know

EXPECTED COMPLETION DATE 2020 to 2040 **PHOTO OP** Take a lift (€2.50) up one of the towers **ADMISSION** €13 **GUIDED TOURS** €4, up to four daily

Local Knowledge

La Sagrada Família Don't Miss List

BY JORDI FAULÍ, DEPUTY ARCHITECTURAL DIRECTOR FOR LA SAGRADA FAMÍLIA

1 PASSION FACADE

Among the Fachada de la Pasión's stand-out features are the angled columns, dramatic scenes from Jesus' last hours, an extraordinary rendering of the Last Supper and a bronze door that reads like a sculptured book. But the most surprising view is from inside the door on the extreme right.

2 MAIN NAVE

The majestic Nave Principal showcases Gaudí's use of tree motifs for columns to support the domes: he described this space as a forest. But it's the skylights that give the nave its luminous quality, even more so once the scaffolding is removed and light will flood down onto the apse and main altar from the skylight 75m above the floor.

3 SIDE NAVE AND NATIVITY TRANSEPT

Although beautiful in its own right, with windows that project light into the interior, this is the perfect place to view the sculpted tree-like columns and get an overall perspective of the main nave. Turn around and you're confronted with the inside of the Nativity Facade, an alternative view that most visitors miss; the stained-glass windows are superb.

4 NATIVITY FACADE

The Fachada del Nacimiento is Gaudí's grand hymn to Creation. Begin by viewing it front-on from a distance, then draw close enough (but to one side) to make out the details of its sculpted figures. The complement to the finely wrought detail is the majesty of the four parabolic towers that reach for the sky and are topped by Venetian stained glass.

5 THE MODEL OF COLÒNIA GÜELL

Among the many original models used by Gaudí in the Museu Gaudí, the most interesting is the church at Colònia Güell. From the side you can visualise the harmony and beauty of the interior, thanks to the model's ingenious use of rope and cloth.

Eat Like a Local

Eating in Barcelona (p85) means getting a taste of genuine Catalan culture and understanding how the people here pass their day. Barcelona is a crossroad of cultures rich in historical influences, where the secret has always been exploration and experimentation from a solid base of traditional cooking to satisfy the five senses. Below: Mercat de la Boqueria; Top Right: *Chocolate con churros*; Bottom Right: Catalonian tapas

Need to Know

COOKING COURSES Cook and Taste (p82) **TOP SURVIVAL TIP** Pace yourself and don't overeat at each stop **BEST PHOTO OP** Mercat de la Boqueria (p90)

2

Local Knowledge

Eating Like a Local Don't Miss List

BY BEGO SANCHIS, OWNER OF COOK & TASTE COOKING SCHOOL

1 BREAKFAST IN MERCAT DE LA BOQUERIA

Mercat de la Boqueria (p90) is the largest of Barcelona's 40 markets and is an obligatory stop for breakfast. Lose yourself in the passageways and let yourself be carried along by the uproar of stallholders and buyers. Your visit is not complete until you've finished with *un desayuno de cuchara* (breakfast eaten with a spoon or fork) from one of the food stalls.

2 PRE-LUNCH SNACK

Stop for a light snack accompanied by a *cava* (sparkling wine) or *vermut* (vermouth) – two local drinks of which Catalans are rightfully proud – at a sunny outdoor table. Where else in the world can you see elegant señoras enjoying their *bocadillo* (filled roll) with a glass of sparkling wine before lunch?

3 LUNCH IN THE BARRIO OF FISHERMEN

Try a seafood rice dish in any bar in the Barrio de Pescadores (Barrio of Fishermen), otherwise known as La Barceloneta (p87). Wander the streets, study the various options and, above all, chose a place where there are far more locals than tourists – this is the best guarantee of authenticity!

4 AFTERNOON TEA

Pause for one of Barcelona's three traditional pastries – a *chocolate con churros* (deep-fried donuts dipped in thick chocolate), *melindro* (a small baked cake) or *ensaimada* (another sweet, baked pastry). The best places are the chocolaterías along Carrer del Pi or, even better, Carrer dels Banys Nous, close to Plaça Sant Josep Oriol in the Barri Gòtic.

5 A TAPAS DINNER

The best way to sample so many different recipes is to base your dinner around tapas until your stomach says enough. You could stay the whole meal in one bar, but most locals hop from one bar to the next, trying the various house specialities in each one.

Explore Gaudí's Barcelona

Few architects have come to define a city quite like Antoni Gaudí in Barcelona. La Sagrada Família (p76) is the master architect's showpiece and is quite simply the most surprising, imaginative cathedral in the world. In the stately streets of L'Eixample, Casa Batlló (p73) is his most beautiful secular creation, closely followed by La Pedrera (p75). Park Güell (p77)

3

4

Parade down La Rambla

La Rambla (p64) connects the Plaça de Catalunya with the waterfront, passing en route numerous distinguished buildings. But it's the life coursing along this pedestrian boulevard that makes La Rambla special, an endless procession of people, street performers, flower sellers, and what can seem like a representative cross-section of the world's peoples.

Wander the Barri Gòtic

5

You'll spend many happy Barcelona hours getting lost in the Barri Gòtic (p65), Barcelona's oldest quarter. There are landmark public buildings (including the cathedral) and some lovely squares to provide breathing space, but what the 'Gothic Quarter' is all about is meandering with neither plan nor pace.

6

Sample Nouveau Catalan Cuisine

The innovation and studied experimentation that has revolutionised Spanish cuisine and earned it world renown finds its true home in Barcelona. In the city's bars and restaurants, you'll find Catalonia's celebrated local staples alongside taste combinations that you never imagined in your wildest dreams. You can eat them as stand-up tapas or sit-down meals.

7

Museu Picasso

Pablo Picasso spent a decade in Barcelona before he decamped to Paris, and the Museu Picasso (p71) is a fitting tribute to his connection with the city. Don't come here expecting his Cubist masterpieces; the gallery focuses on his early years. As long as you come with that understanding, you'll enjoy this priceless insight into one of the towering figures of 20th-century art.

Barcelona's Best...

Places for Art

- **Museu Picasso** (p71) Picasso's early, pre-Cubist works.
- **Fundació Joan Miró** (p82) Showcases one of Spain's finest 20th-century artists.
- **Museu Nacional D'Art de Catalunya** (p77) Titian, Canaletto, Rubens and Gainsborough.
- **Museu d'Art Contemporani de Barcelona** (p69) Avant-garde contemporary art.
- **Fundació Antoni Tàpies** (p75) A homage to the elder statesman of contemporary Catalan art.

Places for a View

- **La Sagrada Família** (p76) Stirring views from the cathedral's towers.
- **Mirador de Colom** (p65) Sweeping coastal and La Rambla views.
- **Casa Batlló** (p73) A swirling facade and a zany rooftop.
- **Camp Nou** (p77) When FC Barcelona are playing at home, this is the place to be for the best view in town.

Places for Innovative Catalan Cooking

- **Tickets** (p88) Gourmet tapas from Ferran Adrià's stable.
- **Tapaç 24** (p87) A reputation for designer tapas.
- **Cal Pep** (p86) One of Barcelona's most celebrated and experimental tapas bars.
- **Cata 1.81** (p87) Delicately presented gourmet tapas served in a bar lined with bottles of quality wine.
- **Alkímia** (p87) Refined Catalan fare from a culinary alchemist.

Plaças in the Ciutat Vella

Plaça Reial (p65) Neoclassical square with Gaudí fountains.

Passeig del Born (p72) Historic square with Barcelona's grandest Gothic church.

Plaça del Rei (p65) Former royal courtyard within sight of the cathedral.

Left: Tapas on display; **Above:** Plaça Reial

LEFT: FLYDIME/GETTY IMAGES ©; ABOVE: JEAN-PIERRE LESCOURRET/GETTY IMAGES ©

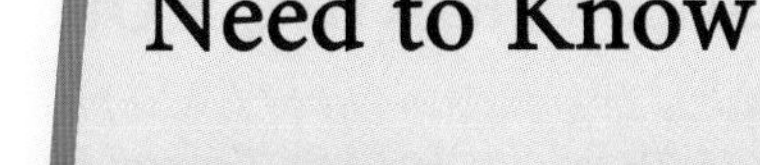

Need to Know

RESOURCES

Oficina d'Informació de Turisme de Barcelona (93 285 38 34; www.barcelonaturisme.com; Plaça de Catalunya 17-S underground; 8.30am-8.30pm) Branch offices around the city.

Le Cool (www.lecool.com) Subscribe for free to this site for weekly events listings.

Barcelona (www.bcn.cat) Barcelona Town Hall, with links.

Barcelona Yellow (www.barcelonayellow.com) Links on everything from Gaudí to gourmet dining.

GETTING AROUND

Air Barcelona's Aeroport del Prat (www.aena.es) has excellent connections with Europe and beyond.

Metro The best way for getting around town, with six lines.

Train Rail links with the rest of Spain and Europe.

BE FOREWARNED

Museums and galleries Most close on Monday (although most Gaudí sites open seven days).

Football Tickets to Barcelona games must be booked 15 days before match day.

Barcelona Walking Tour

Barcelona: it might be cool, it might be fun, it might be relaxed, but visitors could still use a little helping hand in the form of a leisurely walking tour to get the most out of it.

WALK FACTS

- **Start** Plaça de Catalunya
- **Finish** Palau de la Música Catalana
- **Distance** 3.5km
- **Duration** 1½ hours

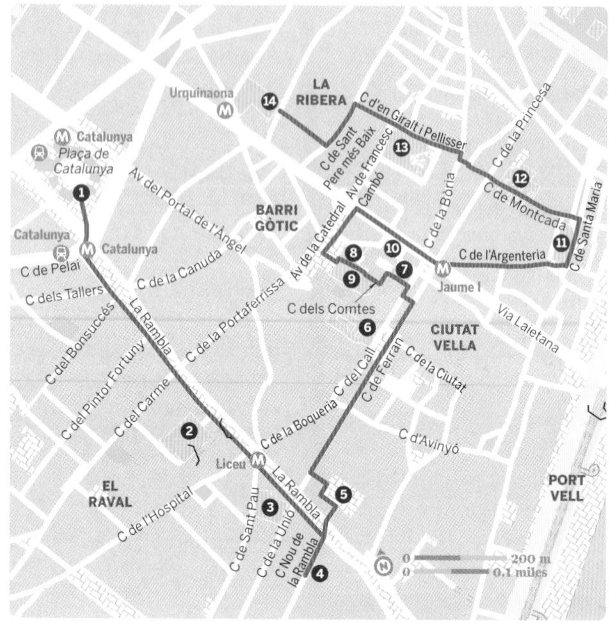

❶ Plaça de Catalunya

There's nothing wrong with following the crowds to start off with, and this bustling square makes a good kick-off point for a leisurely wander down La Rambla.

❷ Mercat de la Boqueria

Seek out some breakfast in one of Europe's best-stocked and most colourful produce markets.

❸ Gran Teatre del Liceu

Barcelona's grand opera house was built in 1847, largely destroyed by fire in 1994, and reopened better than ever in 1999.

❹ Palau Güell

Visit one of Gaudí's earlier efforts. It may lack the playfulness of his later work but is still a fascinating blend of styles and materials.

❺ Plaça Reial

Cross La Rambla via this shady square. The lamp posts next to the central fountain are Gaudí's first known works.

❻ Plaça de Sant Jaume

At the core of the Barri Gòtic, this square has been the political heart of the city for 2000 years.

7 Museu d'Història de Barcelona

You can examine the city's Roman origins in this nearby museum. This is one of Barcelona's most fascinating sights, so set aside at least an hour for the visit at some point during your stay in Barcelona.

8 Museu Frederic Marès

From the complex of buildings huddled around the museum and Plaça del Rei you'll pass the Museu Frederic Marès, which houses an extensive collection from the 20th-century Catalan sculptor and collector.

9 Catedral

Barcelona's *catedral* is one of its most magnificent Gothic structures. The narrow old streets around the cathedral are traffic-free and dotted with occasionally very talented buskers.

10 Roman Walls

Make the loop down Via Laietana to admire what remains of the Roman walls.

11 Església de Santa Maria del Mar

Branch off down Carrer de l'Argenteria and circle Barcelona's finest Gothic church.

12 Museu Picasso

Head up Carrer de Montcada, home to several museums including the must-see Museu Picasso. This collection focuses on his pre-Cubist years.

13 Mercat de Santa Caterina

Proceed north past the Mercat de Santa Caterina, a daring 21st-century reincarnation of a grand 19th-century produce market, on the site of a medieval monastery.

14 Palau de la Música Catalana

Dogleg on to this Modernista high point and World Heritage Site.

Barcelona in ...

ONE DAY

Start your Barcelona adventure by taking a **walking tour** in the medieval warren of winding streets that is the **Barri Gòtic**. Allow plenty of time for admiring **La Catedral**, the **Museu d'Història de Barcelona** and the nearby **Museu Picasso**.

TWO DAYS

The following day, take a walk through Gaudí's unique **Park Güell**, where the artificial can seem more natural than the natural. Next, head to **La Sagrada Família,** Gaudí's breathtaking work in progress.

FOUR DAYS

Start the third day with another round of Gaudí, visiting the extraordinary **Casa Batlló** and **La Pedrera**. Follow this up with some beachside relaxation in **La Barceloneta**. Dedicate the fourth day to **Montjuïc**, with its museums, galleries, fortress, gardens and Olympic stadium.

Rooftop chimneys at Gaudí's La Pedrera (p75)

Discover Barcelona

At a Glance

- **La Rambla** (p64) Barcelona's iconic thoroughfare.
- **Barri Gòtic** (p65) The city's oldest quarter.
- **El Raval** (p69) Slightly seedy inner-city neighbourhood.
- **La Ribera** (p70) Another old quarter; includes hip El Born.
- **La Barceloneta & the Waterfront** (p72) Coastal neighbourhood with beaches, northeast of Port Vell.
- **L'Eixample** (p73) Nineteenth century *barrio*, with Barcelona's best Modernista architecture.

Cloister walkway, Barri Gòtic
JOHN ELK/GETTY IMAGES ©

Sights

La Rambla

Head to Spain's most famous street for that first taste of Barcelona's vibrant atmosphere.

Flanked by narrow traffic lanes and plane trees, the middle of La Rambla is a broad pedestrian boulevard, crowded every day until the wee hours with a cross-section of *barcelonins* and out-of-towners. Dotted with cafes, restaurants, kiosks and news-stands, and enlivened by buskers, pavement artists, mimes and living statues, La Rambla rarely allows a dull moment.

GRAN TEATRE DEL LICEU Arts Centre

(Map p66; ☎93 485 99 14; www.liceubarcelona.com; La Rambla dels Caputxins 51-59; admission with/without guide €10/5; ⏰guided tour 10am, unguided visits 11.30am, noon, 12.30pm & 1pm; Ⓜ Liceu) If you can't catch a night at the opera, you can still have a look around one of Europe's great opera houses, known to locals as the Liceu.

Built in 1847, the Liceu launched such Catalan stars as Josep (aka José) Carreras and Montserrat Caballé. Fire virtually destroyed it in 1994, but city authorities brought it back to life in 1999. You can take a 20-minute quick turn around the main public areas of the theatre or join a one-hour guided tour.

On the guided tour you'll be taken to the grand foyer, with its thick pillars and sumptuous chandeliers, and then up the marble staircase to the Saló dels Miralls

(Hall of Mirrors). With mirrors, ceiling frescoes, fluted columns and high-and-mighty phrases in praise of the arts, it all exudes a typically neobaroque richness worthy of its 19th-century patrons. You'll then be led up to the 4th-floor stalls to admire the theatre itself. The tour also takes in a collection of Modernista art, El Cercle del Liceu.

MIRADOR DE COLOM Viewpoint
(Map p66; ☎93 302 52 24; Plaça del Portal de la Pau; lift adult/child €4/3; ⌚8.30am-8.30pm; Ⓜ Drassanes) High above the swirl of traffic on the roundabout below, Columbus keeps permanent watch, pointing vaguely out to the Mediterranean. Built for the Universal Exhibition in 1888, the monument allows you to zip up 60m in the lift for bird's-eye views back up La Rambla and across the ports of Barcelona.

Barri Gòtic

Barcelona's 'Gothic Quarter', east of La Rambla, is a medieval warren of narrow, winding streets, quaint *plaças* (plazas), and grand mansions and monuments from the city's golden age. Many of its buildings date from the 15th century or earlier.

LA CATEDRAL Church
(Map p66; ☎93 342 82 60; www.website.es/catedralbcn; Plaça de la Seu; admission free, special visit €5, coro admission €2.20; ⌚8am-12.45pm & 5.15-8pm Mon-Sat, special visit 1-5pm Mon-Sat, 2-5pm Sun & holidays; Ⓜ Jaume I) Approached from the broad Avinguda de la Catedral, Barcelona's central place of worship presents a magnificent image. The richly decorated main (northwest) facade, laced with gargoyles and the stone intricacies you would expect of northern European Gothic, sets it quite apart from other churches in Barcelona.

In the first chapel on the right from the northwest entrance, the main Crucifixion figure above the altar is **Sant Crist de Lepant**. It is said Don Juan's flagship bore it into battle at Lepanto and that the figure acquired its odd stance by dodging an incoming cannonball.

In the middle of the central nave is the late-14th-century, exquisitely sculpted timber **coro** (choir stalls). The coats of arms on the stalls belong to members of the Barcelona chapter of the Order of the Golden Fleece.

A broad staircase before the main altar leads you down to the **crypt**, which contains the tomb of Santa Eulàlia, one of Barcelona's two patron saints. The reliefs on the alabaster sarcophagus recount some of her tortures and, along the top strip, the removal of her body to its present resting place.

For a bird's-eye view of medieval Barcelona, visit the cathedral's **roof** and tower by taking the lift (€2.20) from the Capella de les Animes del Purgatori near the northeast transept.

From the southwest transept, exit by the partly Romanesque door (one of the few remnants of the present church's predecessor) to the leafy **claustre** (cloister), with its fountains and flock of 13 geese. The geese supposedly represent the age of Santa Eulàlia at the time of her martyrdom and have, generation after generation, been squawking here since medieval days.

You may visit La Catedral in one of two ways. In the morning or afternoon, entrance is free and you can opt to visit any combination of the choir stalls, chapter house and roof. To visit all three areas, it costs less (and is less crowded) to enter for the so-called 'special visit' between 1pm and 5pm.

PLAÇA REIAL Square
(Map p66; Ⓜ Liceu) One of the most photogenic squares in Barcelona, the Plaça Reial is a delightful retreat from the traffic and pedestrian mobs on nearby La Rambla.

PLAÇA DEL REI Museum Square
(Map p66) Plaça del Reia (King's Sq) is a picturesque plaza where Fernando and Isabel received Columbus following his first New World voyage.

MUSEU D'HISTÒRIA DE BARCELONA Museum
(Map p66; ☎93 256 21 00; www.museuhistoria.bcn.cat; Plaça del Rei; adult/child €7/free, from

Central Barcelona

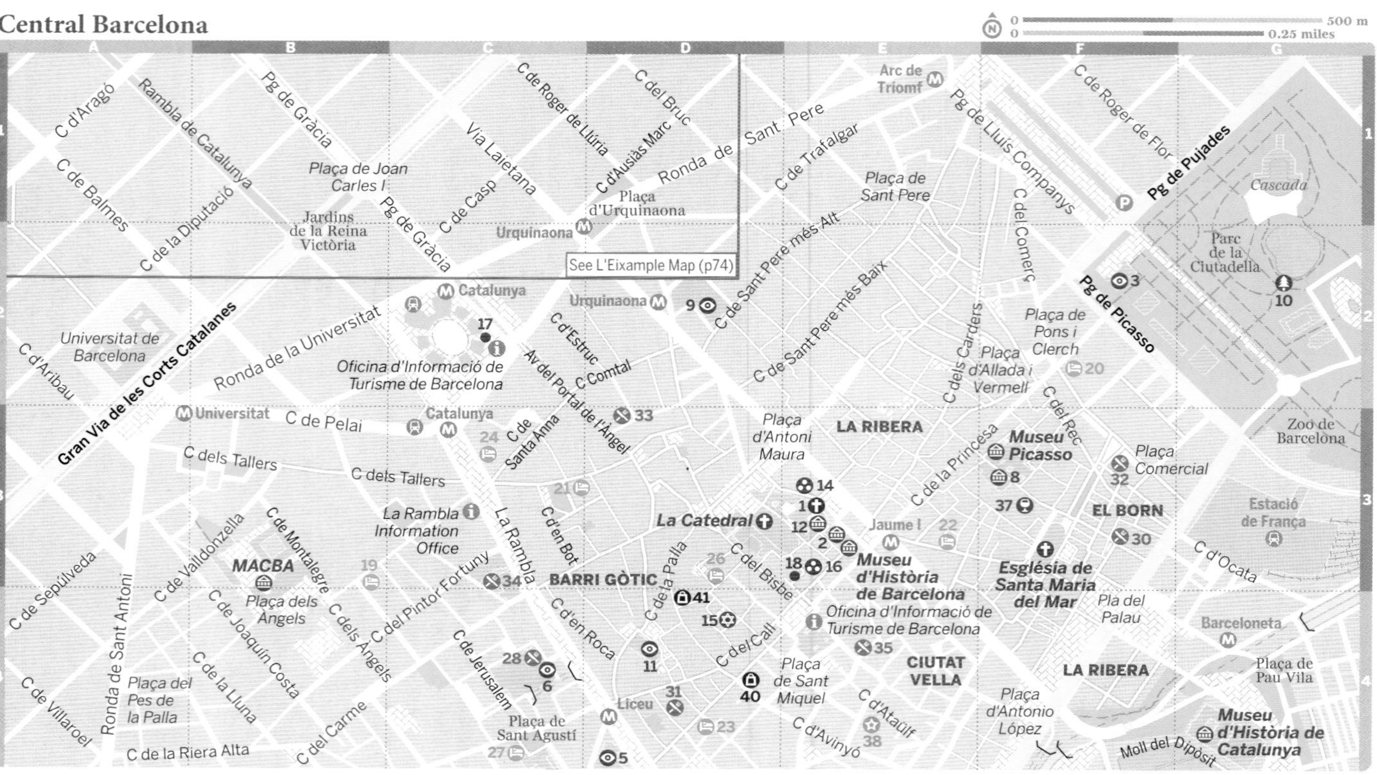

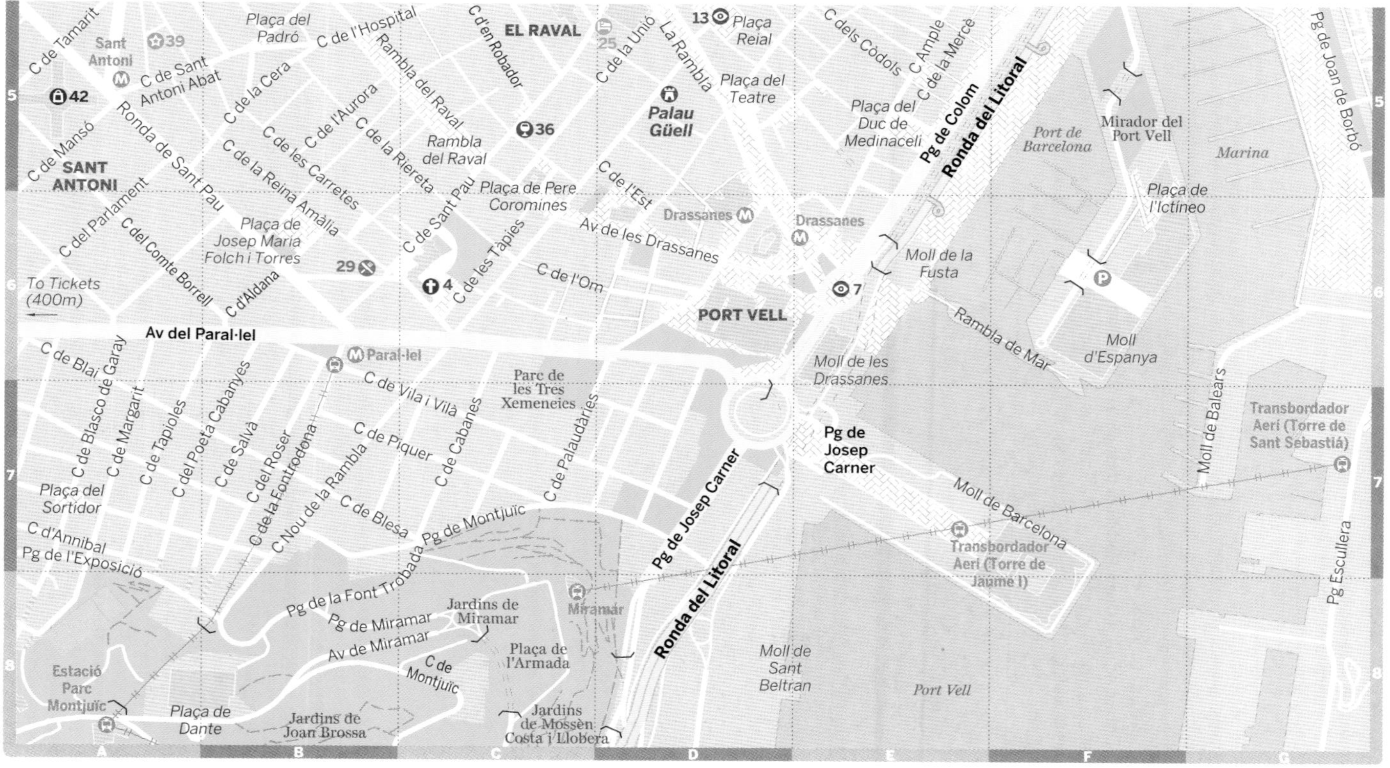
C de Tamarit
Sant Antoni
39
Plaça del Padró
C de l'Hospital
Rambla del Raval
C d'en Robador
EL RAVAL
25
C de la Unió
La Rambla
13
Plaça Reial
C dels Còdols
C Ample
C de la Mercè
42
C de Sant Antoni Abat
C de la Cera
C de l'Aurora
C de la Riereta
36
Palau Güell
Plaça del Teatre
Plaça del Duc de Medinaceli
Pg de Colom
Ronda del Litoral
Port de Barcelona
Mirador del Port Vell
Marina
Pg de Joan de Borbó
C de Mansó
SANT ANTONI
Ronda de Sant Pau
C de les Carretes
C de la Reina Amàlia
Rambla del Raval
C de Sant Pau
Plaça de Pere Coromines
C de l'Est
Drassanes
Plaça de l'Ictíneo
C del Parlament
C del Comte Borrell
Plaça de Josep Maria Folch i Torres
29
C de les Tàpies
Av de les Drassanes
Moll de la Fusta
To Tickets (400m)
C d'Aldana
4
C de l'Om
7
PORT VELL
Rambla de Mar
Moll d'Espanya
Av del Paral·lel
Paral·lel
C de Blai
C de Blasco de Garay
C de Margarit
C de Tapioles
C del Poeta Cabanyes
C de Salvà
C del Roser
C de la Fontrodona
C Nou de la Rambla
C de Vila i Vilà
C de Piquer
C de Cabanes
Parc de les Tres Xemeneies
C de Paladàries
Moll de les Drassanes
Pg de Josep Carner
Moll de Balears
Transbordador Aerí (Torre de Sant Sebastià)
Plaça del Sortidor
C d'Annibal
Pg de l'Exposició
C de Blesa
Pg de Montjuïc
Pg de Josep Carner
Moll de Barcelona
Transbordador Aerí (Torre de Jaume I)
Pg Escullera
Pg de la Font Trobada
Pg de Miramar
Jardins de Miramar
Av de Miramar
Miramar
Ronda del Litoral
Plaça de l'Armada
C de Montjuïc
Moll de Sant Beltran
Port Vell
Estació Parc Montjuïc
Plaça de Dante
Jardins de Joan Brossa
Jardins de Mossèn Costa i Llobera

4pm 1st Sat of month and from 3pm Sun free; 10am-7pm Tue-Sat, 10am-8pm Sun; M Jaume I) One of Barcelona's most fascinating museums takes you back through the centuries to the very foundations of Roman Barcino. You'll stroll over ruins of the old streets, sewers, laundries and wine- and fish-making factories that flourished here following the town's funding by Emperor Augustus around 10 BC.

Enter through **Casa Padellàs** (Map p66), just south of Plaça del Rei. Casa Padellàs was built for a 16th-century noble family in Carrer dels Mercaders and moved here, stone by stone, in the 1930s. It has a courtyard typical of Barcelona's late-Gothic and baroque mansions, with a graceful external staircase up to the 1st floor. Today it leads to a restored Roman tower and a section of Roman wall (whose exterior faces Plaça Ramon de Berenguer el Gran), as well as a section of the house set aside for temporary exhibitions.

Below ground is a remarkable walk through about 4 sq km of excavated ruins, complete with sections of a Roman street, baths and shops, and remains of a Visigothic basilica.

Central Barcelona

Top Sights

	Església de Santa Maria del Mar	F3
	La Catedral	D3
	MACBA	B3
	Museu d'Història de Barcelona	E3
	Museu d'Història de Catalunya	G4
	Museu Picasso	F3
	Palau Güell	D5

Sights

1	Capella Reial de Santa Àgata	E3
2	Casa Padellàs	E3
3	Castell dels Tres Dragons	F2
4	Església de Sant Pau	C6
	Església de Santa Maria del Pi	(see 11)
5	Gran Teatre del Liceu	D4
6	Mercat de la Boqueria	C4
7	Mirador de Colom	E6
	Mirador del Rei Martí	(see 12)
8	Museu Barbier-Mueller d'Art Pre-Colombí	F3
9	Palau de la Música Catalana	D2
	Palau del Lloctinent	(see 12)
10	Parc de la Ciutadella	G2
11	Plaça de Sant Josep Oriol	D4
12	Plaça del Rei	E3
13	Plaça Reial	D5
14	Roman Walls	E3
	Saló del Tinell	(see 12)
15	Sinagoga Major	D4
16	Temple Romà d'August	E3

Activities, Courses & Tours

17	Barcelona Walking Tours	C2
18	Cook and Taste	E3

Sleeping

19	Casa Camper	B3
20	Chic & Basic	F2
21	Hostal Campi	C3
22	Hotel Banys Orientals	E3
23	Hotel California	D4
24	Hotel Continental	C3
25	Hotel España	D5
26	Hotel Neri	D3
27	Hotel San Agustín	C4

Eating

28	Bar Pinotxo	C4
29	Ca L'Isidre	B6
30	Cal Pep	F3
31	Can Culleretes	D4
32	Casa Delfín	F3
33	Els Quatre Gats	D3
34	Granja Viader	C3
	La Vinateria del Call	(see 15)
35	Pla	E4

Drinking

36	Bar Marsella	C5
37	El Xampanyet	F3

Entertainment

38	Harlem Jazz Club	E4
39	Jazz Sí Club	A5
	Palau de la Música Catalana	(see 9)

Shopping

40	La Manual Alpargatera	D4
41	L'Arca de l'Àvia	D4
42	Mercat de Sant Antoni	A5

You'll eventually emerge near the **Saló del Tinell** (Map p66), the banqueting hall of the royal palace and a fine example of Catalan Gothic (built 1359–70).

As you leave the *saló* you'll come to the 14th-century **Capella Reial de Santa Àgata** (Map p66), the palace chapel. Inside, all is bare except for the 15th-century altarpiece and the magnificent techumbre (decorated timber ceiling).

Head down the fan-shaped stairs into Plaça del Rei and look up to observe the **Mirador del Rei Martí** (Map p66), the lookout tower of King Martin, built in 1555, which offers splendid views over the old city.

FREE PALAU DEL LLOCTINENT Historic Site

(Map p66; Carrer dels Comtes; 10am-7pm; M Jaume I) This converted 16th-century palace has a peaceful courtyard, covered with an extraordinary sculpted ceiling made to resemble the upturned hull of a boat.

PLAÇA DE SANT JOSEP ORIOL Square

(Map p66; M Liceu) This small plaza, ringed with tranquil cafes and restaurants, is one of the prettiest in the Barri Gòtic.

Looming over the square is the flank of the **Església de Santa Maria del Pi** (Map p66; 9.30am-1pm & 5-8.30pm; M Liceu), a Gothic church built in the 14th to 16th centuries. The beautiful rose window above its entrance is claimed by some to be the world's biggest.

SINAGOGA MAJOR Synagogue

(Map p66; 93 317 07 90; www.calldebarcelona.org; Carrer de Marlet 5; admission by suggested donation €2.50 ; 10.30am-6.30pm Mon-Fri, to 2.30pm Sat & Sun; M Liceu) In the heart of El Call – Barcelona's medieval Jewish quarter – this was one of four synagogues in the medieval city.

Fragments of medieval and Roman-era walls remain in the small vaulted space that you enter from the street. Also remaining are tanners' wells installed in the 15th century. The second chamber has been spruced up for use as a synagogue.

If You Like... Modernista Architecture

If you like Gaudí's Casa Batlló, you'll also like the following Modernista gems (including some by Gaudí):

1 **COLÒNIA GÜELL**
(93 630 58 07; www.coloniaguellbarcelona.com; Carrer de Claudi Güell 6; adult/student €8/6.60; 10am-7pm Mon-Fri, to 3pm Sat & Sun; FGC lines S4, S7, S8 or S33) Apart from La Sagrada Família, this Utopian textile-workers' complex was Gaudí's last grand project, outside Barcelona at Santa Coloma de Cervelló; his main role was to erect the colony's church.

2 **CASA LLEÓ MORERA**
(Map p74; Passeig de Gràcia 35; M Passeig de Gràcia) On the same block as Casa Batlló, this house is swathed in art nouveau carving on the outside and has a bright, tiled lobby inside; it's by master Catalan architect, Lluís Domènech i Montaner.

3 **COSMOCAIXA**
(Museu de la Ciència; 93 212 60 50; www.fundacio.lacaixa.es; Carrer de Isaac Newton 26; adult/child €3/2; 10am-8pm Tue-Sun; 60, FGC Avinguda Tibidabo) Up the Tibidabo hill overlooking Barcelona, this fine building has been converted into a mind-blowing science museum, complete with a chunk of Amazonian rainforest.

El Raval

MACBA Museum

(Museu d'Art Contemporani de Barcelona; Map p66; 93 412 08 10; www.macba.cat; Plaça dels Àngels 1; adult/concession €7.50/6; 11am-8pm Mon & Wed, to midnight Thu-Fri, 10am-8pm Sat, 10am-3pm Sun & holidays; M Universitat) Designed by Richard Meier and opened in 1995, the MACBA has become the city's foremost contemporary art centre, with captivating exhibitions for the serious art lover. The permanent collection is on the ground floor and dedicates itself to Spanish and Catalan art from the second half of the 20th century, with works by Antoni

Tàpies, Joan Brossa and Miquel Barceló, among others.

PALAU GÜELL Palace

(Map p66; ☎93 317 39 74; www.palauguell.cat; Carrer Nou de la Rambla 3-5; adult/reduced €10/8; ⏱10am-8pm Apr-Sep, 10am-5.30pm Oct-Mar; M Drassanes) Finally reopened in its entirety in May 2010 after nearly 20 years under refurbishment, this is a magnificent example of the early days of Gaudí's fevered architectural imagination.

Up two floors are the main hall and its annexes; central to the structure is the magnificent music room with its rebuilt organ that is played during opening hours. The hall is a parabolic pyramid – each wall an arch stretching up three floors and coming together to form a dome. The family rooms are sometimes labyrinthine and dotted with piercings of light, or grand, stained-glass affairs. The roof is a mad tumult of tiled mosaics and fanciful design in the building's chimney pots.

ESGLÉSIA DE SANT PAU Church

(Map p66; Carrer de Sant Pau 101; ⏱cloister 10am-1pm & 4-7pm Mon-Sat; M Paral·lel) The best example of Romanesque architecture in the city is the dainty little cloister of this church.

La Ribera

PALAU DE LA MÚSICA CATALANA Architecture

(Map p66; ☎902 475485; www.palaumusica.org; Carrer de Sant Francesc de Paula 2; adult/child/student & EU senior €15/free/€7.50; ⏱50min tours every 30 minutes 10am-6pm Easter week & Aug, 10am-3.30pm Sep-Jul; M Urquinaona) This concert hall is a high point of Barcelona's Modernista architecture. It's not exactly a symphony, but more a series of crescendos in tile, brick, sculpted stone and stained glass.

The *palau*, like a peacock, shows off much of its splendour on the outside. Take in the principal facade with its mosaics, floral capitals and the sculpture cluster representing Catalan popular music. Wander inside the foyer and restaurant areas to admire the spangled, tiled pillars. Best of all, however, is the richly colourful auditorium upstairs, with its ceiling of blue-and-gold stained glass and shimmering skylight that slows like a tiny sun.

Narrow alleys criss-cross the historic Barri Gòtic (p65)

Don't Miss Museu Picasso

Set in five contiguous medieval stone mansions, the celebrated Museu Picasso includes more than 3500 artworks from one of the giants of the art world. This collection is uniquely fascinating, concentrating on Picasso's formative years and several specific moments in his later life, but those interested primarily in cubism may not be satisfied.

A visit starts with sketches and oils from Picasso's earliest years in Málaga and A Coruña – around 1893-95.

The enormous *Ciència i Caritat* (Science and Charity) showcases his masterful academic techniques of portraiture.

His first consciously themed adventure, the Blue Period, is well covered. His nocturnal blue-tinted views of *Terrats de Barcelona* (Roofs of Barcelona) and *El Foll* (The Madman) are cold and cheerless, yet somehow spectrally alive.

Among the later works, done in Cannes in 1957, *Las Meninas* is a complex technical series of studies on Diego Velázquez' masterpiece of the same name (which hangs in the Prado in Madrid).

NEED TO KNOW

Map p66; ☎93 256 30 00; www.museupicasso.bcn.es; Carrer de Montcada 15-23; adult/student/senior & child under 16yr €11/6/free, temporary exhibitions adult/student/senior & child under 16yr €6/2.90/free, 3-8pm Sun & 1st Sun of month free; ⏰10am-8pm Tue-Sun & holidays; Ⓜ Jaume I

MUSEU BARBIER-MUELLER D'ART PRE-COLOMBÍ Museum

(**Map p66; ☎93 310 45 16; www.barbier-mueller.ch; Carrer de Montcada 14; adult/student/senior & child under 16yr €3.50/1.70/free, 1st Sun of month free; ⏰11am-7pm Tue-Fri, 10am-7pm Sat, 10am-3pm Sun & holidays; Ⓜ Jaume I**) The wonderfully illuminated artefacts inside the medieval Palau Nadal are part of the treasure-trove of pre-Columbian art collected by Swiss businessman Josef Mueller (who died in 1977) and his son-in-law

Jean-Paul Barbier, who directs the Musée Barbier-Mueller in Geneva.

ESGLÉSIA DE SANTA MARIA DEL MAR Church

(Map p66; ☎93 319 05 16; Plaça de Santa Maria del Mar; ⏰9am-1.30pm & 4.30-8pm; Ⓜ Jaume I) At the southwest end of **Passeig del Born** stands the apse of Barcelona's finest Catalan Gothic church, Santa Maria del Mar (Our Lady of the Sea). Built in the 14th century with record-breaking speed for the time (it took just 54 years), the church is remarkable for its architectural harmony and simplicity.

PARC DE LA CIUTADELLA Park

(Map p66; Passeig de Picasso; ⏰8am-6pm Nov-Feb, to 8pm Oct & Mar, to 9pm Apr-Sep; Ⓜ Arc de Triomf) Come for a stroll, a picnic, a visit to the zoo or to inspect Catalonia's regional parliament, but don't miss a visit to this, the most central green lung in the city. Parc de la Ciutadella is perfect for winding down.

La Barceloneta & the Waterfront

La Barceloneta, laid out in the 18th century and subsequently heavily over-developed, was once a factory workers' and fishermen's quarter. Today the smokestacks are gone (as are most of the fishing families), though an authentic, ungentrified air still permeates these narrow gridlike streets. You'll find some excellent seafood restaurants here and a few bohemianesque neighbourhood bars. Barceloneta meets the sea at the city's sparkling new waterfront, with a beachside promenade extending some 4.5km past artificial beaches, parks and new high-rises to El Fòrum.

On La Barceloneta's seaward side are the first of Barcelona's beaches, which are popular on summer weekends. The pleasant **Passeig Marítim de la Barceloneta** (**Ⓜ Barceloneta or Ciutadella Vila Olímpica**), a 1.25km promenade from La Barceloneta to Port Olímpic, is a haunt for strollers, runners and cyclists.

Left: Palau de la Música Catalana (p70); **Below:** MACBA (p69)
LEFT: LONELY PLANET/GETTY IMAGES ©; BELOW: JEAN-PIERRE LESCOURRET/GETTY IMAGES ©

MUSEU D'HISTÒRIA DE CATALUNYA Museum

(Museum of Catalonian History; Map p66; ☎93 225 47 00; www.mhcat.net; Plaça de Pau Vila 3; adult/child permanent exhibition only €4/3, permanent & temporary exhibitions €5/4, 1st Sun of month free ; ⏰10am-7pm Tue & Thu-Sat, to 8pm Wed, to 2.30pm Sun; Ⓜ Barceloneta) Spanning over 2000 years of Catalan history, this harbourfront museum takes you from the Stone Age through to the early 1980s, with dioramas, artefacts, videos, models and audio recordings helping to conjure up the past.

L'Eixample

Stretching north, east and west of Plaça de Catalunya, L'Eixample (the Extension) was Barcelona's 19th-century answer to overcrowding in the medieval city.

The development of L'Eixample coincided with the city's Modernisme period and so it's home to many Modernista creations. Apart from La Sagrada Família, the principal ones are clustered on or near L'Eixample's main avenue, Passeig de Gràcia.

CASA BATLLÓ Architecture

(Map p74; ☎93 216 03 06; www.casabatllo.es; Passeig de Gràcia 43; adult/senior, student & child 7-18yr/child under 7yr €18.15/€14.55/free; ⏰9am-8pm; Ⓜ Passeig de Gràcia) One of the strangest residential buildings in Europe, this is Gaudí at his hallucinogenic best. The facade, sprinkled with bits of blue, mauve and green tiles and studded with wave-shaped window frames and balconies, rises to an uneven blue-tiled roof with a solitary tower.

The balconies look like the bony jaws of some strange beast and the roof represents Sant Jordi (St George) and the dragon. Even the roof was built to look like the shape of an animal's back, with shiny scales – the 'spine' changes colour as you walk around. If you stare long enough at the building, it seems almost to be a living being.

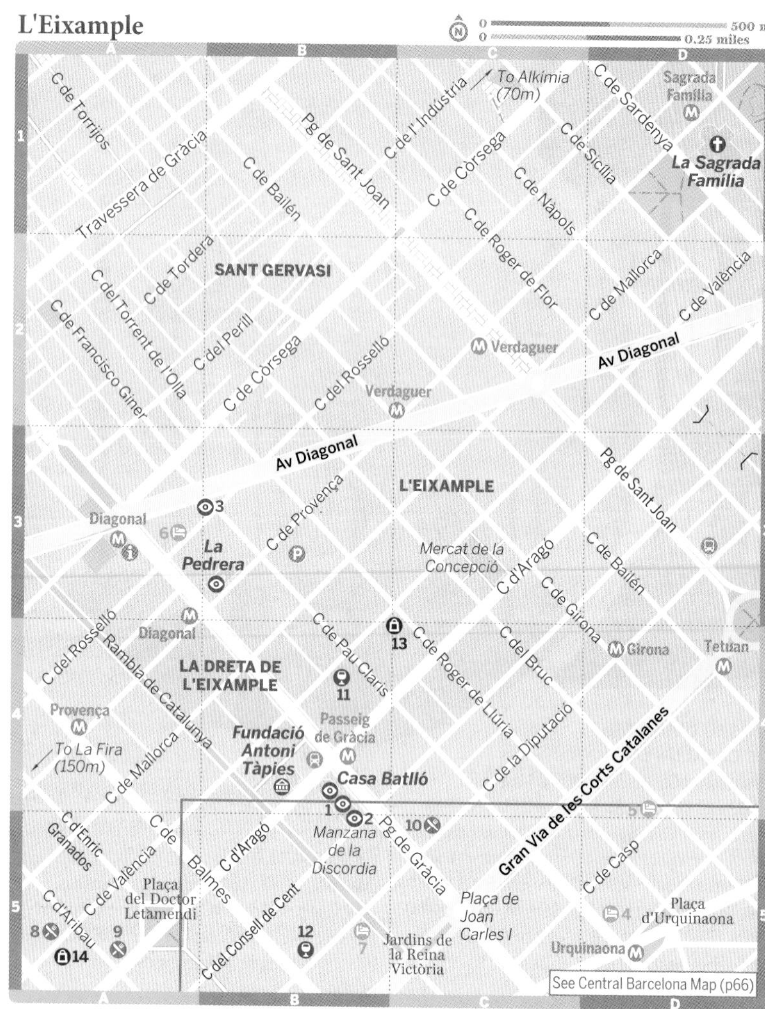

Inside, Gaudí eschewed the straight line, and so the staircase wafts you up to the 1st (main) floor, where the salon looks onto Passeig de Gràcia. Everything swirls: the ceiling is twisted into a vortex around its sun-like lamp; the doors, window and skylights are dreamy waves of wood and coloured glass. Twisting, tiled chimney pots add a surreal touch to the roof.

FREE CASA AMATLLER Architecture

(Map p74; ☎93 487 72 17; www.amatller.org; Passeig de Gràcia 41; ⊙10am-8pm Mon-Sat, to 3pm Sun, guided tour in English noon Fri, in Catalan & Spanish noon Wed; M Passeig de Gràcia) One of Puig i Cadafalch's most striking bits of Modernista fantasy, Casa Amatller combines Gothic window frames with a stepped gable borrowed from Dutch urban architecture. But the busts and reliefs of dragons, knights and other characters dripping off the main facade are pure caprice.

Renovation due for completion in 2013 will see the 1st floor converted into a museum with period pieces, while the

L'Eixample

Top Sights

	Casa Batlló	B4
	Fundació Antoni Tàpies	B4
	La Pedrera	B3
	La Sagrada Família	D1

Sights

1	Casa Amatller	B4
2	Casa Lleó Morera	B5
3	Palau del Baró Quadras	B3

Sleeping

4	Five Rooms	D5
5	Hotel Constanza	D4
6	Hotel Omm	A3
7	Hotel Praktik	B5

Eating

8	Cata 1.81	A5
9	Cinc Sentits	A5
10	Tapaç 24	C5

Drinking

11	Les Gens Que J'Aime	B4
12	Monvínic	B5

Shopping

13	Joan Murrià	C4
14	Xampany	A5

2nd floor will house the Institut Amatller d'Art Hispanic.

LA PEDRERA Architecture

(Casa Milà; Map p74; ☎902 400973; www.fundaciocaixacatalunya.es; Carrer de Provença 261-265; adult/student/child €15/13.50/7.50; 9am-8pm Mar-Oct, to 6.30pm Nov-Feb; M Diagonal) This undulating beast is another madcap Gaudí masterpiece, built in 1905-10 as a combined apartment and office block.

The top-floor apartment, attic and roof, together make up the **Espai Gaudí** (Gaudí Space). The roof is the most extraordinary element, with its giant chimney pots looking like multicoloured medieval knights. One floor below, you can appreciate Gaudí's taste for parabolic arches in a modest **museum** dedicated to his work.

FUNDACIÓ ANTONI TÀPIES Gallery

(Map p74; ☎93 487 03 15; www.fundaciotapies.org; Carrer d'Aragó 255; adult/child under 16yr €7/5.60; 10am-8pm Tue-Sun; M Passeig de Gràcia) The Fundació Antoni Tàpies is both a pioneering Modernista building (completed in 1885) and the major collection of the leading 20th-century Catalan artist, Antoni Tàpies.

The building, designed by Domènech i Montaner, combines a brick-covered iron frame with Islamic-inspired decoration. Tàpies crowned it with the meanderings of his own mind, a work called *Núvol i Cadira* (Cloud and Chair) that spirals above the building like a storm.

FREE **PALAU DEL BARÓ QUADRAS** Architecture

(Casa Asia; Map p74; ☎93 368 08 36; www.casaasia.es; Avinguda Diagonal 373; 10am-8pm Tue-Sat, to 2pm Sun; M Diagonal) Puig i Cadafalch designed Palau del Baró Quadras (built 1902–06) in an exuberant Gothic-inspired style. The main facade is its most intriguing, with a soaring, glassed-in gallery.

Decor inside is eclectic, but dominated by Middle Eastern and Oriental themes.

HOSPITAL DE LA SANTA CREU I DE SANT PAU Architecture

(☎93 317 76 52; www.rutadelmodernisme.com; Carrer de Cartagena 167; guided tour adult/senior & student €10/5; tours 10am, 11am, noon & 1pm in English, others in Catalan, French & Spanish; M Hospital de Sant Pau) Domènech i Montaner outdid himself as architect and philanthropist with this Modernista masterpiece, long considered one of the city's most important hospitals.

The complex, including 16 pavilions – together with the Palau de la Música Catalana, a joint World Heritage Site – is lavishly decorated and each pavilion is unique.

TORRE AGBAR Architecture

(☎93 342 21 29; www.torreagbar.com; Avinguda Diagonal 225; M Glòries) Barcelona's very own cucumber-shaped tower, Jean Nouvel's luminous Torre Agbar (which houses the city water company's headquarters), is the most daring addition to Barcelona's skyline since the first towers of La Sagrada Família went up.

FLICKR/GETTY IMAGES ©

Don't Miss La Sagrada Família

If you have time for only one sightseeing outing, this should be it. La Sagrada Família inspires awe by its sheer verticality, and in the manner of the medieval cathedrals it emulates, it's still under construction after more than 100 years. When completed, the highest tower will be more than half as high again as those that stand today.

The **Nativity Facade** is the artistic pinnacle of the building, mostly created under Gaudí's personal supervision. The three-part portal portrays Christ's birth and childhood. Three sections of the portal represent, from left to right, Hope, Charity and Faith. Among the forest of sculpture on the Charity portal you can see, low down, the manger surrounded by an ox, an ass, the shepherds and kings, and angel musicians.

The southwest **Passion Facade**, on the theme of Christ's last days and death, was built between 1954 and 1978 based on surviving drawings by Gaudí, with four towers and a large, sculpture-bedecked portal. The main series of sculptures, on three levels, are in an S-shaped sequence, starting with the Last Supper at the bottom left and ending with Christ's burial at the top right.

The **Glory Facade** is under construction and will, like the others, be crowned by four towers – the total of 12 representing the Twelve Apostles. Gaudí wanted it to be the most magnificent facade of the church.

Open the same times as the church, the **Museu Gaudí**, below ground level, includes interesting material on Gaudí's life and other works, as well as models and photos of La Sagrada Família.

NEED TO KNOW

Map p74; ☎93 207 30 31; www.sagradafamilia.org; Carrer de Mallorca 401; adult/senior & student/child under 10yr €13/11/free; 🕘9am-8pm Apr-Sep, to 6pm Oct-Mar; Ⓜ Sagrada Família

Gràcia

FREE PARK GÜELL Park

(☎93 413 24 00; Carrer d'Olot 7; admission free; ⏰10am-9pm Jun-Sep, 10am-8pm Apr, May & Oct, 10am-7pm Mar & Nov, 10am-6pm Dec-Feb; 🚌24, Ⓜ Lesseps or Vallcarca) North of Gràcia and about 4km from Plaça de Catalunya, Park Güell is where Gaudí turned his hand to landscape gardening. It's a strange, enchanting place where his passion for natural forms really took flight – to the point where the artificial almost seems more natural than the natural.

Just inside the main entrance on Carrer d'Olot, immediately recognisable by the two Hansel-and-Gretel gatehouses, is the park's newly refurbished Centre d'Interpretaciò, in the **Pavelló de Consergeria**, which is a typically curvaceous former porter's home that hosts a display on Gaudí's building methods and the history of the park.

The spired house to the right of Sala Hipóstila is the **Casa-Museu Gaudí** (www.casamuseugaudi.org; adult/senior & student €5.50/4.50; ⏰10am-8pm), where Gaudí lived for most of his last 20 years (1906–26).

Pedralbes

CAMP NOU Stadium

(☎93 496 36 00; www.fcbarcelona.com; Carrer d'Aristides Maillol; adult/child €23/17; ⏰10am-8pm Mon-Sat, to 2.30pm Sun; Ⓜ Palau Reial) Among Barcelona's most-visited attractions is the high-tech Camp Nou Experience, a multimedia museum exploring the lore of the city's legendary home team, FC Barcelona. Barça is one of Europe's top football clubs, and its museum is a hit with football fans the world over. The best bits of the museum are the photo section, the goal videos and the views out over the stadium.

Unless you see a game, the only way to visit Camp Nou is by purchasing a ticket to the Camp Nou Experience, which (available in 7 languages) provides a look at the museum, followed by a self-guided tour of the stadium. The tour takes in the team's dressing rooms, heads out through the tunnel, onto the pitch and winds up in the presidential box. Set aside about 2½ hours for the whole visit.

If You Like... Roman Barcelona

If you like the signposts to Roman Barcelona in the Museu d'Història dela Ciutat, then journey back in time at these sites:

1 ROMAN WALLS

(Map p66) Third and 4th-century walls rebuilt after the first attacks by Germanic tribes from the north. One section is on the southwest side of Plaça de Ramon Berenguer el Gran, and the other is by the north end of Carrer del Sotstinent Navarro.

2 TEMPLE ROMÀ D'AUGUST

(Map p66; Carrer del Paradis; ⏰10am-8pm Tue-Sun; Ⓜ Jaume I) Four mighty, 1st-century AD columns from the temple stand just beyond the southeast end of the cathedral.

Montjuïc

Montjuïc, the hill overlooking the city centre from the southwest, is dotted with museums, soothing gardens and the main group of 1992 Olympic sites, along with a handful of theatres and clubs.

MUSEU NACIONAL D'ART DE CATALUNYA Museum

(MNAC; ☎93 622 03 76; www.mnac.es; Mirador del Palau Nacional; adult/student/senior & child under 15yr €10/7/free, 1st Sun of month free; ⏰10am-7pm Tue-Sat, 10am-2.30pm Sun & holidays, library 10am-6pm Mon-Fri, to 2.30pm Sat; Ⓜ Espanya) From across the city, the neobaroque silhouette of the Palau Nacional can be seen on the slopes of Montjuïc. Built for the 1929 World Exhibition and restored in 2005, it houses a vast collection of mostly Catalan art

La Sagrada Família

A Timeline

1882 Francesc del Villar is commissioned to construct a neo-Gothic church.

1883 Antoni Gaudí takes over as chief architect, and plans a far more ambitious church to hold 13,000 faithful.

1926 Death of Gaudí; work continues under Domènec Sugrañes. Much of the **apse** (1) and **Nativity Facade** (2) is completed.

1930 **Bell towers** (3) of the Nativity Facade completed.

1936 Construction is interrupted by Spanish Civil War; anarchists destroy Gaudí's plans.

1939-40 Architect Francesc de Paula Quintana i Vidal restores the crypt and meticulously reassembles many of Gaudí's lost models, some of which can be seen in the **museum** (4).

1976 Completion of **Passion Facade** (5).

1986-2006 Sculptor Josep Subirachs adds sculptural details to the Passion Facade including the panels telling the story of Christ's last days, amid much criticism for employing a style far removed from what was thought typical of Gaudí.

2000 **Central nave vault** (6) completed.

2010 Church completely roofed over; Pope Benedict XVI consecrates the church; work begins on a high-speed rail tunnel that will pass beneath the church's **Glory Facade** (7).

2020-40 Projected completion date.

TOP TIPS

Light The best light through the stained-glass windows of the Passion Facade bursts through into the heart of the church in the late afternoon.

Time Visit at opening time on weekdays to avoid the worst of the crowds.

Views Head up the Nativity Facade bell towers for the views, as long queues generally await at the Passion Facade towers.

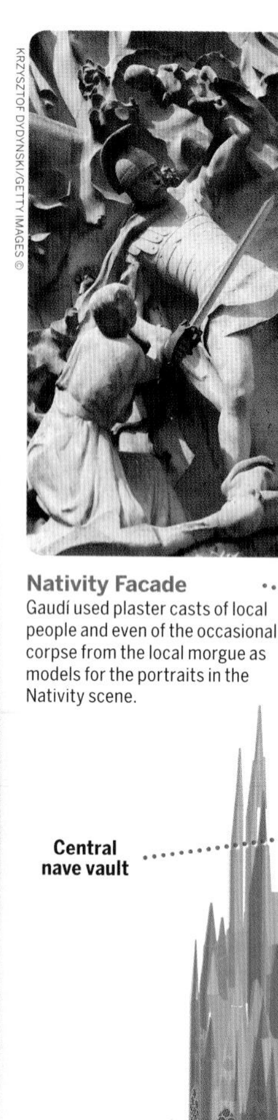

KRZYSZTOF DYDYNSKI/GETTY IMAGES ©

Spiral staircase

Nativity Facade
Gaudí used plaster casts of local people and even of the occasional corpse from the local morgue as models for the portraits in the Nativity scene.

Central nave vault

1

Apse
Built just after the crypt in mostly neo-Gothic style, it is capped by pinnacles that show a hint of the genius that Gaudí would later deploy in the rest of the church.

MICHELLE CHAPLOW/ALAMY ©

Bell towers
The towers (eight completed) of the three facades represent the 12 Apostles. Lifts whisk visitors up one tower of the Nativity and Passion Facades (the latter gets longer queues) for fine views.

Passion Facade
See the story of Christ's last days from Last Supper to burial in an S-shaped sequence from bottom to top of the facade. Check out the cryptogram in which the numbers always add up to 33, Christ's age at his death.

Completed church
Along with the Glory Facade and its four towers, six other towers remain to be completed. They will represent the four Evangelists, the Virgin Mary and, soaring above them all over the transept, a 170m colossus symbolising Christ.

Crypt
The first completed part of the church, the crypt is in largely neo-Gothic style and lies under the transept. Gaudí's burial place here can be seen from the Museu Gaudí.

Museu Gaudí
Jammed with old photos, drawings and restored plaster models that bring Gaudí's ambitions to life, the museum also houses an extraordinarily complex plumb-line device he used to calculate his constructions.

Glory Facade
This will be the most fanciful facade of all, with a narthex boasting 16 hyperboloid lanterns topped by cones that will look something like an organ made of melting ice cream.

Montjuïc

A Day Itinerary

Possibly the site of ancient pre-Roman settlements, Montjuïc today is a hilltop green lung looking over city and sea. Interspersed across varied gardens are major art collections, a fortress, Olympic Stadium and more. A solid one-day itinerary can take in the key spots.

Alight at Espanya metro stop and make for **CaixaForum** 1, always host to three or four free top-class exhibitions. The **Pavelló Mies van der Rohe** 2 across the road is an intriguing look at 1920s futurist housing by one of the 20th century's greatest architects. Uphill, the Romanesque art collection in the **Museu Nacional d'Art de Catalunya** 3 should not be missed. The restaurant here makes a pleasant lunch stop. Escalators lead further up the hill towards the **Estadi Olímpic** 4, scene of the 1992 Olympic Games. The road leads east to the **Fundació Joan Miró** 5, a shrine to the surrealist artist's creativity. Relax in the **Jardins de Mossèn Cinto Verdaguer** 6, the prettiest on the hill, before taking the cable car to the **Castell de Montjuïc** 7. If you pick the right day, you can round off by contemplating the gorgeously kitsch **La Font Màgica** 8 sound and light show.

TOP TIPS

Moving views Take the Transbordador Aeri from La Barceloneta for a bird's eye approach to Montjuïc. Or use the Teleféric de Montjuïc cable car to the Castell for more aerial views.

Summer fun The Castell de Montjuïc is the scene for outdoor summer cinema and concerts (see http://salamontjuic.org).

Beautiful bloomers Bursting with colour and serenity, the Jardins de Mossèn Cinto Verdaguer are exquisitely laid out with bulbs, especially tulips, and aquatic flowers.

CaixaForum

This former factory and barracks designed by Josep Puig i Cadafalch is an outstanding work of Modernista architecture; like a Lego fantasy in brick.

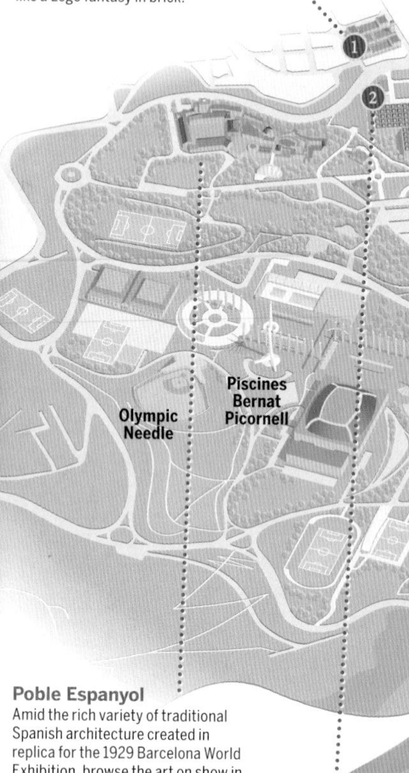

Poble Espanyol

Amid the rich variety of traditional Spanish architecture created in replica for the 1929 Barcelona World Exhibition, browse the art on show in the Fundació Fran Daurel.

Pavelló Mies van der Rohe

Admire the inventiveness of the great German architect Ludwig Mies van der Rohe in this recreation of his avant garde German pavillion for the 1929 World Exhibition.

KRZYSZTOF DYDYNSKI/GETTY IMAGES ©

La Font Màgica

Take a summer evening to behold the Magic Fountain come to life in a unique 15-minute sound and light performance, when the water glows like a cauldron of colour.

TRAVELPIX/ALAMY ©

Museu Nacional d'Art de Catalunya

Make a beeline for the Romanesque art selection and the 12th-century polychrome image of Christ in majesty, which was recovered from the apse of a country chapel in northwest Catalonia.

8

3

Teatre Grec

5

6

4

Estadi Olímpic

Jardí Botànic

7

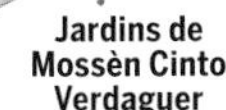

Castell de Montjuïc

Enjoy the sweeping views of the sea and city from atop this 17th-century fortress, once a political prison and long a symbol of oppression.

Fundació Joan Miró

Take in some of Joan Miró's giant canvases, and discover little-known works from his early years in the Sala Joan Prats and Sala Pilar Juncosa.

Museu d'Arqueologia de Catalunya

Seek out the Roman mosaic depicting the Three Graces, one of the most beautiful items in this museum, which was dedicated to the ancient past of Catalonia and neighbouring parts of Spain.

BAB/IMAGEBROCKER ©

BAB/IMAGEBROCKER ©

The Modernistas' Mission

Antoni Gaudí (1852–1926), known above all for La Sagrada Família (p76), was just one, albeit the most imaginative, of a generation of inventive architects who left an indelible mark on Barcelona between 1880 and the 1920s. They were called the Modernistas.

The local offshoot of the Europe-wide phenomenon of art nouveau, Modernisme was characterised by its taste for sinuous, flowing lines and adventurous combinations of materials like tile, glass, brick, iron and steel. But Barcelona's Modernistas were also inspired by an astonishing variety of other styles too: Gothic and Islamic, Renaissance and Romanesque, Byzantine and baroque.

L'Eixample, where most of Barcelona's new building was happening at the time, is home to the bulk of the Modernistas' creations. Others in the city include Gaudí's Palau Güell (p70) and Park Güell (p77); Domènech i Montaner's Palau de la Música Catalana (p70), **Castell dels Tres Dragons** (Map p66) and the **Hotel España restaurant** (Map p66; 93 318 17 58; www.hotelespanya.com; Carrer de Sant Pau 9-11; s €100, d €125-155; ; Liceu); and Puig i Cadafalch's **Els Quatre Gats restaurant** (Map p66; 93 302 41 40; Carrer de Montsió 3; meals: €30-€40; 8am-2am; Urquinaona)

spanning the early Middle Ages to the early 20th century.

The highlight here is the Romanesque art section, considered the most important concentration of early medieval art in the world. Rescued from neglected country churches across northern Catalonia in the early 20th century, the collection consists of huge 11th- and 12th-century frescoes, woodcarvings and painted altar frontals.

FUNDACIÓ JOAN MIRÓ Museum
(www.bcn.fjmiro.es; Plaça de Neptu; adult/senior & child €10/7; 10am-8pm Tue, Wed, Fri & Sat, to 9.30pm Thu, to 2.30pm Sun & holidays; 50, 55, 193, Paral·lel) Joan Miró, the city's best-known 20th-century artistic progeny, bequeathed this art foundation to his hometown in 1971.

The foundation rests amid the greenery of Montjuïc and holds the greatest single collection of the artist's work, comprising some 220 of his paintings, 180 sculptures, some textiles and more than 8000 drawings spanning his entire life.

Courses

COOK AND TASTE Cooking Course
(Map p66; 93 302 13 20; www.cookandtaste.net; Carrer del Paradís 3; half-day workshop €65; Liceu) Learn to whip up a few tapas dishes, paella and a traditional Catalan dessert at this Spanish cookery school.

Tours

BARCELONA WALKING TOURS Walking Tour
(Map p66; 93 285 38 34; www.barcelonaturisme.com; Plaça de Catalunya 17-S; Catalunya) The Oficina d'Informació de Turisme de Barcelona organises guided walking tours, most lasting two hours and starting at the tourist office.

MY FAVOURITE THINGS Tour
(637 265405; www.myft.net; tours €26-32) Offers tours (with no more than 10 participants) based on numerous themes: anything from design to food and rollerblading to sailing.

Sleeping

La Rambla

HOTEL CONTINENTAL Hotel **€€**

(Map p66; ☎93 301 25 70; www.hotelcontinental.com; La Rambla 138; s/d from €92/102; ❄ 📶; M Catalunya) Rooms at this old-fashioned hotel (where George Orwell stayed during the Spanish Civil War) are worn and rather spartan, but have romantic touches such as ceiling fans, brass bedsteads and frilly bedclothes. An extra €20 gets you a room with a small balcony overlooking La Rambla.

Barri Gòtic

HOTEL NERI Design Hotel **€€€**

(Map p66; ☎93 304 06 55; www.hotelneri.com; Carrer de Sant Sever 5; d from €270; ❄ @ 📶; M Liceu) Occupying a beautifully adapted, centuries-old building this stunningly renovated medieval mansion has elegant rooms with designer fittings. There's a fantastic restaurant on the ground floor and a small roof deck for catching some rays.

HOSTAL CAMPI Hostal **€**

(Map p66; ☎93 301 35 45; www.hostalcampi.com; Carrer de la Canuda 4; d €70, s/d without bathroom €35/60; @ 📶; M Catalunya) The best rooms at this friendly, central *hostal* are doubtless the doubles with their own toilets and showers. They are extremely roomy and bright, with attractive tile floors.

HOTEL CALIFORNIA Hotel **€€**

(Map p66; ☎93 317 77 66; www.hotelcaliforniabcn.com; Carrer d'en Rauric 14; s/d €70/120; ❄ @ 📶; M Liceu) A classic, central, gay-friendly establishment, the California offers 31 simple but spotlessly kept rooms in light, neutral colours, with good-sized beds, plasma-screen TVs and a bustling breakfast room.

El Raval

CASA CAMPER Design Hotel **€€€**

(Map p66; ☎93 342 62 80; www.casacamper.com; Carrer d'Elisabets 11; s/d €240/270; ⊖ ❄ @; M Liceu) Run by the well-known Mallorcan shoe people, the Casa Camper has an artfully designed foyer and spacious rooms.

Each is decorated in red, black and white and comes standard with Camper

Gaudí's Park Güell (p77)

Right: Gaudí's Park Güell (p77); **Below:** Mosaic detail at Park Güell

slippers and Vinçon furniture, where you can contemplate the hanging gardens outside your window.

HOTEL SAN AGUSTÍN Hotel **€€**
(Map p66; ☎93 318 16 58; www.hotelsa.com; Plaça de Sant Agustí 3; r from €80-180; ❄@📶; M Liceu) This former 18th-century monastery opened as a hotel in 1840, making it the city's oldest. The location is perfect – a quick stroll off La Rambla on a curious square. Rooms sparkle, and are mostly spacious and light-filled. Consider an attic double with sloping ceiling and bird's-eye views.

La Ribera

CHIC & BASIC Design Hotel **€€**
(Map p66; ☎93 295 46 52; www.chicandbasic.com; Carrer de la Princesa 50; s €96, d €132-192; ❄@; M Jaume I) This is a very cool hotel indeed, with its 31 spotlessly white rooms and fairy-lights curtains that change colour, adding an entirely new atmosphere to the space.

Many beautiful old features of the original building have been retained, such as the marble staircase.

HOTEL BANYS ORIENTALS Boutique Hotel **€€**
(Map p66; ☎93 268 84 60; www.hotelbanysorientals.com; Carrer de l'Argenteria 37; s/d €88/105, ste €130; ❄@; M Jaume I) Cool blues and aquamarines combine with dark-hued floors to lend this boutique hotel a quiet charm. All rooms, on the small side, look onto the street or back lanes. There are more spacious suites in two other nearby buildings.

L'Eixample

HOTEL PRAKTIK Boutique Hotel **€€**
(Map p74; ☎93 343 66 90; www.hotelpraktikrambla.com; Rambla de Catalunya 27; r from €80-170; ❄@📶; M Passeig de Gràcia) This Modernista gem hides a gorgeous little boutique number. The 43 rooms have daring ceramic touches, spot lighting and

contemporary art. There is a chilled reading area and deck-style lounge terrace.

FIVE ROOMS Boutique Hotel **€€**
(Map p74; ☎93 342 78 80; www.thefiverooms.com; Carrer de Pau Claris 72; s/d from €115/135, apt from €175; ❄@; M Urquinaona) On the border between L'Eixample, Five Rooms indeed has five rooms. Each is different, and features include broad, firm beds, stretches of exposed brick wall, restored mosaic tiles and minimalist decor.

HOTEL OMM Design Hotel **€€€**
(Map p74; ☎93 445 40 00; www.hotelomm.es; Carrer de Rosselló 265; d from €360; P❄@; M Diagonal) Design meets plain zany here, with a wild facade that would would no doubt have appealed to Dalí. Light, clear tones dominate in the ultra-modern rooms, of which there are several categories.

HOTEL CONSTANZA Boutique Hotel **€€**
(Map p74; ☎93 270 19 10; www.hotelconstanza.com; Carrer del Bruc 33; s/d €130/150; ❄@; M Girona or Urquinaona) This boutique beauty has stolen the hearts of many a visitor to Barcelona. Design touches abound, and little details like flowers in the bathroom add charm. The terrace is a nice spot to relax with views over the rooftops of L'Eixample.

Eating

Barcelona is something of a foodies' paradise, combining rich Catalan cooking traditions with a new wave of culinary wizards by chefs at the vanguard of *nueva cocina española*.

Barri Gòtic

PLA Fusion **€€**
(Map p66; ☎93 412 65 52; www.elpla.cat; Carrer de la Bellafila 5; mains €18-24; dinner; M Jaume I) One of Gòtic's longstanding favourites, Pla is a stylish, romantically lit medieval den that churns out temptations like oxtail braised in red wine, seared tuna with roasted aubergine, and 'Thai-style' monkfish.

Cafe culture along La Rambla (p64)

ALFREDO MAIQUEZ/GETTY IMAGES ©

LA VINATERIA DELL CALL Spanish **€€**
(Map p66; ☎93 302 60 92; http://lavinateriadelcall.com; Carrer de Sant Domènec del Call 9; small plates €7-11; ⏰dinner; Ⓜ Jaume I) In a magical setting in the former Jewish quarter, this tiny jewelbox of a restaurant serves up tasty Iberian dishes. Portions are small and made for sharing, and there's a good and affordable selection of wines.

CAN CULLERETES Catalan **€€**
(Map p66; ☎93 317 30 22; Carrer Quintana 5; mains €8-14; ⏰lunch & dinner Tue-Sat, lunch Sun; Ⓜ Liceu) Founded in 1786, Barcelona's oldest restaurant is still going strong, with tourists and locals flocking to enjoy its rambling interior, old-fashioned tile-filled decor, and enormous helpings of traditional Catalan food.

El Raval

BAR PINOTXO Tapas **€€**
(Map p66; Mercat de la Boqueria; meals €20; ⏰6am-5pm Mon-Sat Sep-Jul; Ⓜ Liceu) Arguably La Boqueria's best tapas bar sits among the half-dozen or so informal eateries within the market. The popular owner, Juanito, might serve up chickpeas with a sweet sauce of pine nuts and raisins, soft baby squid with cannelini beans, or caramel sweet pork belly.

CA L'ISIDRE Catalan **€€€**
(Map p66; ☎93 441 11 39; www.calisidre.com; Carrer de les Flors 12; mains €20-70; ⏰Mon-Sat, closed Easter & 3 weeks in Aug; Ⓜ Paral·lel) Ca L'Isidre is an old-world gem. Try artichoke hearts stuffed with mushrooms and foie gras, tuna steak with a tomato coulis or lamb's brains with black butter.

GRANJA VIADER Cafe **€**
(Map p66; ☎93 318 34 86; www.granjaviader.cat; Carrer d'en Xuclà 4; ⏰9am-1.45pm & 5-8.45pm Tue-Sat, 5-8.45pm Mon; Ⓜ Liceu) For more than a century, people have flocked down this alley to get to the cups of home-made hot chocolate and whipped cream (ask for a *suís*) ladled out in this classic Catalan-style milk bar-cum-deli.

La Ribera

CAL PEP Tapas **€€**
(Map p66; ☎93 310 79 61; www.calpep.com; Plaça de les Olles 8; mains €8-18; ⏰lunch Tue-Sat, dinner Mon-Fri Sep-Jul; Ⓜ Barceloneta) Ever popular Cal Pep has queues around the square with people trying to get in. And if you want one of the five tables out

the back, you'll need to call ahead. Most people are happy elbowing their way to the bar for some of the tastiest gourmet seafood tapas in town.

CASA DELFÍN Spanish **€**

(Map p66; Passeig del Born 36; mains €4-12; noon-1am; M Barceloneta) One of Barcelona's culinary delights, Casa Delfin is everything you dream of when you think of Catalan (and Mediterranean) cooking. Meaty monkfish roasted in white wine and garlic, mussels and clams with Catalan flatbread and many other dishes are all done to perfection.

La Barceloneta & the Waterfront

CAN MAJÓ Seafood **€€**

(93 221 54 55; Carrer del Almirall Aixada 23; mains €18-24; lunch & dinner Tue-Sat, lunch Sun; 45, 57, 59, 64 or 157, M Barceloneta) Virtually on the beach (with tables outside in summer), Can Majó has a long and steady reputation for fine seafood, particularly its rice dishes and bountiful *suquets* (fish stews).

L'Eixample

TAPAÇ 24 Tapas **€€**

(Map p74; www.carlesabellan.com; Carrer de la Diputació 269; mains €10-20; 9am-midnight Mon-Sat; M Passeig de Gràcia) Carles Abellán runs this basement tapas haven known for its gourmet versions of old faves. Specials include the *bikini* (toasted ham and cheese sandwich – here the ham is cured and the truffle makes all the difference), a thick black *arròs negre de sípia* (squid-ink black rice) and, for dessert, *xocolata amb pa, sal i oli* (balls of chocolate in olive oil with a touch of salt and wafer).

ALKÍMIA Catalan **€€€**

(93 207 61 15; www.alkimia.cat; Carrer de l'Indústria 79; set menu €38-84; lunch & dinner Mon-Fri Sep-Jul; M Verdaguer) Jordi Vila, a culinary alchemist, serves up refined Catalan dishes with a twist in this elegant, white-walled locale well off the tourist trail. Dishes such as his *arròs de nyore i safrà amb escamarlans de la costa* (saffron and sweet-chilli rice with crayfish) earned Vila his first Michelin star.

CINC SENTITS International **€€**

(Map p74; 93 323 94 90; www.cincsentits.com; Carrer d'Aribau 58; mains €10-20; lunch & dinner Tue-Sat ; M Passeig de Gràcia) The 'Five Senses' has earned rave reviews for its indulgent tasting menu (from €49 to €69), a series of small, experimental dishes. A key is the use of fresh local product, such as fish landed on the Costa Brava and top-quality suckling pig from Extremadura.

CATA 1.81 Tapas **€€**

(Map p74; 93 323 68 18; www.cata181.com; Carrer de València 181; tapas €7-12; dinner Mon-Sat; M Passeig de Gràcia) A beautifully designed

Inside Gaudí's La Pedrera (p75)

EKATERINA NOSENKO/GETTY IMAGES ©

eatery, this is the place to come for fine wines and dainty gourmet dishes, such as *raviolis amb bacallà* (salt-cod dumplings) or *truita de patates i tòfona negre* (thick potato tortilla with traces of black truffle).

Montjuïc & Poble Sec

TICKETS Spanish **€€**

(off Map p66; www.ticketsbar.es; Avinguda del Paral·lel 164; tapas from €4-12; ⏲lunch & dinner; Ⓜ Paral·lel) Tickets is the much touted new venture created by rockstar chef Ferran Adrià (of El Bulli fame) and his brother Albert.

It's a fairly flamboyant affair in terms of decor, playing with circus images and theatre lights, while the food has kept some of the El Bulli's whimsical molecular dishes; there's also a more serious seafood bar.

Drinking

BAR MARSELLA Bar

(Map p66; Carrer de Sant Pau 65; ⏲10pm-2am Mon-Thu, 10pm-3am Fri & Sat; Ⓜ Liceu) Hemingway used to slump over an *absenta* (absinthe) in this bar, which has been in business since 1820. It still specialises in absinthe, a drink to be treated with respect.

EL XAMPANYET Wine Bar

(Map p66; Carrer de Montcada 22; ⏲noon-4pm & 7-11pm Tue-Sat, noon-4pm Sun; Ⓜ Jaume I) Nothing has changed for decades in one of the city's best-known *cava* (sparkling wine) bars. Plant yourself at the bar or seek out a table against the decoratively tiled walls for a glass or three of *cava* and an assortment of tapas, such as the tangy *boquerons en vinagre* (white anchovies in vinegar).

MONVÍNIC Wine Bar

(Map p74; ☎932 72 61 87; www.monvinic.com; Carrer de la Diputació 249 ; ⏲wine bar 1.30-11.30pm, restaurant 1.30-3.30pm & 8.30-10.30pm; Ⓜ Passeig de Gracia) One of Spain's best wine bars, Mondvínic has a wine list with more than 3,000 varieties (including 60 by the glass). At the back is the

Left: Tapas bar in Poble Sec; **Below:** Port Vell (Map p53)
LEFT: DIEGO LEZAMA/GETTY IMAGES ©; BELOW: FLY AWAY WITH YOUR IMAGINATION/GETTY IMAGES ©

restaurant that specialises in Mediterranean cuisine, with ingredients sourced locally from Catalan farmers.

LA FIRA Bar

(www.lafiraclub.com; Carrer de Provença 171; admission €8-12; 10.30pm-3am Wed-Sat; FGC Provença) A designer bar with a difference. Wander in past distorting mirrors and ancient fairground attractions from Germany. Put in coins and listen to hens squawk. Speaking of squawking, the music swings wildly from whiffs of house through '90s hits to Spanish pop classics.

LES GENS QUE J'AIME Bar

(Map p74; Carrer de València 286; 6pm-2.30am Sun-Thu, to 3am Fri & Sat; M Passeig de Gràcia) This intimate basement relic of the 1960s follows a deceptively simple formula: chilled jazz music in the background, minimal lighting from vintage lamps and a cosy, scattering of red velvet-backed lounges around tiny tables.

Entertainment

PALAU DE LA MÚSICA CATALANA Live Music

(Map p66; 902 442882; www.palaumusica.org; Carrer de Sant Francesc de Paula 2; box office 10am-9pm Mon-Sat; M Urquinaona) A feast for the eyes, this Modernista delight is also the city's traditional venue for classical and choral music, along with the occasional flamenco, gospel or world-music group.

JAZZ SÍ CLUB Live Music

(Map p66; 93 329 00 20; www.tallerdemusics.com; Carrer de Requesens 2; admission €8, drink included; 6-11pm; M Sant Antoni) A cramped little bar run by the Taller de Músics (Musicians' Workshop) serves as the stage for a varied program of jazz through to some good flamenco (Friday nights). Thursday night is Cuban night, Sunday is rock and the rest are devoted to jazz and/or blues sessions.

HARLEM JAZZ CLUB Live Music
(Map p66; ☎93 310 07 55; www.harlemjazzclub.es; Carrer de la Comtessa de Sobradiel 8; admission €6-15; ⏰8pm-4am Tue-Thu & Sun, to 5am Fri & Sat; Ⓜ Drassanes) This narrow, old-town dive is one of the best spots in town for jazz – along with the occasional Latin, blues or African band.

Shopping

L'ARCA DE L'ÀVIA Vintage, Clothing
(Map p66; ☎93 302 15 98; Carrer dels Banys Nous 20; Ⓜ Liceu) Grandma's chest is indeed full of extraordinary remembrances from the past, including 18th-century embroidered silk vests, elaborate silk kimonos and wedding dresses and shawls from the 1920s.

LA MANUAL ALPARGATERA Shoes
(Map p66; ☎93 301 01 72; http://homepage.mac.com/manualp; Carrer d'Avinyó 7; Ⓜ Liceu) Everyone from Salvador Dalí to Jean Paul Gaultier has ordered a pair of *espadrilles* (rope-soled canvas shoes or sandals) from this famous store, which is the birthplace of the iconic footwear.

JOAN MURRIÀ Food
(Map p74; ☎93 215 57 89; www.murria.cat; Carrer de Roger de Llúria 85; Ⓜ Passeig de Gràcia) Ramon Casas designed the century-old Modernista shop-front ads for this delicious delicatessen. For a century the gluttonous have trembled at this altar of speciality food goods from Catalonia and beyond.

XAMPANY Drink
(Map p74; ☎610 845011; Carrer de València 200; ⏰4.30-10pm Mon-Fri, 10am-2pm Sat; Ⓜ Passeig de Gràcia) Since 1981, this 'Cathedral of Cava' has been a veritable Aladdin's cave of *cava*, with bottles of the stuff crammed high and into every possible chaotic corner of this dimly lit locale.

Information

Tourist Information

In addition to the following listed tourist offices, information booths operate at Estació Nord bus station, Plaça del Portal de la Pau and at the foot of the Mirador a Colom. At least three others are set up at various points around the city centre in summer.

Oficina d'Informació de Turisme de Barcelona as its **main branch** (☎93 285 38 34; www.barcelonaturisme.com; underground at Plaça de Catalunya 17-S; ⏰8.30am-8.30pm; Ⓜ Catalunya) in Plaça de Catalunya. It concentrates on city information and can help book accommodation. The branch in the EU arrivals hall at **Aeroport del Prat**

Exploring Barcelona's Markets

The sprawling **Els Encants Vells** (Fira de Bellcaire; ☎93 246 30 30; www.encantsbcn.com; Plaça de les Glòries Catalanes; ⏰7am-6pm Mon, Wed, Fri & Sat; Ⓜ Glòries), also known as the Fira de Bellcaire, is the city's principal flea market. There is an awful lot of junk, but you can turn up interesting items if you hunt around. The Barri Gòtic is enlivened by an **art and crafts market** (Plaça de Sant Josep Oriol; Liceu) on Saturday and Sunday, the antiques **Mercat Gòtic** (Plaça Nova; Liceu or Jaume I) on Thursday, and a **coin and stamp collectors' market** (Plaça Reial; Liceu) on Sunday morning. The **Mercat de la Boqueria** (Map p66; ☎93 412 13 15; www.boqueria.info; La Rambla 91; ⏰8am-8.30pm Mon-Sat, closed Sun; Ⓜ Liceu) is one of the best-stocked and most colourful produce markets in Europe, while just beyond the western edge of El Raval, the punters at the **Mercat de Sant Antoni** (Map p66; Carrer de Mallorca 157; ⏰7am-8.30pm; Ⓜ Hospital Clínic) dedicate Sunday morning to old maps, stamps, books and cards.

(Aeroport del Prat, terminals 1, 2B & 2A; 9am-9pm) has information on all of Catalonia; a smaller office at the international arrivals hall opens the same hours. The branch at Estació Sants (**8am-8pm; Sants Estació)** has limited city information. There's also a helpful branch in the town hall **(Plaça Sant Jaume; 93 285 38 32; Carrer de la Ciutat 2; 8.30am-8.30pm Mon-Fri, 9am-7pm Sat, 9am-2pm Sun & holidays; M Jaume I)**.

La Rambla Information Office **(www.barcelonaturisme.com; La Rambla dels Estudis 115; 8.30am-8.30pm; M Liceu)**

Palau Robert Regional Tourist Office **(93 238 80 91, from outside Catalonia 902 400012; www.gencat.net/probert; Passeig de Gràcia 107; 10am-8pm Mon-Sat, 10am-2.30pm Sun)** Has a host of material on Catalonia, audiovisual resources, a bookshop and a branch of Turisme Juvenil de Catalunya (for youth travel).

Getting There & Away

Air

Aeroport del Prat **(902 404704; www.aena.es)** is 12km southwest of the centre at El Prat de Llobregat. Barcelona is a big international and domestic destination, with direct flights from North America, as well as many European cities.

Several budget airlines, including Ryanair, use Girona-Costa Brava airport, 11km south of Girona and about 80km north of Barcelona. Buses connect with Barcelona's Estació del Nord bus station.

Bus

Long-distance buses for destinations throughout Spain leave from the Estació del Nord **(902 260606; www.barcelonanord.com; Carrer d'Ali Bei 80; Arc de Triomf)**. A plethora of companies operates services to different parts of the country, although many come under the umbrella of Alsa **(902 422242; www.alsa.es)**. There are frequent services to Madrid, Valencia and Zaragoza (20 or more a day) and several daily departures to such distant destinations as Burgos, Santiago de Compostela and Seville.

Departures from Estació del Nord include the following (where frequencies vary, the lowest figure is usually for Sunday; fares quoted are the lowest available):

DESTINATION	FREQUENCY (PER DAY)	DURATION (HR)	COST (ONE WAY, €)
Burgos	5-6	7½-8½	37
Granada	5-8	12½-14¼	73
Madrid	up to 16	7½-8	30
Seville	1-2	14¾	82
Valencia	up to 14	4-4½	27
Zaragoza	up to 22	3¾	15

Car & Motorcycle

Autopistas (tollways) head out of Barcelona in most directions, including the C31/C32 to the southern Costa Brava; the C32 to Sitges; the C16 to Manresa (with a turn-off for Montserrat); and the AP7 north to Girona, Figueres and France, and south to Tarragona and Valencia (turn off along the AP2 for Lleida, Zaragoza and Madrid). The toll-free alternatives, such as the A2 north to Girona, Figueres and France, and west to Lleida and beyond, or the A7 to Tarragona, tend to be busy and slow.

Train

The main international and domestic station is Estació Sants **(Plaça dels Països Catalans; Sants Estació)**, 2.5km west of La Rambla. Other stops on long-distance lines include Catalunya and Passeig de Gràcia. Information windows operate at Estació Sants and Passeig de Gràcia station.

Eighteen high-speed Tren de Alta Velocidad Española (AVE) trains between Madrid and Barcelona run daily in each direction, nine of them in under three hours. A typical one-way price is €118. The line will eventually run right across Barcelona (via a controversial tunnel) and north to the French frontier. A new high-speed TGV from France connects Paris with Figueres (from €74, 5½ hours). Some other popular runs include the following (fares represent range of lowest fares depending on type of train):

DESTINATION	FREQUENCY (PER DAY)	DURATION (HR)	COST (ONE WAY, €)
Burgos	4	6-7	66-81
Valencia	up to 15	3-4½	36-45
Zaragoza	up to 35	1½-4¼	52-66

Mercat de la Boqueria (see boxed text, p90)

HIROSHI HIGUCHI/GETTY IMAGES ©

Getting Around

The metro is the easiest way of getting around and reaches most places you're likely to visit (although not the airport). For some trips you need buses or FGC suburban trains.

To/From the Airport

The **A1 Aerobús** (**☎93 415 60 20; one way €5.65**) runs from Terminal 1 to Plaça de Catalunya via Plaça d'Espanya, Gran Via de les Corts Catalanes (on the corner of Carrer del Comte d'Urgell) and Plaça de la Universitat (every six to 15 minutes depending on the time of day; 35 minutes) from 6.10am to 1.05am. A2 Aerobús does the same run from Terminal 2, from 6am to 1am. You can buy tickets on the bus.

Renfe's R2 Nord train line runs between the airport and Passeig de Gràçia (via Estació Sants) in central Barcelona (about 35 minutes), before heading out of town. Tickets cost €3.60, unless you have a T-10 multitrip public-transport ticket. The service from the airport starts at 5.42am and ends at 11.38pm daily.

A taxi to/from the centre, about a half-hour ride depending on traffic, costs around €25 to €30.

Sagalés (**☎902 130014; www.sagales.com**) runs the **Barcelona Bus** (**☎902 130014; www.barcelonabus.com**) service between Girona airport and Estació del Nord bus station in Barcelona (one way/return €15/25, 70 minutes).

Car & Motorcycle

Limited parking in the Ciutat Vella is virtually all for residents only, with some metered parking. The narrow streets of Gràcia are not much better. The broad boulevards of L'Eixample are divided into blue and green zones. For nonresidents they mean the same thing: limited meter parking. Fees vary but tend to hover around €3 per hour. Parking stations are also scattered all over L'Eixample, with a few in the old centre too. Prices vary from around €4 to €5 per hour.

Public Transport

Bus

The city transport authority, **Transports Metropolitans de Barcelona** (**TMB; ☎010; www.tmb.net**), runs buses along most city routes every few minutes from 5am or 6am to 10pm or 11pm. Many routes pass through Plaça de Catalunya and/or Plaça de la Universitat.

Metro & FGC

The TMB metro has seven numbered and colour-coded lines. It runs from 5am to midnight Sunday to Thursday and holidays, from 5am to 2am on Friday and days immediately preceding holidays, and 24 hours on Saturday.

Suburban trains run by the Ferrocarrils de la Generalitat de Catalunya **(FGC; ☎93 205 15 15; www.fgc.net)** include a couple of useful city lines. One heads north from Plaça de Catalunya. A branch of it will get you to Tibidabo and another within spitting distance of the Monestir de Pedralbes. The other FGC line heads to Manresa from Plaça d'Espanya and is handy for the trip to Montserrat.

Tickets & Targetas

The metro, FGC trains, *rodalies/cercanías* (Renfe-run local trains) and buses come under one zoned fare regime. Single-ride tickets on all standard transport within Zone 1 (which extends beyond the airport), except on Renfe trains, cost €2.

Targetes are multitrip transport tickets. They are sold at most city-centre metro stations. The prices given here are for travel in Zone 1. Children under four travel free.

Targeta T-10 **(€9.25)** Ten rides (each valid for 1¼ hours) on the metro, buses and FGC trains. You can change between metro, FGC, *rodalies* and buses.

Targeta T-DIA **(€6.95)** Unlimited travel on all transport for one day.

Two-/Three-/Four-/Five-Day Tickets **(€12.80/18.50/23.50/28)** These provide unlimited travel on all transport except the Aerobús; buy them at metro stations and tourist offices.

Taxi

Taxis charge €2.05 flag fall plus meter charges of €0.93 per kilometre (€1.18 from 8pm to 8am and all day on weekends). A further €3.10 is added for all trips to/from the airport, and €1 for luggage bigger than 55cm by 35cm by 35cm. The trip from Estació Sants to Plaça de Catalunya, about 3km, costs about €11. You can call a taxi **(☎Fonotaxi 93 300 11 00, Radiotaxi 93 303 30 33, Radiotaxi BCN 93 225 00 00)** or flag them down in the streets. The call-out charge is €3.40 (€4.20 at night and on weekends).

Catalonia & Eastern Spain

From metropolitan Barcelona spreads a land of such diversity that you could spend weeks discovering it. The stunning cove beaches of the Costa Brava are the jewel in the tourism crown, but for those who need more than a suntan, urban fun and Jewish history is to be found in the medieval city of Girona, while Figueres offers a shrine to Salvador Dalí in the form of its 'theatre-museum'. For something bigger and brasher, Valencia, way off to the south, is one of Spain's most engaging cities, filled with monuments spanning the centuries and an increasingly avant-garde spirit.

Running across the north of the region, the Pyrenees rise to mighty 3000m peaks from a series of green and often remote valleys, dotted with villages that retain a palpable rural and even medieval air.

Add it all together and you get one of the most enticing areas of Spain.

Costa Brava

Catalonia & Eastern Spain

Cuenca
Torrebaja
CUENCA
Río Mijares (Millars)
Costa del
Segorbe
Río Túria
Sagunto
Utiel
Requena
El Picazo
Buñol
Valencia
Río Cabriel
VALENCIA
A7
Sueca
AP7
Río Júcar
Albacete
Gandia
A35
Almansa
Denia
ALBACETE
Cabo de la Nao
Alcoy
Villena
ALICANTE
Benidorm
A31
Río Segura
Costa Blanca
Alicante
Cieza
Elche
Isla de Tabarca
MURCIA
Río Mula
Murcia
A7
A30
Mar Menor
Lorca
Puerto Lumbreras
Cartagena
Costa Cálida
Palma de Mallorca
Mallorca
Ibiza (Eivissa)
Formentera
MEDITERRANEAN SEA
0 100 km
0 50 miles
1 Teatre-Museu Dalí, Figueres
2 The Pyrenees
3 Girona
4 Valencia
5 Zaragoza
6 Cadaqués

Catalonia & Eastern Spain Highlights

1

Teatre-Museu Dalí, Figueres

Dalí said: 'I want my museum to be like a single block, a labyrinth, a great surrealist object. The people who come to see it will leave with the sensation of having had a theatrical dream'. He also described the Teatre-Museu Dalí (p117) as a self-portrait, showing us his desires, enigmas, obsessions and passions.

Need to Know

ANTONI PITXOT Dalí personally appointed Pitxot as director; the 2nd floor has a permanent collection of Pitxot's work **ADMISSION** €11 **WEBSITE** www.salvador-dali.org

Local Knowledge

Teatre-Museu Dalí Don't Miss List

BY ANTONI PITXOT, PAINTER AND DALÍ-APPOINTED DIRECTOR OF THE TEATRE-MUSEU DALÍ

1 TREASURE ROOM

In this room, upholstered in red velvet to give the impression of a jewellery box, Dalí hung the paintings himself to impress visitors with their analogies or contrasts. It's filled with references to the Renaissance, the avant-garde and his obsessions with a scientific approach to form, Gala (his wife and muse) and sex. The star is Atomic Leda with Gala as the centrepiece, Dalí disguised as a swan, and numerous mythological echoes.

2 THE WIND PALACE

The ceiling in this old foyer of the theatre on the 1st floor is full of Dalí's imagery and iconography represented as a golden rain of money. We see Gala and Dalí flying up to the centre of this Wind Palace, their burial ceremony, and Dalí and Gala watching their own idyllic boat trip to a more spiritual dimension.

3 MONSTERS

Dalí's grotesque monsters are phantasmagoric beings that contemplate the theatre-museum from the courtyard. Made of everything from rocks and a whale skeleton from Cape Creus to Figueres plane trees and gargoyles, the monsters embody Dalí's dream to decorate by accumulating instead of selecting.

4 POETRY OF AMERICA ROOM

Apart from Dalí's 1943 masterpiece *Poetry of America* (also known as *The Cosmic Athletes*) in this room, the delicate green-pen drawing *The Argonauts* is worth a closer look to admire the almost imperceptible details of the foot of one of the Argonauts: there are wings in his shoe with gold, rubies and emeralds.

5 MONUMENT TO FRANCESC PUJOLS

Welcoming visitors to the museum at the entrance, this monument to the Catalan philosopher is based on a millenary olive tree and repository of the old feelings of the Catalan people. Everything in the installation links past and tradition to modern times. On top, an atom of hydrogen symbolises Dalí's trust in science.

The Pyrenees

The Pyrenees are Spain's most extensive and soul-stirring mountains. Although they unfold with similar drama across much of the range, if you had to choose just one mountain corner it would have to be the breathtaking Parc Nacional de Ordesa y Monte Perdido (p123), where a dragon's back of limestone peaks skirts the French border.

2

3

Girona

Girona (p111) is a masterpiece of medieva town planning. The old quarter wobbles uphill away from the river, its narrow streets crammed with quirky shops anc tasty restaurants, culminating in the billowing baroque facade of a majestic cathedral. Throw in some beautiful gardens, a handful of galleries and museums, and a festival that turns the entire city into a floral display, and the result is hard to beat. Plaza de la Indepedencia, Girona

KRZYSZTOF DYDYNSKI/GETTY IMAGES ©

4 Sophisticated Valencia

Though less well known than Barcelona, Madrid or Seville, Valencia (p125) deserves its place as one of Spain's most exciting cities. A magnificent cathedral, lovely old quarter, fine beaches and outstanding restaurants are reason enough to visit. But Valencia is also home to the Ciudad de las Artes y las Ciencias (p128), an exceptional showpiece for the exciting new wave of innovative Spanish architecture. L'Umbracle, Ciudad de las Artes y las Ciencias, by architects Santiago Calatrava and Felix Candela

MARTIN LLADO/GETTY IMAGES ©

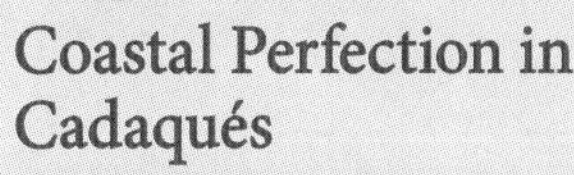

5 Dive into Zaragoza

Every taste is catered for in Zaragoza (p118). For architecture enthusiasts there's a sacred cathedral beloved by pilgrims, as well as the gilded La Seo and the Aljafería, Spain's finest Islamic building outside of Andalucía. History buffs will love the signposts to Roman Caesaraugusta, while Zaragoza nights are the stuff of legend. Basílica de Nuestra Señora del Pilar, Zaragoza

6 Coastal Perfection in Cadaqués

Much of the Spanish coast has lost the battle with tourist developments, but Cadaqués (p114), one-time home of Salvador Dalí and a host of artistic celebrities, has slipped beneath the radar. This is a whitewashed Mediterranean village at its most beguiling, combining hundreds of years of human history with stunning scenery and sophistication.

Catalonia & Eastern Spain's Best...

Places for Roman and Romanesque

- **Tarragona** (p108) Catalonia's premier Roman city.
- **Zaragoza** (p118) Roman remains of Caesaraugusta.
- **El Port de la Selva** (p115) Sublime Romanesque monastery, close to Cadaqués.
- **Montserrat** (p106) Historic monastery under a towering mountain.

Places to Recharge the Batteries

- **Cadaqués** (p114) Dalí's ghost and whitewashed Costa Brava charm.
- **Aínsa** (p124) Dreamy Aragonese hill town.
- **Valles de Echo & Ansó** (p123) The Aragonese Pyrenees' least-trammelled valleys.
- **Sos del Rey Católico** (p124) Hill-town perfection in northwestern Aragón.
- **Ochagavia** (p123) A charming stone village in the mist-shrouded western Pyrenees.

Places to Get Active

- **Parque Nacional de Ordesa y Monte Perdido** (p123) Arguably the best hiking in Spain.
- **Serra del Cadí** (p123) A rock-climber's paradise in the Catalan Pyrenees.
- **Alquézar** (p124) World-class canyoning in Aragón.
- **Val d'Aran** (p123) Skiing and hiking in this remote and peaceful mountain area.

Places for a Great Meal

- **El Celler de Can Roca, Girona** (p114) Rated the no 2 restaurant in the world in 2012.
- **Mas Pau, Figueres** (p116) Michelin-approved Catalan perfection.
- **Casa Pascualillo, Zaragoza** (p121), Considered one of the best tapas bars in Spain.
- **Delicat, Valencia** (p129) City Innovative tapas.
- **Restaurant Txalaka, Girona** (p113) Put a Basque chef in Catalonia and the results are bound to be exceptional.

Left: Catalonian-style Paella; **Above:** View from the hill town of Aínsa, overlooking the Río Cinca

Need to Know

ADVANCE PLANNING

- **Three months before** Make sure you have your accommodation booked if you're arriving during the Las Fallas festival in Valencia.
- **Two months before** Book your accommodation if you're planning to stay along the Costa Brava.

RESOURCES

- **Catalonia** (www.gencat.net/probert) Regional tourist office site for Catalonia.
- **Aragón** (www.turismodearagon.com) Aragón's tourism portal.
- **Valencia City** (www.turisvalencia.es) Everything you need to plan your visit to Valencia City.

GETTING AROUND

- **Air** International airports in Barcelona, Girona (Ryanair's Spanish hub), Valencia and Zaragoza.
- **Bus** Intermittent services in the Pyrenees.
- **Road** Coastal motorways and towards Madrid; small mountain roads in the Pyrenees.
- **Train** Excellent network along the coast with good connections to the rest of Spain (often via Barcelona or Valencia).
- **Train & Boat** In summer, a combination of *rodalies* (local trains) and boats connects the southern Costa Brava with Barcelona.

Catalonia & Eastern Spain Itineraries

Catalonia and the Pyrenees encompass a huge variety of landscapes, sights and experiences. The following routes take you from sunny beaches to energetic cities and tranquil mountain passes, revealing the region's best.

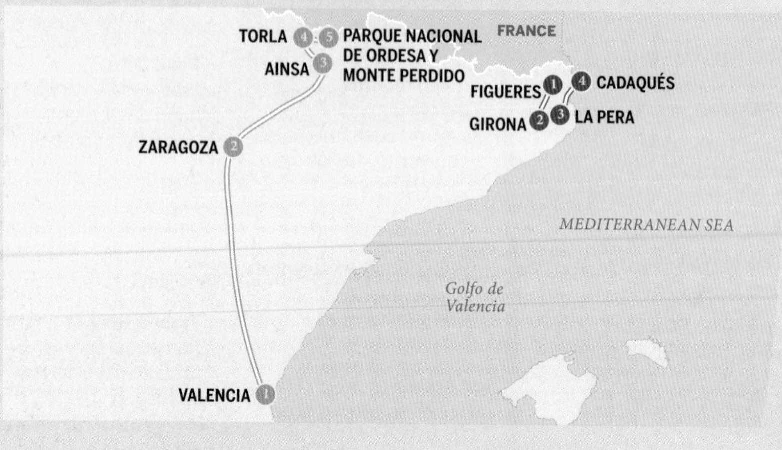

3 DAYS

IN DALÍ'S FOOTSTEPS

Figueres to Cadaqués

Few artists have left such an enduring impression upon the territory they inhabited as Salvador Dalí. Your journey through Dalí's Catalonia begins, just as the great man's life did, in **(1) Figueres**, an unexciting town that may have inspired Salvador to seek refuge in a surreal world of his own making. It nonetheless hosts the mind-blowing Teatre-Museu Dalí, the single-most significant legacy to survive Dalí after his death.

South of Figueres, charming **(2) Girona**, with its beautiful riverside setting, fascinating old quarter and enviable array of sights, is one of the urban highlights of northern Spain and an ideal overnight base for the **(3) Castell de Púbol** in La Pera. This mansion's foundations may belong to the Gothic and Renaissance eras, but Dalí transformed it into a zany epitaph to his muse, Gala.

Away to the northwest, close to mainland Spain's easternmost point, **(4) Cadaqués** is where Dalí spent much of his adult life. It is such a beautiful coastal village that you may feel tempted to do the same. If you can't stay forever then make do with a stroll through the blinding white old quarter and a hunt for the perfect nearby beach and restaurant.

LIFE IN THE INTERIOR

Valencia to Parque Nacional de Ordesa y Monte Perdido

The underexplored province of Aragón may climb steeply up into the Pyrenees, but its central and southern heartland is the soul of inland Spain.

Start in **(1) Valencia,** a vibrant and utterly Mediterranean city. You'd need at least a day or two to soak up the buzz and explore the state of the art museums and intriguing nooks and crannies of the old quarter. Move onto **(2) Zaragoza**, one of Spain's most engaging cities. By day it's a living museum with weighty landmarks to Roman, Islamic and Christian Spain. But once night falls, Zaragoza has perfected the art of tapas, which is a precursor to frenetic nights that are famous throughout the country. The quiet evenings of enchanted **(3) Aínsa**, the quintessential Aragonese hill village, are within sight of the snow-speckled Pyrenees. Aínsa offers a radical change of pace and its central plaza is one of the most impressive small town squares in Spain. Continue the rural feel in **(4) Torla**, gateway to the sublime **(5) Parque Nacional de Ordesa y Monte Perdido**, which is home to some of the finest hiking trails in Spain and the country's most breathtaking high mountain scenery.

Parque Nacional de Ordesa y Monte Perdido (p123)

Discover Catalonia & Eastern Spain

At a Glance

- **Girona** (p111) A quaint river-front town close to the stunning beaches of the Costa Brava.
- **Zaragoza** (p118) Capital of the Aragon region and packed with Christian and Islamic sights.
- **The Pyrenees** (p123) Running from the Mediterranean Sea to the Atlantic Ocean.
- **Valencia** (p125) Dominated by Valencia city, but with a long coastline and hilly coastal hinterland.

Montserrat

INDEPENDENT PHOTOGRAPHER · TOMAS GRIGER/GETTY IMAGES ©

AROUND BARCELONA

Montserrat

Montserrat (Serrated Mountain), 50km northwest of Barcelona, is a 1236m-high mountain of strangely rounded rock pillars, shaped by wind, rain and frost from a conglomeration of limestone, pebbles and sand that once lay under the sea (or else by baby angels, depending on whom you talk to). With the historic Benedictine Monestir de Montserrat, one of Catalonia's most important shrines, cradled at 725m on its side, it's the most popular outing from Barcelona. From the mountain, on a clear day, you can see as far as the Pyrenees. Its caves and many mountain paths make for spectacular rambles, reachable by funiculars.

The *cremallera* (rack-and-pinion train) chugs up the mountainside, arriving just below the monastery, next to the cable car station.

Sights & Activities

MONESTIR DE MONTSERRAT Monastery

(www.abadiamontserrat.net; 9am-6pm) The monastery – the second most important pilgrimage centre in Spain after Santiago de Compostela – was founded in 1025 to commemorate a vision of the Virgin on the mountain, seen by – you've guessed it – shepherds, after which the Black Virgin icon, allegedly carved by St Luke and hidden by St Peter in the mountains, was discovered thanks to said vision.

MUSEU DE MONTSERRAT Museum
(Plaça de Santa Maria; adult/student €6.50/5.50; 10am-6pm) The two-part Museu de Montserrat has an excellent collection, ranging from an Egyptian mummy and Gothic altarpieces to art by El Greco, Monet, Degas and Picasso, as well as modern art and some fantastic 14th-century Russian icons (look for the Last Judgement with detailed punishments awaiting sinners).

Getting There & Away

Take the C16 from Barcelona, then the C58 shortly after Terrassa, followed by the C55 to Monistrol de Montserrat. Leave the car at the free car park at Monistrol Vila and take the *cremallera* up to the top.

The R5 line trains operated by FGC **(www.fgc.net)** run hourly from Plaça d'Espanya station, starting at 8.36am (52 to 56 minutes). They connect with the cable car **(93 835 00 05; www.aeridemontserrat.com; €5/7.90 one way/return; 9.40am-7pm Mar-Oct, 10.10am-5.45pm Mon-Sat, 10.10am-6.45pm Sun & holidays Nov-Feb, 17 minutes)** at the Montserrat Aeri stop and the cremallera **(902 312020; www.cremallerademontserrat.com; one way/return €6/9; 5 minutes)** at the following stop, Monistrol de Montserrat.

Sitges

POP 28,620

Just 35km along the coast from Barcelona, this fishing-village-turned-pumping-beach-resort town has been a favourite with upper-class Barcelonians since the late 19th century, as well as a key location for the burgeoning Modernisme movement which paved the way for the likes of Picasso. A famous gay destination, in July and August Sitges turns into one big beach party with a nightlife to rival Ibiza; the beaches are long and sandy, the tapas bars prolific and the Carnaval Bacchanalian.

Sights & Activities

BEACHES Beach
The main beach is flanked by the attractive seafront Passeig Maritim, dotted with *chiringuitos* (beachside bars) and divided into nine sections with different names, by a series of breakwaters.

MUSEU ROMÀNTIC Museum
(Carrer de Sant Gaudenci 1; adult/student €3.50/2; 9.30am-2pm & 4-7pm Tue-Sat, 10am-3pm Sun) Housed in late-18th-century Can Llopis mansion, the Museu Romàntic recreates with its furnishings and dioramas the lifestyle of a 19th-century Catalan land-owning family, the likes of which would often have made their money in dubious businesses, such as cotton raising using slave labour in South America, and were commonly dubbed *Americanos* or *Indianos*.

FUNDACIÓ STÄMPFLI MUSEU D'ART CONTEMPORANI Gallery
(www.fundacio-stampfli.org; Plaća Ajuntament; adult €3.50; 9.30am-2pm & 4-7pm Fri & Sat, 10am-3pm Sun) This excellent new art gallery opened in late 2010, with a focus on 20th-century art from the 1960s onwards.

Sleeping

HOTEL ROMÀNTIC Boutique Hotel **€€**
(93 894 83 75; www.hotelromantic.com; Carrer de Sant Isidre 33; s/d from €70/100;) These three adjoining 19th-century villas are presented in sensuous Modernista style, with a leafy dining courtyard and friendly service, though the rooms are smallish and could do with sprucing up. Just around the corner is its charming sister hotel, **Hotel La Renaixença** **(93 894 06 43; www.hotelromantic.com; Carrer d'Illa de Cuba 45; s/d from €70/100)**, which is actually better value.

Eating

EL POU Tapas **€€**
(www.elpoudesitges.com; Carrer de Sant Pau 5; meals €30; lunch & dinner Wed-Mon) The tiny wagyu beef burgers at this friendly gourmet tapas place are an absolute delight, and the rest doesn't lag far behind; the

traditional *patatas bravas* (fried potatoes in spicy tomato sauce) sit alongside the likes of *mojama* (salted dried tuna) with almonds, fried aubergine and *xató*; the presentation delights the eye as much as the flavours delight the palate.

EF & GI International **€€**
(www.efgirestaurant.com; Carrer Major 33; meals €35-50; ⌚dinner Tue-Sat mid-Jan–mid-Dec) Fabio and Greg (eF & Gi) are not afraid to experiment and the results are startlingly good: the mostly Mediterranean menu with touches of Asian inspiration throws out such delights as chargrilled beef infused with lemongrass and kaffir lime and tuna loin encrusted with peanuts and calamata olives with mango chutney. Don't skip the dessert, either.

Information

Main Tourist Office (☎93 894 42 51; www.sitgestur.cat; Plaça de E Maristany 2; ⌚10am-2pm & 4-6.30pm Mon-Sat, 10am-2pm Sun)

Getting There & Away

A direct bus run by **Mon-Bus** (www.monbus.cat) goes to Barcelona airport from Passeig de Vilanova in Sitges.

From 6am to 10pm four R2 *rodalies* trains an hour run to Barcelona's Passeig de Gràcia and Estació Sants (€3.60, 27 to 46 minutes).

The best road from Barcelona to Sitges is the C32 tollway.

Tarragona

POP 140,180

The eternally sunny port city of Tarragona is a fascinating mix of Mediterranean beach life, Roman history and medieval alleyways. Easily Catalonia's most important Roman site, Tarragona's number-one attraction is its seaside-facing Roman amphitheatre. The town's medieval heart is one of the most beautiful in Spain, its maze of narrow cobbled streets encircled by steep walls, crowned with a splendid cathedral and its sandstone buildings seemingly suffused with golden light. Add plenty of tempting food options and an array of bars heaving into the wee hours and you get the most exciting urban centre in southern Catalonia.

Sights & Activities

The tourist office dishes out three handy booklets detailing routes around the city taking in Roman, medieval and Modernista sites.

MUSEU D'HISTÒRIA DE TARRAGONA Ruins
(MHT; www.museutgn.com; adult/child per site €3/free, all MHT sites €10/free; ⌚9am-9pm daily Easter-Sep, shorter hr rest of yr) The 'museum' title is somewhat misleading, as this is in fact four separate Roman sites (which since 2000 together have constituted a Unesco World Heritage site), including the museum.

Start exploring with the **Pretori i Circ Romans** (Plaça del Rei), which includes part of the vaults of the Roman circus, where chariot races were once held, ending at the Pretori tower on Plaça de Rei. The circus, 300m long, stretched from here to beyond Plaça de la Font to the west. Nearby Plaça del Fòrum was the location of the provincial forum and political heart of Tarraconensis province.

Near the beach is the crown jewel of Tarragona's Roman sites, the well-preserved **Amfiteatre Romà** (Plaça d'Arce Ochotorena; ⌚9am-9pm Tue-Sat, 9am-3pm Sun Easter-Sep, 9am-5pm Tue-Sat, 10am-3pm Sun & holidays Oct-Easter), where gladiators battled either each other or wild animals to the death. In its arena are the remains of 6th- and 12th-century churches built to commemorate the martyrdom of the Christian bishop Fructuosus and two deacons, who, they say, were burnt alive here in AD 259.

The northwest half of **Fòrum Romà** (Carrer del Cardenal Cervantes) was occupied by a judicial basilica (where legal disputes were settled), from where the rest of the forum stretched downhill to the southwest. Linked to the site by a footbridge is another excavated area which includes a stretch of Roman street. The discovery in 2006 of remains of the foundations of a temple to Jupiter, Juno and Minerva (the major triumvirate of gods at the time of the Roman republic)

Beachfront at Sitges (p107)

POLA DAMONTE/GETTY IMAGES ©

suggests the forum was much bigger and more important than had previously been assumed.

MUSEU NACIONAL ARQUEOLÒGIC DE TARRAGONA Museum

(www.mnat.es; Plaça del Rei 5; adult/child €3.50/free; 10am-8pm Tue-Sat, 10am-2pm Sun & holidays Jun-Sep, shorter hr rest of yr) This excellent museum does justice to the cultural and material wealth of Roman Tarraco. Well laid-out exhibits include part of the Roman city walls, frescoes, sculpture and pottery. In the section on everyday arts you can admire ancient fertility aids, including an outsized stone penis, symbol of the god Priapus.

CATEDRAL Cathedral

(Pla de la Seu; adult/child €4/1.40; 10am-7pm Mon-Sat Jun–mid-Oct, shorter hr rest of yr) Sitting grandly at the top of the old town, Tarragona's cathedral has been undergoing a major facelift for some time (although it's scheduled to be finished in 2012), though the cloisters and museum alone are worth a peek. Built on the site of a Roman temple, the length of its construction (between 1171 and 1331) has endowed it with both Romanesque and Gothic features, as typified by the main facade on Pla de la Seu, and its fortress-like exterior betrays fears of the Moors.

Sleeping

HOTEL PLAÇA DE LA FONT Hotel **€€**

(977 24 61 34; www.hotelpdelafont.com; Plaça de la Font 26; s/d €55/70;) Simple, spic-and-span rooms overlooking a bustling terrace in a you-can't-get-more-central-than-this location, right on the popular Plaça de la Font. If there's no room at the inn, the sister **Hostal La Noria** (**977 23 87 17; Plaça de la Font 53; s/d €30/48**), also on the plaza, has a selection of compact, spartan singles and doubles.

Eating

The quintessential Tarragona seafood experience can be had in **Serrallo**, the town's fishing port. About a dozen bars and restaurants here sell the day's catch, and on summer weekends in particular the place is packed.

Right: Calella de Palafrugell, Costa Brava (p115); **Below:** Parque Nacional de Ordesa y Monte Perdido (p123)

ARCS RESTAURANT Mediterranean **€€**
(☎977 21 80 40; www.restaurantarcs.com; Carrer Misser Sitges 13; menu €23; ⊙lunch & dinner Tue-Sat) Inside a medieval cavern with bright splashes of colour in the form of contemporary art, you are served some wonderful takes on Mediterranean dishes – from *tartar de atún* (tuna carpaccio) and the inspired pumpkin soup with *morcilla* (black pudding) and goat's cheese to the most intense *salmorejo* (a thicker, more savoury gaspacho) outside Andalucía.

AQ Catalan **€€**
(☎977 21 59 54; www.aq-restaurant.com; Carrer de les Coques 7; menus from €18; ⊙lunch & dinner Tue-Sat) This is a bubbly designer haunt with stark colour contrasts (black, lemon and cream linen), slick lines and intriguing plays on traditional cooking, such as *ventresca de tonyina amb ceba caramelitzada, tomáquet, formatge de cabra i olives* (tuna belly meat with caramelised onion, tomato, goat's cheese and olives).

Information

Tourist Office (☎977 25 07 95; www.tarragonaturisme.es; Carrer Major 39; ⊙10am-9pm Mon-Sat, 10am-2pm Sun Jul-Sep, shorter hr rest of yr) Good place for booking guided tours of the city.

Getting There & Away

The bus station is 1.5km northwest of the old town along Rambla Nova, at Plaça Imperial Tarraco. Destinations include Barcelona (€8.10, 1½ hours, 16 daily) and Valencia (€20.20, 3½ hours, seven daily). The local train station is a 10-minute walk along the waterfront to old town while the faster AVE trains arrive at the swanky Camp de Tarragona station, a 15-minute taxi ride from the centre. Departures include Barcelona (€15.90 to €35.10, 35 minutes to 1½ hours, every 30 minutes); Lleida (€7 to €22, 25 minutes to 1¾ hours, 12 daily) and Valencia (€20.30 to €37.30, two to 3½ hours, 13 daily).

GIRONA & THE DALÍ TRIANGLE

Girona

POP 95,720

A tight huddle of ancient arcaded houses, grand churches, climbing cobbled streets and medieval baths, and Catalonia's most extensive and best-preserved Call (medieval Jewish quarter), all enclosed by defensive walls and the lazy Río Onyar, constitute a powerful reason for visiting north Catalonia's largest city, Girona.

Sights

MUSEU D'HISTÒRIA DELS JUEUS DE GIRONA Museum

(Carrer de la Força 8; adult/child €2/free; 10am-8pm Mon-Sat, 10am-2pm Sun Jul & Aug, shorter hr rest of yr) Until 1492 Girona was home to Catalonia's second-most important medieval Jewish community (after Barcelona), and one of the finest Jewish quarters in the country, the Call was centred on the narrow Carrer de la Força for 600 years, until relentless persecution forced the Jews out of Spain. The restored Centre Bonstruc ća Porta, named after Jewish Girona's most illustrious figure – a 13th-century cabbalist philosopher and mystic – houses the excellent Museu d'Història dels Jueus de Girona. The museum shows genuine pride in Girona's Jewish heritage without shying away from the less salubrious aspects, such as persecution by the Inquisition and forced conversions.

CATEDRAL Cathedral

(www.catedraldegirona.org; Plaça de la Catedral; museum adult/child €5/1.20, Sun free; 10am-8pm) The billowing baroque facade of the cathedral seems even grander as it stands at the head of a majestic flight of 86 steps rising from Plaça de la Catedral. Though the beautiful Romanesque **cloister** dates back to the 12th century, most of the building has been repeatedly rebuilt and altered down the centuries, giving the cathedral the

Girona

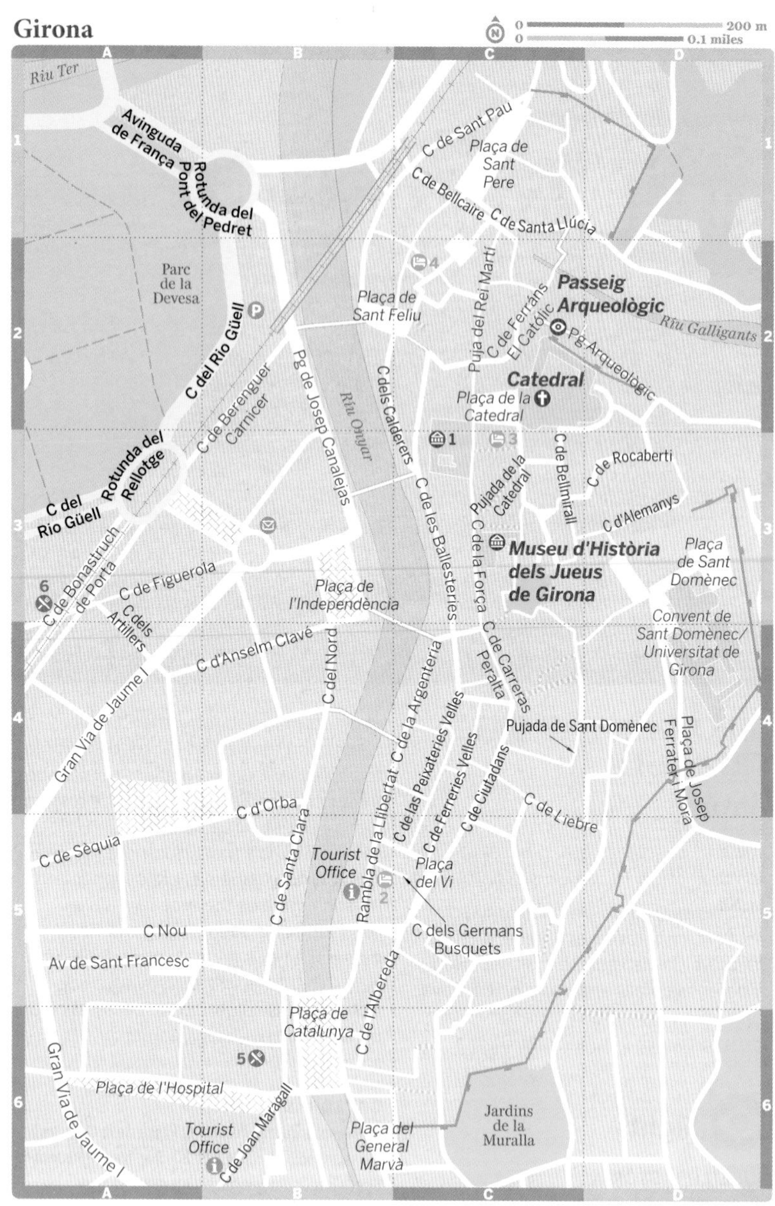

second-widest Gothic nave (23m) in Christendom. The cathedral's **museum**, through the door marked 'Claustre Tresor', contains numerous ecclesiastic treasures, including the masterly Romanesque *Tapís de la Creació* (Tapestry of the Creation) and a Mozarabic illuminated *Beatus* manuscript, dating from 975. The Creation tapestry (under restoration at the time of writing) shows God at the epicentre and in the circle around him the creation of Adam, Eve, the animals, the sky, light and darkness.

Girona

Top Sights

Sights

Sleeping

Eating

PASSEIG ARQUEOLÒGIC Historic Site
(**10am-8pm**) A walk along Girona's medieval walls, also known as the Passeig de la Muralla, is a wonderful way to appreciate the city landscape from above. There are several points of access, the most popular being across the street from the Banys Àrabs, where steps lead up into some heavenly gardens where town and plants merge into one organic masterpiece.

MUSEU D'HISTÒRIA DE LA CIUTAT Museum
(**www.girona.cat; Carrer de la Força 27; adult/student/child €4/2/free; 10am-2pm & 5-7pm Tue-Sat, 10am-2pm Sun & holidays**) The engaging and well-presented City History Museum does Girona's long and impressive history justice, its displays covering everything from the city's Roman origins, through the siege of the city by Napoleonic troops to the *sardana* (Catalonia's national folk dance) tradition.

Sleeping

BED & BREAKFAST BELLS OFICIS B&B **€€**
(**972 22 81 70; www.bellsoficis.com; Carrer dels Germans Busquets 2; r incl breakfast €40-85;**) Up the wobbly-winding staircase of a 19th-century building right in the heart of Girona you'll discover six very desirable rooms, lovingly restored by knowledgeable Javi and his wife. Some have unusual pebble art in the bathrooms, while others have views over the street.

CASA CÚNDARO Boutique Hotel **€€**
(**972 22 35 83; www.casacundaro.com; Pujada de la Catedral 9; d €60-80;**) The understated exterior of this medieval Jewish house, run by a friendly family, hides five sumptuous rooms and four self-catering apartments – all combining original exposed stone walls with modern luxuries such as satellite TV. The location right next to the cathedral is either a boon or a bane, depending on whether you enjoy the sound of church bells.

HOTEL LLEGENDES DE GIRONA Hotel **€€€**
(**972 22 09 05; www.llegendeshotel.com; Portal de la Barca 4; d €123, 'Fountain of Lovers' room €288; P**) The rooms at this restored 18th-century building are supremely comfortable, with all manner of hi-tech gadgets, and the all-glass bathrooms have huge rain showers. This incongruous blend of modernity and antiquity includes a guide to tantric sex positions in each room; three of the rooms even have an 'Eros' sofa to try them out on.

Eating

RESTAURANT TXALAKA Basque **€€**
(**972 22 59 75; Carrer Bonastruc de Porta 4; mains €17-23, pintxos €2.50-4; closed Sun**) For sensational Basque cooking and *pintxos* (tapas) washed down with *txakoli* (the fizzy white wine from the Basque coast) poured from a great height, don't miss this popular local spot. Just load up your plate with the likes of garlic prawns, fresh anchovy *montaditos*, marinated wild mushrooms and octopus dusted in paprika, and pay according to the number of *montadito* sticks/dishes.

L'ALQUERIA Catalan **€€**
(**972 22 18 82; www.restaurantalqueria.com; Carrer de la Ginesta 8; mains €18-22; lunch & dinner Wed-Sat, lunch only Tue & Sun**) This

smart minimalist *arrocería* serves the finest *arrós negre* (rice cooked in cuttlefish ink) and *arrós a la Catalan* in the city, as well as around 20 other superbly executed rice dishes, including paellas.

Information

Tourist Office (☎972 22 65 75; www.girona.cat/turisme; Rambla de la Llibertat 1; ⏰8am-8pm Mon-Fri, 8am-2pm & 4-8pm Sat, 9am-2pm Sun)

Getting There & Away

Girona-Costa Brava airport (www.barcelona-girona-airport.com), Ryanair's Spanish hub, is located 11km south of the centre, with **Sagalés Barcelona Bus** (www.sagales.com) connecting it to Girona's main bus/train station (€2.60, 25 minutes, hourly), as well as Barcelona's Estació del Nord (€15/25 one way/return; 1¼ hours). A **taxi** (☎872 97 50 00) to central Girona costs around €22/25 day/night.

Sarfa (www.sarfa.com) buses serve Cadaques (€5.50, 1¾ hours, two to three daily) via Roses (€3.70, 1¼ hours) and Tossa de Mar (€8.50, 55 minutes). The bus station is next to the train station.

Girona is on the train line between Barcelona (from €9.70, 1½ hours, up to 20 daily) and Figueres (€4.80 to €14.10, 25 to 40 minutes, up to 16 daily). Trains also run to Portbou (from €5.40, one hour, 13 daily), with some continuing on to Cerbère in France.

Cadaqués & Around

POP 2900

If you have time for only one stop on the Costa Brava, make it Cadaqués. A whitewashed village around a rocky bay, its narrow, hilly streets perfect for wandering, it and the surrounding area have a special magic – a fusion of wind, sea, light and rock – that isn't dissipated even by the throngs of summer visitors.

A portion of that magic owes itself to Salvador Dalí, who spent family holidays in Cadaqués during his youth, and lived much of his later life at nearby Port Lligat.

Cooking Up a Three-Star Storm

Although celebrity chef Ferran Adrià closed the famous **El Bulli** restaurant's doors in 2011, fear not, gourmets! Catalonia still has three three-star Michelin establishments, all eager to slip into El Bulli's place.

El Celler de Can Roca (☎972 22 21 57; www.cellercanroca.com; Carrer Can Sunyer 48; 5/9 course menus €130/160; ⏰lunch & dinner Tue-Sat), the second-best restaurant in the world as of 2012, located 2km west of central Girona in a refurbished country house, is run by three brothers – Joan, Josep and Jordi – who focus on 'emotional cuisine' through their ever-changing takes on Mediterranean dishes. The style is playful – how about a 'dry gambini' (with a prawn serving the olive role in a dry martini)?

Can Fabes (☎93 867 28 51; www.canfabes.com; Carrer de Sant Joan 6, Sant Celoni; meals €180, tasting menus €105-195; ⏰lunch & dinner Wed-Sat, lunch Sun, closed Jan) has long attracted a steady stream of 'gastronauts' from Barcelona to Sant Celoni, 50km from Girona. Chef Santi Santamaria (the first Catalan chef ever to be awarded three Michelin stars) is a local boy who started up here in 1981. Dishes based on local, seasonal products (seafood landed at Blanes, for example) are at the core of his cooking.

Sant Pau (☎93 760 06 62; www.ruscalleda.com; Carrer Nou 10, Sant Pol de Mar; menus €146; ⏰lunch & dinner Tue-Wed, Fri & Sat, dinner Thu, closed May & Nov), another foodie fave, is a beautifully presented mansion whose garden overlooks the Mediterranean in Sant Pol de Mar, 50km from Girona. Carme Ruscalleda is the driving force, with Eastern touches, such as tempura, making an appearance on an otherwise Catalan menu.

Thanks to Dalí and other luminaries, such as his friend Federico García Lorca, Cadaqués pulled in a celebrity crowd for decades. One visit by the poet Paul Éluard and his Russian wife, Gala, in 1929 caused an earthquake in Dalí's life: he ran off to Paris with Gala (who was to become his lifelong obsession and, later, his wife) and joined the surrealist movement. In the 1950s the crowd he attracted was more jet-setting – Walt Disney, the Duke of Windsor and Greek shipowner Stavros Niarchos. In the 1970s Mick Jagger and Gabriel García Márquez popped by. Today the crowd is not quite as famous, and leans heavily towards day-tripping French from across the border, but the enchantment of Cadaqués' atmosphere remains.

Sights

MUSEU DE CADAQUÉS Museum

(Carrer de Narcís Monturiol 15; adult/child €5/3.50; 10am-1.30pm & 4-7pm Mon-Sat Apr-Jun, shorter hr rest of yr) Dalí features strongly in the works of art displayed here, as do his contemporaries, also connected to Cadaques, such as Picasso.

CASA MUSEU DALÍ Museum

(972 25 10 15; www.salvador-dali.org; adult/child €11/free; by advance reservation only) Located by a peaceful cove in Port Lligat, a tiny fishing settlement a 1.25km walk from Cadaqués, the Casa Museu Dalí – the lifelong residence of Salvador Dalí – started life as a mere fisherman's hut. It was steadily altered and enlarged by Dalí, who lived here with his wife from 1930 to 1982, and is now a fascinating insight into the lives of the (pun intended!) surreal couple. If the Teatre-Museu Dalí is the mask that the showman presented to the world, then this is an intimate glimpse of his actual face. This splendid, bizarre whitewashed structure is a mishmash of cottages and sunny terraces, linked together by narrow labyrinthine corridors and containing an assortment of bizarre furnishings, each chosen with great care.

Compulsory small group tours are conducted by multilingual guides; booking ahead is essential.

If You Like... Costa Brava Villages

If you like Cadaqués, we think you'll also enjoy exploring these other villages of the Costa Brava:

1 **CALELLA DE PALAFRUGELL** Low-slung buildings strung Aegean-style around a bay of rocky points and small, pretty beaches.

2 **LLAFRANC** A smallish bay but a longer stretch of sand, cupped on either side by pine-dotted craggy coast.

3 **TAMARIU** A small crescent cove surrounded by pine stands, offering some of the most translucent waters on Spain's Mediterranean coast.

4 **AIGUABLAVA** Glowing blue water and a backdrop of pine trees – this is the Mediterranean at its absolute pinnacle of beauty.

5 **FORNELLS** On one of the Costa Brava's most picturesque bays with a marina, beach and transparent azure water.

6 **PERATALLADA** Warm stone houses and beautifully preserved narrow streets inland from the coast.

7 **BESALÚ** Delightfully well-preserved medieval town with a Tolkienesque fortified bridge.

8 **EL PORT DE LA SELVA** Home to the Monestir de Sant Pere de Rodes, one of Catalonia's finest Romanesque monasteries.

Sleeping

HOSTAL VEHÍ Pensión **€€€**
(☎972 25 84 70; www.hostalvehi.com; Carrer de l'Església 5; s/d without bathroom €30/55, d with bathroom €77; ❄📶) Near the church in the heart of the old town, this simple *pensión* with clean-as-a-whistle rooms, run by a friendly family, tends to be booked up for July and August. It's a pain to get to if you have a lot of luggage and the wi-fi policy is annoying, but it's easily the cheapest deal in town, and also about the best.

Eating & Drinking

ES BALUARD Seafood **€€**
(☎972 25 81 83; www.esbaluard-cadaques.net; Riba Nemesi Llorens; mains €16-22) The family that runs this old-school restaurant that's set into the old sea wall clearly worships at the throne of Poseidon, because the tastiest of his subjects wind up on your plate. Fish dishes drawing on local market produce, such as the *anchoas de Cadaqués* and *gambitas de Roses*, dominate the menu and you shouldn't shy away from the *crema catalana*, either.

L'HOSTAL Bar
(Passeig del Mar 8; ⏰10pm-5am Sun-Thu, 10pm-6am Fri & Sat) One evening in the 1970s, an effusive Dalí called this beachside bar the *lugar más bonito del mundo* (the most beautiful place on earth). Photos of the artist adorn the walls and live bands play most nights.

Information

Tourist Office (☎972 25 83 15; Carrer del Cotxe 2; ⏰9am-9pm Mon-Sat, 10am-1pm & 5-8pm Sun late Jun–mid-Sep, shorter hr rest of yr)

Getting There & Away

Sarfa buses connect Cadaqués to Barcelona (€23.70, 2¾ hours, two to five daily), Figueres (€5.30, one hour, three to seven daily) via Castelló d'Empúries, and Girona (€3.50, 1¾ hours, two to three daily).

Figueres

POP 44,765

Twelve kilometres inland from the Golf de Roses, Figueres is a pleasant enough town with an unmissable attraction. Salvador Dalí was born in Figueres in 1904 and although his career took him to Madrid, Barcelona, Paris and the USA, he remained true to his roots.

In the 1960s and '70s he created here the extraordinary Teatre-Museu Dalí – a monument to surrealism and a legacy that outshines any other Spanish artist, both in terms of popularity and sheer flamboyance. Whatever your feelings about the complex, egocentric Dalí, this museum is worth every cent and minute you can spare.

Sleeping & Eating

HOTEL DURÁN Hotel **€€**
(☎972 50 12 50; www.hotelduran.com; Carrer de Lasauca 5; s/d from €74/89; P❄📶) Staying at this mid-19th-century hotel is very much in keeping with the Dalí theme as he and his wife used to frequent the place themselves. The rooms are modern with forgettable soft beige, brown and white decor but the restaurant is like a royal banquet hall, with smooth service and and a fantasic €20 lunch menu which features such expertly prepared delights as seared tuna steak and rabbit loin.

MAS PAU Catalan **€€**
(☎972 54 61 54; www.maspau.com; Avinyonet de Puigventós; meals €65-90; ⏰lunch & dinner Wed-Sat, dinner Tue, lunch Sun) Five kilometres southwest of Figueres along the road to Besalú, this enchanting 16th-century *masia* (farmhouse), made of rough-hewn stone and set amid soothing gardens, is run by Toni and Xavier – both formerly of Ferran Adrià's El Bulli. This Michelin-starred restaurant offers a seasonal menu with an emphasis on fresh local ingredients; the pork trotter crackling stuffed with crayfish and acorn-fed duck with chestnuts are both inspired dishes.

GREGOR SCHUSTER/GETTY IMAGES ©; SALVADOR DALI, FUNDACIÓ GALA-SALVADOR DALI/VEGAP. LICENSED BY VISCOPY, 2013 ©

Don't Miss Teatre-Museu Dalí

The first name that comes into your head when you lay your eyes on this red castle-like building, topped with the artist's trademark giant eggs and stylised Oscar-like statues, and studded with plaster-covered croissants, is Dalí.

Choice exhibits include **Taxi Plujós** (Rainy Taxi), composed of an early Cadillac, surmounted by statues. Put a coin in the slot and water washes all over the occupant of the car. The **Sala de Peixateries** (Fish Shop Room) holds a collection of Dalí oils, including the famous *Autoretrat Tou amb Tall de Bacon Fregit* (Soft Self-Portrait with Fried Bacon) and *Retrat de Picasso* (Portrait of Picasso). Beneath the former stage of the theatre is the crypt with Dalí's plain tomb, located at 'the spiritual centre of Europe' as Dalí modestly described it.

Gala – Dalí's wife and lifelong muse – is seen throughout – from the *Gala Mirando el Mar Mediterráneo* (Gala Looking at the Mediterranean Sea) on the 2nd level, which also appears to be a portrait of Abraham Lincoln from afar, to the classic *Leda Atómica* (Atomic Leda).

A separate entrance (same ticket and times) leads into the Owen Cheatham collection of 37 jewels, designed by Dalí, called **Dalí Joies** (Dalí Jewels). Dalí did these on paper (his first commission was in 1941) and the jewellery was made by specialists in New York. Each piece, ranging from the disconcerting *Ull del Temps* (Eye of Time) through to the *Cor Reial* (Royal Heart), is unique.

In August the museum opens at night (admission €12, 10pm to 1am) for a maximum of 500 people (booking essential); ticket price includes a glass of *cava* (sparking wine).

NEED TO KNOW

www.salvador-dali.org; Plaça de Gala i Salvador Dalí 5; admission incl Dalí Joies & Museu de l'Empordá adult/child €12/free; 9am-8pm Jul-Sep, 9.30am-6pm Mar-Jun & Oct, shorter hr rest of yr

Information

Tourist Office (☎972 50 31 55; www.figueresciutat.com; Plaça del Sol; ⏰9am-8pm Mon-Sat, 10am-2pm Sun Jul-Sep, shorter hr rest of yr)

Getting There & Away

Sarfa buses serve Cadaqués (€4.80, one hour, up to eight daily).

There are hourly train connections to Girona (€4, 30 minutes) and Barcelona (from €9.40, 1¾ hours) and to Portbou and the French border (€2 to €2.30, 25 minutes).

Castell de Púbol

Two kilometres away from the village of La Pera, just south of the C66 and 22km northwest of Palafrugell, the **Castell de Púbol** (www.salvador-dali.org; Plaça de Gala Dalí; adult/student & senior €8/5; ⏰10am-8pm daily mid-Jun–mid-Sep, shorter hr rest of yr) forms the southernmost point of northeast Catalonia's 'Salvador Dalí triangle', other elements of which include the Teatre-Museu Dalí in Figueres, and his home in Port Lligat.

Having promised to make his wife, Gala – his muse and the love of his life – 'queen of the castle', in 1969 Dalí finally found the ideal residence to turn into Gala's refuge, since at the age of 76, she no longer desired Dalí's hectic lifestyle. It's a semi-dilapidated Gothic and Renaissance stronghold which includes a 14th-century church in the quiet village of Púbol.

The sombre castle, its stone walls covered with creepers, is almost the antithesis of the flamboyance of the Teatre-Museu Dalí or the Dalí's seaside home: Gala had it decorated exactly as she wished and received only whom she wished. Legend has it that Dalí himself had to apply for written permission to visit her here.

The interior reflects her tastes: her bedroom is simple and almost unadorned; the 'everlasting' flowers that she was so fond of prevail everywhere and a gallery upstairs showcases a splendid collection of dresses designed for her by the likes of Piere Cardin, Christian Dior and Elizabeth Arden. A slightly creepy mannequin, designed to look like Gala, sits with its back to the visitor.

Dalí touches nevertheless creep in: a radiator cover with radiators painted over the top, spindly-legged elephant statues in the exuberant garden, a see-through table with ostrich legs with a stuffed horse visible below, a melted clock on a coathanger in the guest room, and a stuffed giraffe staring at Gala's tomb in the crypt.

To get here, catch one of the frequent Palafrugell-bound buses from Girona (€2.50; 40 minutes), alight at the second La Pera stop along the C66 and walk the 2km to the castle, or else take a train from Girona to Flaça (hourly, € 2.95, 12 to 15 minutes) and then catch a taxi for the last 4km.

ZARAGOZA

POP 674,725

Zaragoza (Saragossa) rocks and rolls. The feisty citizens of this great city, on the banks of the mighty Río Ebro, make up over half of Aragón's population and they live a fairly hectic lifestyle with great tapas bars and raucous nightlife. But Zaragoza is so much more than just a city that loves to live the good life: it also has a host of historical sights spanning all the great civilisations (Roman, Islamic and Christian) that have left their indelible mark on the Spanish soul.

Sights

FREE **BASÍLICA DE NUESTRA SEÑORA DEL PILAR** Church

(Plaza del Pilar; lift admission €2; ⏰7am-8.30pm, lift 10am-1.30pm & 4-6.30pm Tue-Sun) Brace yourself for the saintly and the solemn in this great baroque cavern of Catholicism. The faithful believe that it was here on 2 January 40 that Santiago (St James the Apostle) saw the Virgin Mary descend atop a marble *pilar* (pillar). A chapel was built around the remaining

CESAR LUCAS ABREU/GETTY IMAGES ©

Don't Miss Aljafería

La Aljafería is Spain's finest Islamic-era edifice outside Andalucía. It's not in the league of Granada's Alhambra or Córdoba's Mezquita, but it's a glorious monument nonetheless.

Inside the main gate, cross the rather dull introductory courtyard into a second, the **Patio de Santa Isabel**, once the central courtyard of the Islamic palace. Here you're confronted by the delicate interwoven arches typical of the geometric mastery of Islamic architecture. Opening off the stunning northern porch is a small, octagonal **oratorio** (prayer room), with a magnificent horseshoe-arched doorway leading into its *mihrab* (prayer niche indicating the direction of Mecca).

Moving upstairs, you pass through rooms of the **Palacio Mudéjar**, added by Christian rulers in the 12th to 14th centuries, then to the Catholic Monarchs' **palace**, which, as though by way of riposte to the Islamic finery below, contains some exquisite Mudéjar coffered ceilings, especially in the lavish **Salón del Trono** (Throne Room).

Spanish-language guided tours lasting 50 minutes run throughout the day and are included in the admission price; they generally start half past the hour.

NEED TO KNOW

Off Map p120; Calle de los Diputados; adult/under 12yr €3/free, free Sun; ⏲10am-2pm Sat-Wed, 4.30-8pm Mon-Wed, Fri & Sat Jul & Aug, shorter hours rest of year

pilar, followed by a series of ever-more-grandiose churches, culminating in the enormous basilica that you see today.

The legendary **pilar** is hidden in the Capilla Santa, inside the east end of the basilica. A tiny oval-shaped portion of the *pilar* is exposed on the chapel's outer west side. A steady stream of people line up to brush lips with its polished and seamed cheek, which even popes have air-kissed. Parents also line up from 1.30pm to 2pm and from 6.30pm to 7.30pm to have their babies blessed next to the Virgin.

Zaragoza

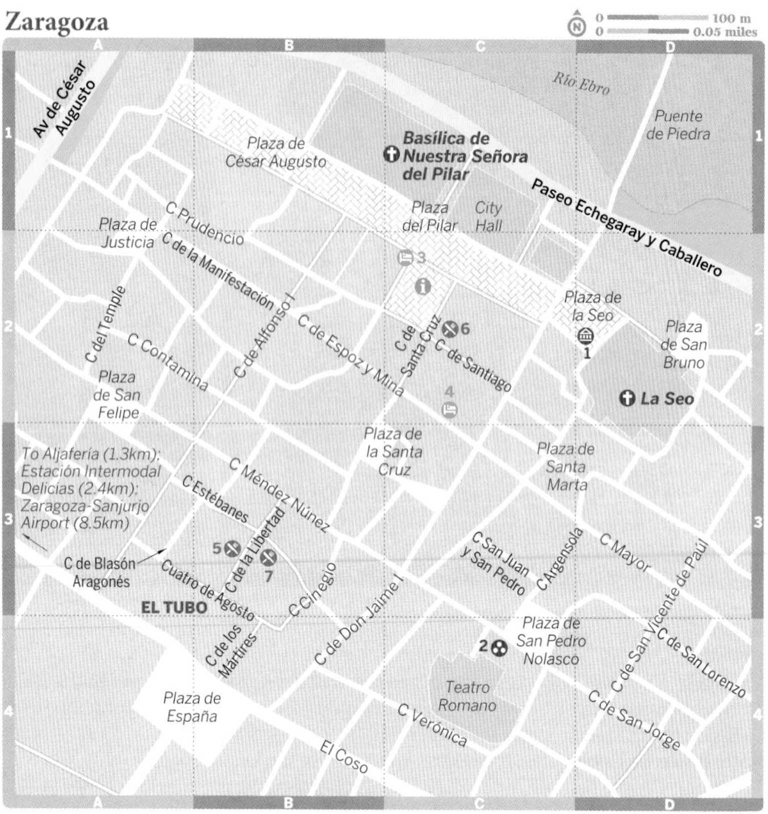

Zaragoza

Top Sights

Basílica de Nuestra Señora del Pilar	C1
La Seo	D2

Sights

1 Museo del Foro de Caesaraugusta	D2
2 Museo del Teatro de Caesaraugusta	C4

Sleeping

3 Hotel Las Torres	C2
4 Hotel Sauce	C2

Eating

5 Casa Pascualillo	B3
6 Mery Limón Gastrobar	C2
7 Taberna Doña Casta	B3

LA SEO Church

(Catedral de San Salvador; Plaza de la Seo; admission €4; 10am-6pm Tue-Fri, 10am-2pm & 3-6pm Sat, 10-11.30am & 2.30-6pm Sun Jun-Sep) Dominating the eastern end of Plaza del Pilar is the Catedral de San Salvador, more popularly known as La Seo. Built between the 12th and 17th centuries, it displays a fabulous spread of architectural styles from Romanesque to baroque – it's Zaragoza's finest example of Christian architecture. It stands on the site of Islamic Zaragoza's main mosque (which in turn stood upon the temple of the Roman forum). The northwest facade is a Mudéjar masterpiece, deploying classic dark brickwork and colourful ceramic decoration in eye-pleasing geometric patterns.

MUSEO DEL FORO DE CAESARAUGUSTA Museum

(Plaza de la Seo 2; admission €2.50; 9am-8.30pm Tue-Sat, 10am-2pm Sun Jun-Sep, shorter hours rest of year) The trapezoid building on Plaza de la Seo is the entrance to an excellent reconstruction of part of Roman Caesaraugusta's forum, now well below ground level. The remains of porticoes, shops, a great *cloaca* (sewer) system, and a limited collection of artefacts from the 1st century AD are on display.

MUSEO DEL TEATRO DE CAESARAUGUSTA Ruin, Museum

(Calle de San Jorge 12; admission €3.50; 9am-8.30pm Tue-Sat, to 1.30pm Sun) Discovered during the excavation of a building site in 1972, the ruins of Zaragoza's Teatro Romano (Roman theatre) are the focus of this interesting museum. The theatre once seated 6000 spectators, and great efforts have been made to help visitors reconstruct the edifice's former splendour, including evening projections of a **virtual performance** on the stage; get there early to ensure a place.

Sleeping

HOTEL LAS TORRES Hotel €€

(976 39 42 50; www.hotellastorres.com; Plaza del Pilar 11; s/d incl breakfast from €75/85;) The rooms are designer cool with dazzling white furnishings and daring wallpaper in the public spaces; they're not averse to the odd chandelier in the midst of all this modern chic. The bathrooms have hydromassage showers, and the views of the square and basilica from the balconies attached to most rooms are simply stunning. Our only complaint? Two years after it opened, the fittings in some of the rooms are already showing considerable wear and tear.

HOTEL SAUCE Hotel €

(976 20 50 50; www.hotelsauce.com; Calle de Espoz y Mina 33; s/d €53.50/58;) This small hotel has good rooms with a mix of styles from traditional and cosy to a modern, classy look. Bookings are advisable. Breakfast costs €8.

Eating

The tangle of lanes in El Tubo, immediately north of Plaza de España, is home to one of Spain's richest gatherings of tapas bars.

CASA PASCUALILLO Tapas €

(Calle de la Libertad 5; mains €5-14; lunch & dinner Tue-Sat, lunch Sun) When *Metropoli*, the respected weekend magazine of *El Mundo* newspaper, set out to find the best 50 tapas bars in Spain a few years

Baqueira/Beret ski resort, Val d'Aran (p123)

GONZALO AZUMENDI/GETTY IMAGES ©

back, it's no surprise that Casa Pascualillo made the final cut. The bar groans under the weight of enticing tapas varieties; the house speciality is El Pascualillo, a 'small' *bocadillo* (filled roll) of *jamón*, mushrooms and onion. There's also a more formal restaurant attached.

MERY LIMÓN GASTROBAR International **€€**
(www.merylimon.com; Calle de Santiago 30; mains €6-14, menú del día €15) This terrific little bar has an unusual menu divided into three parts – Italian, New York and Mediterranean. But what really stands out is the *menú del día* (daily set menu), which combines seven small dishes from the cutting-edge of Spanish gastronomy and wines to go with them.

TABERNA DOÑA CASTA Tapas **€€**
(Calle Estébanes 6; Tue-Sun) If you like your tapas without too many frills, this enduringly popular and informal *taberna* (tavern) could become your culinary home in Zaragoza. The bottle of wine and six tapas for €23 is a terrific way to meet all your gastronomic needs at a reasonable price. Its specialities are *croquetas* (croquettes) and egg-based dishes.

Information

Municipal Tourist Office (976 20 12 00; www.zaragozaturismo.es; Plaza del Pilar; 9am-9pm mid-Jun–mid-Oct, 10am-8pm mid-Oct–mid-Jun) Has branch offices around town, including the train station.

Oficina de Turismo de Aragón (www.turismodearagon.com; Avenida de César Augusto 25; 9am-2pm & 5-8pm Mon-Fri, from 10am Sat & Sun) Around 500m southwest along Av de César Augusto from the western end of Plaza de César Augusto.

Getting There & Away

AIR The **Zaragoza-Sanjurjo airport** (976 71 23 00), 8.5km west of the city centre, has direct **Ryanair** (www.ryanair.com) flights to/from London (Stansted), Brussels (Charleroi), Paris (Beauvais), Milan (Bergamo), Lanzarote and Seville. **Iberia** (www.iberia.es) and **Air Europa** (www.aireuropa.com) also operate a small number of domestic and international routes.

Exploring the Pyrenees

The main entry point into the Parque Nacional de Ordesa y Monte Perdido is Torla, 3km south of the southwest corner of the national park. Private vehicles may not drive from Torla to Pradera de Ordesa during Easter week and from July to mid-September. During these periods a shuttle bus (one way/return €3/4.50) runs between Torla's Centro de Visitantes and Pradera de Ordesa. During the same periods, a one-way system is enforced on part of the Escalona-Sarvisé road. From the Puyarruego turn-off, 2km out of Escalona, to a point about 1km after the road diverges from the Bellos valley, only northwestward traffic is allowed. Southeastward traffic uses an alternative, more southerly road.

You can find information centres in the following villages. From November to March they are only open on weekends:

Torla (974 48 64 72; 9am-2pm & 4-7pm)

Bielsa (974 50 10 43; 9am-2pm & 3.15-6pm)

Tella (974 48 64 72; 9am-2pm & 3.15-6pm)

Escalona (974 50 51 31; 9am-2pm & 3.15-6pm)

BUS Dozens of bus lines fan out across Spain from the bus station attached to the Estación Intermodal Delicias train station. The following companies are the more useful ones:

Alosa (**☎902 210700; www.alosa.es**) Up to eight buses to/from Huesca (€7.30, one hour) and Jaca (€14.50, 2½ hours).

ALSA (**☎902 422242; www.alsa.es**) Frequent daily buses to/from Madrid (from €15.29, 3¾ hours) and Barcelona (€14.49, 3¾ hours).

TRAIN Zaragoza's futuristic, if rather impersonal, **Estación Intermodal Delicias** (**Calle Rioja 33**) is connected by almost hourly high-speed AVE services to Madrid (€60.10, 1¼ hours) and Barcelona (€65.80, from 1½ hours). There are also services to Valencia (€29.80, 4½ hours).

Getting Around

Airport Buses (**☎902 360065; €1.70**) run to/from Paseo María Agustín 7 – which crosses Avenida de César Augusto around 500m southwest of Plaza de España – via the bus/train station every half-hour (every hour on Sunday).

Buses 34 and 51 travel between the city centre and the Estación Intermodal Delicias; the former travels along the Avenida de César Augusto.

THE PYRENEES

Leaving behind Zaragoza's parched flatlands, a hint of green tinges the landscape and there's a growing anticipation of very big mountains somewhere up ahead. And they are big. The Pyrenees boast several peaks well over the 3000m mark and they're among the most dramatic and rewarding on the Spanish side of the range.

Parque Nacional de Ordesa y Monte Perdido

This is where the Spanish Pyrenees really take your breath away. At the heart of it all is a dragon's back of limestone peaks skirting the French border, with a southeastward spur that includes Monte Perdido (3348m), the third-highest peak in the Pyrenees.

If You Like... Mountains

If you like the Parque Nacional de Ordesa y Monte Perdido, we think you'll also like these stirring mountain areas:

1. **VAL D'ARAN** A verdant valley , Catalonia's northernmost outpost, surrounded by spectacular 2000m-plus mountains and studded with ski resorts, including Baquiera/Beret.

2. **VALLES DE ECHO & ANSÓ** Lush, little-visited valleys with old stone villages climbing deep into the Aragonese Pyrenees.

3. **VALL FERRERA** At the heart of the Parc Natural de l'Alt Pirineu (Catalonia's biggest nature reserve), with pretty villages and good walking.

4. **SERRA DEL CADÍ** Picturesque pre-Pyrenees range with ravines and peaks famous for rock climbing.

5. **VALLE DEL RONCAL** Awash in greens and often concealed in mists, this is the most beautiful corner of the western Pyrenees.

6. **OCHAGAVÍA** Grey slate, stone and cobblestone village in the lush, green western Pyrenees.

Activities

For a range of walking options in the park, pick up a copy of the *Senderos* maps and route descriptions for the four sectors (Ordesa, Añisclo, Escuaín and Pineta) from any of the information offices. The Circo de Soaso is a classic day walk that follows the Valle de Ordesa to Circo de Soaso, a rocky balcony whose centrepiece is the Cola de Caballo (Horsetail) waterfall.

If You Like... Aragón's Villages

If you like Aínsa, Aragón has many similarly charming villages to offer:

1 SOS DEL REY CATÓLICO If this gorgeous medieval hilltop village in northwestern Aragón were in Tuscany, it would be world-famous.

2 ALBARRACÍN Albarracín offers epic fortress walls and ancient, maze-like streets with centuries-old buildings leaning over them. West of Teruel.

3 ALQUÉZAR A beautiful stone village, Alquézar is draped along a ridgeline and famous as a destination for canyoning.

4 DAROCA A sleepy medieval town with a castle.

Torla

POP 327

Torla is a lovely Alpine-style village of stone houses with slate roofs, although it does get overrun in July and August. Most people use Torla as a gateway to the national park, but the setting is also delightful, the houses clustered above Río Ara with a backdrop of the national park's mountains.

Sleeping

HOTEL VILLA DE TORLA Hotel €€
(**☎974 48 61 56; www.hotelvilladetorla.com; Plaza de Aragón 1; s €35-45, d €52-69; ⏲mid-Mar–Dec; 🏊**) The rooms here are tidy – some are spacious and stylish, others have floral bedspreads and look a little tired. But the undoubted highlight is the swimming pool and the bar terrace, from where there are lovely views.

Eating

RESTAURANTE EL DUENDE Aragonese €€
(**☎974 48 60 32; www.elduenderestaurante.com; Calle de la Iglesia; mains €14.60-20.55**) This charming place is the best of many restaurants in town, with fine local cuisine, an extensive menu and eclectic decor in a lovely 19th-century building.

Aínsa

POP 2232

The beautiful hilltop village of medieval Aínsa (L'Aínsa in the local dialect), which stands above the modern town of the same name, is one of Aragón's gems, a stunning village hewn from uneven stone.

Sights

IGLESIA DE SANTA MARÍA Church
(**belfry admission €1; ⏲belfry 11am-1.30pm & 4-7pm Sat & Sun, longer hr Jul & Aug**) The restored Romanesque Iglesia de Santa María, rising above the northeastern corner of Plaza Mayor, lights up when you pop €1 into a box, with five minutes of Gregorian chants thrown in.

CASTLE Castle
(**ecomuseum admission €4; ⏲ecomuseum 11am-2pm Wed-Fri, 10am-2pm & 4-7pm Sat & Sun Easter-Oct**) The castle and fortifications off the western end of the Plaza de San Salvador mostly date from the 1600s, though the main tower is 11th century; there are some reasonable views from the wall.

Sleeping

HOTEL LOS SIETE REYES Hotel €€
(**☎974 50 06 81; www.lossietereyes.com; Plaza Mayor; d €70-129; ❄📶**) Set in one of the most charming stone buildings overlooking Plaza Mayor, this temple of style has stunning bathrooms, polished floorboards,

Detour: Teruel

One of Spain's most attractive provincial cities, compact Teruel is an open-air museum of ornate Mudéjar monuments. But this is very much a living museum where the streets are filled with life – a reflection of a city reasserting itself with cultural attitude.

Teruel's **cathedral** (Plaza de la Catedral; adult/child €3/2; 11am-2pm & 4-8pm) is a rich example of the Mudéjar imagination at work with its kaleidoscopic brickwork and colourful ceramic tiles. Inside, the astounding Mudéjar ceiling of the nave is covered with paintings that add up to a medieval cosmography – from musical instruments and hunting scenes to coats of arms and Christ's crucifixion.

The most impressive of Teruel's Mudéjar towers is the **Torre de El Salvador** (www.teruelmudejar.com; Calle El Salvador; adult/concession €2.50/1.80; 10am-2pm & 4-8pm), an early-14th-century extravaganza of brick and ceramics built around an older Islamic minaret.

Teruel is on the highway and railway between Zaragoza and Valencia.

exposed stone walls, flat-screen TVs and some lovely period detail wedded to a contemporary designer look. The attic rooms are enormous, but all are spacious and some have lovely mountain views, while others look out over the Plaza Mayor.

Eating

RESTAURANTE CALLIZO Modern Spanish **€€**

(974 50 03 85; http://restcallizo.restaurantesok.com; Plaza Mayor; set menus €25-42; closed Mon & dinner Sun) This place is definitely something special, cleverly combining traditional cuisine with culinary innovation on its constantly changing menu. The set menus are gastronomic journeys of the highest order; it also offers a (pricey) children's menu.

Information

Municipal Tourist Office (974 50 07 67; www.ainsasobrarbe.net; Avenida Pirenáica 1; 9am-9pm) Inconveniently situated in the new town down the hill, but with an outpost in the Museo de Oficios y Artes Tradicionales.

Regional Tourist Office (974 50 05 12; www.turismosobrarbe.com; Plaza del Castillo 1, Torre Nordeste; 10am-2pm & 4-7pm) Extremely helpful; within the castle walls.

Getting There & Away

Alosa (902 21 07 00; www.alosa.es) runs daily buses to/from Barbastro (€5.40, one hour) and Torla (€4, one hour).

VALENCIA

POP 815,000

Valencia, Spain's third-largest city, for ages languished in the long shadows cast by Madrid, Spain's political capital, and Barcelona, the country's cultural and economic powerhouse. No longer. Stunning public buildings have changed the city's skyline – Sir Norman Foster's **Palacio de Congresos**, David Chipperfield's award-winning **Veles i Vents** structure beside the inner port, and, on the grandest scale of all, the Ciudad de las Artes y las Ciencas, designed in the main by Santiago Calatrava, local boy made good.

Sights & Activities

Western Valencia

BIOPARC Zoo

(www.bioparcvalencia.es; Avenida Pio Baroja 3; adult/child €24/17; 10am-dusk) 'Zoo' is far too old-fashioned and inept a term for this wonderful, innovative, ecofriendly

Valencia

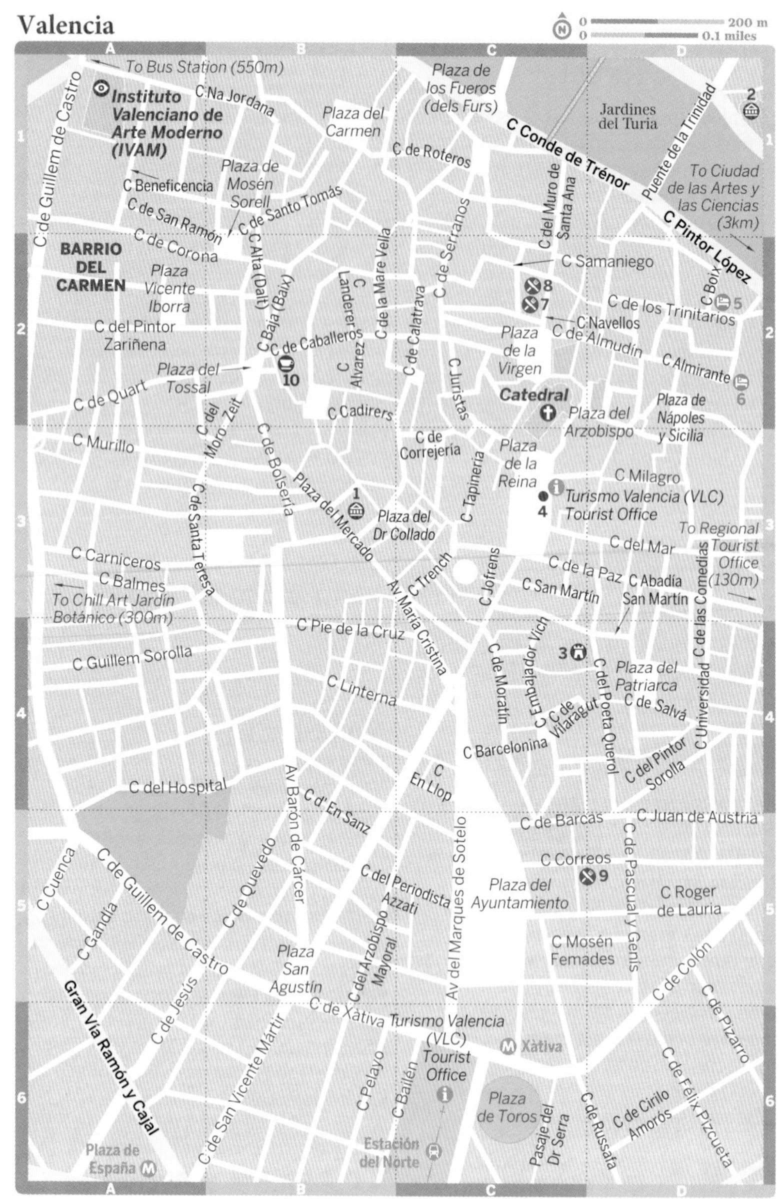

and gently educational space where wild animals apparently (fear not: only apparently) roam free as you wander from savannah to Equatorial Africa and Madagascar, where large-eyed lemurs gambol around your ankles.

MUSEO DE HISTORIA DE VALENCIA Museum

(Calle Valencia 42; adult/child €2/1; ⌚10am-7pm Tue-Sat, 10am-3pm Sun) This museum, very hands-on and with plenty of film and video, plots more than 2000 years of the

Valencia

Top Sights

Catedral ... C2
Instituto Valenciano de Arte Moderno (IVAM) ... A1

Sights

1 La Lonja ... B3
2 Museo de Bellas Artes ... D1
Museo Nacional de Cerámica ... (see 3)
3 Palacio del Marqués de Dos Aguas ... C4

Activities, Courses & Tours

4 Art Valencia ... C3

Sleeping

5 Ad Hoc Monumental ... D2
6 Caro Hotel ... D2

Eating

7 Delicat ... C2
8 Seu-Xerea ... C2
9 Vuelve Carolina ... D5

Drinking

10 Sant Jaume ... B2

city's history. Ask to borrow the museum's informative folder in English.

Central Valencia

CATEDRAL Cathedral

(Plaza de la Virgen; adult/child incl audioguide €4.50/3; 10am-4.45pm or 5.45pm Mon-Sat, 2-4.45pm Sun) Valencia's cathedral is a microcosm of the city's architectural history: the Puerta del Palau on the eastern side is pure Romanesque; the dome, tower and Puerta de los Apóstoles on Plaza de la Virgen are Gothic; the presbytery and main entrance on Plaza de la Reina are resplendently baroque.

Don't miss the rich, recently revealed Italianate frescoes above the main altarpiece. In the flamboyant Gothic **Capilla del Santo Cáliz**, right of the main entrance, is what's claimed to be the **Holy Grail**, the chalice from which Christ sipped during the Last Supper.

LA LONJA Historic Building

(adult/child €2/1; 10am-7pm Tue-Sat, 10am-3pm Sun) This splendid late-15th-century building, a Unesco World Heritage Site, was originally Valencia's silk and commodity exchange. Highlights are the colonnaded hall with its twisted Gothic pillars and the 1st-floor Consulado del Mar with its stunning coffered ceiling.

INSTITUTO VALENCIANO DE ARTE MODERNO (IVAM) Art

(www.ivam.es; Calle Guillem de Castro 118; adult/child €2/1; 10am-8pm Tue-Sun) IVAM (*'ee-bam'*) hosts excellent temporary exhibitions and houses an impressive permanent collection of 20th-century Spanish art.

FREE **MUSEO DE BELLAS ARTES** Museum

(Calle San Pío V 9; 10am-7pm Tue-Sun, 11am-5pm Mon) Bright and spacious, the Museo de Bellas Artes ranks among Spain's best. Highlights include the grandiose *Mosaic of the Nine Muses*, a collection of magnificent late-medieval altarpieces, and works by El Greco, Goya, Velázquez, Murillo and Ribalta, plus artists such as Sorolla and Pinazo of the Valencian Impressionist school.

PALACIO DEL MARQUÉS DE DOS AGUAS Palace

(Calle Poeta Querol 2) A pair of wonderfully extravagant rococo caryatids curl around the main entrance of this over-the-top palace. Inside, the **Museo Nacional de Cerámica** **(adult/child €3/free; 10am-2pm & 4-8pm Tue-Sat, 10am-2pm Sun)** displays ceramics from around the world – and especially of the renowned local production centres of Manises, Alcora and Paterna.

MUSEO FALLERO Museum

(Plaza Monteolivete 4; adult/child €2/1; 10am-7pm Tue-Sat, 10am-3pm Sun) Each Fallas festival, one of the thousands of *ninots* (satirical papier-mâché effigies) that pose at the base of each *falla* (huge statues of papier-mâché and polystyrene) is saved from the flames by popular vote. Those reprieved over the years are displayed here.

Tours

VALENCIA GUÍAS Tour

(96 385 17 40; www.valenciaguias.com; Paseo de la Pechina 32) Daily three-hour guided

KIMBERLEY COOLE/GETTY IMAGES ©

Don't Miss Ciudad de las Artes y las Ciencias

The aesthetically stunning City of Arts & Sciences occupies a massive 350,000-sq-metre swathe of the old Turia riverbed.

For most families with young children the **Oceanogràfic** (adult/child €24.90/18.80; 10am-6pm or 8pm) is the highlight of a visit to Valencia's City of Arts & Sciences. There are polar zones, a dolphinarium, a Red Sea aquarium, a Mediterranean seascape – and a couple of underwater tunnels, one 70m long, where the fish have the chance to gawp back at visitors.

The unblinking heavy-lidded eye of the **Hemisfèric** (adult/child €7.85/6.10) is at once planetarium, IMAX cinema and laser show. Optional English soundtrack for all films.

The interactive science museum, **Museo de las Ciencias Príncipe Felipe** (adult/child €7.85/6.10; 10am-7pm or 9pm), stretches like a giant whale skeleton within the City of Arts & Sciences, with plenty of touchy-feely things for children and displays for all ages.

Brooding over the riverbed like a giant beetle, its shell shimmering with translucent mosaic tiles, the **Palau de les Arts Reina Sofia** is an ultramodern arts complex, grafted onto the City of Arts & Sciences. With seating for 4400, it's exceeded in capacity only by the Sydney Opera House.

Take bus 35 from Plaza del Ayuntamiento or bus 95 from Torres de Serranos or Plaza de América. Oceanogràfic

NEED TO KNOW

Ciudad de las Artes y las Ciencias (City of Arts & Sciences; reservations 902 10 00 31; www.cac.es; combined ticket adult/child €31.50/24)

Palau de les Arts Reina Sofia (www.lesarts.com; Av. del Professor López Piñero)

bicycle tours in English (€25 including rental and snack; minimum two persons). Also two-hour walking tours in Spanish and English (adult/child €15/free), leaving the Plaza de la Reina tourist office at 10am each Saturday.

ART VALENCIA Walking Tour
(**☎96 310 61 93; www.artvalencia.com**) Two-hour walking tours (€13.50) in English and Spanish departing 11am Friday from the Plaza de la Reina tourist office.

Sleeping

CARO HOTEL Hotel **€€€**
(**☎96 305 90 00; www.carohotel.com; Calle Almirante 14; r €140-200;**) This spanking new hotel, housed in a sumptuous 19th-century mansion, sits atop some 2000 years of Valencian history. Its recent restoration has revealed a hefty hunk of the Arab wall, Roman column bases and Gothic arches. Each room is furnished in soothing dark shades and is unique in design. Bathrooms have sensuous, circular bathtubs, bathrobes and sexy Bulgari toiletries.

CHILL ART JARDÍN BOTÁNICO Boutique Hotel **€€**
(**off Map p126; ☎96 315 40 12; www.hoteljardinbotanico.com; Calle Doctor Peset Cervera 6; s/d from €85/90;**) Welcoming and megacool, this intimate – only 16 rooms – hotel is furnished with great flair. Candles flicker in the lounge and each bedroom has original artwork. You'll understand why the Instituto Valenciano de Arte Moderno (IVAM), an easy walk away, regularly selects it as a venue for its guests.

AD HOC MONUMENTAL Hotel **€€**
(**☎96 391 91 40; www.adhochoteles.com; Calle Boix 4; s €65-101, d €76-125;**) Friendly Ad Hoc offers comfort and charm deep within the old quarter and also runs a splendid small restaurant (dinner Monday to Saturday). The late-19th-century building has been restored to its former splendour with great sensitivity, revealing original ceilings, mellow brickwork and solid wooden beams.

Eating

Central Valencia

DELICAT Tapas, Fusion **€**
(**☎96 392 33 57; seudelicat@hotmail.es; Calle Conde Almodovar 4; mains €4-11, menus €12; Tue-Sun**) At this particularly friendly, intimate option (there are only nine tables, plus the terrace in summer), Catina, up front, and her partner, Paco, on full view in the kitchen, offer an unbeatable value five-course menu of samplers for lunch and a range of truly innovative tapas anytime.

SEU-XEREA Fusion, Mediterranean **€€**
(**☎96 392 40 00; www.seuxerea.com; Calle Conde Almodóvar 4; mains around €20, menus €19-45; Tue-Sat**) Recently renovated, this

Valencia for Children

Beaches, of course. The nearest is the combined beach of Malvarrosa and Las Arenas (the latter meaning 'sand'), a shortish bus or tram ride from Valencia's centre. The **high-speed tram** itself is fun: feel the G-force as it surges along.

The other great playground, year-round, is the diverted Río Turia's former 9km riverbed. Of its formal playgrounds, the giant **Gulliver** (**Jardines del Turia; admission free; 10am-8pm Sep-Jun, 10am-2pm & 5-9pm Jul & Aug; 19, 95**), in the Jardines del Turia, just asks to be clambered all over.

The **Jardín Botánico** (**http://www.jardibotanic.org; Calle de Quart 80; adult/child €2/1; 10am-dusk**) is altogether more peaceful; mind the cacti and feral cats, play hide-and-seek among the trees, and keep an eye out for frogs in the fountain.

Las Fallas

The exuberant, anarchic swirl of **Las Fallas de San José** (www.fallas.es) – fireworks, music, festive bonfires and all-night partying – is a must if you're visiting Valencia in mid-March.

The *fallas* themselves are huge sculptures of papier mâché on wood (with, increasingly, environmentally damaging polystyrene), built by teams of local artists. Despite Spain's deep economic recession, in 2012 the combined cost of their construction was well over €8 million. Each neighbourhood sponsors its own *falla*, and when the town wakes after the *plantà* (overnight construction of the *fallas*) on the morning of 16 March, more than 350 have sprung up. Reaching up to 15m in height, with the most expensive costing in 2012 €400,000, these grotesque, colourful effigies satirise celebrities, current affairs and local customs.

Around-the-clock festivities include street parties, paella-cooking competitions, parades, open-air concerts, bullfights and free firework displays. Valencia considers itself the pyrotechnic capital of the world and each day at 2pm from 1 to 19 March a *mascletà* (over five minutes of deafening thumps and explosions) shakes the window panes of Plaza del Ayuntamiento.
After midnight on the final day each *falla* goes up in flames – backed by yet more fireworks.

welcoming restaurant is favourably quoted in almost every English-language press article about Valencia City. The creative, regularly changing, rock-reliable à la carte menu features dishes both international and deep rooted in Spain.

VUELVE CAROLINA Mediterranean **€€**
(☎96 321 86 86; www.vuelvecarolina.com; Calle Correos 8; mains €12-16, menus €30; ⏱Mon-Sat) This new, popular place (reservations are essential) could be a ship's hull. Walls, the bar and just about everything are of stripped pine, subtly lit. The crockery, with plates shaped like fretted leaves and oval glasses, also speaks style. The cuisine is correspondingly original with subtle, creative dishes such as a starter of thick, creamy yoghurt enfolding a single, succulent mussel.

Las Arenas

On weekends locals in their hundreds head for Las Arenas, just north of the port, where a long line of restaurants overlooking the beach all serve up authentic paella in a three-course meal costing around €20.

TRIDENTE Fusion **€€**
(☎96 356 77 77; Paseo de Neptuno 2; mains €16, menus €29-49; ⏱lunch & dinner Mon-Sat, lunch Sun) Begin with an aperitif on the broad beachfront terrace of Tridente, restaurant of Neptuno hotel, then move inside, where filtered sunlight bathes its soothing cream decor. There's an ample à la carte selection but you won't find details of the day's menus in front of you – they're delivered orally by the maître d', who speaks good English. Dishes with their combinations of colours and blending of sweet and savoury are delightfully presented and portions are generous.

Drinking

The Barrio del Carmen has both the grungiest and grooviest collection of bars. On weekends, Calle de Caballeros, the main street, seethes with punters seeking *la marcha* (the action).

SANT JAUME Cafe, Bar

(Plaza del Tossal) At this converted pharmacy, you can still see the old potion bottles and jars ranged behind the counter. Its 1st floor is all quiet crannies and poky passageways.

UBIK CAFÉ Cafe, Bar

(http://ubikcafe.blogspot.com.es; Calle Literato Azorín 13) This child-friendly cafe, bar and bookshop is a comfy place to lounge and browse. It has a short, well-selected list of wines and serves cheese and cold meat platters, salads and plenty of Italian specialities.

Entertainment

BLACK NOTE Jazz

(http://blacknoteclub.com; Calle Polo y Peyrolón 15; ⏰from 11.30pm) Valencia City's most active jazz venue, Black Note has live music daily except Sunday and good canned jazz. Admission, including first drink, ranges from free to €15, depending on who's grooving.

CAFÉ MERCEDES JAZZ Jazz

(www.cafemercedes.es; Calle de Sueca 27; ⏰10pm-3.30am Thu-Sun) This attractive contemporary cafe offers the best from the local jazz scene. Entry is free to jam sessions and less than €10 when a recognised combo is billed.

WAH WAH Club

(www.wahwahclub.es; Calle Campoamor 52; ⏰10pm-3am Thu-Sat) For many clubbers, Wah Wah remains Valencia's hottest venue for live music, especially underground and international indie.

Information

Call 902 12 32 12 throughout the region for tourist information (at premium rates).

Regional Tourist Office (☎96 398 64 22; www.comunitatvalenciana.com; Calle de la Paz 48; ⏰9am-8pm Mon-Sat, 10am-2pm Sun) A fount of information about the Valencia region.

Turismo Valencia (VLC) Tourist Office (☎96 315 39 31; www.turisvalencia.es; Plaza de la Reina 19; ⏰9am-7pm Mon-Sat, 10am-2pm Sun) Has several other branches around town, including the train station and airport arrivals area.

Plaza de la Virgen (Map p126), Valencia

Detour: Cartagena

Easy to slot into a journey between Valencia and Granada, Cartagena is a city that feels old. Stand on the battlements of the castle that overlooks this city and you can literally see layer upon layer of history spread below you.

As archaeologists continue to strip back more and more of the town's old quarter to reveal a long-buried – and fascinating – Roman and Carthaginian heritage, the city is finally starting to get the recognition it deserves as one of the most historically and culturally fascinating places on the east coast of Spain.

The **Museo Teatro Romano** (Plaza del Ayuntamiento 9; adult/child €6/3; 10am-8pm Tue-Sat, 10am-2pm Sun) is the city's finest museum. The tour transports visitors from the initial museum on Plaza del Ayuntamiento, via escalators and an underground passage beneath the ruined cathedral, to the magnificent, recently restored Roman theatre dating from the 1st century BC. Other Roman sites include the **Augusteum** (Calle Caballero; adult/child €2.50/free; 4-7.30pm Tue-Sun), which has an exhibition on the Roman Forum. The **Decumanos** (Calle Honda; adult/child €2/free; 10am-2.30pm Tue-Sun) has evocative remains of one of the town's main Roman streets linking the port with the forum, and including an arcade and thermal baths. The **Casa de la Fortuna** (Plaza Risueño; adult/child €2.50/free; 10am-2.30pm Tue-Sun) consists of fascinating remains of an aristocratic Roman villa dating back to the 2nd and 3rd centuries, complete with murals and mosaics, and part of an excavated road. Finally, the **Muralla Púnica** (Calle de San Diego; adult/child €3.50/free; 10am-2.30pm & 4-7.30pm), built around a section of the old Punic wall, concentrates on the town's Carthaginian and Roman legacy.

From Valencia you'll probably have to change bus or train in Alicante or Murcia in order to get to Cartagena.

Getting There & Away

Air

Valencia's **Aeropuerto de Manises** (96 159 85 00) is 10km west of the city centre along the A3, towards Madrid. It's served by metro lines 3 and 5.

Budget flights serve major European destinations such as Paris, Milan, Geneva, Amsterdam and Brussels. The following airlines fly to/from Ireland and the UK:

EasyJet London (Gatwick)

Ryanair Year-round: London (Stansted) Summer only: Bristol, Dublin, East Midlands, Manchester.

Bus

Valencia's **bus station** (96 346 62 66) is beside the riverbed on Avenida Menéndez Pidal. Bus 8 connects it to Plaza del Ayuntamiento.

Avanza (www.avanzabus.com) operates hourly bus services to/from Madrid (€27.50 to €34.50, four hours).

ALSA (www.alsa.es) has up to 10 daily buses to/from Barcelona (€27 to €32, 4½ hours).

Train

From Valencia's Estación del Norte, major destinations include the following:

DESTINATION	PRICE (€)	DURATION (HR)	FREQUENCY
Alicante	17-29	1¾	10
Barcelona	40-44	3 to 3½	at least 12
Madrid	63-80	1¾	up to 15

Getting Around

Valencia has an integrated bus, tram and metro network.

Tourist offices of Turismo Valencia (VLC) sell the Valencia Tourist Card (€15/20/25 per one/two/three days), entitling you to free urban travel and discounts at participating sights, shops and restaurants.

To/From the Airport

Metro lines 3 and 5 connect the airport, central Valencia and the port. A taxi into the city centre costs around €17 (there's a supplement of €2.50 above the metered fee for journeys originating at the airport).

Car & Motorcycle

Street parking is a pain. There are large underground car parks beneath Plazas de la Reina and Alfonso el Magnánimo and, biggest of all, near the train station, covering the area between Calle Xàtiva and the Gran Vía.

Public Transport

Most buses run until about 10pm, with seven night services continuing until around 1am. Buy a Bonobús Plus, a touch-sensitive, rechargeable card (€9.50 for 10 journeys), sold at major metro stations, most tobacconists and some newspaper kiosks or pay as you get on (€1.50).

The high-speed tram is a pleasant way to get to the beach and port. Pick it up at Pont de Fusta or where it intersects with the metro at Benimaclet.

Metro (**www.metrovalencia.es**) lines cross town and serve the outer suburbs. The closest stations to the city centre are Ángel Guimerá, Xàtiva (for the train station), Colón and Pont de Fusta.

Taxi

Call Radio-Taxi (**☎96 370 33 33**) or Valencia Taxi (**☎96 357 13 13**).

Camino de Santiago & Basque Spain

This is the Spain that most foreign visitors have yet to discover. Spain's north coast and its hinterland are home to some of the most dramatic scenery in the country, from the Pyrenees of Navarra to wild coastline with picture-perfect villages.

The diversity and culinary innovation of the Basque Country finds expression in two cities: magnificent San Sebastián, one of the world's most beautiful seaside cities, and Bilbao, whose stirring Guggenheim Museum has become the symbol for the region. Away from the coast is the wine country of La Rioja and the stunning cathedral cities of Burgos and León. Above all else this is pilgrim territory: the Camino de Santiago, a medieval pilgrimage trail running from the French border right across north Spain, is undergoing a huge resurgence of interest. It all culminates in Santiago de Compostela, whose cathedral is as splendid as it is spiritually significant.

Museo Guggenheim (p153) by architect Frank Gehry, Bilbao

Picking grapes, Galicia

OLIVER STREWE/GETTY IMAGES ©

Camino de Santiago & Basque Spain

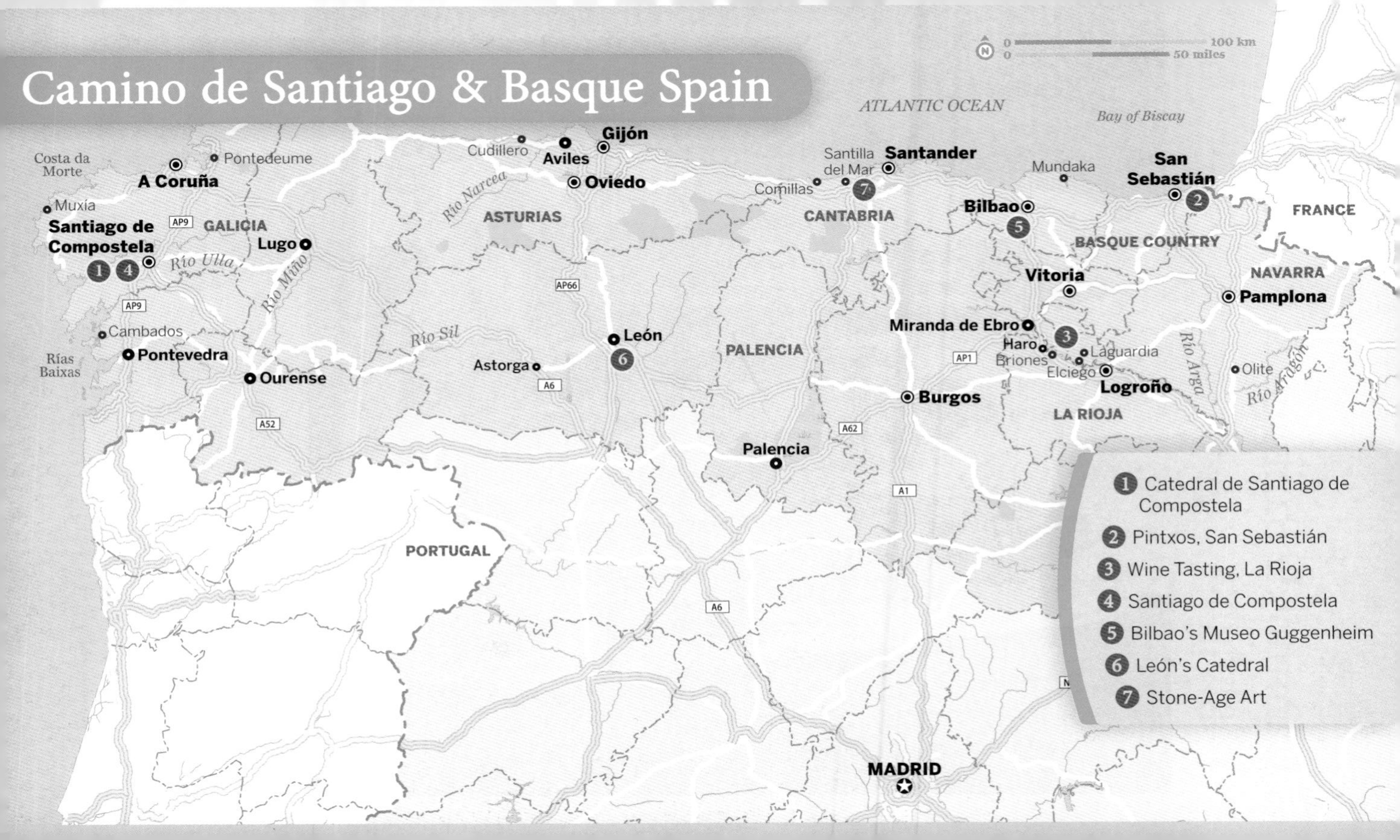

1 Catedral de Santiago de Compostela
2 Pintxos, San Sebastián
3 Wine Tasting, La Rioja
4 Santiago de Compostela
5 Bilbao's Museo Guggenheim
6 León's Catedral
7 Stone-Age Art

0 100 km
0 50 miles
ATLANTIC OCEAN
Bay of Biscay
Costa da Morte
Muxía
Santiago de Compostela
A Coruña
Pontedeume
GALICIA
AP9
Lugo
Río Ulla
Río Miño
Cambados
Rías Baixas
Pontevedra
Ourense
A52
Cudillero
Aviles
Gijón
Oviedo
Río Narcea
ASTURIAS
AP66
Río Sil
Astorga
A6
León
Santilla del Mar
Comillas
Santander
CANTABRIA
PALENCIA
Palencia
A62
Burgos
A1
AP1
Mundaka
Bilbao
San Sebastián
BASQUE COUNTRY
Vitoria
Miranda de Ebro
Haro
Briones
Laguardia
Elciego
Logroño
LA RIOJA
Río Arga
Olite
Río Aragón
NAVARRA
Pamplona
FRANCE
PORTUGAL
MADRID

Camino de Santiago & Basque Spain Highlights

1

Catedral de Santiago de Compostela

Ernest Hemingway described Santiago's cathedral (p178) as the building which meant the most to him in all the world. It's an intense, eclectic monument loaded with spiritual symbolism. Thanks to its Unesco World Heritage status, it has become the focal point for the regeneration of Santiago de Compostela's old town.

Above Right: El Pórtico de la Gloria; Below Right: Statue of St James

Need to Know

TOP FESTIVAL Feast of Saint James (25 July) **PEAK PILGRIM SEASON** June to August **BEST PHOTO OP** Take the cathedral rooftop tour

Catedral de Santiago de Compostela Don't Miss List

BY IÑAKI GAZTELUMENDI, SANTIAGO TOURISM GURU

1 OBRADOIRO FACADE

I've lived in Santiago all my life, but it's still a privilege to see the overwhelmingly baroque Fachada del Obradoiro every day. Study it closely, but also step back into the middle of the plaza where the 360-degree views are a journey through the evolution of art, from the Middle Ages to the 18th century.

2 MAIN ENTRANCE

I'm always surprised how many people rush inside. Pause instead to contemplate the splendour of the El Pórtico de la Gloria, where I have a special weakness for the 24 elders of the apocalypse with musical instruments. Inside, near the Altar Mayor, the figure of Maestro Mateo moves me with its simplicity amid the extravagant beauty elsewhere.

3 PLAZA DE LA QUINTANA

Of the four plazas that connect the cathedral to the rest of the old town, Plaza de la Quintana is the most enigmatic, divided as it is between Quintana of the Dead and Quintana of the Living. Seek out the subtly beautiful granite panel on the monastery facade of the Mosteiro de San Paio de Antealtares.

4 THE CATHEDRAL'S ROOF

As you climb through the labyrinth of staircases, you'll see the great eras of the cathedral's architectural history. But the cathedral was built not just through the genius of its architects, but rather through the labour of local people, and from the summit the panoramic views are a reminder that the cathedral is the centrepiece of a living, breathing city.

5 EL PALACIO GELMÍREZ

Don't miss the interior of this palace, an annex to the cathedral, with its numerous Romanesque gems. I particularly like the kitchen and dining room with their scenes of Galician banquets. It's rare to find two main pillars of Santiago life (gastronomy and the social life that grew up around the cathedral) in one place.

Pintxos in San Sebastián

San Sebastián (p155) is a culinary Mecca: if you love food you must come here. The city holds 18 Michelin stars (and counting), more per capita than any other city in the world. It all owes a debt to the New Basque Cuisine Movement, which has lightened up traditional dishes and emphasised the remarkable local products.

Need to Know

DON'T BE PUT OFF Not all places have *pintxos* lined up along the bar – if it's made to order it's worth the wait **PEAK TIMES** Just before lunch and dinner

2

Local Knowledge

Pintxos in San Sebastián Don't Miss List

BY GABRIELLA RANELLI, COOKING SCHOOL TEACHER AND GASTRONOMIC TOUR LEADER

1 THE PINTXO CRAWL

The *pintxos* tradition is to go from bar to bar trying one *pintxo* and a drink in each spot, then moving on. The idea is to try the house speciality in each one. Don't count on sitting down. It's more like a movable cocktail party.

2 CALLE DE FERMÍN CALBETÓN & CALLE DE 31 DE AGOSTO

If you only have one day, you can't miss Calle de Fermin Calbetón or Calle de 31 de Agosto in the Parte Vieja (Old Town). Any place with a lot of people is probably a good bet, but remember that if you come at any time other than before lunch and before dinner, an empty bar might just mean that you are off schedule.

3 GROS

The other great area for *pintxos* in San Sebastián is in Gros, east of the Parte Vieja across the Río Urumea. Gros is where you will find more wine bars and sophisticated contemporary *pintxos*. The pace is slower here and people might linger longer in some of the bars on this side because the wine lists are especially tempting. Don't forget to try the cider.

4 GILDA

The most emblematic *pintxo* in San Sebastian is the Gilda. Its base always consists of pickled guindilla peppers (a mild green chilli), anchovies and olives and is traditionally served piled on a plate and doused in extra-virgin olive oil. But this being San Sebastián, some bars do creative variations on the theme.

5 TXAKOLI DE GETARIA

The perfect (and most traditional) accompaniment to many *pintxos* in San Sebastián is a glass of *txacoli*, the tart local white wine, which is often poured into your glass from a great height. And not just any *txacoli:* it really should be Txakoli de Getaria, which is produced west of San Sebastián. It goes especially well with a shrimp brochette.

Wine Tasting in La Rioja

Get out the *copas* (glasses) for La Rioja (p162) and for some of the best red wines produced in the country. Wine goes well with the region's ochre earth and vast blue skies. Under these skies lie space-age bodegas, vineyard tours (and tastings), fascinating museums charting th history of wine, great value hotels and some magnificently scenic countryside. Autumn vineyards, La Rioja

3

4

Santiago de Compostela

The cathedral city of Santiago de Compostela (p174) is one of the most sacred cities in the Catholic world. This much-coveted destination for pilgrims along the Camino de Santiago is laden with spiritual significance, and its staggering cathedral cannot fail to leave you moved. Santiago's monumental splendour co-exists alongside the wonderful food culture for which Galicia is famed.

/GETTY IMAGES ©

Bilbao & Museo Guggenheim

5

It wasn't so long ago that tourists gave industrial Bilbao a wide berth, but then along came Frank Gehry's Museo Guggenheim (p153), a shimmering, titanium fish stuffed with cutting-edge modern art, and suddenly Bilbao was the place to be. But as well as Guggenheim art, Bilbao also has a clutch of other fantastic galleries and museums and a *pintxo* culture second only to San Sebastián's.

LUIS DAVILLA/CONTRIBUTOR/GETTY IMAGES ©

6

Marvel at León's Catedral

Spain has some extraordinary cathedrals, but few combine delicacy and grandeur to such sublime effect as León's Catedral (p171). Prettily proportioned on the outside, and a kaleidoscope of colour within, the cathedral's 128 stained-glass windows will leave you breathless. The quiet slap of sandals on flagstones is also a reminder that this is an important staging post for pilgrims along the Camino de Santiago.

7

Stone-Age Art

When Bilbao's Guggenheim and Madrid's Museo del Prado were just twinkles in someone's eye, Spain was producing world-class art galleries – and none come more spectacular than the prehistoric cave paintings of Altamira (p155).

Camino de Santiago & Basque Spain's Best...

Places to Eat

- **Arzak** (p159) Three Michelin stars and the granddaddy of *nueva cocina vasca*.
- **La Cuchara de San Telmo** (p160) The king of San Sebastián *pintxo* bars.
- **Cervecería Morito** (p169) An old style bar with totally up to date tapas.
- **La Fabula** (p170) innovative slimmed-down dishes in a bright, modern setting.

Places for a Local Drop

- **Briones** (p165) Home to one of Spain's most interactive wine museums.
- **Laguardia** (p165) Charming hill-town in the heart of La Rioja wine country with plenty of wineries to visit nearby.
- **Asturian bars** (p165) Cider is an Asturian obsession – learn all about it at the Museo de la Sidra in Nava.

Daring Architecure

- **Museo Guggenheim** (p153) The building that changed the way we build.
- **Hotel Marques de Riscal** (p164) Frank Gehry turns his hand to village improvements.
- **Bodegas Ysios** (p164) A wave-like structure rolling across the Riojan landscape.
- **León Catedral** (p171) The house of God on a huge scale.
- **Burgos Catedral** (p168) Masterpiece of Gothic art.
- **Santiago de Compostela Catedral** (p178) The magnificent reward at the end of the road.

Places for City Life

- **San Sebastián** (p155) Gorgeous city, perfect beach and extraordinary food.
- **Santiago de Compostela** (p**174**) Cathedral city beloved by pilgrims and aesthetes alike.
- **León** (p171) Full of energy and with one of the finest cathedrals in Spain.
- **Bilbao** (p148) Gritty city with the Guggenheim, one of the iconic buildings of the modern age.
- **Burgos** (p168) Home of *El Cid*, a glittering cathedral and a pretty streetscape.

Left: Asturian barman pouring cider; **Above:** San Sebastián

Need to Know

ADVANCE PLANNING

- **Two months before** Book your table at Arzak.
- **One month before** Book summertime accommodation in San Sebastián.

RESOURCES

- **Basque Country** (www.basquecountry-tourism.com) Informative site for the Basque Country.
- **Navarra** (www.turismo.navarra.es) Everything you need to know about Navarra.
- **La Rioja** (www.lariojaturismo.com) Official tourist office site for La Rioja.
- **Castilla y León** (www.turismocastillayleon.com) Informative site for north-central Spain.
- **Galicia** (www.turgalicia.es) Excellent window on Galicia.

GETTING AROUND

- **Air** International airports in Bilbao, Santander, Oviedo, Santiago de Compostela, A Coruña and Vigo.
- **Train** Renfe (www.renfe.es) trains connect to the rest of Spain, FEVE (v runs along the coast.
- **Bus** Intermittent services where trains don't reach.

BE FOREWARNED

- **Accommodation** Can be hard to find in San Sebastián (May to September) and Santiago de Compostela (July).
- **Arzak** The Basque Country's most celebrated restaurant closes the last two weeks in June and November.
- **Summer** Book your coastal accommodation months in advance.

Camino de Santiago & Basque Spain Itineraries

The two big hitters of Spain's little-trodden northern regions are the beaches, galleries and divine food of the great Basque cities of Bilbao and San Sebastián, and the Camino de Santiago pilgrimage route.

3 DAYS

BASQUE CITIES

Bilbao to Pamplona

Basque culture is one of the oldest in Europe, but **(1) Bilbao** offers confirmation that a willingness to embrace the outrageously modern is central to the Basque psyche. This is a town of fiercely guarded Basque traditions, not least in the seven streets of the Parte Vieja (old town) where Bilbao was born. Not far away, the futuristic Museo Guggenheim is one of Europe's most extraordinary architectural innovations and deserves a full day of appreciation.

For the remaining two days, lose yourself in **(2) San Sebastián**, a gorgeous seaside city arrayed around a near-perfect beach. In the impossibly narrow lanes of the old town, bar tops groan under the weight of *pintxos* (Basque tapas), from basic Basque staples to the experimental high cuisine in miniature for which the region has become famous. Elsewhere in town, Michelin-starred restaurants provide a more formal but equally delicious dining experience.

Finally, head an hour inland from San Sebastián to **(3) Pamplona**, the capital of Navarra and a city renowned the world over for the legendary bull run held each morning during its annual Sanfermines festival.

THE CAMINO DE SANTIAGO

Pamplona to Santiago de Compostela

There are many different *caminos* (routes) to Santiago de Compostela. The most trodden route begins on the French-Spanish Basque country border, tumbles out of the Pyrenees and really gets into gear in **(1) Pamplona**, a city that hosts a crazy bull-running festival.

Next, saunter through La Rioja, Spain's most prestigious wine-producing region. A good base for the area is **(2) Laguardia**, a medieval hilltop town surrounded by vineyards. One of the best bodegas, in the nearby village of **(3) Elciego**, is the Guggenheim-esque Bodegas Marqués de Riscal. Also along the Río Ebro, **(4) Briones** has the astonishing Dinastía Vivanco, arguably La Rioja's best wine museum.

Rising up from the plains of central Castilla y León is **(5) Burgos**, dominated by its cathedral - this is your next stop, followed by glorious **(6) León** and its sparkling cathedral windows. Moving ever westward, celebrate the completion of your journey with hundreds of foot-weary pilgrims in front of the great altar of the cathedral of **(7) Santiago de Compostela**, a sacred city whose golden granite buildings grow a jacket of moss in the seemingly constant drizzle.

San Sebastián's Parte Vieja

Discover Camino de Santiago & Basque Spain

At a Glance

Zubizuri footbridge by architect Santiago Calatrava, across the Río de Nervión, Bilbao

BASQUE COUNTRY

Bilbao

POP 354,200

Bilbao (Bilbo in Basque) had a tough upbringing. Growing up in an environment of heavy industry and industrial wastelands, it was abused for years by those in power and had to work hard to get anywhere. But, like the kid from the estates who made it big, Bilbao's graft paid off when a few wise investments left it with a shimmering titanium fish called the Museo Guggenheim and a horde of arty groupies around the world.

Sights

MUSEO DE BELLAS ARTES Art Gallery

(Fine Arts Museum; Map p150; www.museobilbao.com; Plaza del Museo 2; adult/child €6/free, free Wed; 10am-8pm Tue-Sun) A mere five minutes from Museo Guggenheim is Bilbao's Museo de Bellas Artes. More than just a complement to the Guggenheim, it often seems to actually exceed its more famous cousin for content.

The museum houses a compelling collection that includes everything from Gothic sculptures to 20th-century pop art. As with the Guggenheim, it's the temporary exhibitions (see website for upcoming exhibitions) that are the real hit though.

CASCO VIEJO Old Town

The compact Casco Viejo, Bilbao's atmospheric old quarter, is full of charming streets, boisterous bars and plenty of quirky and independent shops. At the

Detour: Guernica

Guernica (Basque: Gernika) is a state of mind. At a glance it seems no more than a modern and ugly country town. Apparently, prior to the morning of 26 April 1937, Guernica wasn't quite so ugly, but the horrifying events of that day meant that the town was later reconstructed as fast as possible with little regard for aesthetics. Franco, who'd been having some problems with the Basques, decided to teach them a lesson by calling in his buddy Hitler. On that fateful morning planes from Hitler's Condor Legion flew backwards and forwards over the town demonstrating their new found concept of saturation bombing. In the space of a few hours, the town was destroyed and many people were left dead or injured.

The tragedy of Guernica gained international resonance with Picasso's iconic painting *Guernica,* which has come to symbolise the violence of the 20th century. A copy of the painting now hangs in the entrance hall of the UN headquarters in New York, while the original hangs in the Centro de Arte Reina Sofía (p200) in Madrid.

Guernica's seminal experience is a visit to the **Museo de la Paz de Gernika (Guernica Peace Museum; www.peacemuseumguernica.org; Plaza Foru 1; adult/child €5/2; 10am-2pm & 4-7pm Tue-Sat, 10am-2pm Sun)**, where audiovisual displays calmly reveal the horror of war and hatred, both in the Basque Country and around the world.

Guernica is an easy day trip from Bilbao by ET/FV train from Atxuri train station (€2.80, one hour). Trains run every half-hour.

heart of the Casco are Bilbao's original seven streets, Las Siete Calles, which date from the 1400s.

EUSKAL MUSEOA Museum

(Museo Vasco; Map p150; www.euskal-museoa.org; Plaza Miguel Unamuno 4; adult/child €3/free, free Thu; 11am-5pm Tue-Sat, 11am-2pm Sun) This museum is probably the most complete museum of Basque culture and history in all of Spain. The story kicks off back in the days of prehistory and from this murky period the displays bound rapidly through to the modern age.

The main problem with the museum is that, unless you speak Spanish (or perhaps you studied Euskara at school?), it's all a little meaningless as there are no English or French translations.

MUSEO MARÍTIMO RÍA DE BILBAO Museum

(Map p150; www.museomaritimobilbao.org; Muelle Ramón de la Sota 1; adult/child €5/free; 10am-8pm Tue-Sun, to 6pm weekdays in winter) This space-age maritime museum, appropriately sited down on the waterfront, uses bright and well-thought-out displays to bring the watery depths of Bilbao and Basque maritime history to life.

Sleeping

PENSIÓN ITURRIENEA OSTATUA Boutique Hotel €€

(Map p150; 944 16 15 00; www.iturrieneaostatua.com; Calle de Santa María 14; r €50-70;) Easily the most eccentric hotel in Bilbao, it's part farmyard, part old-fashioned toyshop, and a work of art in its own right. The nine rooms here are so full of character that there'll be barely enough room for your own!

HOSTAL BEGOÑA Boutique Hotel €

(Map p150; 944 23 01 34; www.hostalbegona.com; Calle de la Amistad 2; s/d from €50/55; @) The owners of this outstanding place don't need voguish labels for their very stylish and individual creation. Begoña speaks for itself with colourful

Bilbao

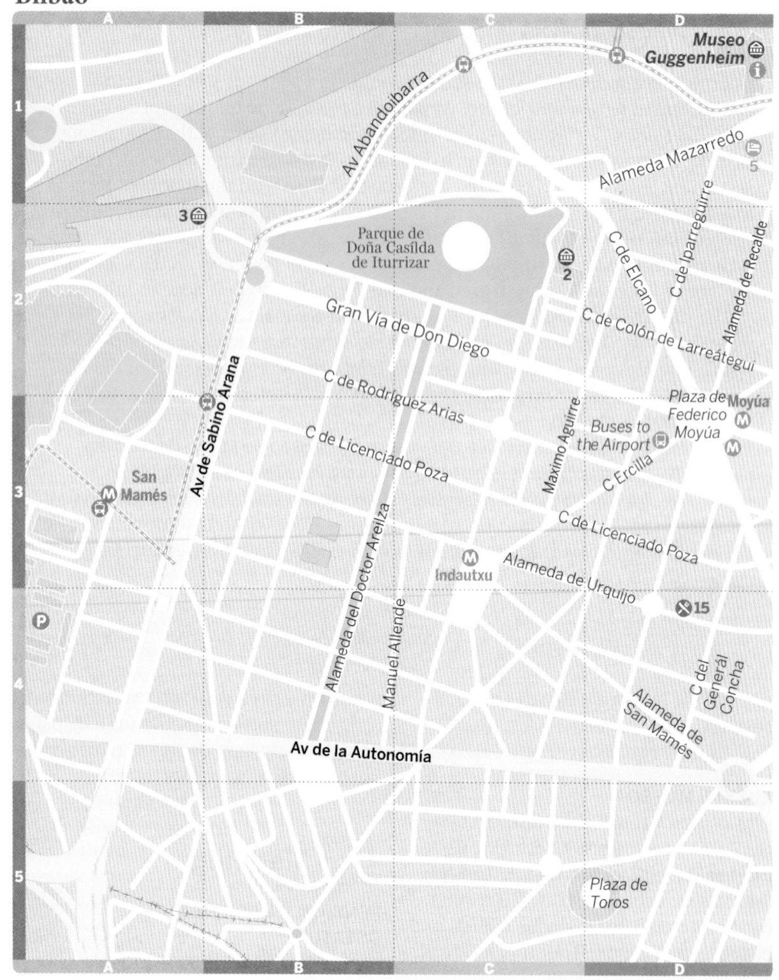

rooms decorated with modern artworks, all with funky tiled bathrooms and wrought-iron beds.

BARCELÓ NERVIÓN Hotel **€**

(Map p150; ☎944 45 47 00; www.barcelonervion.com; Paseo Campo Volantin 11; s/d from €51/55; P ❄ @ ☎) OK, it's a chain hotel and, yes, whilst the rooms are cheap, they do charge over the odds for everything else. But let's be fair: hotels of this quality don't come much cheaper than this. The rooms are smart, comfortable and spacious and they'll throw in a baby cot for no extra charge. The location, on the riverfront and equidistant to the old town and the Guggenheim, is ideal.

GRAN HOTEL DOMINE Design Hotel **€€€**

(Map p150; ☎944 25 33 00; www.granhoteldominebilbao.com; Alameda Mazarredo 61; r from €132; P ❄ @ ≋) Designer chic all the way, from the Javier Mariscal interiors to the Phillipe Starck and Arne Jacobsen fittings – and that's just in the loos. This

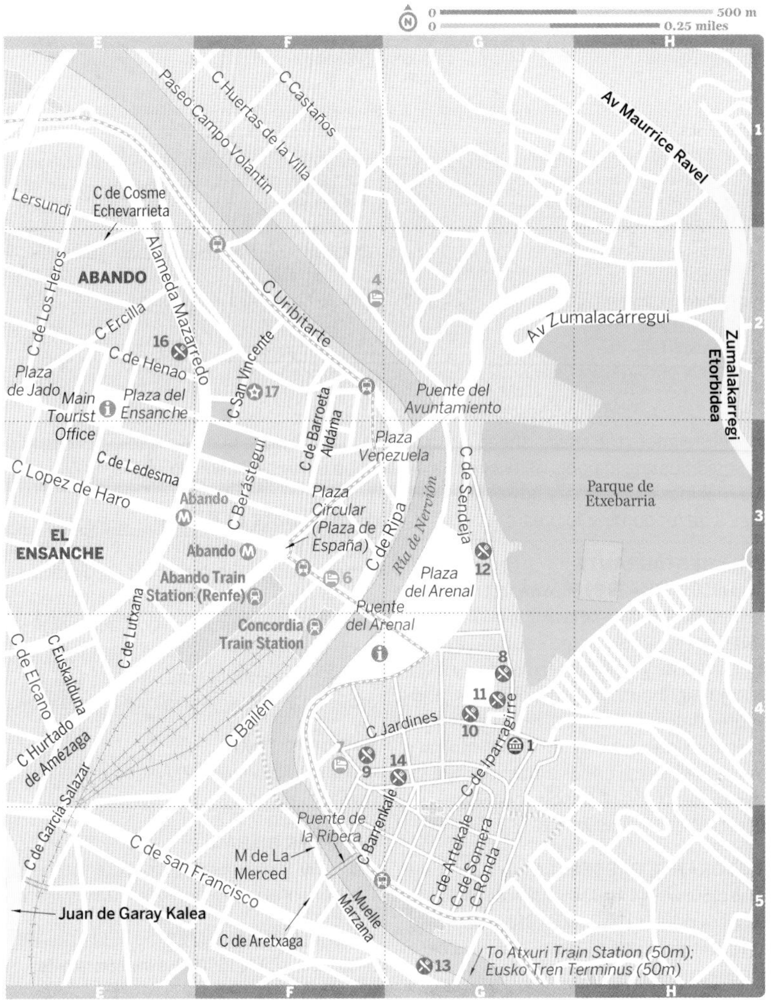

stellar showpiece of the Silken chain has views of the Guggenheim from some of its pricier rooms, a giant column of rounded beach stones reaching for the heavens and a water feature filled with plates and glasses. Yes, it's a little different!

Eating

In the world of trade and commerce, the Basques are an outward-looking lot, but when it comes to food they refuse to believe that any other people could possibly match their culinary skills (and they may well have a point). This means that eating out in Bilbao is generally a choice of Basque, Basque or Basque food. Still, life could be worse and there are some terrific places to eat.

RIO-OJA Basque €
(Map p150; ☎944 15 08 71; Calle de Perro 4; mains €8-11) An institution that shouldn't be missed. It specialises in light Basque seafood and heavy inland fare, but to

Bilbao

Top Sights

	Museo Guggenheim	D1

Sights

1	Euskal Museoa	G4
2	Museo de Bellas Artes	C2
3	Museo Marítimo Ría de Bilbao	A2

Sleeping

4	Barceló Nervión	F2
5	Gran Hotel Domine	D1
6	Hostal Begoña	F3
7	Pensión Iturrienea Ostatua	F4

Eating

8	Bar Gure Toki	G4
9	Berton Sasibil	F4
10	Café-Bar Bilbao	G4
11	Casa Victor Montes	G4
12	Claudio: La Feria del Jamón	G3
13	Mina Restaurante	G5
14	Rio-Oja	G4
15	Ristorante Passerela	D4
	Sorginzulo	(see 8)
16	Zortziko Restaurante	E2

Entertainment

17	Kafe Antzokia	F2

most foreigners the snails, sheep brains or squid floating in pools of its own ink are the makings of a culinary adventure story they'll be recounting for years.

MINA RESTAURANTE Basque **€€€**
(Map p150; ☎944 79 59 38; www.restaurantemina.es; Muelle Marzana; tasting menu from €61) Offering unexpected sophistication and fine dining in an otherwise fairly grimy neighbourhood, this riverside, and appropriately fish-based, restaurant has been making waves in the Bilbao culinary world, with some critics citing it as the new *número uno* of Basque cooking. Reservations are essential.

RISTORANTE PASSERELA Italian **€€**
(Map p150; ☎944 44 03 46; Alameda de Urquijo 30; menú del día €12.50, mains €10-14) Opened in 1980 this is one of the oldest, and best regarded, Italian restaurants in Bilbao. In proper Italian style you order a plate of fresh pasta to start and then follow up with a meat or fish course, followed by a sticky Sicilian dessert. After which you'll probably get busy making plans for a holiday in Italy.

ZORTZIKO RESTAURANTE Basque **€€€**
(Map p150; ☎944 23 97 43; Alameda Mazarredo 17; menus from €60; ⏰Tue-Sat; ✍) Michelin stared chef Daniel García presents immaculate modern Basque cuisine in a formal 1920's style French dining room. The highly inventive menu changes frequently but can include such delicacies as citrus soup or mussel cannelloni.

Pintxo Bars in Bilbao

There are literally hundreds of *pintxo* bars throughout Bilbao, but the Plaza Nueva on the edge of the Casco Viejo offers especially rich pickings, as do Calle de Perro and Calle Jardines. Some of the city's long-time standouts (all charge from around €2.50 per *pintxo*) are listed below.

BAR GURE TOKI Pintxos
(Map p150; Plaza Nueva 12) A simple line in creative pintxos.

CAFÉ-BAR BILBAO Pintxos
(Map p150; Plaza Nueva 6) Cool blue southern tile work and warm northern atmosphere.

CASA VICTOR MONTES Basque **€€**
(Map p150; ☎944 15 70 67; www.victormontesbilbao.com; Plaza Nueva 8; mains €15) As well known for its pintxos as its full meals.

SORGINZULO Pintxos
(Map p150; Plaza Nueva 12) A matchbox-sized bar with an exemplary spread of pintxos.

BERTON SASIBIL Pintxos
(Map p150; Calle Jardines 8) Screens informative films on the crafting of the same superb *pintxos* that you're munching on.

CLAUDIO: LA FERIA DEL JAMÓN Pintxos
(Map p150; Calle Esperanza 9-18) A creaky old place full of ancient furnishings.

OLIVER STREWE/GETTY IMAGES ©

Don't Miss Museo Guggenheim

Opened in September 1997, Bilbao's Museo Guggenheim sensationally lifted modern architecture and Bilbao into the 21st century. It boosted the city's already inspired regeneration, stimulated further development and placed Bilbao firmly in the world art and tourism spotlight.

Some might say, probably quite rightly, that structure overwhelms function here and that the Guggenheim is more famous for its architecture than its content. But Canadian architect Frank Gehry's inspired use of flowing canopies, cliffs, promontories, ship shapes, towers and flying fins is irresistible.

Heading inside, the interior of the Guggenheim is purposefully vast. The cathedral-like atrium is more than 45m high. Light pours in through the glass cliffs. Permanent exhibits fill the ground floor and include such wonders as mazes of metal and phrases of light reaching for the skies.

For most people, though, it is the temporary exhibitions that are the main attraction (check the website for upcoming shows).

Admission prices vary depending on special exhibitions and time of year. The prices we have quoted are the maxiumn (and most common); the last ticket sales are half an hour before closing. Excellent self-guided audio tours in various languages are free with admission and there is a special children's audio guide.

The Artean Pass is a joint ticket for the Guggenheim and the Museo de Bellas Artes (p148) which, at €13.50 for adults, offers significant savings. It's available from either museum.

NEED TO KNOW

Map p150; www.guggenheim-bilbao.es; Avenida Abandoibarra 2; adult/child €13/free; 10am-8pm, closed Mon Sep-Jun

Entertainment

KAFE ANTZOKIA Live Music
(Map p150; www.kafeantzokia.com; Calle San Vicente 2) This is the vibrant heart of contemporary Basque Bilbao, featuring international rock bands, blues and reggae, but also the cream of Basque rock-pop. Weekend concerts run from 10pm to 1am, followed by DJs until 5am. Cover charge for concerts can range from about €12 upwards. During the day it's a cafe, restaurant and cultural centre all rolled into one and has frequent exciting events on.

Tourist Information

Tourist Office (944 79 57 60) Main office **(Plaza del Ensanche 11; 9am-2pm & 4-7.30pm Mon-Fri)**; Airport (**944 71 03 01; Airport; 9am-9pm Mon-Sat, 9am-3pm Sun)**; Guggenheim **(Alameda Mazarredo 66; 10am-7pm Mon-Sat, 10am-6pm Sun, shorter hrs Sep-Jun)**; Teatro Arriaga **(Plaza Arriaga; 9.30am-2pm & 4-7.30pm daily)** Bilbao's friendly tourist-office staffers are extremely helpful, well informed and, above all, enthusiastic about their city. At all offices ask for the free bimonthly *Bilbao Guía,* with its entertainment listings plus tips on restaurants, bars and nightlife.

Getting There & Away

Air

Bilbao's airport (**902 40 47 04; www.aena.es)** is near Sondika, to the northeast of the city. A number of European flag carriers serve the city and of the budget airlines EasyJet **(www.easyjet.com)** and Vueling **(www.vueling.com)** cover the widest range of destinations.

Bus

Bilbao's main bus station, Termibus, is west of the centre. There are regular services to the following destinations:

DESTINATION	FARE (€)	DURATION (HR)
Barcelona	44	7-8
Madrid	28.50	4.75
Pamplona	14	2.75
San Sebastián	10	1

Building facades in Bilbao's Casco Viejo (Old Quarter; p148)

Detour: Altamira

Spain's finest prehistoric art, the wonderful paintings of bison, horses and other animals in the Cueva de Altamira, 2km southwest of Santillana del Mar, was discovered in 1879 by Cantabrian historian and scientist Marcelino Sanz de Sautuola and his eight-year-old daughter María Justina. By 2002 Altamira had attracted so many visitors that the cave was closed to prevent deterioration of the art, but a replica cave in the **Museo de Altamira** (museodealtamira.mcu.es; adult/child, EU senior or student €3/free, Sun & from 2.30pm Sat free; 9.30am-8pm Tue-Sat, to 3pm Sun & holidays; P) now enables everyone to appreciate the inspired, 14,500-year-old paintings. Excellent other displays, in English and Spanish, cover prehistoric humanity and cave art around the world, from Altamira to Australia.

Train

The Abando train station is just across the river from Plaza Arriaga and the Casco Viejo. There are frequent trains to the following destinations:

DESTINATION	FARE (€)	DURATION (HR)
Barcelona	65	6¾
Burgos	22.50	3
Madrid	from 50.50	5
Valladolid	from 31	4

Getting Around

To/From the Airport

The **airport bus** (Bizkaibus A3247; €1.30, 30 minutes) departs from a stand on the extreme right as you leave arrivals. It runs from the airport every 20 to 30 minutes from 6.20am to midnight. There is also a direct hourly bus from the airport to San Sebastián (€15.70, 1¼ hours). It runs from 7.45am to 11.45pm.

Taxis from the airport to the Casco Viejo cost about €24.

San Sebastián

POP 183,300

It's said that nothing is impossible. This is wrong. It's impossible to lay eyes on San Sebastián (Basque: Donostia) and not fall madly in love. This stunning city is everything that grimy Bilbao is not: cool, svelte and flirtatious by night, charming and well mannered by day. Best of all is the summer fun on the beach. For it's setting, form and attitude, Playa de la Concha is the equal of any city beach in Europe. Then there's Playa de Gros (also known as Playa de la Zurriola), with its surfers and sultry beach goers. As the sun falls on another sweltering summer's day, you'll sit back with a drink and an artistic *pintxo* and realise that, yes, you too are in love with sexy San Sebastián.

Sights

BEACHES & ISLA DE SANTA CLARA Beach

Fulfilling almost every idea of how a perfect city beach should be formed, **Playa de la Concha** and its westerly extension, **Playa de Ondarreta**, are easily among the best city beaches in Europe.

Less popular, but just as showy, **Playa de Gros** (Playa de la Zurriola), east of Río Urumea, is the city's main surf beach.

AQUARIUM Aquarium

(www.aquariumss.com; Plaza Carlos Blasco de Imaz 1; adult/child €12/6; 10am-8pm Mon-Fri, 10am-9pm Sat & Sun) In the city's excellent aquarium you'll fear for your life as huge sharks bear down on you and be tripped out by fancy fluoro jellyfish. The highlights of a visit are the cinema-screen–sized deep ocean and coral reef exhibits and the long tunnel, around which swim monsters of the deep.

San Sebastián

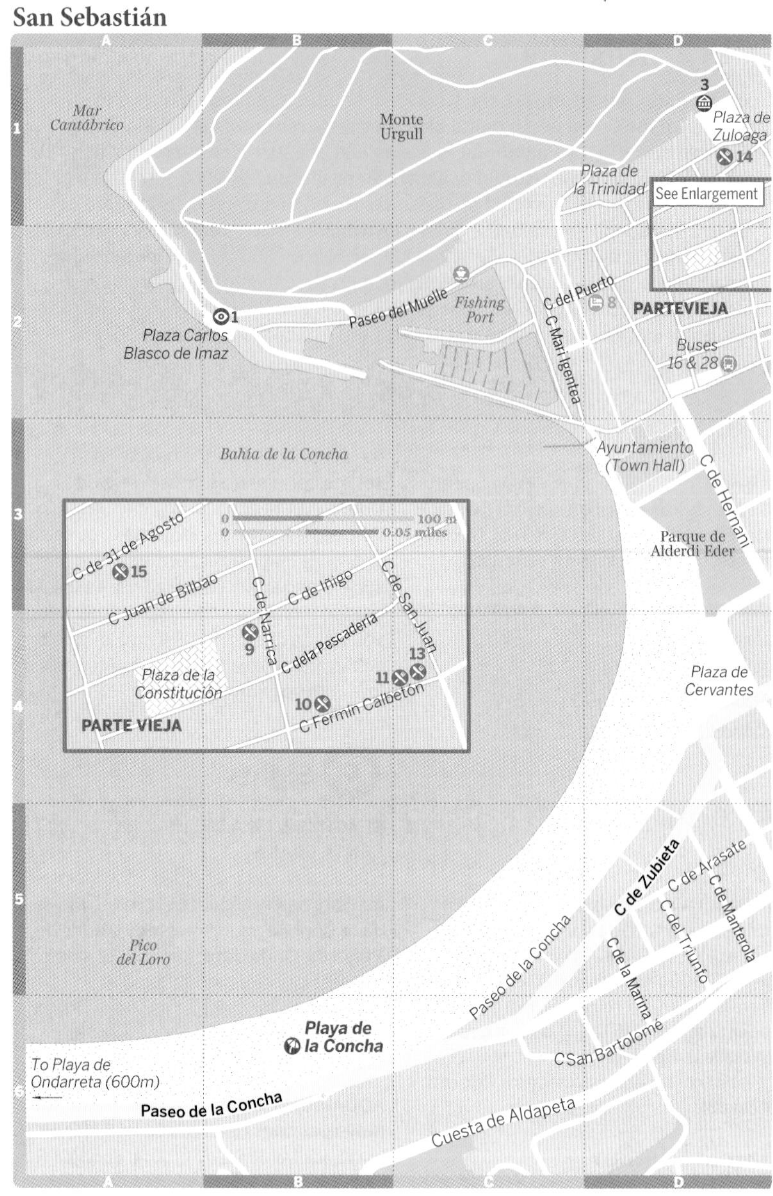

SAN TELMO MUSEOA Museum
(☎943 48 15 80; www.santelmomuseoa.com; Plaza Zuloaga 1; adult/child €5/free, free to all Tue; ⏲10am-8pm Tue-Sun) Both the oldest and newest museum in the Basque country the San Telmo museum has existed since 1902 – sort of. It was actually closed for many years but after major renovation work it has recently reopened and is now a museum of Basque culture and society.

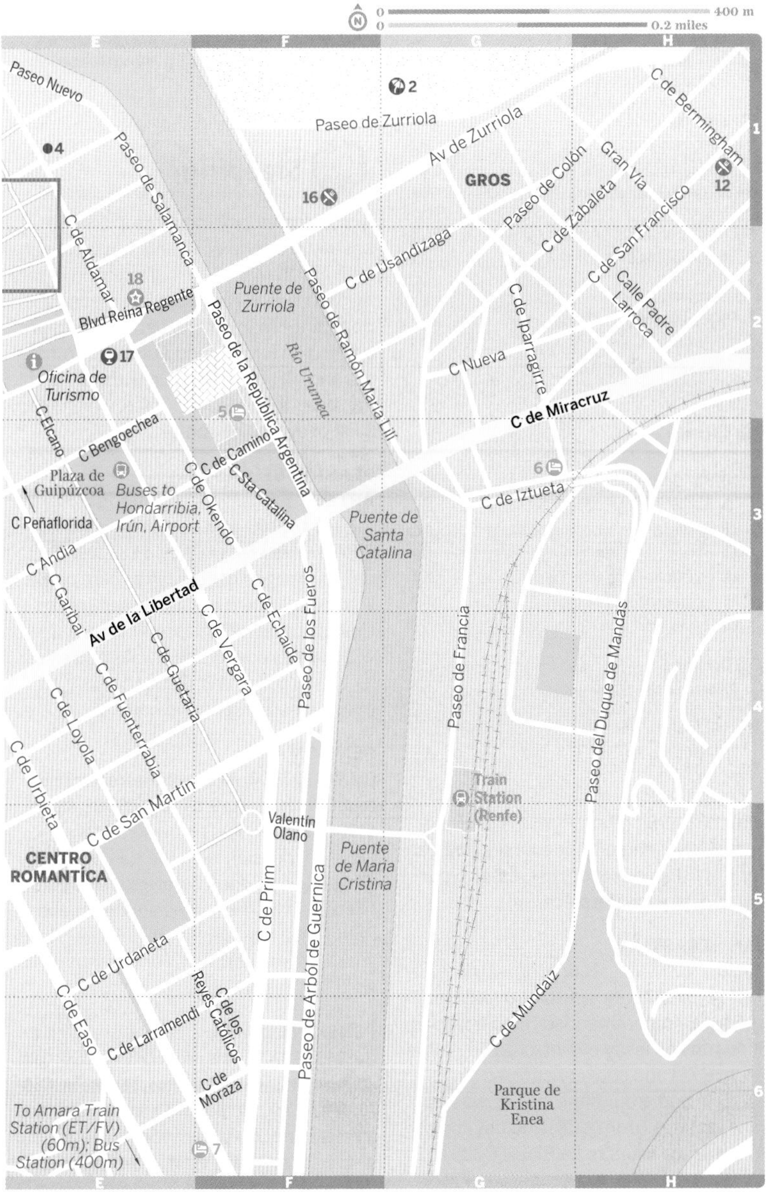

0 400 m
0 0.2 miles
E F G H
1 2 3 4 5 6
Paseo Nuevo
2
Paseo de Zurriola
Av de Zurriola
C de Bermingham
4
Paseo de Salamanca
GROS
Paseo de Colón
Gran Vía
12
16
C de Zabaleta
C de San Francisco
C de Aldamar
C de Usandizaga
18
Puente de Zurriola
Paseo de Ramón María Lili
Calle Padre Larroca
Blvd Reina Regente
Paseo de la República Argentina
C de Iparragirre
Río Urumea
C Nueva
17
Oficina de Turismo
5
C de Miracruz
C Elcano
C Bengoechea
C de Camino
C Sta Catalina
6
Plaza de Guipúzcoa
C de Okendo
Buses to Hondarribia, Irún, Airport
C de Iztueta
C Peñaflorida
Puente de Santa Catalina
C Andia
C Garibai
Av de la Libertad
C de Echaide
Paseo de los Fueros
C de Vergara
C de Guetaria
Paseo de Francia
Paseo del Duque de Mandas
C de Fuenterrabia
C de Loyola
C de Urbieta
C de San Martín
Train Station (Renfe)
Valentín Olano
CENTRO ROMANTÍCA
Puente de Maria Cristina
C de Prim
Paseo de Arbol de Guernica
C de Urdaneta
C de Mundaiz
C de Easo
C de Larramendi
C de los Reyes Católicos
C de Moraza
Parque de Kristina Enea
To Amara Train Station (ET/FV) (60m); Bus Station (400m)
7

Courses & Tours

The tourist office runs a whole array of different city tours (including a running tour!) starting at €10.

PINTXO.SANSE Cooking Course
(☎902 44 34 42; www.sansebastianreservas.com; course €120) The food of San Sebastián has a legendary status and it's those little parcels of delight, *pintxos*, that really set hearts aflutter. In association

San Sebastián

Top Sights
Playa de la Concha B6

Sights
1 Aquarium B2
2 Playa de Gros G1
3 San Telmo Museoa D1

Activities, Courses & Tours
4 San Sebastián Food E1

Sleeping
5 Hotel Maria Cristina F2
6 Pensión Aida G3
7 Pensión Bellas Artes F6
8 Pensión Edorta D2

Eating
9 Astelena B4
10 Bar Borda Berri B4
11 Bar Goiz-Argi C4
12 Bergara Bar H1
13 Bodegón Alejandro C4
14 La Cuchara de San Telmo D1
15 Restaurante Alberto A3
16 Restaurante Ni Neu F1

Drinking
17 Museo del Whisky E2

Entertainment
18 Altxerri Jazz Bar E2

with the tourist office, Pintxo.Sanse runs personalised three-hour courses (in Spanish, English and French) in creating your own culinary masterpiece.

SAN SEBASTIÁN FOOD Tour, Cooking Course
(**☎634 759 503; www.sansebastianfood.com**) The highly recommended San Sebastián Food runs an array of *pintxo* tasting tours (from €75) and cookery courses (from €135) in and around the city, as well as wine tastings (from €25) and day-long wine-tasting tours to La Rioja (€225).

SABORES DE SAN SEBASTIÁN Tour
(**Flavours of San Sebastián; ☎902 44 34 42; www.sansebastianreservas.com; tour €18; 11.30am Tue & Thu Jul & Aug**) The tourist office runs the Sabores de San Sebastián, a two-hour tour (in Spanish and English, French tours are available on request) of some of the city's *pintxo* haunts. Tours are also held with less frequency outside of high season – contact the tourist office for dates.

Sleeping

Accommodation standards in San Sebastián are generally good, but prices are high and availability in high season is very tight. In fact, with the city's increasing popularity, many of the better places are booked up for July and August months in advance. If you do turn up without a booking, head to the tourist office, which keeps a list of available rooms.

PENSIÓN BELLAS ARTES Boutique Hotel **€€**
(**☎943 47 49 05; www.pension-bellasartes.com; Calle de Urbieta 64; s €69-89, d €89-109;**) To call this magnificent place a mere *pensión* is to do it something of a disservice. Its rooms (some with glassed-in balconies), with their exposed stone walls and excellent bathrooms, should be the envy of many a more-expensive hotel.

PENSIÓN AIDA Boutique Hotel **€€**
(**☎943 32 78 00; www.pensionesconencanto.com; Calle de Iztueta 9; s €60, d €82-88, studios €130-150;** @) The owners of this excellent *pensión* read the rule book on what makes a good hotel and have complied exactly. The rooms are bright and bold, full of exposed stone and everything smells fresh and clean. For our money, we'd say this one is very hard to beat.

PENSIÓN EDORTA Boutique Hotel **€€**
(**☎943 42 37 73; www.pensionedorta.com; Calle del Puerto 15; r €80-90, r without bathroom €60-70;**) A fine *pensión* with rooms that are all tarted up in brash modern colours, but with a salute to the past in the stone walls and ceilings. It's very well cared for and well situated.

HOTEL MARIA CRISTINA Historic Hotel **€€€**
(**☎943 43 76 00; www.starwoodhotels.com; Paseo de la República Argentina 4; s/d from €245/322;** P @) In case you're won-

dering what sort of hotels Lonely Planet authors normally stay in, the absolutely impeccable Maria Cristina, with its huge and luxurious rooms, is not one of them. However, don't be downhearted, because instead of hanging out with us, you'll get to mix with royalty and Hollywood stars. Yes, we know, it's disappointing.

Eating

With fourteen Michelin stars (including three restaurants with the coveted three stars) for a population of 183,000, San Sebastián stands atop a pedestal as one of the culinary capitals of the planet. As if that alone wasn't enough, the city is overflowing with bars – almost all of which have bar tops weighed down under a mountain of tapas (known as *pintxos* here) that almost every Spaniard will (sometimes grudgingly) tell you are the best in country. These statistics alone make San Sebastián's CV look pretty impressive. But it's not just us who thinks this: a raft of the world's best chefs, including such luminaries as Catalan super chef Ferran Adrià, have said that San Sebastián is quite possibly the best place on the entire planet to eat.

BODEGÓN ALEJANDRO Seafood **€€**
(☎943 42 71 58; Calle de Fermín Calbetón 4; menú del día from €23, mains €15-18; closed Mon & dinner Sun) This highly regarded restaurant, with a pleasant casual style, has a menu from which you can select such succulent treats as tripe with veal cheeks,

Three Shining Stars

The Basque Country seems to be engaged in an eternal battle with Catalonia for the title of the best foodie region in Spain and, just like in Catalonia, the Basque Country is home to an impressive number of restaurants that have been awarded a coveted three Michelin stars, as well as many more with one or two stars. Of the three star places all are in and around San Sebastián.

Arzak (☎943 27 84 65; www.arzak.info; Avenida Alcalde Jose Elosegui 273; meals around €175; closed Sun-Mon & Nov & late Jun) Acclaimed chef Juan Mari Arzak takes some beating when it comes to *nueva cocina vasca* (Basque nouvelle cuisine) and his restaurant is, not surprisingly, considered one of the best places to eat in Spain. Arzak is now assisted by his daughter Elena and they never cease to innovate. Reservations, well in advance, are obligatory. The restaurant is about 1.5km east of San Sebastián.

Martín Berasategui Restaurant (☎943 36 64 71; www.martinberasategui.com; Calle Loidi 4, Lasarte-Oria; meals around €120; closed Sun dinner, Mon-Tue & Dec-mid-Jan) This superlative restaurant, about 9km southwest of San Sebastián, is considered by foodies to be one of the best restaurants in the world. The chef, Martín Berasategui, doesn't approach cooking in the same way as the rest of us. He approaches it as a science and the results are tastes you never knew existed. Reserve well ahead.

Akelaŕe (☎943 31 12 09; www.akelarre.net; Paseo Padre Orcolaga 56; tasting menu €145; closed Sun dinner, Mon-Tue & Dec–mid-Jan) This is where chef Pedro Subijana creates cuisine that is a feast to all five senses (and possibly a few senses we haven't yet named!). As with most of the region's top *nueva cocina vasca* restaurants, the emphasis here is on using fresh, local produce and turning it into something totally unexpected. It's in the suburb of Igeldo just west of the city.

baby tomatoes stuffed with squid or just plain old baked lobster. Oh, what choices!

RESTAURANTE NI NEU Contemporary Basque **€€€**
(☎943 00 31 62; www.restaurantenineu.com; Avenida de Zurriola 1; menus €18-38) The former Michelin-starred Kursaal has been rebranded as the Restaurante Ni Neu and, although the old chef and his star have gone, the food quality remains much the same with plenty of light, fluffy and utterly modern dishes that leave you hoping never to eat boring old fashioned meat and two veg again!

RESTAURANTE ALBERTO Seafood **€**
(☎943 42 88 84; Calle de 31 de Agosto 19; menus €15; closed Tue) A charming old seafood restaurant with a fishmonger-style window display of the day's catch. It's small and friendly and the pocket-sized dining room feels like it was once someone's living room. The food is earthy (well, ok salty) and good and the service swift.

Pintxo Bars in San Sebastián

No other city in Spain has made such a culture out of the creation, and consumption of *pintxos* and for many people the overriding memory of their stay in San Sebastián will be that of late nights in the *pintxo* bars.

The following *pintxo* bars all charge between €2.50 to €3.50 for one *pintxo*.

LA CUCHARA DE SAN TELMO Contemporary Basque
(Calle de 31 de Agosto 28) This unfussy, hidden-away (and hard to find) bar offers miniature *nueva cocina vasca* from a supremely creative kitchen. Unlike many San Sebastián bars this one doesn't have any *pintxos* laid out on the bar top; instead you must order from the blackboard menu behind the counter. Don't miss delights such as *carrílera de ternera al vino tinto* (calf cheeks in red wine), with meat so tender it starts to dissolve almost before it's past your lips.

Left: Playa de la Concha, San Sebastián (p155); **Below:** Market produce, San Sebastián

LEFT: WALTER BIBIKOW/GETTY IMAGES ©; BELOW: DALLAS STRIBLEY/GETTY IMAGES ©

BAR BORDA BERRI Pintxos

(Calle Fermín Cabetón 12) You won't find any *pintxos* sprawled across the bar counter at this outstanding little bar, which many locals swear blind is now the best in the city. Instead you must order them freshly made from the blackboard menu behind the bar. The bar staff are happy to offer advice on the day's best choice, but otherwise the house specials are pig's ears and delicious calf cheeks.

BERGARA BAR Pintxos

(General Artetxe 8) The neighbourhood of Gros is a growing powerhouse in the battle of the *pintxos* and many locals now prefer to take their nibbles here and leave the old town to the tourists. The Bergara Bar, which sits on the edge of a busy square, is one of the most highly regarded *pintxo* bars in Gros and has a mouth watering array of delights piled onto the bar counter as well as others chalked up onto the board. There are several other really good bars in the vicinity.

ASTELENA Basque

(Calle de Iñigo 1) The *pintxos* draped across the counter in this bar, tucked into the corner of Plaza de la Constitución, stand out as some of the best in the city. Many of them are a fusion of Basque and Asian inspirations, but the best of all are perhaps the foie gras-based treats.

BAR GOIZ-ARGI Basque

(Calle de Fermín Calbetón 4) *Gambas a la plancha* (prawns cooked on a hotplate) are the house speciality. Sounds simple, we know, but never have we tasted prawns cooked quite as perfectly as this.

Drinking & Entertainment

MUSEO DEL WHISKY Bar

(Alameda Boulevard 5) Appropriately named, this Irish/Scottish-style bar is

If You Like… Seaside Villages

If you like seaside villages we think you'll like these:

1 **SANTILLANA DEL MAR** This honey coloured stone village, a little way inland, is so postcard pretty it hardly seems real.

2 **LASTRES** Precarious cliffside fishing village with some 16th-century churches thrown in, east of Gijón.

3 **COMILLAS** Cobbled streets, a golden beach and a Gaudí-designed building, west of Santillana del Mar.

4 **PONTEDEUME** Medieval Galician hillside town overlooking the Eume estuary northeast of A Coruña.

5 **COMBARRO** Postcard-perfect village set around a bay close to Pontevedra.

6 **BAIONA** Medium-sized town with a village feel and spectacular seaside fortress in Galicia's far southwest.

7 **MUXÍA** A quaint village in Galicia's extreme west.

full of bottles of Scotland's finest (3000 bottles to be exact) as well as a museum's worth of whisky related knick-knacks – old bottles, tacky mugs and glasses and a nice, dusty, museum-like atmosphere.

ALTXERRI JAZZ BAR Live Music
(www.altxerri.com; Blvd Reina Regente 2) This jazz and blues temple has regular live gigs by local and international stars. Jamming sessions take over on nights with no gig and there's an in-house art gallery.

Information

Oficina de Turismo (**☎943 48 11 66; www.sansebastianturismo.com; Alameda del Boulevard 8; ⏰9.30am-1.30pm & 3.30-7pm Mon-Thu, 10am-7pm Fri & Sat, 10am-2pm Sun**) This friendly office offers comprehensive information on the city and the Basque Country in general.

Getting There & Away

Air

The city's **airport** (**☎902 404704; www.aena.es**) is 22km out of town, near Hondarribia. There are regular flights to Madrid and Barcelona and occasional charters to other major European cities. Biarritz, just over the border in France, is served by Ryanair and EasyJet, among various other budget airlines, and is generally much cheaper to fly into.

Bus

The main bus station is a 20-minute walk south of the Parte Vieja, between Plaza de Pío XII and the river. Local bus 28 and 26 connects the bus station with Alameda del Boulevard (€1.40, 10 minutes).

There are daily bus services to the following:

DESTINATION	FARE (€)	DURATION (HR)
Biarritz (France)	6.60	1¼
Bilbao	10.10	1
Bilbao airport	15.70	1¼
Madrid	from 33.60	5-6
Pamplona	7.29	1

Train

The main **Renfe train station** (**Paseo de Francia**) is just across Río Urumea, on a line linking Paris to Madrid. There are several services daily to Madrid (from €54.20, five hours) and two to Barcelona (from €63.30, six hours).

LA RIOJA

Get out the *copas* (glasses) for La Rioja and some of the best red wines produced in the country. Wine goes well with the region's ochre earth and vast blue skies, which seem far more Mediterranean than the Basque greens further north. In fact, it's hard not to feel as if you're in a different country altogether.

Logroño

POP 153,000

Logroño doesn't feel the need to be loud and brash. Instead it's a stately town with a heart of tree-studded squares, narrow streets and hidden corners. There are few monuments here, but there is a monumentally good selection of *pintxos* (tapas) bars. In fact, Logroño is quickly gaining a culinary reputation to rival anywhere in Spain.

Sights

CATEDRAL DE SANTA MARÍA DE LA REDONDA Cathedral

(Calle de Portales; 8am-1pm & 6-8.45pm Mon-Sat, 9am-2pm & 6.30-8.45pm Sun) The Catedral de Santa María de la Redonda started life as a Gothic church before maturing into a full-blown cathedral in the 16th century. Inside you'll find it a little dark and overpowering. Outside it seems lighter and friendlier, thanks, no doubt, to the huge square in which it proudly sits.

Sleeping

HOTEL MARQUÉS DE VALLEJO Design Hotel **€€**

(941 24 83 33; www.hotelmarquesdevallejo.com; Calle del Marqués de Vallejo 8; s/d €76/97; P) From the driftwood art and photographic flashlights in the communal spaces to the lollipops and raunchy red pouffes in the rooms, a huge amount of thought and effort has gone into the design of this stylish, modern and very well-priced hotel.

Eating

Logroño is a *pintxo* lover's delight and at only around €2 to €4 a pop, sampling all the different flavours isn't going to break the bank either. Most of the action takes place on Calle Laurel and Calle de

Bar Soriano (p164), Logroño

ANGUS OBORN/GETTY IMAGES ©

San Juan, where, among the dozens of possible tapas bars, you will find these standouts:

BAR SORIANO Tapas €

(Travesía de Laurel 2) The smell of frying food will suck you into this bar, which has been serving up the same delicious mushroom tapas, topped with a shrimp, for more than 30 years.

LA TABERNA DE BACO Tapas €

(Calle de San Agustín 10) This place has a cracking list of around 40 different *pintxos*, including *bombitas* (potatoes stuffed with mushrooms) and *rabas de pollo* (fried chicken slices marinated in spices and lemon juice).

Getting There & Away

Buses bounce off to the following:

DESTINATION	FARE (€)	DURATION (HR)
Bilbao	12.80	2¾
Burgos	7.43	2¼
Pamplona	8.38	1-1¾

By train, Logroño is regularly connected to the following:

DESTINATION	FARE (€)	DURATION (HR)
Bilbao	21.90	2½
Burgos	14.90-35	1¾
Madrid	58.30	3¼
Zaragoza	14.90-36	2½

The New Guggenheim(s)

'If Bilbao has one, we want one too', scream the villages of rural La Rioja. Impressed by the effect El Goog had on Bilbao's international standing and apparently unconcerned by the size and wealth difference between the big industrial city and their small farming communities, two villages have got themselves a Guggenheim lookalike.

When the owner of the Bodegas Marqués de Riscal, in the village of **Elciego**, decided he wanted to create something special, he certainly didn't hold back. The result is the spectacular Frank Gehry–designed **Hotel Marqués de Riscal** (945 18 08 80; www.starwoodhotels.com/luxury; r from €304; P ❄ wifi). Costing around €85 million to construct and now managed by the Starwood chain, the building is a flamboyant wave of multicoloured titanium sheets that stands in utter contrast to the creaky old village behind it. If you want a closer look, you have three options. The easiest is to join one of the bodega's **wine tours** (945 18 08 88; www.marquesderiscal.com; tour €10) – it's necessary to book in advance. You won't get inside the building, but you will get to see its exterior from some distance. A much closer look can be obtained by reserving a table at one of the two superb in-house restaurants; the Michelin approved **Restaurante Marqués de Riscal** (945 18 08 80; menú from €70; closed Sun & Jan) or the **Bistró 1860** (945 18 08 80; menú €55). For the most intimate look at the building, you'll need to reserve a room for the night, though be prepared to part with some serious cash!

But what one Riojan bodega can do, another can do better and just a couple of kilometres to the north of Laguardia is the **Bodegas Ysios** (www.ysios.com; Camino de la Hoya, Laguarida). Designed by Santiago Calatrava as a 'temple dedicated to wine', it's wave-like roof made of aluminium and cedar wood matches the flow of the rocky mountains behind it. Daily **tours** (945 60 06 40; per person €6) of the bodega are by appointment only.

Briones

POP 900 / ELEV 501M

One man's dream has put the small, obscenely quaint village of Briones firmly on the Spanish wine and tourism map. The sunset-gold village crawls gently up a hillside and offers commanding views over the surrounding vine-carpeted plains. It's on these plains where you will find the fantastic **Dinastía Vivanco** (Museo de la Cultura del Vino; www.dinastiavivanco.com; adult/child €7.50/free; ⏲10am-6pm Tue-Thu & Sun, 10am-8pm Fri & Sat). Over several floors and numerous rooms, you will learn all about the history and culture of wine and the various processes that go into its production.

Laguardia

POP 1490 / ELEV 557M

It's easy to spin back the wheels of time in the medieval fortress town of Laguardia, or the 'Guard of Navarra' as it was once appropriately known, sitting proudly on its rocky hilltop. The walled old quarter, which makes up most of the town, is virtually traffic-free and is a sheer joy to wander around.

Sleeping & Eating

POSADA MAYOR DE MIGUELOA Historic Hotel **€€**
(☎945 62 11 75; www.mayordemigueloa.com; Calle Mayor 20; s/d €96/121; ❄ 📶) For the ultimate in gracious La Rioja living, this old mansion-hotel is irresistible. The in-house **restaurant**, which is open to non-guests, is superb and offers original twists on local cuisine with meals starting at about €20.

Tourist Office (☎945 60 08 45; www.laguardia-alava.com; Calle Mayor 52; ⏲10am-2pm & 4-7pm Mon-Fri, 10am-2pm & 5-7pm Sat, 10.45am-2pm Sun) Has a list of bodegas that can be visited in the local area.

If You Like... Wine

If you like the Dinastía wine museum in Briones, we think you'll also like these other wine attractions:

1 **HARO**
The unattractive capital of La Rioja wine country has a Museo del Vino and winery visits.

2 **MUSEO DEL VINO, OLITE**
Outstanding wine museum in one of Navarra's most charming small towns.

3 **MUSEO DE LA SIDRA, NAVA**
Fine museum in the capital of Asturian cider production.

4 **CAMBADOS**
Pretty seaside capital of Galicia's Albariño wine country with a fine wine festival at the end of July.

5 **RIBADAVIA**
The headquarters of the Ribeiro wine.

CAMINO DE SANTIAGO

Pamplona

POP 195,800 / ELEV 456M

Senses are heightened in Pamplona (Basque: Iruña), capital of the fiercely independent Kingdom of Navarra, alert constantly to the fearful sound of thundering bulls clattering like tanks down cobbled streets and causing mayhem and bloodshed all the way.

Of course, visit outside the eight days in July when the legendary festival of Sanfermines (the running of the bulls) takes over the minds and souls of a million people and the closest you'll come to a bull is in a photograph.

For those who do venture here outside fiesta time, you will find Pamplona a fascinating place. And for those of you who come during fiesta week? Welcome to one of the biggest and most famous festivals in the world. It'll be a week that you'll never forget – as long as you stay sober enough to remember it.

Sights

CATEDRAL Cathedral
(Calle Dormitalería; guided tour per adult/child €5/free; 10am-6pm Mon-Sat) Pamplona's main cathedral stands on a rise just inside the city ramparts amid a dark thicket of narrow streets. The cathedral is a late-medieval Gothic gem spoiled only by its rather dull neoclassical facade, an 18th-century appendage.The real joy is the Gothic **cloister**, where there is marvellous delicacy in the stonework.

MUSEO DE NAVARRA Museum
(www.cfnavarra.es/cultura/museo; Calle Cuesta de Santo Domingo 47; adult €2, free Sat afternoon & Sun; 9.30am-2pm & 5-7pm Tue-Sat, 11am-2pm Sun) Housed in a former medieval hospital, this superb museum has an eclectic collection of archaeological finds (including a number of fantastic Roman mosaics unearthed mainly in southern Navarra), as well as a selection of artworks including Goya's *Marqués de San Adrián*.

MUSEO DEL ENCIERRO Museum
(www.museoencierro.com; Calle Mercaderes 17; adult/child €8/free; 10am-2pm & 4-8pm Mon-Fri, 11am-8pm Sat-Sun) You can live out a virtual-reality version of the *encierros* (running of the bulls through town) at this new museum. A visit guides you through the history and culture of the *encierro* and San Fermín in general, after which you can don special glasses and step – or rather run – straight into the middle of a hectic bullrun in a 3D film.

Sleeping

During Sanfermines, hotels raise their rates mercilessly – all quadruple their normal rack rates and many increase them fivefold – and it can be near impossible to get a room without reserving between six months and a year in advance.

PALACIO GUENDULAIN Historic Hotel **€€€**
(948 22 55 22; www.palacioguendulain.com; Calle Zapatería 53; d incl breakfast from €133.92; P ❄ 📶) To call this stunning hotel, inside the converted former home of the viceroy of New Granada, sumptuous is an understatement. On arrival, you're greeted by a museum-piece 17th-century carriage decked in gold, and a collection of classic cars lie scattered about the courtyard under the watchful eye of the viceroy's private chapel. The rooms contain *Princess and the Pea*-soft beds, enormous showers and regal armchairs.

Laguardia (p165)
WALTER BIBIKOW/GETTY IMAGES ©

The Running of the Bulls

Liberated, obsessive or plain mad is how you might describe aficionados (and there are many) who regularly take part in Pamplona's **Sanfermines** (Fiesta de San Fermín), a nonstop cacophony of music, dance, fireworks and processions – and the small matter of running alongside a handful of agitated, horn-tossing *toros* (bulls) – that takes place from 6 to 14 July each year.

El encierro, the running of the bulls from their corrals to the bullring for the afternoon bullfight, takes place in Pamplona every morning during Sanfermines. Six bulls are let loose from the Coralillos de Santo Domingo to charge across the square of the same name. They continue up the street, veering onto Calle de los Mercaderes from Plaza Consistorial, then sweep right onto Calle de la Estafeta for the final charge to the ring. Devotees, known as *mozos* (the brave or foolish, depending on your point of view), race madly with the bulls, aiming to keep close – but not too close. The total course is some 825m long and lasts little more than three minutes.

Those who prefer to be spectators rather than action men (and we use the word 'men' on purpose here as, technically, women are forbidden from running, although an increasing number are doing it anyway) bag their spot along the route early. Some people rent a space on one of the house balconies overlooking the course. Whichever the vantage point, it's all over in a few blurred seconds.

Each evening a traditional bullfight is held. Sanfermines winds up at midnight on 14 July with a candlelit procession, known as the **Pobre de Mí** (Poor Me), which starts from Plaza Consistorial.

Concern has grown about the high numbers of people taking part in recent *encierros*. Since records began in 1924, 16 people have died during Pamplona's bullrun. Many of those who run are full of bravado (and/or drink) and have little idea of what they're doing. For dedicated *encierro* news, check out www.sanfermin.com.

Animal rights groups oppose bullrunning as a cruel tradition, and the participating bulls will almost certainly all be killed in the afternoon bullfight. The PETA-organised anti-bullfighting demonstration, the **Running of the Nudes**, takes place two days before the first bullrun.

HOTEL PUERTA DEL CAMINO Boutique Hotel **€€**
(948 22 66 88; www.hotelpuertadelcamino.com; Calle Dos de Mayo 4; s/d from €89/95; P ❄) A very stylish hotel inside a converted convent (clearly the nuns appreciated the finer things in life!) beside the northern gates to the old city. The functional rooms have clean, modern lines and it's positioned in one of the prettier, and quieter, parts of town.

Eating & Drinking

BASERRI Basque **€**
(948 22 20 21; Calle de San Nicolás 32; menú del día €14) This place has won enough *pintxo* awards that we could fill this entire book listing them. In fact, it's staggering to know that so many food awards actually exist! As you'd expect from such a certificate-studded bar, the *pintxos* and full meals are superb.

CASA OTAÑO Basque **€€**
(☎948 22 50 95; Calle de San Nicolás 5; mains €15-18) A little pricier than many on this street but worth the extra. Its formal atmosphere is eased by the dazzling array of pink and red flowers spilling off the balcony. Great dishes range from the locally caught trout to heavenly duck dishes. The €17.50 *menú del día* is good value.

CAFÉ IRUÑA Historic Cafe
(Plaza del Castillo 44) Opened on the eve of Sanfermines in 1888, Café Iruña's dominant position, powerful sense of history and frilly belle-époque decor make this by far the most famous and popular watering hole in the city. As well as caffeine and alcohol, it also has a good range of *pintxos* and light meals.

Information

Tourist Office (☎848 42 04 20; www.turismo.navarra.es; Avda Roncesvalles 4; ⏰Mon-Fri 9am-7pm, Sat 10am-2pm & 4-7pm, Sun 10am-2pm) This extremely well-organised office, just opposite the statue of the bulls in the new town, has plenty of information about the city and Navarra. There are a couple of summer-only tourist info booths scattered throughout the city.

Getting There & Away

Air

Pamplona's airport (☎948 16 87 00), about 7km south of the city, has regular flights to Madrid and Barcelona. Bus 16 (€1.20) travels between the city (from the bus station and Calle de las Navas de Tolosa) and to the suburb of Noáia, from where it's about a 200m walk to the airport. A taxi costs about €15.

Bus

From the main bus station (Calle Conde Oliveto 8), buses leave for most towns throughout Navarra, although service is restricted on Sunday.

Regular bus services travel to:

DESTINATION	FARE (€)	DURATION (HR)
Bilbao	14.15	2
Logroño	8.38	1¾
San Sebastián	7.29	1

Train

Pamplona's train station is linked to the city centre by bus 9 from Paseo de Sarasate every 15 minutes. Tickets are also sold at the Renfe agency (Calle de Estella 8; ⏰9am-1.30pm & 4.30-7.30pm Mon-Fri, 9am-1pm Sat).

Trains run to/from the following:

DESTINATION	FARE (€)	DURATION (HR)	FREQUENCY
Madrid	57.90	3	4 daily
San Sebastián	from 21.20	2	2 daily

Burgos

POP 179,250 / ELEV 861M

The extraordinary Gothic cathedral of Burgos is one of Spain's glittering jewels of religious architecture and it looms large over the city and skyline. On the surface, conservative Burgos seems to embody all the stereotypes of a north-central Spanish town, with sombre grey-stone architecture, the fortifying cuisine of the high *meseta* (plateau) and a climate of extremes. But this is a city that rewards deeper exploration: below the surface lie good restaurants and, when the sun's shining, pretty streetscapes that extend far beyond the landmark cathedral.

Sights

CATEDRAL Cathedral
(Plaza del Rey Fernando; adult/child €5/2.50; ⏰9.30am-6.30pm) The Unesco World Heritage–listed cathedral is a masterpiece that's probably worth the trip to Burgos on its own. It had humble origins as a modest Romanesque church, but work began on a grander scale in 1221. Remarkably, within 40 years most of the French Gothic structure that you see today had been completed.

The cathedral's twin towers, which went up later in the 15th century, each represent 84m of richly decorated Gothic fantasy and they're surrounded by a sea of similarly intricate spires.

The main altar is a typically overwhelming piece of gold-encrusted extravagance, while directly beneath the star-vaulted central dome lies the **tomb of El Cid**. Another highlight is the **Escalera Dorada** (Gilded Stairway; 1520) on the cathedral's northwestern flank, the handiwork of Diego de Siloé. The **Capilla del Condestable**, on the eastern end of the ambulatory behind the main altar, is a remarkable late-15th-century production.

Sleeping

HOTEL NORTE Y LONDRES Historic Hotel **€€**

(☎947 26 41 25; www.hotelnorteylondres.com; Plaza de Alonso Martínez 10; s/d €66/100; P @ 📶) Set in a former 16th-century palace and with understated period charm, this fine hotel promises spacious rooms with antique furnishings, polished wooden floors and pretty balconies; those on the 4th floor are more modern.

HOTEL LA PUEBLA Boutique Hotel **€€**

(☎947 20 00 11; www.hotellapuebla.com; Calle de la Puebla 20; s/d €50/65; ❄ @ 📶) This boutique hotel adds a touch of style to the Burgos hotel scene. The rooms aren't huge and most don't have views, but they're softly lit, beautifully designed and supremely comfortable. They come in a range of styles, from colourful to minimalist black and white.

HOTEL MESON DEL CID Historic Hotel **€€**

(☎947 20 87 15; www.mesondelcid.es; Plaza de Santa María 8; s/d €70/100; P ⊖ ❄ 📶) Facing the cathedral, this hotel occupies a centuries-old building. Rooms have Regency-style burgundy-and-cream fabrics, aptly combined with dark-wood furnishings and terracotta tiles.

Eating

CERVECERÍA MORITO Tapas **€**

(Calle de la Sombrerería 27; tapas €3, raciones €5-7) Cervecería Morito is the undisputed king of Burgos tapas bars and it's always crowded, deservedly so. A typical order is *alpargata* (lashings of cured ham with bread, tomato and olive oil) or the *pincho de morcilla* (small tapa of local blood sausage). The presentation is surprising nouvelle, especially the visual feast of salads.

Basque street festival

SIMON GREENWOOD/GETTY IMAGES ©

LA FABULA Modern Castilian **€€**
(947 26 30 92; Calle de la Merced; menú del día €15, meals €25-30) With local celebrity chef Isabel Alvarez at the helm, fabulous La Fabula offers innovative slimmed-down dishes in a bright, modern dining room filled with classical music. The menu includes tasty rice dishes and creative flights of fancy such as pyramids of wild mushroom with a pinch of salty nougat.

LA FAVORITA Tapas **€€**
(www.lafavorita-taberna.com; Calle de Avellanos 8; tapas from €2; 10am-midnight Mon-Fri, noon-1.30am Sat & Sun) Away from the main Burgos tapas hub and close to the cathedral, La Favorita has a barn-like interior of exposed brick and wooden beams, and attracts slicked-back-hair businessmen at midday. The emphasis is on local cured meats and cheeses (try the cheese platter for €11.90), and wine by the glass starts at €1.50.

Only in Spain...

Spain's weird and wonderful fiestas have always left the rest of the world shaking their heads, from the Running of the Bulls in Pamplona to the tomato-throwing extravaganza of La Tomatina in Buñol. But surely there's no festival quite as strange as the baby-jumping festival of **Castrillo de Murcia**, a small village just south of the A231, 25km west of Burgos.

Every year since 1620, this tiny village of around 250 inhabitants has marked the feast of Corpus Cristi by lining up the babies of the village on a mattress, while grown men dressed as 'El Colacho', a figure representing the devil, leap over up to six prostrate and, it must be said, somewhat bewildered babies at a time. Like all Spanish rites, it does have a purpose: the ritual is thought to ward off the devil. But why jumping over babies? We have no idea and the villagers aren't telling. They do, however, assure us that no baby has been injured in the recorded history of the fiesta.

Drinking

CAFÉ ESPAÑA Cafe
(Calle de Lain Calvo 12; 10am-11pm) With its old-world elegance, Café España has been a bastion of the Burgos cafe scene for more than 80 years. A pianist plays jazz here most weekends.

CAFÉ DE LAS ARTES Bar, Cafe
(Calle de Lain Calvo 31; 10am-midnight) An artsy vibe and occasional live music.

Information

Municipal Tourist Office (947 28 88 74; www.aytoburgos.es; Plaza de Santa María; 10am-8pm) Pick up its 24-hour, 48-hour and 72-hour guides to Burgos; they can also be downloaded as PDFs online.

Regional Tourist Office (www.turismocastillayleon.com; Plaza de Alonso Martínez 7; 9am-8pm Sun-Thu, 9am-9pm Fri & Sat)

Getting There & Away

The **bus station** (Calle de Miranda 4) is south of the river, in the newer part of town. The new train station is a considerable hike northeast of the town centre - bus 2 (€0.95) connects the train station with Plaza de España.

BUS Regular buses run to Madrid (€17.07, three hours, up to 20 daily), Bilbao (€12.16, two hours, eight daily) and León (€14.50, two hours, three daily).

TRAIN Destinations include Madrid (from €31.45, 2½ to 4½ hours, seven daily), Bilbao (from €19.30, three hours, four daily), León (from €20.80, two hours) and Salamanca (from €19.85, 2½ hours, three daily).

Renfe (947 20 91 31; Calle de la Moneda 21; 9.30am-1.30pm & 4.30-7.30pm Mon-Fri), the national rail network, has a convenient sales office in the centre of town.

León

POP 132,740 / ELEV 527M

León is a wonderful city, combining stunning historical architecture with an irresistible energy. Its standout attraction is the cathedral, one of the most beautiful in all of Spain. By day you'll encounter a city with its roots firmly planted in the soil of northern Castile, with its grand monuments, loyal Catholic heritage and role as an important staging post along the Camino de Santiago.

By night León is taken over by its large student population, who provide it with a deep-into-the-night soundtrack of revelry that floods the narrow streets and plazas of the picturesque old quarter, the Barrio Húmedo.

If You Like... Cathedrals

If you like the cathedrals in León and Burgos, the cathedrals in the following towns should also appeal:

1 **PALENCIA**
One of the largest Castilian cathedrals, with a treasure trove of religious art and ornate chapels. One of the most stunning chapels is the Capilla El Sagrario.

2 **PLASENCIA**
Two cathedrals in one – Gothic and plateresque from the 16th century, and Romanesque from the 13th century. The Capilla de San Pablo contains the dramatic 1569 Caravaggio painting of John the Baptist.

3 **ASTORGA**
Plateresque on the outside and mainly Gothic on the inside with a stunning altarpiece by Gaspar Becerra.

Sights

CATEDRAL Cathedral

(www.catedraldeleon.org; adult/concession/child €5/4/free; 8.30am-1.30pm & 4-8pm Mon-Sat, 8.30am-2.30pm & 5-8pm Sun) León's 13th-century cathedral, with its soaring towers, flying buttresses and truly breathtaking interior, is the city's spiritual heart. Whether spotlit by night or bathed in the glorious northern sunshine, the cathedral, arguably Spain's premier Gothic masterpiece, exudes a glorious, almost luminous quality.

The extraordinary **facade** has a radiant rose window, three richly sculpted doorways and two muscular towers. After going through the main entrance, lorded over by the scene of the Last Supper, an extraordinary gallery of **vidrieras** (stained-glass windows) awaits. French in inspiration and mostly executed from the 13th to the 16th centuries, the windows evoke an atmosphere unlike that of any other cathedral in Spain; the kaleidoscope of coloured light is offset by the otherwise gloomy interior.

Other treasures include a silver urn on the altar, by Enrique de Arfe, containing the remains of San Froilán, León's patron saint. Also note the magnificent choir stalls and the recently restored frescoes in the **Capilla de Santa Teresa**. The peaceful, light-filled **claustro** (cloister; admission €1), with its 15th-century frescoes, is a perfect complement to the main sanctuary and an essential part of the cathedral experience.

REAL BASÍLICA DE SAN ISIDORO Church

Even older than León's cathedral, the Real Basílica de San Isidoro provides a stunning Romanesque counterpoint to the former's Gothic strains, with extraordinary frescoes the main highlight among many.

The main **basilica** is a hotchpotch of styles, but the two main portals on the southern facade are pure Romanesque. Of particular note is the **Puerta del Perdón** (on the right, and under restoration when we visited), which has been attributed to Maestro Mateo, the

León

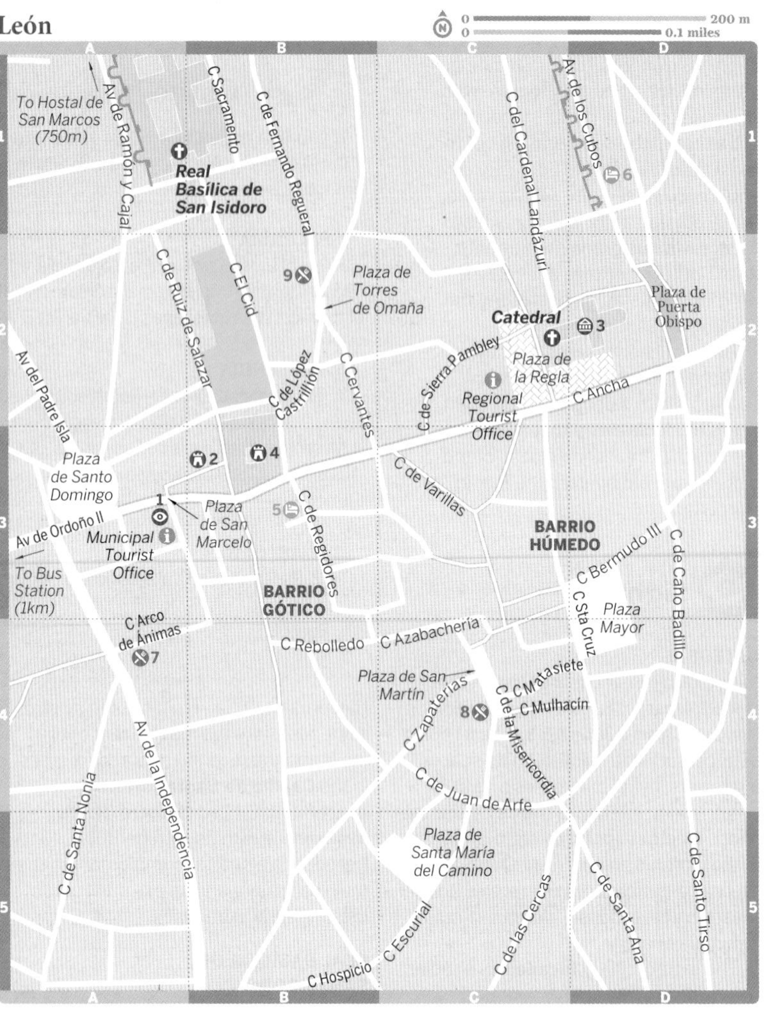

León

Top Sights

Catedral C2
Real Basílica de San Isidoro A1

Sights

1 Ayuntamiento A3
2 Casa de Botines B3
3 Claustro D2
4 Palacio de los Guzmanes B3

Sleeping

5 La Posada Regia B3
6 Q!H D1

Eating

7 Alfonso Valderas A4
8 El Llar C4
9 El Picoteo de la Jouja B2

Detour: Picos de Europa

These jagged, deeply fissured mountains straddling southeast Asturias, southwest Cantabria and northern Castilla y León amount to some of the finest walking country, and some of the most spectacular country of any kind, in Spain.

A star attraction of the Picos' central massif is the gorge that divides it from the western Macizo El Cornión. The popular Garganta del Cares (Cares Gorge) trail can be busy in summer, but the walk is always an exciting experience. This part of the Picos also has plenty of less heavily tramped paths and climbing challenges. Arenas de Cabrales is a popular base with a lot of accommodation, but Poncebos, Sotres, Bulnes and Caín also have sleeping options.

genius of the cathedral at Santiago de Compostela. The attached **Panteón Real** houses the remaining sarcophagi, which rest with quiet dignity beneath a canopy of some of the finest **Romanesque frescoes** in Spain.

BARRIO GÓTICO Historic Quarter

On the fringes of León's Old Town, Plaza de San Marcelo is home to the **ayuntamiento** (town hall), which occupies a charmingly compact Renaissance-era palace. The Renaissance theme continues in the form of the splendid **Palacio de los Guzmanes** (1560), where the facade and patio stand out; the latter is accessible only on a free guided tour that leaves most hours. Next door is Antoni Gaudí's contribution to León's skyline, the castle-like, neo-Gothic **Casa de Botines** (1893).

Sleeping

LA POSADA REGIA Historic Hotel **€€**

(☎987 21 31 73; www.regialeon.com; Calle de Regidores 9-11; s/d €65/120; ❄ 📶) You won't find many places better than this in northern Spain. The secret is a 14th-century building, magnificently restored (wooden beams, exposed brick and understated antique furniture), with individually styled rooms, character that overflows into the public areas, and supremely comfortable beds and bathrooms.

HOSTAL DE SAN MARCOS Historic Hotel **€€€**

(☎987 23 73 00; www.parador.es; Plaza de San Marcos 7; d from €198; ❄ @ 📶) León's sumptuous *parador* is one of the finest hotels in Spain. With palatial rooms fit for royalty and filled with old-world luxury and decor, this is one of the Parador chain's flagship properties, and as you'd expect, the service and attention to detail is faultless.

Q!H Hotel **€€**

(☎987 87 55 80; www.qhhoteles.com; Avenida de los Cubos 6; s/d €45/60; ❄ 📶 🏊) This boutique spa hotel is located within confessional distance of the cathedral. The historic 19th-century building provided a suitable aesthetic canvas for the sharp modern design of the interior. Rooms have cathedral views, a bold accented colour scheme and steely grey bathrooms.

Eating

EL LLAR Tapas **€€**

(Plaza de San Martín 9; meals €25-30; 🖉) This old León *taberna* is a great place to *tapear* (eat tapas) with its innovative selection of *raciones* that includes baked potatoes filled with wild mushrooms and prawns *au gratin*.

EL PICOTEO DE LA JOUJA Tapas **€**

(Plaza de Torres de Omaña) This intimate little bar has earned a loyal following for its concentration on traditional local tapas

(try the six tapas for €13.50) and local wines, including some from the nearby Bierzo region.

ALFONSO VALDERAS Seafood **€€**
(987 20 05 05; Calle Arco de Ánimas 1; mains €13.65-18.90; lunch & dinner Mon-Sat, lunch Sun) The city's most famous restaurant for *bacalao* (salt cod) prepared around 20 different ways. If this is your first encounter with this versatile fish, order it *al pil-pil* (with a mild chilli sauce).

Information

Municipal Tourist Office (987 87 83 27; Plaza de San Marcelo; 9.30am-2pm & 5-7.30pm)

Regional Tourist Office (987 23 70 82; www.turismocastillayleon.com; Calle el Cid 2; 9am-8pm)

Getting There & Away

The train and bus stations lie on the western bank of Río Bernesga, off the western end of Avenida de Ordoño II.

BUS From the bus station (Paseo del Ingeniero Sáez de Miera) there are buses to Madrid (€22.60, 3½ hours, seven daily), Astorga (€3.40, one hour, 12 daily), Burgos (€14.50, two hours, three daily), Ponferrada (€8.20, two hours, 14 daily) and Valladolid (€9.23, two hours, six daily).

CAR & MOTORCYCLE Parking bays (€9 to €13 for 12 hours) are found in the streets surrounding Plaza de Santo Domingo.

TRAIN Regular daily trains travel to Valladolid (from €12.65, two hours), Burgos (from €20.80, two hours), Oviedo (from €8.20, two hours), Madrid (from €34.75, 4¼ hours) and Barcelona (from €70.70, nine hours).

SANTIAGO DE COMPOSTELA

POP 79,000 / ELEV 260M

Locals say the arcaded, stone streets of Santiago de Compostela are at their most beautiful in the rain, when the old city glistens. Most would agree, however, that it's hard to catch the Galician capital

Left: Garganta del Cares, Picos de Europa (p173); **Below:** Arenas de Cabrales, Picos de Europa

LEFT: ROB COUSINS/GETTY IMAGES ©; BELOW: GONZALO AZUMENDI/GETTY IMAGES ©

in a bad pose. Whether you're wandering the medieval streets of the old city, nibbling on tapas in the taverns, or gazing down at the rooftops from atop the cathedral, Santiago seduces.

The faithful believe that Santiago Apóstol (St James the Apostle) preached in Galicia and, after his death in Palestine, was brought back by stone boat and buried here. The tomb was supposedly rediscovered in about 814 by a religious hermit following a guiding star (hence, it's thought the name 'Compostela' derives from the Latin *campus stellae*, field of the star). The Asturian king Alfonso II had a church erected above the holy remains, pilgrims began flocking to it and by the 11th century the pilgrimage was becoming a major European phenomenon, bringing a flood of funds into the city.

Today an average of 150,000 pilgrims and countless thousands of other visitors make the journey here each year.

Sights

MUSEO DA CATEDRAL Museum

(www.catedraldesantiago.es; Praza do Obradoiro; adult/student & pilgrim/child €5/3/free; 10am-2pm & 4-8pm, closed Sun afternoon) The Cathedral Museum, entered to the right of the cathedral's Obradoiro facade, spreads over four floors and includes the cathedral's large, 16th-century, Gothic/plateresque cloister. You'll see a sizeable section of Maestro Mateo's original carved stone choir (destroyed in 1603 but recently pieced back together), an impressive collection of religious art (including the *botafumeiros*, in the 2nd-floor library), the lavishly decorated 18th-century *sala capitular* (chapter house) and, off the cloister, the Panteón de Reyes, which contains tombs of kings of medieval León.

Santiago de Compostela

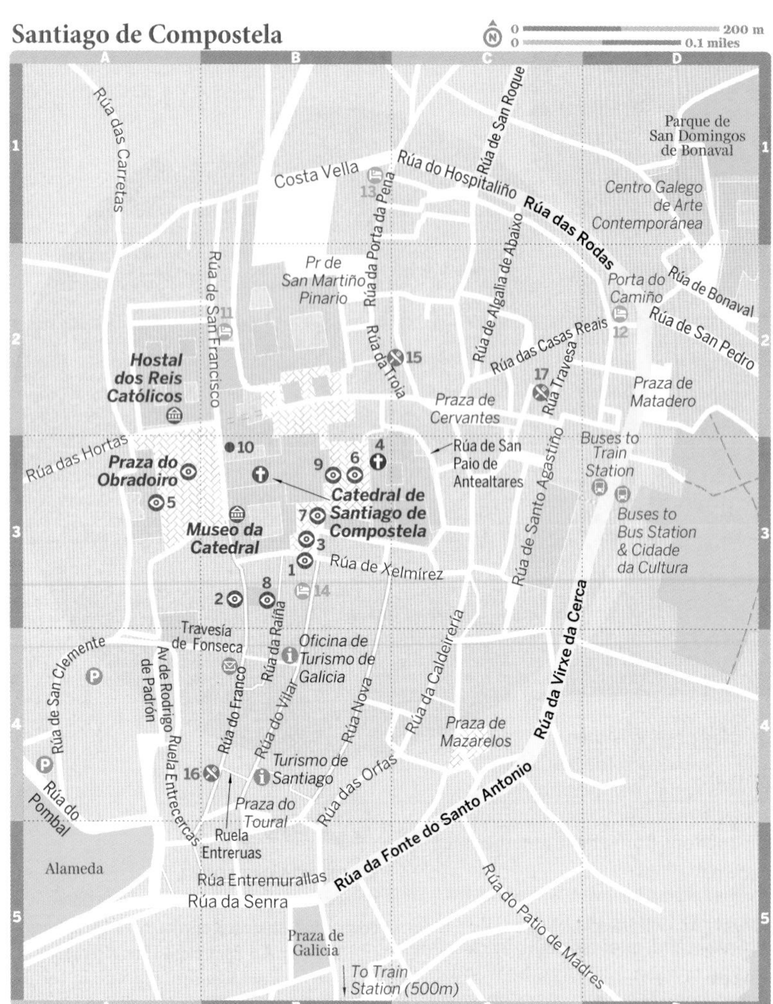

AROUND THE CATHEDRAL Square

The cathedral is surrounded by handsome plazas that invite you to wander through them. The grand **Praza do Obradoiro** (Workshop Plaza) earned its name from the stonemasons' workshops set up there while the cathedral was being built. At its northern end, the Renaissance **Hostal dos Reis Católicos** (admission €3; noon-2pm & 4-6pm Sun-Fri) was built in the early 16th century by order of the Catholic Monarchs, Isabel and Fernando, as a refuge for pilgrims and a symbol of the crown's power in this ecclesiastical city. Along the western side of Praza do Obradoiro is the elegant 18th-century **Pazo de Raxoi**, now the city hall.

South of the cathedral, stop in cafe-lined **Praza de Fonseca** to look into the **Colexio de Fonseca** (admission free; 11am-2pm & 5-8.30pm Tue-Sat, 11am-2pm Sun) with a beautiful Renaissance courtyard; it was the original seat of Santiago's university (founded in 1495).

Around the corner, **Praza das Praterías** (Silversmiths' Square) is marked by the

Santiago de Compostela

Top Sights

Catedral de Santiago de Compostela ... B3
Hostal dos Reis Católicos ... A2
Museo da Catedral ... B3
Praza do Obradoiro ... A3

Sights

1 Casa do Cabildo ... B3
2 Colexio de Fonseca ... B3
3 Fuente de los Caballos ... B3
4 Mosteiro de San Paio de Antealtares ... B3
5 Pazo de Raxoi ... A3
6 Praza da Quintana ... B3
7 Praza das Praterías ... B3
8 Praza de Fonseca ... B3
9 Puerta Santa ... B3

Activities, Courses & Tours

10 Cathedral Rooftop Tour ... B3

Sleeping

11 Casa-Hotel As Artes ... B2
12 Hotel Casas Reais ... D2
13 Hotel Costa Vella ... B1
14 Hotel Rúa Villar ... B3

Eating

15 Bierzo de Enxebre ... C2
16 Mesón Ó 42 ... B4
17 O Curro da Parra ... C2

Fuente de los Caballos fountain (1829), with the cathedral's south facade at the top of the steps. Curiously, the **Casa do Cabildo** (Praza das Praterías), on the lower side of the square, is no more than a 3m-deep facade, erected in 1758 to embellish the plaza.

Following the cathedral walls, you enter **Praza da Quintana**, lined by the long, stark wall of the **Mosteiro de San Paio de Antealtares** (Praza da Quintana), founded by Alfonso II for Benedictine monks to look after Santiago's relics.

CIDADE DA CULTURA DE GALICIA Cultural Centre

(City of Culture of Galicia; www.cidadedacultura.org; 8am-11pm, building interiors 10am-2pm & 4-8pm, museum closed Mon ; P) This vast prestige project is taking shape atop Monte Gaiás, a hill about 1.5km southeast of the Old Town, to the designs of American Peter Eisenman. The first sections, the Library and Archive of Galicia, opened in 2011 after 10 years of building, delays and administrative rethinks. The concept is full of symbolism – the overall shape resembles a giant stone wave sliced into sections and is intended to be vaguely similar to a conch shell (symbol of the Camino de Santiago), while the passageways between the buildings are meant to recall the streets trodden by pilgrims arriving in Santiago. The Museo de Galicia, opened in 2012, added a new venue for events and exhibitions including assorted concerts (the museum has no permanent collection). You can reach the City of Culture on bus 9 (hourly Monday to Friday until 10.35pm and Saturday until 1.35pm) or bus C11 (5.35pm and 8.05pm Saturday and four times on Sunday), northbound from a stop opposite the market on Rúa da Virxe da Cerca.

Tours

Turismo de Santiago (p179) offers a range of two-hour walking tours in English and/or Spanish that give a fascinating glimpse into the stories behind Santiago's old stone walls. From April to September, a general Old-Town tour in English (€10) starts from Praza das Praterías at 4pm Thursday to Saturday and noon on Sunday.

Sleeping

HOTEL COSTA VELLA Boutique Hotel **€€**

(981 56 95 30; www.costavella.com; Rúa da Porta da Pena 17; s €59, d €81-97;) The tranquil, thoughtfully designed rooms (some with glassed-in galleries), friendly welcome and lovely garden cafe make this a wonderful option.

WIN-INITIATIVE/GETTY IMAGES ©

Don't Miss Catedral de Santiago de Compostela

The grand heart of Santiago, the cathedral soars above the city centre in a splendid jumble of moss-covered spires and statues. Built piecemeal over several centuries, its beauty is a mix of Romanesque with baroque and Gothic flourishes.

The Obradoiro facade is also the cathedral's main entrance, but owing to restoration work inside, it is likely to be closed until at least 2014.

The artistically unparalleled **Pórtico de la Gloria** (Galician: Porta da Gloria), just inside the Obradoiro entrance, features 200 Romanesque sculptures by Maestro Mateo, who was placed in charge of the cathedral-building program in the late 12th century. The restoration work means, unfortunately, that you may well find the Pórtico partly shrouded in scaffolding.

At the western end of the cathedral's main nave, to the right of the elaborate, Churrigueresque **Altar Mayor** (Main Altar), a small staircase leads up to a 13th-century **statue of Santiago**, which the faithful queue up to kiss or embrace. From here you emerge on the left side, then descend some steps to contemplate the **Cripta Apostólica**, which we are assured is Santiago's tomb. Behind the Altar Mayor is the **Puerta Santa** (Holy Door), which opens onto Praza da Quintana and is cracked open only in holy years (next in 2021).

A special pilgrims' Mass is usually celebrated at noon daily, with other Masses usually at 9.30am or 10am daily, 1.15pm Sunday, 6pm Saturday and Sunday, and 7.30pm daily. Touristic visits are not allowed during these services.

For unforgettable bird's-eye views of the cathedral interior, and of the city from the cathedral roof, take the **cathedral rooftop tour** (981 55 29 85; www.catedraldesantiago.es; per person €10; 10am-2pm & 4-8pm), which starts in the Pazo de Xelmírez to the left of the cathedral's Obradoiro facade.

NEED TO KNOW

www.catedraldesantiago.es; Praza do Obradoiro; 7am-9pm

HOTEL CASAS REAIS Boutique Hotel €€
(981 55 57 09; www.casasreais.es; Rúa das Casas Reais 29; d incl breakfast €90;) The 11 bright, contemporary rooms here are originally and discreetly themed after different real or pop-culture monarchs. White linen, mirrors and galleries all help to maximise light and this is undoubtedly one of the most attractive of Santiago's recent wave of new hotels in old buildings.

CASA-HOTEL AS ARTES Boutique Hotel €€
(981 55 52 54; www.asartes.com; Travesía de Dos Puertas 2; r €95-105; @) On a quiet street close to the cathedral, As Artes' seven lovely stone-walled rooms exude a romantic rustic air.

HOTEL RÚA VILLAR Hotel €€
(981 51 98 58; www.hotelruavillar.com; Rúa do Vilar 8-10; s €85, d €105-140;) Rúa Villar is in an artfully restored 18th-century building whose upstairs focal point is a central sitting area capped with a splendid stained-glass skylight. Service is attentive and the 16 rooms, with soft beds, are cosy and inviting, if not spacious. Original work by first-rank modern Spanish artists adorns the walls, and the classy restaurant (mains €12 to €22, menus €16) specialises in daily fresh seafood.

Eating

O CURRO DA PARRA Contemporary Galician €€
(www.ocurrodaparra.com; Rúa do Curro da Parra 7; mains €14-20, tapas €5-8; closed Mon) With a neat little stone-walled dining room upstairs and a narrow tapas and wine bar below, this relative newcomer serves up a broad range of thoughtfully created, market-fresh fare. On weekday lunchtimes it serves a great-value €11 *menú mercado* (market menu).

BIERZO DE ENXEBRE Leonese €€
(www.bierzoenxebre.es; Rúa da Troia 10; raciones €8-14; closed Tue) The cuisine at this busy and atmospheric spot is that of El Bierzo, a rural area of northwest Castilla y León, meaning excellent grilled and cured meats, but also cheeses, pies and vegetables.

MESÓN Ó 42 Galician €€
(www.restauranteo42.com; Rúa do Franco 42; raciones €6-14, mains €16-19; closed Sun evening) With a solid list of favourite local *raciones* like *empanadas* (pies), shellfish, octopus and tortillas, as well as fish, meat and rice dishes, this popular place stands out from the crowd with well-prepared food and good service.

Information

Oficina de Turismo de Galicia (www.turgalicia.es; Rúa do Vilar 30-32; 10am-8pm Mon-Fri, 11am-2pm & 5-7pm Sat, 11am-2pm Sun) The scoop on all things Galicia as well as on the Camino de Santiago.

Turismo de Santiago (981 55 51 29; www.santiagoturismo.com; Rúa do Vilar 63; 9am-9pm, to 7pm Nov-Mar) The efficient main municipal tourist office.

Getting There & Away

Air

Santiago's **Lavacolla airport** (981 54 75 00; www.aena.es) is 11km east of the city. Airlines and destinations include:

Air Berlin (www.airberlin.com) Germany

Aer Lingus (www.aerlingus.com) Dublin

easyJet (www.easyjet.com) Geneva

Iberia (www.iberia.com) Madrid, Barcelona, Bilbao

Ryanair (www.ryanair.com) Barcelona, Frankfurt, London, Madrid, Málaga, Milan, Valencia

Volotea (www.volotea.com) Venice

Vueling Airlines (www.vueling.com) Barcelona, Paris

Bus

The **bus station** (981 54 24 16; www.tussa.org; Praza de Camilo Díaz Baliño;) is about a 20-minute walk northeast of the city centre.

Right: Seafood pintxo dish, San Sebastián; **Below:** Costa da Morte

Castromil-Monbus runs to A Coruña (€6, 50 to 90 minutes, 15 or more daily), Pontevedra (€5.85, 50 to 90 minutes, 14 or more daily), Ourense (€9, 1½ to two hours, four or more daily) and many other places in Galicia. Empresa Freire heads to Lugo (€8.50, two hours, five or more daily).

ALSA operates further afield, including to Oviedo (€27.63, 5¼ to 8¾ hours, five or more daily), Santander (€46 to €66, eight to 10 hours, three daily), León (€27.91, six hours, one daily) and Madrid (€44.13 to €63.45, 7¾ to 10 hours, seven or more daily).

Train

The **train station** (**☎ 981 59 18 59; Rúa do Hórreo**) is about a 15-minute walk south from the Old Town. Regional trains run roughly every hour up and down the coast, linking Santiago with Vigo (€8.55 to €10.20, 1½ to 1¾ hours), Pontevedra (€5.65 to €6.75, one hour) and A Coruña (€5.65 to €6.75, 35 minutes). A daytime Talgo and an overnight Trenhotel head to Madrid (€50.60 to €53.60, 6¼ to 9½ hours).

Getting Around

Santiago is walkable, although it's a bit of a hike from the train and bus stations to the city centre. Private vehicles are barred from the Old Town from about 10am to dusk for most of the summer. Underground car parks around its fringes generally charge about €16 per 24 hours.

Up to 37 Empresa Freire buses (€3, 35 minutes) run daily between Lavacolla airport and Rúa do Doutor Teixeiro, in the new town southwest of Praza de Galicia, via the bus station. Taxis charge around €20.

Costa da Morte

Rocky headlands, winding inlets, small fishing towns, narrow coves, wide sweeping bays and many a remote, sandy beach – this is the eerily beautiful 'Coast

of Death'. For some the most enchanting part of Galicia, this relatively isolated and unspoilt shore runs from Muros, at the mouth of the Ría de Muros, around to Caión, just before A Coruña. It's a coast of legends, like the one about villagers who put out lamps to lure passing ships on to deadly rocks. Despite its many lighthouses, this treacherous coast has certainly seen a lot of shipwrecks, and the idyllic landscape can undergo a rapid transformation when ocean mists blow in.

Cabo Fisterra is the western edge of Spain, at least in popular imagination. The real westernmost point is Cabo de la Nave, 5km north, but that doesn't keep throngs of people from heading out to this beautiful, windswept cape, which is also kilometre 0 of the 86km Fisterra variant of the Camino de Santiago walk. Pilgrims ending their journeys here ritually burn smelly socks, T-shirts etc on the rocks just past the lighthouse.

One of the appealing rural hotels could be just the ticket as a base for exploring the region. Many are listed at the useful www.turismocostadamorte.com.

Public transport is limited and having your own wheels makes it far easier to get about. The area's sinuous highways aren't the easiest to navigate, but it's a marvellous area to get lost in.

Madrid & Around

No city on earth is more alive than Madrid. This beguiling place has a sheer energy that carries a simple message: this city knows how to live. In recent years Madrid has transformed itself into Spain's premier style centre and its calling cards are many: astonishing art galleries, relentless nightlife, an exceptional live music scene, a feast of fine restaurants and tapas bars, and a population that's mastered the art of the good life.

Away from the capital, the endless horizons of Central Spain's thinly populated high *meseta* (plateau) are where you'll find some of Spain's most engaging towns. Renaissance Salamanca, lovely little Segovia, and Toledo are places where history seems written on every stone. These areas will give you a real insight into the soul of Spain.

Plaza Mayor (p196), Madrid

Madrid & Around

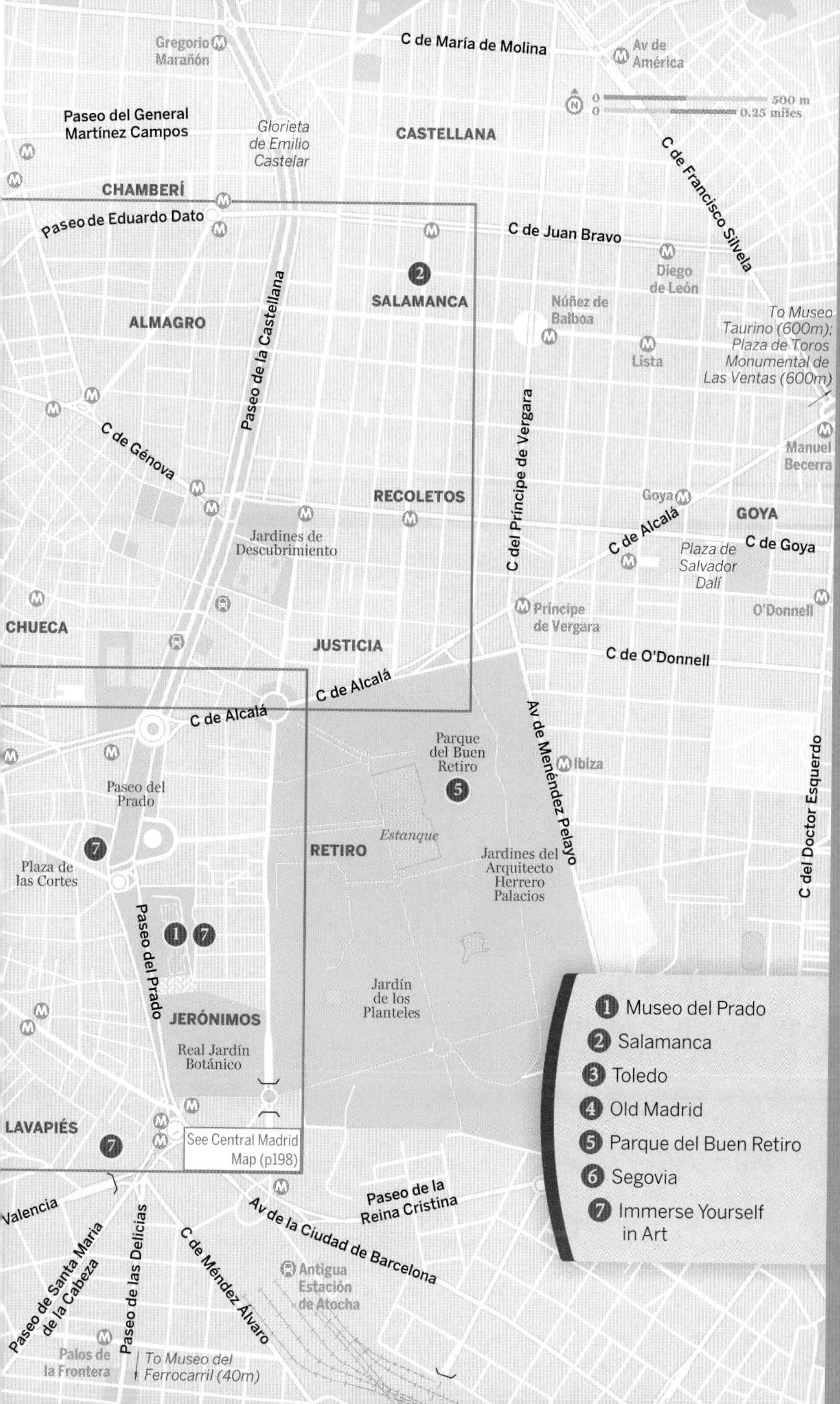

C de María de Molina
Gregorio Marañón
Av de América
500 m
0.25 miles
Paseo del General Martínez Campos
Glorieta de Emilio Castelar
CASTELLANA
C de Francisco Silvela
CHAMBERÍ
Paseo de Eduardo Dato
C de Juan Bravo
Diego de León
SALAMANCA
Núñez de Balboa
Lista
ALMAGRO
Paseo de la Castellana
To Museo Taurino (600m); Plaza de Toros Monumental de Las Ventas (600m)
Manuel Becerra
C de Génova
C del Príncipe de Vergara
RECOLETOS
Goya
GOYA
Jardines de Descubrimiento
C de Alcalá
Plaza de Salvador Dalí
C de Goya
Príncipe de Vergara
O'Donnell
CHUECA
JUSTICIA
C de O'Donnell
C de Alcalá
C de Alcalá
Parque del Buen Retiro
Av de Menéndez Pelayo
Ibiza
Paseo del Prado
C del Doctor Esquerdo
Estanque
RETIRO
Jardines del Arquitecto Herrero Palacios
Plaza de las Cortes
Paseo del Prado
Jardín de los Planteles
JERÓNIMOS
Real Jardín Botánico
LAVAPIÉS
See Central Madrid Map (p198)
Valencia
Paseo de la Reina Cristina
Av de la Ciudad de Barcelona
Paseo de Santa María de la Cabeza
Paseo de las Delicias
C de Méndez Álvaro
Antigua Estación de Atocha
Palos de la Frontera
To Museo del Ferrocarril (40m)
1 Museo del Prado
2 Salamanca
3 Toledo
4 Old Madrid
5 Parque del Buen Retiro
6 Segovia
7 Immerse Yourself in Art

Madrid & Around Highlights

1

Museo del Prado

Founded in 1819 by Fernando VII, El Prado (p206) ranks among the world's best museums and is the key to understanding painters such as Hieronymus Bosch (El Bosco), El Greco, Velázquez and Goya. One visit is never enough. Bottom Right: *La Maja Desnuda* by Goya

Need to Know

ADMISSION €12 **FREE ENTRY** 6pm to 8pm Tuesday to Saturday, 5pm to 7pm Sunday **SELF-GUIDED TOURS** See the museum's website for one- to three-hour itineraries

Local Knowledge

Museo del Prado Don't Miss List

BY LEONARDO HERNÁNDEZ, MEMBER OF FRIENDS OF THE PRADO AND REGULAR PRADO VISITOR

1 EDIFICIO JERÓNIMOS

The museum's extension, designed by Spanish architect Rafael Moneo, is worth visiting on its own. Highlights include the Sala de las Musas (Room of the Muses), the giant doors by Cristina Iglesias, the upper garden and El Claustro de los Jerónimos (Jerónimos' Cloister).

2 LA RENDICIÓN DE BREDA (LAS LANZAS), BY DIEGO VELÁZQUEZ

Velázquez's masterpiece shows the moment in 1625 in which Ambrosio Spinola, a Spanish general, accepted the surrender of the Dutch town of Breda after a long siege. The Spanish novelist Arturo Pérez-Reverte mixed fantasy and reality in his novel *The Sun over Breda,* claiming that his character Captain Alatriste appeared in the painting but was later mysteriously erased by Velázquez.

3 LA FAMÍLIA DE CARLOS IV, BY FRANCISCO DE GOYA

This painting is a small fragment of Spanish history transferred to canvas. It shows the royal family in 1800 with Fernando (later Fernando VII) dressed in blue on the left. His fiancée has not yet been chosen, which may be why Goya depicts her with no facial definition.

4 EL DESCENDIMIENTO, BY ROGER VAN DER WEYDEN

This 1435 painting is unusual, both for its size and for the recurring crossbow shapes in the painting's upper corners, which are echoed in the bodies of Mary and Christ. Once the central part of a triptych, the painting is filled with drama and luminous colours.

5 LA CONDESA DE VILCHES, BY FEDERICO MADRAZO

The painter was a friend of the model, which may be why he is able to transmit all her grace and sensuality. The light blue dress, the tone of her skin, the brightness in her eyes, and the smile slightly pointed suggest a timeless sympathy that endures through the centuries.

Salamanca

Salamanca (p233) is monumental (as recognised by Unesco) and very cultural (it was Europe's Capital of Culture in 2002), but the full Salamanca experience requires a little local knowledge. Behind the grand facades, it's all about discovering secret corners and learning new ways to look at its well-known sights.

Need to Know

LOCATION 2½ hours northwest of Madrid **BEST PHOTO OP** Out over the old town from Puerta de la Torre **TOP SURVIVAL TIP** Take a post-lunch siesta

2

Local Knowledge

Salamanca Don't Miss List

BY BEATRIZ CASTAÑO & JUAN OLAZABAL, ADOPTED CHARROS (SALAMANCA NATIVES)

1 LA PLAZA MAYOR

By all means admire the plaza's 88 arches adorned with busts of the great and good, and the way the sun turns the plaza's local sandstone to gold. But the essence of Salamanca, where life is performance, is to take up residence at one of the outdoor tables and watch all the life of Salamanca flow through the plaza (pictured left).

2 THE CATHEDRALS & PLAZA ANAYA

Apart from the cathedrals' landmark architectural features, look for the astronaut mischievously carved into the Catedral Nueva's northern door during restorations, and the cracks and broken stained-glass windows from the 1755 earthquake. Right outside, students pass the afternoon, sometimes in song, in Plaza Anaya, one of Salamanca's most charming corners.

3 THE UNIVERSITY FACADE

The facade of Salamanca's prestigious university is a plateresque masterpiece. But the devil lies in the detail. Trying to find the famous frog of Salamanca is a local rite of passage: according to local legend, the student who fails to find it will fail in their studies. But its origins probably lie in lust – it's actually a symbol of female sexuality...

4 TAPAS ALONG CALLE VAN DYCK

Tapas is a Salamanca passion and Calle de Van Dyck, north of the old town, is the most emblematic tapas street, where it's all about Salamanca's famous pork products, especially *embutidos* (cured meats). Hop from bar to bar and try the *pincho moruno* (marinated kebab), *lomo* (cured pork sausage), *jamón* and *chanfaina* (a paella accompanied with various pork cuts).

5 STAYING OUT AS LONG AS YOUR BODY LASTS

When the Plaza Mayor clock announces the onset of night, the party begins. A quarter of people in Salamanca are students, which means that the city never sleeps. The most famous drink is *el garrafón* (any alcohol of low quality), which suits a student's budget, but be warned – the hangovers can last for days.

Wander through Monumental Toledo

On a hilltop southwest of Madrid, picturesque Toledo (p224) is like a window on the Spanish soul. There are so many monuments to the city's polyglot Christian, Jewish and Muslim pas across the city that it has the quality of a living museum: this is one place where comparisor to the great cities of North Africa and the Middle East are not misplaced.

3

4

Explore Old Madrid

One of the most beautiful city squares in the world, Plaza Mayor (p196) also serves as a gateway to the old-world elegance of Madrid's oldest *barrios* (neighbourhoods). The grandeur of th Palacio Real is offset by the tangle of medieval lanes in La Latina, punctuate by some of Madrid's most intimate an charming little plazas, among them Plaza de la Villa and Plaza de la Paja.

Plaza Mayor, Madrid

MATTES RENÃ/GETTY IMAGES ©

5 Parque del Buen Retiro

Once a royal playground, the Parque del Buen Retiro (p201) is a haven from city life in the heart of one of Europe's noisiest cities. On Sundays it throngs with people, musicians and a happy buzz, while during the rest of the week it's quiet, an ideal time for tracking down its elegant if quirky collection of monuments.

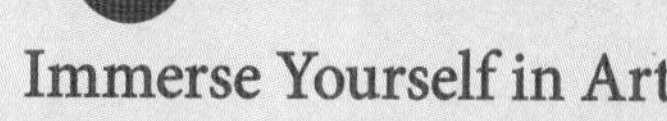

6 Discover Disneyland in Segovia

The old town of Segovia (p236) has monuments that span Spanish history. At one end stands one of Europe's best-preserved Roman aqueducts, while at the other is the fairy-tale (yet fortress-like) Alcázar (p237), which inspired the designers of Disneyland's famous castle. In between, stunning religious buildings and fine restaurants stand watch over the lively streets. El Acueducto (p236), Segovia

7 Immerse Yourself in Art

Within a mile of each other, Madrid's three world-class art galleries – the Museo del Prado (p206), Museo Thyssen-Bornemisza (p201) and Centro de Arte Reina Sofía (p200) – have made the city one of Europe's most important artistic capitals. Spanish icons share wall space with a host of European masters, but you'll find little-known artistic gems all across Madrid.

Pablo Picasso's *Guernica*, Centro de Arte Reina Sofía, Madrid

Madrid & Around's Best...

Galleries for Art-Lovers

- **Museo del Prado** (p206) Goya, Velázquez and much more.
- **Museo Thyssen-Bornemisza** (p201) Stunning showpiece of European masters.
- **Centro de Arte Reina Sofía** (p200) Picasso's *Guernica*, Miró and Dalí.
- **Real Academia de Bellas Artes de San Fernando** (p205) Little-known gallery with big-name masterpieces.

Tapas Bars

- **Almendro 13** (p212) Traditional tapas in La Latina.
- **Casa Alberto** (p212) One of Madrid's longest-standing and most traditional *tabernas* (taverns).
- **Sula Madrid** (p213) Innovative tapas and a sleek and sophisticated atmosphere.
- **Mercado de San Miguel** (p207) Billing itself as a 'culinary cultural centre' and who are we to argue?
- **Alfileritos 24** (p229) Innovative dishes served in 14th Century surrounds.

Places with a View

- **Toledo** (p224) Cross the Puente de Alcántara for a fairytale view of Toledo.
- **Plaza Mayor at night, Salamanca** (p234) One of Spain's most beautiful squares.
- **Segovia** (p236) Head 2km north of town for the photo opportunity to impress the folks back home.
- **Windmills of Consuegra** (p238) Don Quijote's famous windmills in all their glory.

Signposts to the Past

- **Old Madrid** (p196) Plaza Mayor sits in the heart of the oldest quarter of Madrid.
- **Toledo** (p224) Churches, synagogues and mosques.
- **Acueducto, Segovia** (p236) An astonishing feat of Roman engineering.
- **Ávila** (p230) Magnificent 12th century defensive walls.

Left: Tapas bar, Madrid;
Above: Windmills at sunset, Consuegra

Need to Know

RESOURCES

- **Centro de Turismo Madrid** (www.esmadrid.com) Tourist information for Madrid, with branches across the city.
- **Turismo Madrid** (www.turismomadrid.es) Portal of the regional Comunidad de Madrid tourist office that's especially good for areas outside the city but still within the Comunidad de Madrid.
- **Le Cool** (www.madrid.lecool.com) Weekly updates on upcoming events in Madrid with an emphasis on the alternative, offbeat and avant-garde.
- **Castilla y León** (www.turismocastillayleon.com) Informative site for north-central Spain.
- **Castilla-La Mancha** (www.turismocastillalamancha.com) Castilla-La Mancha's tourism portal.

GETTING AROUND

- **Air** Madrid's Barajas Airport (www.aena.es) has excellent connections with Europe and beyond.
- **Train** Extensive rail system connecting most of Central Spain.
- **Bus** Wherever trains don't go.
- **Road** Good network of motorways, with smaller connecting roads.
- **Madrid Metro** Best for getting anywhere in town, including the airport.
- **Madrid Taxis** Some of the cheapest in Europe.

BE FOREWARNED

- **Museums and galleries** Most close on Monday.
- **Centro de Arte Reina Sofía** Opens Monday, closes Tuesday.
- **Madrid restaurants** Many close during August and on Mondays the rest of the year.

Historic Madrid Walking Tour

Madrid has world-class art galleries and other sights, but as much as anything this is a city to savour, taste, smell and enjoy by simply exploring its streets, plazas and parks. This walking tour will help you get the most out of Madrid.

WALK FACTS

- **Start** Plaza de la Puerta del Sol
- **Finish** Plaza de la Cibeles
- **Distance** 5km
- **Duration** 3 to 4 hours

❶ Plaza de la Puerta del Sol

Start in the pulsating, geographic centre of Spain, the Plaza de la Puerta del Sol and head northwest along Calle del Arenal.

❷ Iglesia de San Ginés

This is one of Madrid's oldest places of Christian worship and houses some fine paintings.

❸ Chocolatería de San Ginés

Down a narrow lane just behind the church, Chocolatería de San Ginés is justifiably famous for its chocolate con churros (deep-fried Spanish donuts with chocolate), the ideal Madrid indulgence at any hour of the day.

❹ Iglesia de San Pedro El Viejo

With it's clearly Mudéjar bell tower, this 15th-century church is one of the few remaining windows onto the world of medieval Madrid.

❺ Plaza de la Paja

Linger for awhile in the charming Plaza de la Paja and then twist down through lanes of La Morería to Calle de Bailén.

6 Jardines de las Vistillas

Have a soothing *cerveza* (beer) at one of the wonderful *terrazas* (cafes with outdoor tables) that fringe the Jardines de las Vistillas and enjoy the view towards the Sierra de Guadarrama.

7 Palacio Real

Overlooking the Plaza de Oriente, the Palacio Real was Spain's seat of royal power for centuries.

8 Plaza de Oriente

Plaza de Oriente is a splendid arc of greenery and graceful architecture which could be Madrid's most agreeable plaza. You'll find yourself surrounded by gardens, the Palacio Real and the Teatro Real, and peopled by an ever-changing cast of *madrileños* at play.

9 Plaza de España

Follow the walkway extension of Calle de Bailén, which leads into Plaza de España surrounded by monumental towers. The eastern flank of the square marks the start of the Gran Vía.

10 Gran Vía

It's difficult to imagine Madrid without the Gran Vía, a Haussmannesque boulevard that was slammed through tumble down slums in the 1910s and 1920s and is now known for its chi-chi shops.

11 Metrópolis Building

At the southern end of Gran Vía the stunning French-designed Metrópolis building has a winged statue of victory sitting atop its dome.

12 Plaza de la Cibeles

Head downhill to Plaza de la Cibeles, a place that evokes the splendour of imperial Madrid.

Madrid in...

ONE DAY

Begin in the **Plaza Mayor** with its architectural beauty. Wander down **Calle Mayor** and head for the **Palacio Real** and the **Plaza de Oriente**. From here amble along to the incomparable **Museo del Prado**, one of Europe's best art galleries. Catch your breath in the **Parque del Buen Retiro** before heading up along **Gran Vía** and into **Chueca** for Madrid's famously noisy and eclectic nightlife.

THREE DAYS

Three days is a minimum for getting a real taste of Madrid. Spend a morning each on days two and three at **Centro de Arte Reina Sofía** and **Museo Thyssen-Bornemisza**. Otherwise, pause in **Plaza de la Cibeles** to admire some of the best architecture in Madrid as you work your way north to the **Gran Café de Gijón**, one of Madrid's grand old cafes. A quick metro ride across town takes you to the astonishing Goya frescoes in the **Ermita de San Antonio de la Florida**. On another day, head for **La Latina** and the great restaurants and tapas bars along **Calle de la Cava Baja**.

Palacio Real (p197)

Discover Madrid & Around

At a Glance

- **Los Austrias, Sol & Centro** (p196) Madrid's grandest monuments.
- **La Latina & Lavapiés** (p211) Great tapas bars and restaurants.
- **Huertas & Atocha** (p200) Centro de Arte Reina Sofía.
- **Paseo del Prado & El Retiro** (p201) Art galleries and the Parque del Buen Retiro.
- **Malasaña & Chueca** (p216) Nightlife and shopping.

Segovia's Old Town (p236)

DANITA DELIMONT/GETTY IMAGES ©

MADRID

Sights

Madrid has three- of the finest art galleries in the world: if ever there existed a golden mile of fine art, it would have to be the combined charms of the Museo del Prado, the Centro de Arte Reina Sofía and the Museo Thyssen-Bornemisza. Beyond the museums' walls, the combination of stately architecture and feel-good living has never been easier to access than in the beautiful plazas, where *terrazas* (cafes with outdoor tables) provide a front-row seat for Madrid's fine cityscape and endlessly energetic streetlife. Throw in some outstanding city parks (the Parque del Buen Retiro, in particular) and areas like Chueca, Malasaña and Salamanca, which each have their own identity, and you'll quickly end up wondering why you decided to spend so little time here.

Los Austrias, Sol & Centro

These *barrios* are where the story of Madrid began. As the seat of royal power, this is where the splendour of imperial Spain was at its most ostentatious and where Spain's overarching Catholicism was at its most devout – think expansive palaces, elaborate private mansions, ancient churches and imposing convents amid the clamour of modern Madrid.

PLAZA MAYOR Square

(Map p198; Plaza Mayor; M Sol) Ah, the history the plaza has seen! Designed in 1619 by Juan Gómez de Mora and built in typical

Herrerian style, of which the slate spires are the most obvious expression, its first public ceremony was suitably auspicious – the beatification of San Isidro Labrador (St Isidro the Farm Labourer), Madrid's patron saint. Thereafter it was as if all that was controversial about Spain took place in this square. Bullfights, often in celebration of royal weddings or births, with royalty watching on from the balconies and up to 50,000 people crammed into the plaza, were a recurring theme until 1878. Far more notorious were the *autos-da-fé* (the ritual condemnations of heretics during the Spanish Inquisition) followed by executions – burnings at the stake and deaths by garrotte on the north side of the square, hangings to the south. These days, the plaza is an epicentre of Madrid life, from the outdoor tables to the life coursing across its cobblestones.

The grandeur of the plaza is due in large part to the warm colours of the uniformly ochre apartments, with 237 wrought-iron balconies offset by the exquisite frescoes of the 17th-century **Real Casa de la Panadería** (Royal Bakery).

PALACIO REAL Palace

(Map p198; ☎91 454 88 00; www.patrimonionacional.es; Calle de Bailén; adult/concession €10/5, guide/audioguide/pamphlet €7/4/1, EU citizens free 5-8pm Wed & Thu; ⏰10am-8pm Apr-Sep, to 6pm Oct-Mar; M Ópera) Spain's lavish Palacio Real is a jewelbox of a palace, although it's used only occasionally for royal ceremonies; the royal family moved to the modest Palacio de la Zarzuela years ago.

The official tour leads through 50 of the palace rooms, which hold a good selection of Goyas, 215 absurdly ornate clocks, and five Stradivarius violins still used for concerts and balls. The **main stairway** is a grand statement of imperial power, leading first to the Halberdiers' rooms and eventually to the sumptuous **Salón del Trono** (Throne Room), with its crimson-velvet wall coverings and Tiepolo ceiling. Shortly after, you'll reach the **Salón de Gasparini**, with its exquisite stucco ceiling and walls resplendent with embroidered silks.

PLAZA DE ORIENTE Square

(Map p198; Plaza de Oriente; M Ópera) A royal palace that once had aspirations to be the Spanish Versailles. Sophisticated cafes watched over by apartments that cost the equivalent of a royal salary. The **Teatro Real**, Madrid's opera house and one of Spain's temples to high culture. Some of the finest sunset views in Madrid... Welcome to Plaza de Oriente, a living, breathing monument to imperial Madrid.

CAMPO DEL MORO & JARDINES DE SABATINI Gardens

In proper palace style, lush gardens surround the Palacio Real. To the north

Madrid Card

If you intend to do some intensive sightseeing and travelling on public transport, it might be worth looking at the **Madrid Card** (**☎91 360 47 72; www.madridcard.com; 1/2/3 days adult €39/49/59, child age 6-12 €20/28/34**). It includes free entry to more than 50 museums in and around Madrid (some of these are already free, but it does include the Museo del Prado, Museo Thyssen-Bornemisza, Centro de Arte Reina Sofía, Estadio Santiago Bernabéu and Palacio Real); free walking tours; and discounts for a number of restaurants, shops, bars and car rental. The Madrid Card can be bought online, or in person at the tourist offices on Plaza Mayor or Terminal 4 in Barajas Airport, the Metro de Madrid ticket office in Terminal 2 of the airport, the Museo Thyssen-Bornemisza, and in some tobacconists and hotels.

Central Madrid

are the formal French-style **Jardines de Sabatini** (9am-9pm May-Sep; Ópera). Directly behind the palace are the fountains of the **Campo del Moro** (Map p198; 91 454 88 00; www.patrimonionacional.es; Paseo de la Virgen del Puerto; 10am-8pm Mon-Sat, 9am-8pm Sun & holidays Apr-Sep, 10am-6pm Mon-Sat, 9am-6pm Sun & holidays Oct-Mar; Príncipe Pío), so named because this is where the Muslim army camped before a 12th-century attack on the Alcázar. Now, shady paths, a thatch-roofed pagoda and palace views are the main attractions.

CONVENTO DE LAS DESCALZAS REALES Convent

(Convent of the Barefoot Royals; Map p198; www.patrimonionacional.es; Plaza de las Descalzas 3; adult/child €7/4, incl Convento de la Encarnación €10/5, EU citizens free Wed & Thu afternoon; 10.30am-2pm & 4-6.30pm Tue-Sat, 10am-3pm Sun; Ópera, Sol) The grim plateresque walls of the Convento de las Descalzas Reales offer no hint that behind the facade lies a sumptuous stronghold of the faith. Founded in 1559 by Juana of Austria, the widowed daughter of the Spanish king

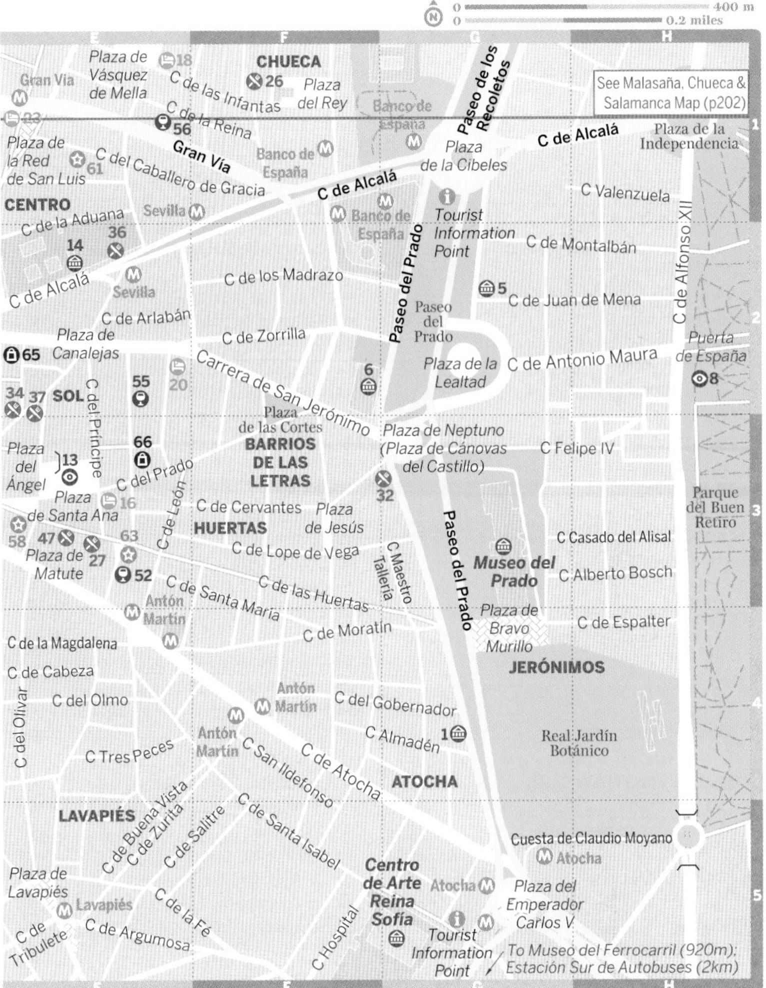

Carlos I, the convent quickly became one of Spain's richest religious houses thanks to gifts from Juana's noble friends. On the obligatory guided tour you'll see a gaudily frescoed Renaissance stairway, a number of extraordinary tapestries based on works by Rubens, and a wonderful painting entitled *The Voyage of the 11,000 Virgins*.

La Latina

EL RASTRO Market

(Map p198; Ribera de Curtidores; 8am-3pm Sun; M La Latina) This crowded Sunday flea market was, back in the 17th and 18th centuries, largely a meat market – *rastro* means 'stain', in reference to the trail of blood left behind by animals dragged down the hill. The road leading through the market, Ribera de Curtidores, translates as Tanners' Alley and further evokes this sense of a slaughterhouse past. On Sunday mornings this is *the* place to be, with all of Madrid (in all its diversity) here in search of a bargain.

Central Madrid

Top Sights

Centro de Arte Reina Sofía G5
Museo del Prado G3
Plaza Mayor C3

Sights

1 Caixa Forum G4
2 Campo del Moro A2
3 Convento de las Descalzas Reales C1
4 El Rastro C5
5 Museo Naval G2
6 Museo Thyssen-Bornemisza F2
7 Palacio Real A2
8 Parque del Buen Retiro H2
9 Plaza de la Paja B3
10 Plaza de la Puerta del Sol D2
11 Plaza de la Villa B3
12 Plaza de Oriente B1
13 Plaza de Santa Ana E3
14 Real Academia de Bellas Artes de San Fernando E2

Activities, Courses & Tours

15 Visitas Guiadas Oficiales B3

Sleeping

16 Hotel Alicia E3
17 Hotel Meninas C1
18 Hotel Óscar E1
19 Hotel Plaza Mayor D3
20 Hotel Urban E2
21 Mario Room Mate C1
22 Posada del Dragón C3
23 Praktik Metropol E1

Eating

24 Almendro 13 .... B4
25 Amaya C3
26 Bocaito F1
27 Casa Alberto E3
28 Casa Labra D2
29 Casa Lucas B4
30 Casa Revuelta C3
31 Ene Restaurante B3
32 Estado Puro G3
33 Juana La Loca B4
34 La Casa del Abuelo E2
35 La Chata C4
36 La Terraza del Casino E2
37 La Trucha E2
38 Las Bravas D3
39 Mercado de San Miguel C3
40 Naïa Restaurante B3
41 Posada de la Villa C3
42 Restaurante Sobrino de Botín C3
43 Taberna La Bola B1
44 Taberna Matritum C4
45 Txacolina C4
46 Txirimiri B4
47 Vi Cool E3

Drinking

48 Café del Real B2
49 Chocolatería de San Ginés C2
50 Chocolatería Valor C1
51 Delic B4
52 El Imperfecto E3
53 Gaudeamus Café D5
54 La Escalera de Jacob D4
55 La Venencia E2
56 Museo Chicote E1

Entertainment

57 Café Berlin C1
58 Café Central E3
59 ContraClub A4
60 Corral de la Morería A4
61 Costello Café & Niteclub E1
62 Las Carboneras C3
63 Populart E3

Shopping

64 El Flamenco Vive B2
El Rastro .... (see 4)
65 Gil E2
66 María Cabello E3

Huertas & Atocha

CENTRO DE ARTE REINA SOFÍA Museum

(Map p198; ☎91 774 10 00; www.museoreinasofia.es; Calle de Santa Isabel 52; adult/concession €6/free, free Sun, 7-9pm Mon-Fri & 2.30-9pm Sat ; ⏰10am-9pm Mon-Sat, 10am-2.30pm Sun; M Atocha) Home to Picasso's *Guernica*, arguably Spain's single most famous artwork, the Centro de Arte Reina Sofía is Madrid's premier collection of contemporary art. In addition to plenty of paintings by Picasso, other major drawcards are works by Salvador Dalí (1904–1989) and

Joan Miró (1893–1983). The collection principally spans the 20th century up to the 1980s (for more recent works, check to see if the **Museo Municipal de Arte Contemporáneo** (Map p202; ☎91 588 59 28; www.munimadrid.es/museoartecontemporaneo; Calle del Conde Duque 9-11; Ⓜ Plaza de España, Ventura Rodríguez, San Bernardo), which was closed for renovations at the time of writing, has reopened). The occasional non-Spaniard artist makes an appearance (including Francis Bacon's *Lying Figure;* 1966), but most of the collection is strictly peninsular.

In addition to Picasso's *Guernica,* which is worth the admission fee on its own, don't neglect the artist's preparatory sketches in the rooms surrounding room 206; they offer an intriguing insight into the development of this seminal work.

The work of Joan Miró (1893–1983) is defined by often delightfully bright primary colours, but watch out also for a handful of his equally odd sculptures.

The Reina Sofía is also home to 20 or so canvases by Salvador Dalí, of which the most famous is perhaps the surrealist extravaganza that is *El Gran Masturbador* (1929).

Paseo del Prado & El Retiro

MUSEO THYSSEN-BORNEMISZA Museum
(Map p198; ☎902 760 511; www.museothyssen.org; Paseo del Prado 8; adult/child €9/free; 🕙10am-7pm Tue-Sun; Ⓜ Banco de España) One of the most extraordinary private collections of predominantly European art in the world, the Museo Thyssen-Bornemisza is a worthy member of Madrid's 'Golden Triangle' of art. Where the Museo del Prado or Centro de Arte Reina Sofía enable you to study the body of work of a particular artist in depth, the Thyssen is the place to immerse yourself in a breathtaking breadth of artistic styles. Most of the big names are here, sometimes with just a single painting, but the Thyssen's gift to Madrid and the art-loving public is to have them all under one roof.

PARQUE DEL BUEN RETIRO Gardens
(Map p198; 🕙6am-midnight May-Sep, to 11pm Oct-Apr; Ⓜ Retiro, Príncipe de Vergara, Ibiza, Atocha) The glorious gardens of El Retiro are as beautiful as any you'll find in a European city. Littered with marble monuments, landscaped lawns, the occasional elegant building and abundant greenery, it's quiet and contemplative during the week but comes to life on weekends.

The focal point for so much of El Retiro's life is the *estanque* (artificial lake), which is watched over by the massive ornamental structure of the **Monument to Alfonso XII** on the east side, complete with marble lions. Hidden among the trees south of the lake is

Paintings in the Centro de Arte Reina Sofía

Guernica (Pablo Picasso; 1937)

Naturaleza Muerta (Pablo Picasso; 1912)

El Gran Masturbador (Salvador Dalí; 1929)

Muchacha en la Ventana (Salvador Dalí; 1925)

Monumento Imperial a la Mujer Niña (Salvador Dalí; 1929)

Pastorale (Joan Miró; 1923–24)

Danseuse Espagnole (Joan Miró; 1928)

L'atelier aux Sculptures (Miquel Barceló; 1993)

Los Cuatro Dictadores (Eduardo Arroyo; 1963)

Retrato de Josette (Juan Gris; 1916)

Cartes et Dés (Georges Braque; 1914)

El Peine del Viento I (Eduardo Chillida; 1962)

Homenaje a Mallarmé (Jorge Oteiza; 1958)

Pintura (Antoni Tàpies; 1955)

Otoños (Pablo Palazuelo; 1952)

Malasaña, Chueca & Salamanca

the **Palacio de Cristal** (91 574 66 14; 11am-8pm Mon-Sat, to 6pm Sun May-Sep, 10am-6pm Mon-Sat, 10am-4pm Sun Oct-Apr), a magnificent metal-and-glass structure that is arguably El Retiro's most beautiful architectural monument.

Salamanca

FREE MUSEO ARQUEOLÓGICO NACIONAL Museum

(Map p202; http://man.mcu.es; Calle de Serrano 13; 9.30am-8pm Tue-Sat, to 3pm Sun; M Serrano) The showpiece National Archaeology Museum contains a sweeping accumulation of artefacts behind its towering facade. The large collection includes stunning mosaics taken from Roman villas across Spain, intricate Muslim-era and Mudéjar handiwork, sculpted figures such as the *Dama de Ibiza* and *Dama de Elche*, examples of Romanesque and Gothic architectural styles and a partial copy of the prehistoric cave paintings of Altamira (Cantabria).

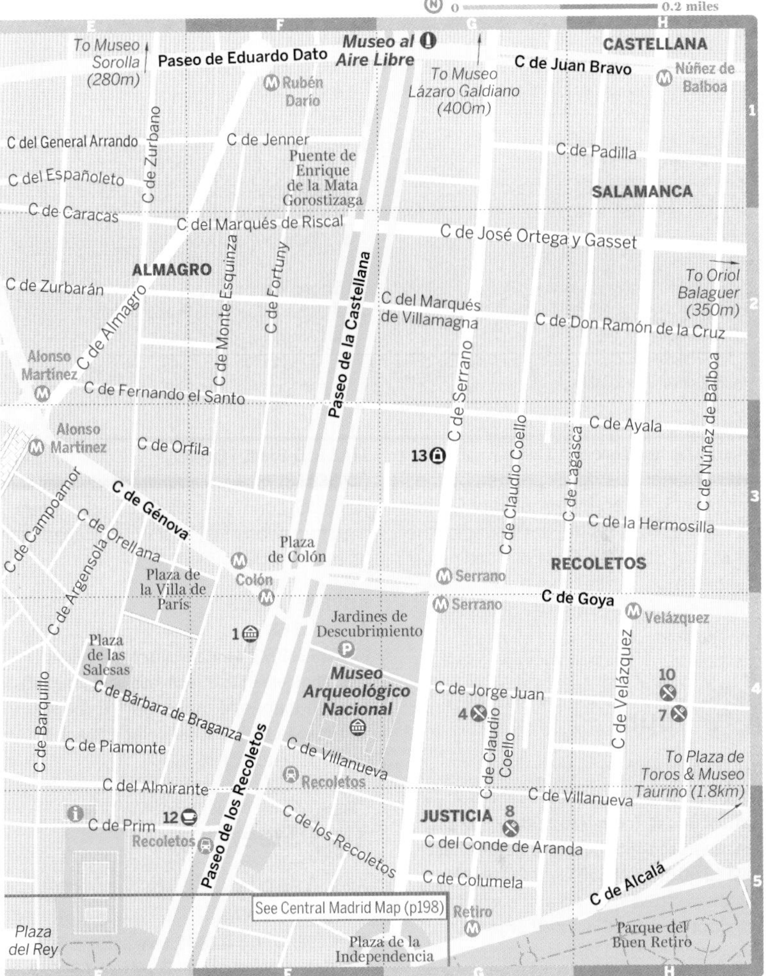

MUSEO LÁZARO GALDIANO Museum
(off Map p202; ☎91 561 60 84; www.flg.es; Calle de Serrano 122; adult/concession €6/3, last hr free; ⊙10am-4.30pm Wed-Sat & Mon, to 3pm Sun; **M** Gregorio Marañón) In an imposing early-20th-century Italianate stone mansion, the Museo Lázaro Galdiano has some 13,000 works of art and objets d'art. Apart from works by Bosch, Zurbarán, Goya, Claudio Coello, El Greco and Constable, this is a rather oddball assembly of all sorts of collectables.

Chamberí & Argüelles

FREE **ERMITA DE SAN ANTONIO DE LA FLORIDA** Art
(Map p184; Glorieta de San Antonio de la Florida 5; ⊙9.30am-8pm Tue-Fri, 10am-2pm Sat & Sun, hours vary Jul & Aug; **M** Príncipe Pío) The frescoed ceilings of the Ermita de San Antoniode la Florida are one of Madrid's most surprising secrets. Recently restored and also known as the **Panteón de Goya**, the southern of the two small chapels is

Malasaña, Chueca & Salamanca

one of the few places to see Goya's work in its original setting, as painted by the master in 1798 on the request of Carlos IV. The frescoes on the dome depict the miracle of St Anthony, who is calling on a young man to rise from the golden grave and absolve his father, unjustly accused of his murder.

Tours

VISITAS GUIADAS OFICIALES Guided Tour
(Official Guided Tours; Map p198; 902 221 424; www.esmadrid.com; Plaza Mayor 27; adult/child €3.90/free; M Sol) Over 20 highly recommended walking and cycling tours conducted in Spanish and English. Organised by the Centro de Turismo de Madrid (p221).

WELLINGTON SOCIETY Walking Tour
(609 143203; www.wellsoc.org; tours €50-85) A handful of quirky historical tours laced with anecdotes and led by the inimitable Stephen Drake-Jones. Membership costs €50 and includes a day or evening walking tour.

INSIDER'S MADRID Walking Tour
(91 447 38 66; www.insidersmadrid.com; tours from €60) An impressive range of tailor-made tours, including walking, tapas, flamenco and bullfighting tours.

MADRID BIKE TOURS Cycling
(680 581 782; www.madridbiketours.com; 4hr tours €55) Londoner Mike Chandler offers a guided two-wheel tour of Madrid as well as tours further afield.

ADVENTUROUS APPETITES Walking Tour
(639 331073; www.adventurousappetites.com; 4hr tours €50; 8pm-midnight Mon-Sat) English-language tapas tours through central Madrid. Prices include the first drink but exclude food.

Sleeping

Los Austrias, Sol & Centro

HOTEL MENINAS Boutique Hotel **€€**
(Map p198; 91 541 28 05; www.hotelmeninas.com; Calle de Campomanes 7; s/d from €99/119; M Ópera) This is a classy, cool choice. Opened in 2005, it's the sort of place where an interior designer licked their lips and created a master work of understated, minimalist luxury. The colour scheme is black, white and grey, with splashes of colour. Flat-screen TVs in every room, modern bathroom fittings, internet access, and even a laptop in some rooms, round out the clean lines and latest innovations.

PRAKTIK METROPOL Boutique Hotel **€€**
(Map p198; 91 521 29 35; www.hotelpraktikmetropol.com; Calle de la Montera 47; s/d from

€65/79; ❄📶; **M** Gran Vía) You'd be hard-pressed to find better value anywhere in Europe than here in this recently overhauled hotel. The rooms have a fresh, contemporary look with white wood furnishings, and some (especially the corner rooms) have brilliant views down to Gran Vía and out over the city. It's spread over six floors and there's a roof terrace if you don't have a room with a view.

HOTEL PLAZA MAYOR Hotel **€€**
(Map p198; ☎91 360 06 06; www.h-plazamayor.com; Calle de Atocha 2; s/d from €55/85; ❄📶; M Sol, Tirso de Molina) We love this place. Sitting just across from the Plaza Mayor, here you'll find stylish decor, helpful staff and charming original elements of this 150-year-old building. The rooms are attractive, some with a light colour scheme and wrought-iron furniture. The attic rooms (doubles from €130) boast dark wood and designer lamps, and have lovely little terraces with wonderful rooftop views of central Madrid.

MARIO ROOM MATE Boutique Hotel **€€**
(Map p198; ☎91 548 85 48; www.room-matehoteles.com; Calle de Campomanes 4; s €80-125, d €100-150; ❄📶; M Ópera) Entering this swanky boutique hotel is like crossing the threshold of Madrid's latest nightclub: staff dressed all in black, black walls and swirls of red lighting in the lobby. Rooms can be small, but have high ceilings, simple furniture and light tones contrasting smoothly with muted colours and dark surfaces. Some rooms are pristine white; others have splashes of colour with zany murals.

La Latina & Lavapiés

POSADA DEL DRAGÓN Boutique Hotel **€€**
(Map p198; ☎91 119 14 24; www.posadadeldragon.com; Calle de la Cava Baja 14 ; r from €91; ❄📶; M La Latina) At last, a boutique hotel in the heart of La Latina. This restored 19th-century inn sits on one of our favourite Madrid streets (and one of the best streets for tapas in the country), and

If You Like... Spanish Art

You don't have to be in Spain long to realise that Spaniards everywhere consider art almost essential to life. Every reasonable sized town (and quite a few villages!) seems to have an art gallery of some description, but it's in and around Madrid where the passion for art runs strongest. Here's some others you shouldn't miss.

1 **MUSEO AL AIRE LIBRE**
(Map p202; www.munimadrid.es/museoairelibre; cnr Paseo de la Castellana & Paseo de Eduardo Dato; ⏲24hr; M Rubén Darío) This fascinating open-air collection of 17 abstract sculptures includes works by the renowned Basque artist Eduardo Chillida, the Catalan master Joan Miró, as well as Eusebio Sempere and Alberto Sánchez.

2 **REAL ACADEMIA DE BELLAS ARTES DE SAN FERNANDO**
(Map p198; ☎91 524 08 64; http://rabasf.insde.es; Calle de Alcalá 13; adult/child €5/free, free Wed; ⏲9am-3pm Tue-Sat, to 2.30pm Sun Sep-Jun, hours vary Jul & Aug; M Sol, Sevilla) In any other city, the Royal Fine Arts Academy would be a stand-out attraction, but in Madrid it too often gets forgotten in the rush to the Prado, Thyssen or Reina Sofía.

3 **CAIXA FORUM**
(Map p198; www.fundacio.lacaixa.es; Paseo del Prado 36; ⏲10am-8pm; M Atocha) This extraordinary structure is one of Madrid's most eye-catching architectural innovations. The exhibitions here are always worth checking out and include cover photography, painting and multimedia shows.

4 **MUSEO SOROLLA**
(off Map p202; www.museosorolla.mcu.es; Paseo del General Martínez Campos 37; adult/child €3/free, free Sun; ⏲9.30am-8pm Tue-Sat, 10am-3pm Sun; M Iglesia, Gregorio Marañón) The Valencian artist Joaquín Sorolla immortalised the clear Mediterranean light of the Valencian coast. His Madrid house now contains the most complete collection of the artist's works.

KRZYSZTOF DYDYNSKI/GETTY IMAGES ©

Don't Miss Museo del Prado

Welcome to one of the world's premier art galleries. The more than 7000 paintings held in the Museo del Prado's collection (although only around 1500 are currently on display) are like a window onto the historical vagaries of the Spanish soul, at once grand and imperious in the royal paintings of Velázquez, darkly tumultuous in *Las Pinturas Negras* (Black Paintings) of Goya, and outward-looking with sophisticated works of art from all across Europe. Spend as long as you can at the Prado or, better still, plan to make a couple of visits because it can be a little overwhelming if you try to absorb it all at once.

Francisco José de Goya y Lucientes (Goya) is found on all three floors of the Prado, but we recommend starting at the southern end of the ground or lower level. In room 89, Goya's *El Dos de Mayo* and *El Tres de Mayo* rank among Madrid's most emblematic paintings; they bring to life the 1808 anti-French revolt and subsequent execution of insurgents in Madrid. Alongside, in rooms 87 and 88, are some of his darkest and most disturbing works, *Las Pinturas Negras* (Black Paintings); they are so called in part because of the dark browns and black that dominate, but more for the distorted animalesque appearance of their characters.

There are more Goyas on the 1st floor in rooms 69 to 73. Among them are two more of Goya's best-known and most intriguing oils: *La Maja Vestida* and *La Maja Desnuda*.

Diego Rodriguez de Silva y Velázquez (Velázquez) is another of the grand masters of Spanish art who brings so much distinction to the Prado. Of all his works, *Las Meninas* (room 50) is what most people come to see. Completed in 1656, it is more properly known as *La Família de Felipe IV* (The Family of Felipe IV). Hieronymus Bosch's *Garden of Earthly Delights*

NEED TO KNOW

Map p198; www.museodelprado.es; Paseo del Prado; adult/child €12/free, free 6-8pm Mon-Sat & 5-7pm Sun, audioguides €3.50; 🕙10am-8pm Mon-Sat, 10am-7pm Sun; Ⓜ Banco de España

rooms either look out over the street or over the pretty internal patio. The rooms? Some are on the small side, but bold, brassy colour schemes and designer everything distract (for the most part).

Huertas & Atocha

HOTEL ALICIA Boutique Hotel **€€**
(Map p198; 91 389 60 95; www.room-matehoteles.com; Calle del Prado 2; d €100-175, ste from €200; ; M Sol, Sevilla, Antón Martín) One of the landmark properties of the designer Room Mate chain of hotels, Hotel Alicia overlooks Plaza de Santa Ana with beautiful, spacious rooms. The style (the work of designer Pascua Ortega) is a touch more muted than in other Room Mate hotels, but the supermodern look remains intact, the downstairs bar is oh-so-cool, and the service is young and switched on.

HOTEL URBAN Luxury Hotel **€€€**
(Map p198; 91 787 77 70; www.derbyhotels.com; Carrera de San Jerónimo 34; r from €225; ; M Sevilla) This towering glass edifice is the epitome of art-inspired designer cool. With its clean lines and original artworks from Africa and Asia (there's a small museum dedicated to Egyptian art in the basement), it's a wonderful antidote to the more classic charm of Madrid's five-star hotels of longer standing. Dark-wood floors and dark walls are offset by plenty of light, while the dazzling bathrooms have wonderful designer fittings – the washbasins are sublime.

Malasaña & Chueca

HOTEL ÓSCAR Boutique Hotel **€€**
(Map p198; 91 701 11 73; www.room-matehoteles.com; Plaza de Vázquez de Mella 12; d €90-200, ste €150-280; ; M Gran Vía) Outstanding. Hotel Óscar belongs to the highly original Room Mate chain of hotels, and the designer rooms ooze style and sophistication. Some have floor-to-ceiling murals, the lighting is always funky, and the colour scheme is asplash with pinks, lime greens, oranges or more-minimalist black and white.

HOTEL ABALÚ Boutique Hotel **€€**
(Map p202; 91 531 47 44; www.hotelabalu.com; Calle del Pez 19; d/apt from €84/110; ; M Noviciado) Malasaña's very own boutique hotel is an oasis of style amid the *barrio's* timeworn feel. Suitably located on cool Calle del Pez, each room here has its own design drawn from the imagination of Luis Delgado, from retro chintz to Zen, Baroque and pure white (and most aesthetics in between).

Eating

Los Austrias, Sol & Centro

MERCADO DE SAN MIGUEL Tapas **€**
(Map p198; www.mercadodesanmiguel.es; Plaza de San Miguel; tapas from €1; 10am-midnight Sun-Wed, to 2am Thu-Sat; M Sol) One of Madrid's oldest and most beautiful markets,

Paintings in the Museo del Prado

Las Meninas (Velázquez)

La Rendición de Breda (Velázquez)

La Maja Desnuda & *La Maja Vestida* (Goya)

El Tres de Mayo (Goya)

Las Pinturas Negras (*Black Paintings;* Goya)

El Jardín de las Delicias (*The Garden of Earthly Delights;* Hieronymus Bosch)

Adam & Eve (Adán y Eva, Dürer)

El Lavatorio (Tintoretto)

La Trinidad (El Greco)

David Vencedor de Goliath (Caravaggio)

El Sueño de Jacob (Ribera)

Las Tres Gracias (*The Three Graces,* Rubens)

Artemisa (Rembrandt)

Museo del Prado

Plan of Attack

Begin on the 1st floor with **Las Meninas** 1 by Velázquez. Although alone worth the entry price, it's a fine introduction to the 17th-century golden age of Spanish art; nearby are more of Velázquez' royal paintings and works by Zurbarán and Murillo. While on the 1st floor, seek out Goya's **La Maja Vestida and La Maja Desnuda** 2 with more of Goya's early works in neighbouring rooms. Downstairs at the southern end of the Prado, Goya's anger is evident in the searing **El Dos de Mayo** and **El Tres de Mayo** 3, and the torment of Goya's later years finds expression in the adjacent rooms with his **Pinturas Negras** 4, or Black Paintings. Also on the lower floor, Hieronymus Bosch's weird and wonderful **Garden of Earthly Delights** 5 is one of the Prado's signature masterpieces. Returning to the 1st floor, El Greco's **Adoration of the Shepherds** 6 is an extraordinary work, as is Peter Paul Rubens' **Las Tres Gracias** 7, which forms the centrepiece of the Prado's gathering of Flemish masters. (This painting may have been moved to the 2nd floor.) A detour to the 2nd floor takes in some lesser-known Goyas, but finish in the **Edificio Jerónimos** 8 with a visit to the cloisters and the outstanding bookshop.

Also Visit:

Nearby are Museo Thyssen-Bornemisza and Centro de Arte Reina Sofía. They form an extraordinary trio of galleries.

TOP TIPS

Book online Purchase your ticket online (www.museodelprado.es), save €1 and avoid the queues

Best time to visit As soon after opening time as possible

Free tours The website (www.museodelprado.es/coleccion/que-ver/) has self-guided tours for one- to three-hour visits

PETER BARRITT/ALAMY ©

Las Tres Gracias (Rubens)
A late Rubens masterpiece, *The Three Graces* is a classical and masterly expression of Rubens' preoccupation with sensuality, here portraying Aglaia, Euphrosyne and Thalia, the daughters of Zeus.

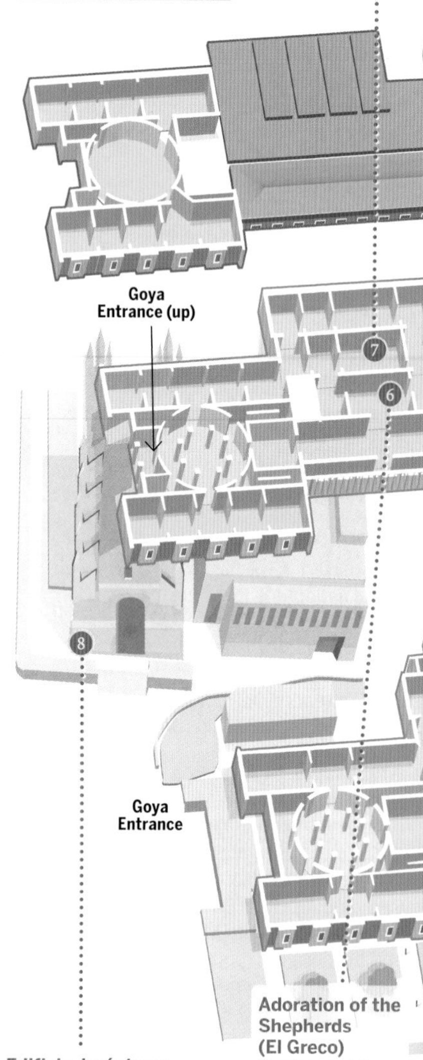

Edificio Jerónimos
Opened in 2007, this state-of-the-art extension has rotating exhibitions of Prado masterpieces held in storage for decades for lack of wall space, and stunning 2nd-floor granite cloisters that date back to 1672.

Adoration of the Shepherds (El Greco)
There's an ecstatic quality to this intense painting. El Greco's distorted rendering of bodily forms came to characterise much of his later work.

RICHARD NEBESKY/GETTY IMAGES ©

Las Meninas (Velázquez)

This masterpiece depicts Velázquez and the Infanta Margarita, with the king and queen whose images appear, according to some experts, in mirrors behind Velázquez.

GIANNI DAGLI ORTI/ALAMY ©

La Maja Vestida & La Maja Desnuda (Goya)

These enigmatic works scandalised early-19th-century Madrid society, fuelling the rumour mill as to the woman's identity and drawing the ire of the Spanish Inquisition. (La Maja Vestida pictured above.)

El Dos de Mayo & El Tres de Mayo (Goya)

RICHARD NEBESKY/ GETTY IMAGES ©

Few paintings evoke a city's sense of self quite like Goya's portrayal of Madrid's valiant but ultimately unsuccessful uprising against French rule in 1808. (El Dos de Mayo pictured here.)

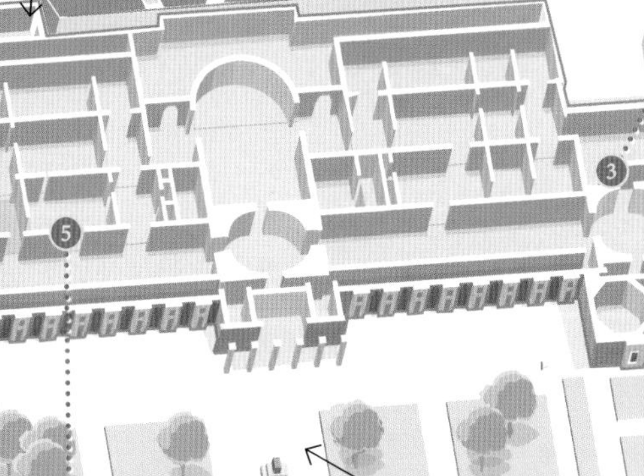

The Garden of Earthly Delights (Bosch)

A fantastical painting in triptych form, this overwhelming work depicts the Garden of Eden and what the Prado describes as 'the lugubrious precincts of Hell' in exquisitely bizarre detail.

Las Pinturas Negras (Goya)

PETER BARRITT/ALAMY ©

Las Pinturas Negras are Goya's darkest works. *Saturno Devorando a Su Hijo* evokes a writhing mass of tortured humanity, while *La Romería de San Isidro* and *El Akelarre* are profoundly unsettling.

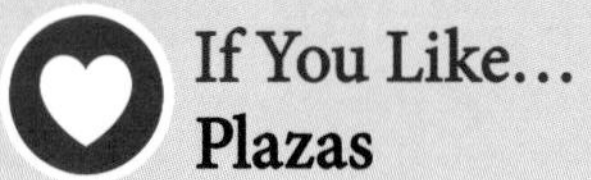

If You Like... Plazas

If you like the Plaza Mayor, we think you'll easily fall in love with these other central Madrid plazas:

1 **PLAZA DE LA VILLA**
(Map p198; Plaza de la Villa; M Ópera) Intimate square enclosed on three sides by 17th-century *barroco madrileño* (Madrid-style baroque architecture: a pleasing amalgam of brick, exposed stone and wrought iron) .

2 **PLAZA DE SANTA ANA**
(Map p198; Plaza de Santa Ana; M Sevilla, Sol, Antón Martín) A delightful confluence of elegant architecture and irresistible energy, and the focal point of Huertas' intellectual life.

3 **PLAZA DE LA PAJA**
(Map p198) Feels like you've stumbled upon a village square in the heart of the city.

4 **PLAZA DE LA PUERTA DEL SOL**
(Map p198; Plaza de la Puerta del Sol; M Sol) The official centrepoint of Spain is a gracious hemisphere of elegant facades and often overwhelming crowds.

the Mercado de San Miguel has undergone a stunning major renovation and bills itself as a 'culinary cultural centre'. Within the early-20th-century glass walls, the market has become an inviting space strewn with tables. You can order tapas and sometimes more substantial plates at most of the counter-bars, and everything here (from caviar to chocolate) is as tempting as the market is alive.

RESTAURANTE SOBRINO DE BOTÍN Castilian €€€
(Map p198; ☎91 366 42 17; www.botin.es; Calle de los Cuchilleros 17; mains €18.50-28; M La Latina, Sol) It's not every day that you can eat in the oldest restaurant in the world (the *Guinness Book of Records* has recognised it as the oldest – established in 1725). And it has also appeared in many novels about Madrid, from Ernest Hemingway to Frederick Forsyth. The secret of its staying power is fine *cochinillo* (roast suckling pig; €24) and *cordero asado* (roast lamb; €24) cooked in wood-fired ovens.

LA TERRAZA DEL CASINO
Contemporary Spanish €€€
(Map p198; ☎91 521 87 00; www.casinodemadrid.es; Calle de Alcalá 15; set menus from €100; ⊙lunch & dinner Mon-Fri, dinner Sat; M Sevilla) Perched atop the landmark Casino de Madrid building, this temple of haute cuisine is overseen, albeit from afar, by Ferran Adrià (Spain's premier celebrity chef), but is mostly in the hands of his acolyte Paco Roncero. It's all about culinary experimentation, with a menu that changes as each new idea emerges from the laboratory and moves into the kitchen.

TABERNA LA BOLA Madrileño €€
(Map p198; ☎91 547 69 30; www.labola.es; Calle de la Bola 5; mains €16-24; ⊙lunch & dinner Mon-Sat, lunch Sun, closed Aug; M Santo Domingo) In any poll of food-loving locals seeking the best and most traditional Madrid cuisine, Taberna La Bola (going strong since 1870 and run by the sixth generation of the Verdasco family) always features near the top. We're inclined to agree and, if you're going to try *cocido a la madrileña* (meat-and-chickpea stew; €19.50) while in Madrid, this is a good place to do so.

Tapas

Los Austrias, Sol and Centro are all prime hunting grounds for memorable tapas bars. **Amaya** (Map p198; ☎91 366 82 07; Plaza de la Provincia 3; meals €25-30; ⊙noon-5pm & 8pm-late Tue-Sat, noon-5pm Sun; M Sol) combines traditional Spanish flavours with some surprising twists. For *bacalao* (cod), **Casa Labra** (Map p198; ☎91 532 14 05; www.casalabra.es; Calle de Tetuán 11; tapas from €1; ⊙9.30am-3.30pm & 5.30-11pm; M Sol) has been around since 1860 and was a favourite of the poet Federico García Lorca. However, many *madrileños* won't eat *bacalao* anywhere except **Casa Revuelta**

(Map p198; ☎91 366 33 32; Calle de Latoneros 3; tapas from €2.60; ⏰10.30am-4pm & 7-11pm Tue-Sat, 10.30am-4pm Sun, closed Aug; Ⓜ Sol, La Latina), clinched by the fact that the owner painstakingly extracts every fish bone in the morning.

La Latina & Lavapiés

POSADA DE LA VILLA Madrileño **€€€**
(Map p198; ☎91 366 18 80; www.posadadelavilla.com; Calle de la Cava Baja 9; mains €20-28; ⏰lunch & dinner Mon-Sat, lunch Sun, closed Aug; Ⓜ La Latina) This wonderfully restored 17th-century *posada* (inn) is something of a local landmark. The atmosphere is formal, the decoration sombre and traditional (heavy timber and brickwork), and the cuisine decidedly local – roast meats, *cocido* (meat and chickpea stew), *callos* (tripe) and *sopa de ajo* (garlic soup).

NAÏA RESTAURANTE Fusion **€€**
(Map p198; ☎91 366 27 83; www.naiarestaurante.com; Plaza de la Paja 3; mains €12-19; ⏰lunch & dinner Tue-Sun; Ⓜ La Latina) On the lovely Plaza de la Paja, Naïa has a real buzz about it, with a cooking laboratory overseen by Carlos López Reyes, modern Spanish cuisine and a chill-out lounge downstairs. The emphasis throughout is on natural ingredients, healthy food and exciting tastes.

Madrid for Children

Madrid has plenty to keep the little ones entertained. A good place to start is **Casa de Campo** (Ⓜ Batán), where there are swimming pools, the **Zoo Aquarium de Madrid** (☎902 345014; www.zoomadrid.com; Casa de Campo; adult/child €21.35/17.60; ⏰10.30am-8.30pm Jul & Aug, reduced hours Sep-Jun; 🚌37 from Intercambiador de Príncipe Pío, Ⓜ Casa de Campo) and the **Parque de Atracciones** (☎91 463 29 00; www.parquedeatracciones.es; Casa de Campo; >120cm/90-120cm/<90cm €29.90/23.90/free; ⏰noon-midnight Sun-Fri, to 1am Sat Jul & Aug, reduced hours Sep-Jun; 🚌37 from Intercambiador de Príncipe Pío, Ⓜ Batán) amusement park, which has a 'Zona Infantil' with sedate rides for the really young. To get to Casa de Campo, take the **Teleférico** (☎91 541 11 18; www.teleferico.com; one-way/return €3.85/5.60; ⏰noon-9pm Mon-Fri, to 9.30pm Sat & Sun Jun-Aug, reduced hours Sep-May; Ⓜ Argüelles), one of the world's most horizontal cable cars, which putters for 2.5km out from the slopes of La Rosaleda.

Another possibility is **Faunia** (☎91 301 62 10; www.faunia.es; Avenida de las Comunidades 28; adult/child €25.50/19.50; ⏰10am-8pm Mon-Fri & 10am-9pm Sat & Sun Jun-Aug, reduced hours Sep-May; Ⓜ Valdebernardo), a modern animal theme park with an 'Amazon Jungle' and a 'Polar Ecosystem'. Faunia is located east of the M-40, about 7km from the city centre.

The **Museo del Ferrocarril** (☎902 228822; www.museodelferrocarril.org; Paseo de las Delicias 61; adult/child €5.09/3.56; ⏰10am-3pm Tue-Thu & Sun, 10am-8pm Fri & Sat, closed Aug; Ⓜ Delicias) is home to old railway cars, train engines and more. The free **Museo Naval** (Map p198; ☎91 523 87 89; www.armada.mde.es/museonaval; Paseo del Prado 5; ⏰10am-7pm Tue-Sun; Ⓜ Banco de España) will appeal to those fascinated by ships.

The **Museo de Cera** (Map p202; ☎91 319 26 49; www.museoceramadrid.com; Paseo de los Recoletos 41; adult/child €17/12; ⏰10am-2.30pm & 4.30-8.30pm Mon-Fri, 10am-8.30pm Sat & Sun; Ⓜ Colón) is Madrid's modest answer to Madame Tussaud's, with more than 450 wax characters.

Other possibilities include seeing Real Madrid play at the Estadio Santiago Bernabéu (p219), wandering through the soothing greenery of the Parque del Buen Retiro (p201), where in summer there are puppet shows and boat rides, or skiing at **Madrid Xanadú** (☎902 36 13 09; www.madridsnowzone.com; Calle Puerto de Navacerrada; per hr adult/child €22/19, day pass €36/33, equipment rental €18; ⏰10am-midnight; 🚌528, 534).

ENE RESTAURANTE Contemporary Spanish **€€**

(Map p198; 91 366 25 91; www.enerestaurante.com; Calle del Nuncio 19; mains €11-22, brunch €22; lunch & dinner daily, brunch 12.30-4.30pm Sat & Sun; M La Latina) Just across from Iglesia de San Pedro El Viejo, one of Madrid's oldest churches, Ene is anything but old world. The design is cutting edge and awash with reds and purples, while the young and friendly waiters circulate to the tune of lounge music. The food is Spanish-Asian fusion and there are also plenty of *pintxos* (Basque tapas) to choose from.

Tapas

Madrid's home of tapas is La Latina, especially along Calle de la Cava Baja and the surrounding streets. **Almendro 13** (Map p198; 91 365 42 52; Calle del Almendro 13; mains €7-15; 12.30-4pm & 7.30pm-midnight Sun-Thu, 12.30-5pm & 8pm-1am Fri & Sat; M La Latina) is famous for quality rather than frilly elaborations, with cured meats, cheeses, tortillas and *huevos rotos* (literally, 'broken eggs') the house specialities. Down on Calle de la Cava Baja, **Txacolina** (Map p198; 91 366 48 77; Calle de la Cava Baja 26; tapas from €3; dinner Mon & Wed-Fri, lunch & dinner Sat, lunch Sun; M La Latina) does Basque 'high cuisine in miniature', although these are some of the biggest *pintxos* (Basque tapas) you'll find; wash it all down with a *txacoli*, a sharp Basque white. On the same street, **Casa Lucas** (Map p198; 91 365 08 04; www.casalucas.es; Calle de la Cava Baja 30; tapas/raciones from €5/12; lunch & dinner Thu-Tue, dinner Wed; M La Latina) and **La Chata** (Map p198; 91 366 14 58; Calle de la Cava Baja 24; mains €8-20; lunch & dinner Thu-Mon, dinner Wed; M La Latina) are also hugely popular. Not far away, **Juana La Loca** (Map p198; 91 364 05 25; Plaza de la Puerta de Moros 4; tapas from €4, mains €8-19; lunch & dinner Tue-Sun, dinner Mon; M La Latina) does a magnificent *tortilla de patatas* (potato and onion omelette), as does **Txirimiri** (Map p198; 91 364 11 96; www.txirimiri.es; Calle del Humilladero 6; tapas from €4; lunch & dinner Mon-Sat, closed Aug; M La Latina). **Taberna Matritum** (Map p198; 91 365 82 37; Calle de la Cava Alta 17; mains €13-18; lunch & dinner Wed-Sun, dinner Mon & Tue; M La Latina) serves great tapas and desserts by the master chocolatier Oriol Balaguer.

Huertas & Atocha

CASA ALBERTO Spanish **€€**

(Map p198; 91 429 93 56; www.casaalberto.es; Calle de las Huertas 18; mains €16-20; lunch & dinner Tue-Sat, lunch Sun; M Antón Martín) One of the most atmospheric old *tabernas* of Madrid, Casa Alberto has been around since 1827. The secret to its staying power is vermouth on tap, excellent tapas at the bar and fine sit-down meals; Casa Alberto's *rabo de toro* (bull's tail) is famous among aficionados. As the antique wood-panelled decoration will

Cafe scene, Madrid

suggest straight away, the *raciones* have none of the frilly innovations that have come to characterise Spanish tapas.

VI COOL Contemporary Spanish **€€** (Map p198; ☎91 429 49 13; www.vi-cool.com; Calle de las Huertas 12; mains €8-18; ⏲lunch & dinner daily; Ⓜ Antón Martín) Catalan master chef Sergi Arola is one of the most restless and relentlessly creative culinary talents in the country. Dishes are either tapas or larger *raciones*, ranging from his trademark *Las Bravas de Arola* (a different take on the well-loved Spanish dish of roast potatoes in a spicy tomato sauce), to fried prawns with curry and mint.

Tapas

In Huertas, **La Casa del Abuelo** (Map p198; ☎91 000 01 33; www.lacasadelabuelo.es; Calle de la Victoria 12; raciones from €9.50; ⏲8.30am-midnight Sun-Thu, 8am-1am Fri & Sat; Ⓜ Sol) is famous for *gambas a la plancha* (grilled prawns) or *gambas al ajillo* (prawns sizzling in garlic on little ceramic plates) and a *chato* (small glass) of the heavy, sweet El Abuelo red wine; they cook over 200kg of prawns here on a good day. For *patatas bravas* (fried potatoes lathered in a spicy tomato sauce), **Las Bravas** (Map p198; ☎91 522 85 81; Callejón de Álvarez Gato 3; raciones €3.50-10; ⏲lunch & dinner; Ⓜ Sol, Sevilla) is the place, while **La Trucha** (Map p198; ☎91 532 08 90; Calle de Núñez de Arce 6; mains €8.50-13.50; ⏲lunch & dinner; Ⓜ Sol) has a counter overloaded with enticing Andalucian tapas and 95 items on the menu.

Salamanca

SULA MADRID Contemporary Spanish **€€€** (Map p202; ☎91 781 61 97; www.sula.es; Calle de Jorge Juan 33; mains €23.50-27.50, set menus €30-60; ⏲lunch & dinner Mon-Sat; Ⓜ Velázquez) A gastronomic temple that combines stellar cooking with clean-lined sophistication, Sula Madrid – a superstylish tapas bar, top-notch restaurant and ham-and-champagne tasting centre all rolled into one – is one of our favourite top-end restaurants in Madrid. And we're not the only ones: when master chef Ferran Adrià was asked to nominate his favourite restaurant, he chose Sula.

LA GALETTE Spanish **€€** (Map p202; ☎91 576 06 41; Calle del Conde de Aranda 11; mains €9.50-19.50; ⏲lunch & dinner Mon-Sat, lunch Sun; 🥕; Ⓜ Retiro) This lovely little restaurant combines an intimate dining area with checked tablecloths and cuisine that the owner describes as 'baroque vegetarian'. The food (both veg and non-veg) is a revelation, blending creative flavours with a strong base in traditional home cooking. The *croquetas de manzana* (apple croquettes) are a house speciality.

Tapas

In Salamanca, **Biotza** (Map p202; www.biotzarestaurante.com; Calle de Claudio Coello 27; tapas €2.50-3.50; ⏲9am-midnight Mon-Thu, to 1am Fri & Sat; Ⓜ Serrano) offers creative Basque *pintxos* in stylish surrounds, while **La Colonial de Goya** (Map p202; www.restauranterincondegoya.es; Calle de Jorge Juan 34; tapas €3-4.50; ⏲8am-midnight Mon-Fri, noon-1am Sat & Sun; Ⓜ Velázquez) serves up a staggering choice of *pintxos*, including 63 varieties of canapés. Further south, along the Paseo del Prado, there's only one choice for tapas and it's one of Madrid's best: **Estado Puro** (Map p198; ☎91 330 24 00; www.tapasenestadopuro.com; Plaza de Cánovas del Castillo 4; tapas €5-12.50; ⏲11am-1am Tue-Sat, to 4pm Sun; Ⓜ Banco de España, Atocha).

Malasaña & Chueca

LA MUSA Spanish, Fusion **€€** (Map p202; ☎91 448 75 58; www.lamusa.com.es; Calle de Manuela Malasaña 18; mains €7-15; ⏲9am-1am Mon-Thu, 9am-2am Fri, 1pm-2am Sat, 1pm-1am Sun; Ⓜ San Bernardo) Snug yet loud, a favourite of Madrid's hip young crowd yet utterly unpretentious, La Musa is all about designer decor, lounge music on the sound system and fun food (breakfast, lunch and dinner) that will live long in the memory. The menu is divided into three types of tapas – hot, cold and BBQ; among the hot varieties is the fantastic *jabalí con ali-oli de miel y sobrasada* (wild boar with honey mayonnaise and

Right: La Casa del Abuelo, Huertas (p213); **Below:** Tapas in La Latina
BELOW: DIEGO LEZAMA/GETTY IMAGES ©; RIGHT: DIEGO LEZAMA/GETTY IMAGES ©

sobrasada – a soft, mildly spicy sausage from Mallorca).

Tapas

Chueca is another stellar tapas *barrio*. Don't miss **Bocaito** (Map p198; ☎91 532 12 19; www.bocaito.com; Calle de la Libertad 4-6; tapas from €3.50, mains €12-20; ⊙lunch & dinner Mon-Fri, dinner Sat; M Chueca, Banco de España), another purveyor of Andalucian *jamón* (ham) and seafood and a favourite haunt of filmmaker Pedro Almodóvar. **Bodega de La Ardosa** (Map p202; ☎91 521 49 79; Calle de Colón 13; tapas & raciones €3.50-11; ⊙8.30am-1am; M Tribunal) is extremely popular for its *salmorejo* (cold, tomato-based soup), *croquetas*, *patatas bravas* and *tortilla de patatas*, while **Casa Julio** (Map p202; ☎91 522 72 74; Calle de la Madera 37; 6/12 croquetas €5/10; ⊙lunch & dinner Mon-Sat; M Tribunal) is widely touted as the home of Madrid's best *croquetas*.

Drinking

Los Austrias, Sol & Centro

CHOCOLATERÍA DE SAN GINÉS Cafe
(Map p198; Pasadizo de San Ginés 5; ⊙9.30am-7am; M Sol) One of the grand icons of the Madrid night, this *chocolate con churros* (Spanish donuts with chocolate) cafe sees a sprinkling of tourists throughout the day, but locals usually pack it out in their search for sustenance on their way home from a nightclub sometime close to dawn. They close for only two hours a day, and only then to give it a quick scrub. Only in Madrid...

CAFÉ DEL REAL Cocktail Bar, Cafe
(Map p198; Plaza de Isabel II 2; ⊙9am-1am Mon-Thu, to 3am Fri & Sat; M Ópera) A cafe and cocktail bar in equal parts, this intimate little place serves up creative coffees and a few cocktails to the soundtrack of chill-out music. The best seats are upstairs, where the low ceilings, wooden beams

and leather chairs are a great place to pass an afternoon with friends.

CHOCOLATERÍA VALOR Cafe
(Map p198; www.chocolateriasvalor.es; Postigo de San Martín; 9am-10.30pm Sun, 8am-10.30pm Mon-Thu, 8am-1am Fri, 9am-1am Sat; M Callao) It may be Madrid tradition to indulge in *chocolate con churros* around sunrise on your way home from a nightclub, but for everyone else who prefers a more reasonable hour, this is possibly the best *chocolatería* in town. They serve traditional *churros,* but they're only the side event to the astonishing array of chocolates in which to dip them.

La Latina & Lavapiés

GAUDEAMUS CAFÉ Cafe
(Map p198; www.gaudeamuscafe.com; Calle de Tribulete 14, 4th fl; 3pm-midnight Mon-Sat; M Lavapiés) What a place! Decoration that's light and airy, with pop-art posters of Audrey Hepburn and James Bond. A large terrace with views over the Lavapiés rooftops. A stunning backdrop of a ruined church atop which the cafe sits. With so much else going for it, it almost seems incidental that it also serves great teas, coffees and snacks (and meals). The cafe is around 300m southwest of Plaza de Lavapiés along Calle de Tribulete; look for the glass doors.

DELIC Bar, Cafe
(Map p198; www.delic.es; Costanilla de San Andrés 14; 11am-2am Fri-Sun & Tue-Thu, 7pm-2am Mon; M La Latina) We could go on for hours about this long-standing cafe-bar, but we'll reduce it to its most basic elements: nursing an exceptionally good *mojito* (€8) or three on a warm summer's evening at Delic's outdoor tables on one of Madrid's prettiest plazas is one of life's great pleasures.

LA ESCALERA DE JACOB Cocktail Bar
(Map p198; www.laescaleradejacob.es; Calle de Lavapiés 11; concerts from €6; 8pm-2am Wed & Thu, 8pm-2.30am Fri, 11am-2.30am Sat, 5pm-1am Sun; M Antón Martín, Tirso de Molina) As much a cocktail bar as a live music

venue or theatre, 'Jacob's Ladder' is one of Madrid's most original stages. Magicians, storytellers, children's theatre, live jazz and other genres are all part of the mix. This alternative slant on life makes for some terrific live performances, and regardless of what's on, it's worth stopping by here for their creative cocktails that you won't find anywhere else – the *fray aguacate* (Frangelico, vodka, honey, avocado and vanilla) should give you an idea of how far they go.

Huertas & Atocha

LA VENENCIA Bar

(Map p198; Calle de Echegaray 7; ⌚1-3.30pm & 7.30pm-1.30am; Ⓜ Sol) This is how sherry bars should be – old-world vibe, drinks poured straight from the dusty wooden barrels, and none of the frenetic activity for which Huertas is famous. La Venencia is a *barrio* classic, with fine sherry from Sanlúcar and manzanilla from Jeréz, accompanied by a small selection of tapas with an Andalucian bent. Otherwise, there's no music, no flashy decorations; it's all about you, your *fino* (sherry) and your friends.

EL IMPERFECTO Bar, Live Music

(Map p198; Plaza de Matute 2; ⌚3pm-2am Mon-Thu, to 2.30am Fri & Sat; Ⓜ Antón Martín) Its name notwithstanding, the 'Imperfect One' is our ideal Huertas bar, with live jazz most Tuesdays at 9pm and a drinks menu as long as a saxophone, ranging from cocktails (€7) and spirits to milkshakes, teas and creative coffees.

Malasaña & Chueca

MUSEO CHICOTE Cocktail Bar

(Map p198; www.museo-chicote.com; Gran Vía 12; ⌚6pm-3am Mon-Thu, to 4am Fri & Sat; Ⓜ Gran Vía) The founder of this Madrid landmark is said to have invented more than a hundred cocktails, which the likes of Hemingway, Ava Gardner, Grace Kelly, Sophia Loren and Frank Sinatra have all enjoyed at one time or another. It's still frequented by film stars and top socialites, and it's at its best after midnight, when a lounge atmosphere takes over, couples cuddle on the curved benches and some of the city's best DJs do their stuff. We don't say this often, but if you haven't been here, you haven't really been to Madrid – it's that much of an icon.

CAFÉ COMERCIAL Cafe

(Map p202; Glorieta de Bilbao 7; ⌚7.30am-midnight Mon-Thu, 7.30am-2am Fri, 8.30am-2am Sat, 9am-midnight Sun; Ⓜ Bilbao) This glorious old Madrid cafe proudly fights a rearguard action against progress with heavy leather seats, abundant marble and old-style waiters. Café Comercial, which dates back to 1887, is the largest of the *barrio's* old cafes and has changed little since those days, although the clientele has broadened to include just about anyone, from writers and their laptops to old men playing chess.

GRAN CAFÉ DE GIJÓN Cafe

(Map p202; www.cafegijon.com; Paseo de los Recoletos 21; ⌚7am-1.30am; Ⓜ Chueca, Banco de España) This graceful old cafe has been serving coffee and meals since 1888 and has long been a favourite with Madrid's literati for a drink or a meal – *all* of Spain's great literary figures of the 20th century came here for coffee and *tertulias* (literary discussions).

Entertainment

All of the following publications and websites provide comprehensive, updated listings of showings at Madrid's theatres, cinemas and concert halls:

EsMadrid Magazine (www.esmadrid.com) Monthly tourist-office listings for concerts and other performances; available at tourist offices, some hotels and online.

In Madrid (www.in-madrid.com) Monthly English-language expat publication given out free (check the website for locations) with lots of information about what to see and do in town.

La Netro (www.madrid.lanetro.com) Comprehensive online guide to Madrid events.

What's on When (www.whatsonwhen.com) The Madrid page covers the highlights of sport and cultural activities, with information on getting tickets.

Live Music & Flamenco

Madrid may not be the spiritual home of flamenco, and its big names may feel more at home in the atmospheric flamenco taverns of Andalucía, but Madrid remains one of Spain's premier flamenco stages.

CORRAL DE LA MORERÍA Flamenco

(Map p198; ☎91 365 84 46; www.corraldelamoreria.com; Calle de la Morería 17; admission incl drink €42-45; ⏰8.30pm-2.30am, shows 9.30pm & 11.30pm Sun-Fri, 7pm, 10pm & midnight Sat; Ⓜ Ópera) This is one of the most prestigious flamenco stages in Madrid, with 50 years' experience as a leading flamenco venue and top performers most nights. The stage area has a rustic feel, and tables are pushed up close. We'd steer clear of the restaurant, which is overpriced (from €43), but the performances have a far better price:quality ratio.

LAS CARBONERAS Flamenco

(Map p198; ☎91 542 86 77; www.tablaolascarboneras.com; Plaza del Conde de Miranda 1; admission €30; ⏰shows 8.30pm & 10.30pm Mon-Thu, 8.30pm & 11pm Fri & Sat; Ⓜ Ópera, Sol, La Latina) Like most of the *tablaos* around town, this place sees far more tourists than locals, but the quality is nonetheless unimpeachable. It's not the place for gritty, soul-moving spontaneity, but it's still an excellent introduction and one of the few places that flamenco aficionados seem to have no complaints about.

LAS TABLAS Flamenco

(off Map p202; ☎91 542 05 20; www.lastablasmadrid.com; Plaza de España 9; admission €27; ⏰shows 10.30pm Sun-Thu, 8pm & 10pm Fri & Sat; Ⓜ Plaza de España) Las Tablas has a reputation for quality flamenco and reasonable prices; it could just be the best choice in town. Most nights you'll see a classic flamenco show, with plenty of throaty singing and soul-baring dancing.

CAFÉ CENTRAL Jazz

(Map p198; ☎91 369 41 43; www.cafecentralmadrid.com; Plaza del Ángel 10; admission €10-15; ⏰1.30pm-2.30am Sun-Thu, to 3.30am Fri & Sat; Ⓜ Antón Martín, Sol) In 2011, the respected jazz magazine *Down Beat* included this art-deco bar on the list of the world's best jazz clubs, the only place in Spain to earn the prestigious accolade (said by some to be the jazz equivalent of earning a Michelin star). With well over 9000 gigs

Tapas bar, Plaza de la Paja (p210)

NGOLF POMPE/GETTY IMAGES ©

under its belt, it rarely misses a beat. Big international names like Chano Domínguez, Tal Farlow and Wynton Marsalis have all played here, and you'll hear everything from Latin jazz and fusion to tango and classical jazz.

POPULART Jazz

(Map p198; ☎91 429 84 07; www.populart.es; Calle de las Huertas 22; admission free; 🕐6pm-2.30am Sun-Thu, to 3.30am Fri & Sat; M Antón Martín, Sol) One of Madrid's classic jazz clubs, this place offers a low-key atmosphere and top-quality music, which is mostly jazz with occasional blues, swing and even flamenco thrown into the mix.

CAFÉ BERLIN Jazz

(Map p198; ☎91 521 57 52; Calle de Jacometrezo 4; admission €8; 🕐7pm-2.30am Tue-Sun Sep-Jul; M Callao, Santo Domingo) El Berlín has been something of a Madrid jazz stalwart since the 1950s and it's the kind of place that serious jazz fans rave about as the most authentic in town – it's all about classic jazz here, with none of the fusion performances that you find elsewhere. The art-deco interior ads to the charm and the headline acts are a who's-who of world jazz; in the past Al Foster (Miles Davis' drummer), Santiago de Muela and the Calento Jazz Orchestra have all taken to the stage.

COSTELLO CAFÉ & NITECLUB Live Music

(Map p198; www.costelloclub.com; Calle del Caballero de Gracia 10; admission €5-10; 🕐6pm-1am Sun-Wed, to 2.30am Thu-Sat; M Gran Vía) Very cool. Costello Café & Niteclub is smooth-as-silk ambience wedded with an innovative mix of pop, rock and fusion in Warholesque surrounds. There's live music at 9.30pm every night except Sundays, with resident and visiting DJs keeping you on your feet until closing time from Thursday to Saturday.

CONTRACLUB Live Music

(Map p198; ☎91 365 55 45; www.contraclub.es; Calle de Bailén 16; admission €6-12; 🕐10pm-6am Wed-Sat; M La Latina) ContraClub is

Left: Flamenco artists perform at Corral de la Morería (p217); **Below:** Latin jazz band, Populart

LEFT: BRUCE YUANYUE BI/GETTY IMAGES ©; BELOW: LONELY PLANET/GETTY IMAGES ©

a crossover live music venue and nightclub, with live flamenco on Wednesday and an eclectic mix of other live music (jazz, blues, world music and rock) from Thursday to Saturday. After the live acts (which start at 10.30pm), the resident DJs serve up equally eclectic beats (indie, pop, funk and soul) to make sure you don't move elsewhere.

Football

ESTADIO SANTIAGO BERNABÉU Football

(902 291709, 91 398 43 00; www.realmadrid.com; Avenida de Concha Espina 1; tour adult/child €19/13; 10am-7pm Mon-Sat, 10.30am-6.30pm Sun, except match days; M Santiago Bernabéu) The home of **Real Madrid**, Estadio Santiago Bernabéu is a temple to football and is one of the world's great sporting arenas; watching a game here is akin to a pilgrimage for sports fans. When the players strut their stuff with 80,000 passionate *madrileños* in attendance, you'll get chills down your spine. If you're fortunate enough to be in town when Real Madrid wins a major trophy, head to Plaza de la Cibeles and wait for the all-night party to begin.

For a self-guided **tour** of the stadium, buy your ticket at ticket window 10 (next to Gate 7). The tour takes you through the extraordinary **Exposición de Trofeos** (Trophy Exhibit), the presidential box, the press room, dressing rooms and the players' tunnel, and even onto the pitch itself. On match days, tours cease five hours before the game is scheduled to start, although the Exposición de Trofeos is open until two hours before game time.

Tickets for matches start at around €40 and run up to the rafters for major matches. Unless you book through a ticket agency, turn up at the ticket office at Gate 42 on Avenida de Concha Espina early in the week before a scheduled game. Tickets can also be bought online

Bullfighting

Love it or loath it, bullfighting is still a big part of Madrid life, and from the **Fiesta de San Isidro** in mid-May until the end of October, Spain's top bullfighters come to swing their capes at **Plaza de Toros Monumental de Las Ventas** (**☎91 725 18 57; Calle de Alcalá 237; admission free; tour adult/child €9/6; ⏰10am-2pm & 3-7pm Jul-Sep, 10am-6pm Oct-Jun; Ⓜ Las Ventas**), one of the largest rings in the bullfighting world. In one afternoon, there are generally six bulls and three toreros dressed in the dazzling *trajede luces* (suit of lights). It's a one-sided event – the death of the bull is close to inevitable – but it's still a dangerous business, as well as a festive occasion for aficionados. For a more in-depth discussion of bullfighting, turn to p349.

at www.realmadrid.com, while the all-important telephone number for booking tickets (which you later pick up at Gate 42) is ☎902 324324, which only works if you're calling from within Spain.

The stadium is north of the city, along the Paseo de la Castellana, around 3.5km north of the Plaza de la Cibeles.

Shopping

EL RASTRO Market

(Map p198; Calle de la Ribera de Curtidores; ⏰8am-3pm Sun; Ⓜ La Latina, Puerta de Toledo, Tirso de Molina) A Sunday morning at El Rastro is a Madrid institution. You could easily spend an entire morning inching your way down the Calle de la Ribera de Curtidores and through the maze of streets that hosts El Rastro flea market every Sunday morning. Cheap clothes, luggage, old flamenco records, even older photos of Madrid, faux designer purses, grungy T-shirts, household goods and electronics are the main fare. For every 10 pieces of junk, there's a real gem (a lost masterpiece, an Underwood typewriter) waiting to be found.

A word of warning: pickpockets love El Rastro as much as everyone else, so keep a tight hold on your belongings and don't keep valuables in easy-to-reach pockets.

EL FLAMENCO VIVE Flamenco

(Map p198; www.elflamencovive.es; Calle Conde de Lemos 7; ⏰10.30am-2pm & 5-9pm Mon-Sat; Ⓜ Ópera) This temple to flamenco has it all, from guitars and songbooks to well-priced CDs, polka-dotted dancing costumes, shoes, colourful plastic jewellery and literature about flamenco.

GIL Accessories

(Map p198; Carrera de San Jerónimo 2; ⏰9.30am-1.30pm & 4.30-8pm Mon-Sat; Ⓜ Sol) You don't see them much these days, but the exquisite fringed and embroidered *mantones* and *mantoncillos* (traditional Spanish shawls worn by women on grand occasions) and delicate *mantillas* (Spanish veils) are stunning and uniquely Spanish gifts. Gil also sells *abanicos* (Spanish fans). Inside this dark shop, dating back to 1880, the sales clerks still wait behind a long counter to attend to you; the service hasn't changed in years and that's no bad thing.

MARÍA CABELLO Wine

(Map p198; Calle de Echegaray 19; ⏰9.30am-2.30pm & 5.30-9pm Mon-Fri, 10am-2.30pm & 6.30-9.30pm Sat; Ⓜ Sevilla, Antón Martín) All wine shops should be like this. This family-run corner shop really knows its wines and the interior has scarcely changed since 1913, with wooden shelves and even a faded ceiling fresco. There are fine wines in abundance (mostly Spanish, and a few foreign bottles), with some 500 labels on show or tucked away out the back.

AGATHA RUIZ DE LA PRADA Fashion

(Map p202; www.agatharuizdelaprada.com; Calle de Serrano 27; ⏰10am-8.30pm Mon-Sat; Ⓜ Serrano) This boutique has to be seen to be believed, with pinks, yellows and oranges everywhere you turn. It's fun and exuberant, but not just for kids. It also has serious and highly original fashion.

ORIOL BALAGUER Food

(www.oriolbalaguer.com; Calle de José Ortega y Gasset 44; ⌚9am-9pm Mon-Sat, to 2.30pm Sun; Ⓜ Nuñez de Balboa) Catalan pastry chef Oriol Balaguer has a formidable CV – he worked in the kitchens of Ferran Adrià in Catalonia and won the prize for the World's Best Dessert (his 'Seven Textures of Chocolate') in 2001. His chocolate boutique is presented like a small art gallery, except that it's dedicated to exquisite, finely crafted chocolate collections and cakes. You'll never be able to buy ordinary chocolate again.

PATRIMONIO COMUNAL OLIVARERO Food

(Map p202; www.pco.es; Calle de Mejía Lequerica 1; ⌚10am-2pm & 5-8pm Mon-Fri, 10am-2pm Sat; Ⓜ Alonso Martínez) To catch the essence of the country's olive-oil varieties (Spain is the world's largest producer), Patrimonio Comunal Olivarero is perfect. With examples of the extra-virgin variety (and nothing else) from all over Spain, you could spend ages agonising over the choices.

Information

Centro de Turismo de Madrid (☎91 588 16 36; www.esmadrid.com; Plaza Mayor 27; ⌚9.30am-8.30pm; Ⓜ Sol) Excellent city tourist office with a smaller office underneath Plaza de Colón and information points at Plaza de la Cibeles **(Plaza de la Cibeles; ⌚9.30am-8.30pm; Ⓜ Banco de España)**, Plaza de Callao **(Plaza del Callao; ⌚9am-midnight; Ⓜ Callao)**, outside the Centro de Arte Reina Sofía **(cnr Calle de Santa Isabel & Plaza del Emperador Carlos V; ⌚9.30am-8.30pm; Ⓜ Atocha)** and at the T4 terminal at Barajas airport.

Getting There & Away

Air

Madrid's Barajas Airport **(☎902 404 704; www.aena.es; Ⓜ Aeropuerto T1, T2 & T3; Aeropuerto T4)** lies 15km northeast of the city.

Bus

Estación Sur de Autobuses **(☎91 468 42 00; www.estaciondeautobuses.com; Calle de Méndez Álvaro 83; Ⓜ Méndez Álvaro)**, just south of the M30 ring road, is the city's principal bus station. To get here, take Calle de Méndez Alvaro around 2km southeast of Atocha train station. It serves most destinations to the south and many in other parts of the country. Most bus companies have a ticket office here, even if their buses depart from elsewhere.

Car & Motorcycle

Madrid is surrounded by two main ring roads, the outermost M40 and the inner M30; there are also two partial ring roads, the M45 and the more-distant M50. The R5 and R3 are part of a series of toll roads built to ease traffic jams.

El Rastro flea market, Madrid
KRZYSZTOF DYDYNSKI/GETTY IMAGES ©

Train

Madrid is served by two main train stations. The bigger of the two is Puerta de Atocha (**M Atocha Renfe**), at the southern end of the city centre, while Chamartín (**M Chamartín**) lies in the north of the city. The bulk of trains for Spanish destinations depart from Atocha, especially those going south. International services arrive at and leave from Chamartín. For bookings, contact Renfe (**902 240202; www.renfe.es**) at either train station.

High-speed **Tren de Alta Velocidad Española (AVE)** services connect Madrid with Seville (via Córdoba), Valladolid (via Segovia), Toledo, Valencia (via Cuenca), Málaga and Barcelona (via Zaragoza and Huesca or Tarragona). Most high-speed services operate from Madrid's Puerta de Atocha station. The Madrid–Segovia/Valladolid service leaves from the Chamartín station.

Getting Around

To/From the Airport

A **taxi** to the city centre will cost you around €25 (up to €35 from T4), depending on traffic and where you're going; in addition to what the meter says, you pay a €5.50 airport supplement.

Exprés Aeropuerto **(Airport Express; www.emtmadrid.es; €5; 24hr)** The recently inaugurated Exprés Aeropuerto runs between Puerta de Atocha train station and the airport. Buses run every 13 to 23 minutes from 6am to 11.30pm, and every 35 minutes throughout the rest of the night. The trip takes 40 minutes. From 11.55pm until 5.35am, departures are from the Plaza de Cibeles, not the train station.

Metro **(www.metromadrid.es)** Line 8 of the Metro runs from the airport to the Nuevos Ministerios transport interchange on Paseo de la Castella, where line 8 connects with lines 10 and 6. It operates from 6.05am to 2am. A one-way ticket to/from the airport costs €4.50 (10-trip Metrobús ticket €12).The journey to Nuevos Ministerios takes around 15 minutes, around 25 minutes from T4.

Bus

Buses operated by Empresa Municipal de Transportes de Madrid **(EMT; 902 507 850; www.emtmadrid.es)** travel along most city routes regularly between about 6.30am and 11.30pm. There are 26 night-bus *búhos* (owls) routes operating from midnight to 6am, with all routes originating in Plaza de la Cibeles.

Metro

Madrid's modern metro (p222), Europe's second-largest, is a fast, efficient and safe way to navigate Madrid, and generally easier than getting to grips with bus routes. There are 11 colour-coded lines in central Madrid, in addition to the modern southern suburban MetroSur system, as well as lines heading east to the major population centres of Pozuelo and Boadilla del Monte. The metro operates from 6.05am to 2am, although there is talk of ceasing the service at midnight. A single ticket costs €1.50; a 10-ride Metrobús ticket is €12.

Taxi

You can pick up a taxi at ranks throughout town or simply flag one down. Flag fall is €2.15 from 6am to 10pm daily, €2.20 from 10pm to 6am Sunday to Friday, and €3.10 from 10pm Saturday to 6am Sunday. You pay between €1 and €1.20 per kilometre depending on the hour. Several supplementary charges, usually posted inside the taxi, apply; these include €5.50 to/from the airport; €3 from taxi ranks at train and bus stations, and €3 to/from the Parque Ferial Juan Carlos I. There's no charge for luggage.

Radio-Teléfono Taxi (**91 547 82 00; www.radiotelefono-taxi.com**)

AROUND MADRID

San Lorenzo de El Escorial

POP 18,447 / ELEV 1032M

The imposing palace and monastery complex of San Lorenzo de El Escorial is an impressive place, rising up from the foothills of the mountains that shelter Madrid from the north and west. The one-time royal getaway is now a prim little town overflowing with quaint shops, restaurants and hotels catering primarily to throngs of weekending *madrileños*. The fresh, cool air here has been drawing city dwellers since the complex was first ordered to be built by Felipe II in the 16th century. Most visitors come on a day trip from Madrid.

Sights

The main entrance to the **Real Monasterio de San Lorenzo** (☎91 890 78 18; www.patrimonionacional.es; adult/concession €10/5, guide/audioguide €7/4, EU citizens free 5-8pm Wed & Thu; ⏰10am-8pm Apr-Sep, 10am-6pm Oct-Mar, closed Mon) is on its western facade. Above the gateway a statue of St Lawrence stands guard, holding a symbolic gridiron, the instrument of his martyrdom (he was roasted alive on one). From here you'll first enter the **Patio de los Reyes**, which houses the statues of the six kings of Judah.

Directly ahead lies the sombre **basilica**. As you enter, look up at the unusual flat vaulting by the choir stalls. Once inside the church proper, turn left to view Benvenuto Cellini's white Carrara marble statue of Christ crucified (1576).

The remainder of the ground floor contains various treasures, including some tapestries and an El Greco painting – impressive as it is, it's a far cry from El Greco's dream of decorating the whole complex. Continue downstairs to the northeastern corner of the complex. You pass through the **Museo de Arquitectura** and the **Museo de Pintura**. The former tells (in Spanish) the story of how the complex was built; the latter contains a range of 16th- and 17th-century Italian, Spanish and Flemish art.

Head upstairs into a gallery around the eastern part of the complex known as the **Palacio de Felipe II** or **Palacio de los Austrias**. You'll then descend to the 17th-century **Panteón de los Reyes** (Crypt of the Kings), where almost all Spain's monarchs since Carlos I are interred.

Information

Tourist Office (☎91 890 53 13; www.sanlorenzoturismo.org; Calle de Grimaldi 4; ⏰10am-2pm & 3-6pm Tue-Sat, 10am-2pm Sun)

Getting There & Away

Every 15 minutes (every 30 minutes on weekends) buses 661 and 664 run to El Escorial (€3.55, one hour) from platform 30 at the Intercambiador de Autobuses de Moncloa in Madrid.

Real Monasterio de San Lorenzo

Right: Parque del Buen Retiro (p201), Madrid; **Below:** Old Town gate, Toledo
BELOW: OLIVER STREWE/GETTY IMAGES ©; RIGHT: LONELY PLANET/GETTY IMAGES ©

San Lorenzo de El Escorial is 59km northwest of Madrid and it should take about 40 minutes to drive there. Take the A6 highway to the M600, then follow the signs to El Escorial.

A few dozen Renfe (902 240202; www.renfe.es) C8 *cercanías* make the trip daily from Madrid's Atocha or Chamartín train station to El Escorial (€1.65, one hour).

Toledo

POP 83,110 / ELEV 655M

Though one of the smaller of Spain's provincial capitals, Toledo looms large in the nation's history and consciousness as a religious centre, bulwark of the Spanish church, and once-flourishing symbol of a multicultural medieval society. The Old Town today is a treasure chest of churches, museums, synagogues and mosques set amongst a labyrinth of narrow streets, plazas and hidden inner patios in a lofty setting high above Río Tajo.

Sights

CATEDRAL Cathedral
(Plaza del Ayuntamiento; adult/child €7/free; 10.30am-6.30pm Mon-Sat, 2-6.30pm Sun) Toledo's cathedral reflects the city's historical significance as the heart of Catholic Spain.

From the earliest days of the Visigothic occupation, the current site of the cathedral has been a centre of worship. During Muslim rule, it contained Toledo's central mosque, destroyed in 1085. Dating from the 13th century and essentially a Gothic structure, the cathedral is nevertheless a melting pot of styles, including Mudéjar and Renaissance.

The heavy interior, with sturdy columns dividing the space into five naves, is on a monumental scale. Every one of the numerous side chapels has artistic treasures.

The **tesoro**, however, deals in treasure of the glittery kind. It's dominated by the extraordinary Custodia de Arfe: with 18kg

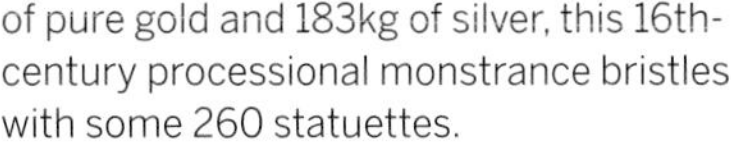

of pure gold and 183kg of silver, this 16th-century processional monstrance bristles with some 260 statuettes.

The high altar sits in the extravagant **Capilla Mayor**, whose masterpiece is the *retablo* (altarpiece), with painted wooden sculptures depicting scenes from the lives of Christ and the Virgin Mary; it's flanked by royal tombs. The oldest of the cathedral's magnificent stained-glass pieces is the rose window above the **Puerta del Reloj**. Behind the main altar lies a mesmerising piece of 18th-century *churrigueresco* (lavish Baroque ornamentation), the **Transparente**, which is illuminated by a light well carved into the dome above.

The highlight of all, however, is the **sacristía** (sacristy), which contains a gallery with paintings by such masters as El Greco, Zurbarán, Caravaggio, Titian, Rafael and Velázquez.

ALCÁZAR Fortress, Museum

(Museo del Ejército; Calle Alféreces Provisionales; adult/child €5/free; ⏲10am-9pm Thu-Tue Jun-Sep, to 7pm Oct-May) At the highest point in the city looms the foreboding Alcázar. Abd ar-Rahman III raised an *al-qasr* (fortress) here in the 10th century, which was thereafter altered by the Christians. Alonso Covarrubias rebuilt it as a royal residence for Carlos I, but the court moved to Madrid and the fortress eventually became a military academy.

Rebuilt under Franco, it has recently been reopened as an absolutely enormous military museum, with strict staff barking orders adding to the martial experience.

SINAGOGA DEL TRÁNSITO Synagogue

(http://museosefardi.mcu.es; Calle Samuel Leví; adult/child €3/1.50, with Museo del Greco €5; ⏲9.30am-8pm Tue-Sat Apr-Sep, to 6.30pm Oct-Mar, 10am-3pm Sun) This magnificent synagogue was built in 1355 by special permission of Pedro I. Toledo's former *judería* (Jewish quarter) was once home to 10 synagogues and comprised some 10% of the walled city's area. The synagogue now houses the **Museo Sefardí**.

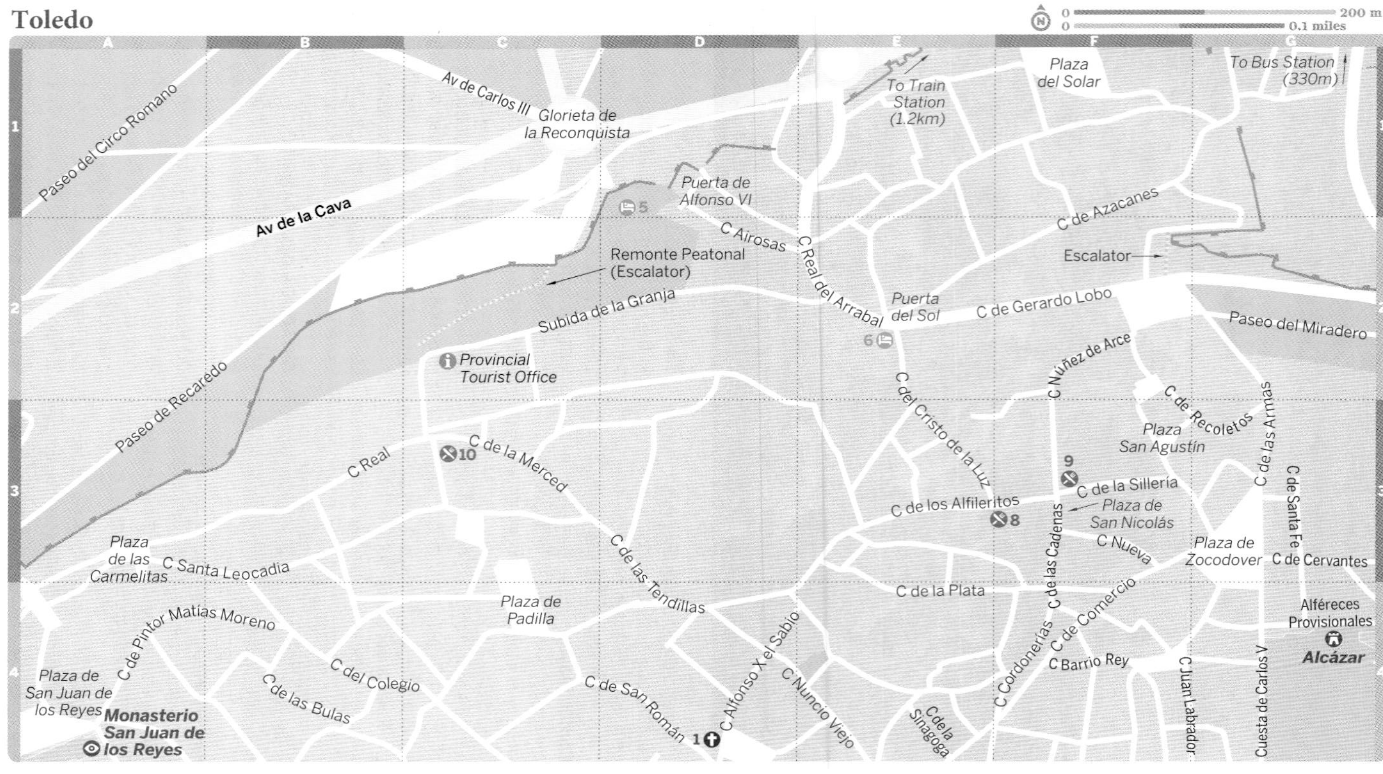
Toledo
0 200 m
0 0.1 miles
A
B
C
D
E
F
G
1
2
3
4
Paseo del Circo Romano
Av de la Cava
Av de Carlos III
Glorieta de la Reconquista
Puerta de Alfonso VI
5
C Airosas
Remonte Peatonal (Escalator)
Subida de la Granja
Paseo de Recaredo
Provincial Tourist Office
C Real
10
C de la Merced
Plaza de las Carmelitas
C Santa Leocadia
C de Pintor Matías Moreno
Plaza de San Juan de los Reyes
Monasterio San Juan de los Reyes
C del Colegio
C de las Bulas
Plaza de Padilla
C de las Tendillas
C de San Román
1
C Alfonso X el Sabio
C Nuncio Viejo
C de la Sinagoga
To Train Station (1.2km)
C Real del Arrabal
Puerta del Sol
6
C del Cristo de la Luz
C de los Alfileritos
8
C de la Plata
C Cordonerías
C de las Cadenas
9
C de la Sillería
Plaza de San Nicolás
C Nueva
C de Comercio
C Barrio Rey
Plaza del Solar
C de Azacanes
Escalator
C de Gerardo Lobo
C Núñez de Arce
C de Recoletos
Plaza San Agustín
Plaza de Zocodover
C Juan Labrador
To Bus Station (330m)
Paseo del Miradero
C de las Armas
C de Santa Fe
C de Cervantes
Alféreces Provisionales
Alcázar
Cuesta de Carlos V

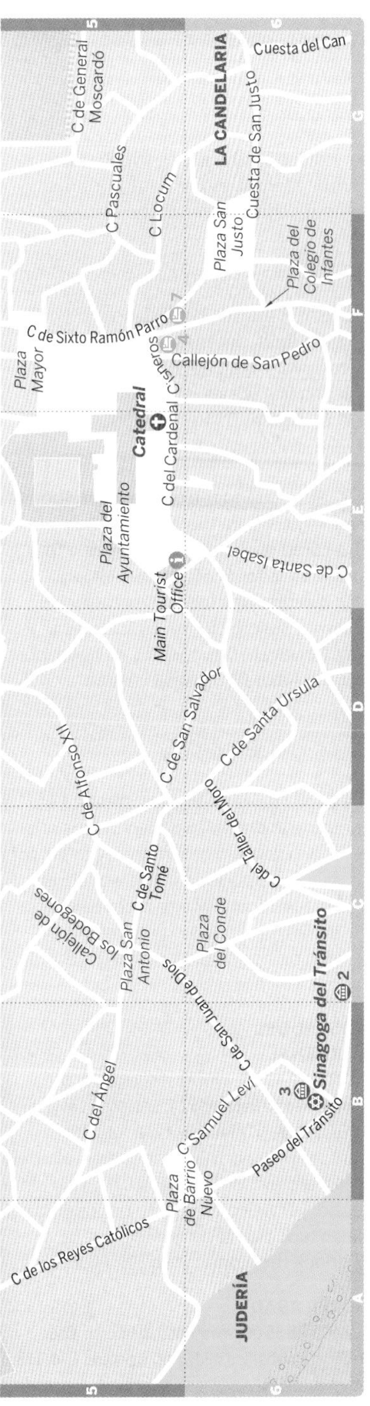

Toledo

Top Sights

Sights

Sleeping

Eating

Exhibits provide an insight into the history of Jewish culture in Spain, and include archaeological finds, a memorial garden, costumes and ceremonial artefacts.

MUSEO DEL GRECO Museum, Gallery

(925 22 44 05; http://museodelgreco.mcu.es; Paseo del Tránsito; adult/child €3/1.50, with Sinagoga del Tránsito €5; 9.30am-8pm Tue-Sat Apr-Sep, to 6.30pm Oct-Mar, 10am-3pm Sun) In the early 20th century, an aristocrat bought up what he thought was El Greco's house and did a stunning job of returning it to period style. He was wrong, but this museum is well worth visiting anyway. As well as the house itself, with its lovely patio, there are excavated cellars from a Jewish-quarter palace and a good selection of paintings, including a set of the apostles by El Greco, a Zurbarán, and works by El Greco's son and various followers.

MONASTERIO SAN JUAN DE LOS REYES Monastery

(Calle San Juan de los Reyes 2; admission €2.50; 10am-6.45pm) This imposing 15th-century Franciscan monastery and church of San Juan de los Reyes was provocatively founded in the heart of the Jewish quarter

Toledo Top Tips

TAKE THE ESCALATOR

A **remonte peatonal** (7am-10pm Mon-Fri, 8am-2am Sat, 8am-11pm Sun), which starts near the Puerta de Alfonso VI and ends near the Monasterio de Santo Domingo El Antiguo, is a good way to avoid the steep uphill climb to reach the historic quarter of town.

PULSERA TURÍSTICA

The Pulsera Turística is a bracelet (€8) that gets you into six key Toledo sights, all of which cost €2.50 on their own. There's no time limit, but make sure it doesn't fall off! Buy the bracelet at any of the sights covered, which are Monasterio San Juan de los Reyes, Sinagoga de Santa María la Blanca, Iglesia de Santo Tomé, Iglesia del Salvador, Iglesia San Ildefonso and Mezquita Cristo de la Luz.

TOP VISTAS

For superb city views, head over the Puente de Alcántara to the other side of Río Tajo and head along the road that rises to your right, where the vista becomes more marvellous with every step. You can also climb the towers at the **Iglesia San Ildefonso** (Iglesia de los Jesuitas; Plaza Juan de Mariana 1; admission €2.50; 10am-6.45pm), surely one of the few churches to boast a Coke machine, for more camera-clicking views of the cathedral and Alcázar. For a meal with superb city panoramas, you can't beat **La Ermita** (www.laermitarestaurante.com; Carretera de Circunvalación; mains €18-22, degustation menu €48), with a short quality menu of elaborate Spanish cuisine.

by the Catholic Kings Isabel and Fernando to demonstrate the supposed supremacy of their faith.

The highlight is the amazing two-level cloister, a harmonious fusion of late ('flamboyant') Gothic downstairs and Mudéjar architecture upstairs, with superb statuary, arches, vaulting, elaborate pinnacles and gargoyles surrounding a lush garden with orange trees and roses.

Sleeping

CASA DE CISNEROS Boutique Hotel **€€**
(925 22 88 28; www.hostal-casa-de-cisneros.com; Calle Cardenal Cisneros; s/d incl breakfast €55/75;) Right by the cathedral, this lovely 16th-century house was once the home of the cardinal and Grand Inquisitor Cisneros (often known as Ximénes). It's a top choice, with cosy, seductive rooms with original wooden beams and walls and voguish bathrooms. Guests get to visit and sip a wine in the wonderful downstairs space where archaeological works have revealed the remains of Roman baths and part of an 11th-century Moorish palace.

HOSTAL DEL CARDENAL Historic Hotel **€€**
(925 22 49 00; www.hostaldelcardenal.com; Paseo de Recaredo 24; s/d incl breakfast €90/120;) This wonderful 18th-century mansion has soft ochre-coloured walls, arches and columns. The rooms are grand, yet welcoming, with dark furniture, plush fabrics and parquet floors. Several overlook the glorious terraced gardens.

HOTEL ABAD Hotel **€€**
(925 28 35 00; www.hotelabad.com; Calle Real del Arrabal 1; d midweek/weekend €74/123;

P) Compact, pretty, and pleasing, this hotel sits on the lower slopes of the Old Town and offers good value, with prices usually lower than those we list here. Rooms blend modern comfort with exposed old brick very successfully; some have small balconies, but those at the back are notably quieter.

LA POSADA DE MANOLO Boutique Hotel **€€**
(925 28 22 50; www.laposadademanolo.com; Calle de Sixto Ramón Parro 8; s/d incl breakfast €46/76;) This memorable hotel has themed each floor with furnishings and decor reflecting one of the three cultures of Toledo: Christian, Islamic and Jewish. There are stunning views of the Old Town and cathedral from the terrace.

Eating

ALFILERITOS 24 Modern Spanish **€€**
(www.alfileritos24.com; Calle de los Alfileritos 24; mains €15-21, bar food €6-11; bar food 9.30am-midnight, to 1am Fri & Sat) The 14th-century surroundings of columns, beams and barrel-vault ceilings are snazzily coupled with modern artwork and bright dining rooms in an atrium space spread over four floors. The menu demonstrates an innovative flourish in the kitchen, with dishes like red-tuna tartare with seaweed and guacamole, and loins of venison with baked-in-the-bag Reineta apple.

LA ABADÍA Tapas **€**
(www.abadiatoledo.com; Plaza de San Nicolás 3; raciones €4-15) In a former 16th-century palace, this atmospheric bar and restaurant is ideal for romancing couples. Arches, niches and subtle lighting are spread over a warren of brick-and-stone-clad rooms. The menu includes lightweight dishes and tapas portions – perfect for small (distracted) appetites.

TABERNA EL EMBRUJO Tapas **€€**
(Calle Santa Leocadia 6; raciones €8-22) Near the top of the escalator up to the Old Town, this friendly bar has an appealing stone-clad dining area and an outdoor terrace across the street. It does a great line in high-quality deli-style tapas, with tasty tomato salads, delicious foie and toothsome seafood options, all served with a smile.

Information

Main Tourist Office (925 25 40 30; www.toledo-turismo.com; Plaza del Ayuntamiento; 10am-6pm)

Provincial Tourist Office (www.diputoledo.es; Subida de la Granja; 10am-5pm Mon-Sat, to 3pm Sun)

El Acueducto (p236), Segovia
OLIVER STREWE/GETTY IMAGES ©

Old city walls and cathedral, Ávila

MAREMAGNUM/GETTY IMAGES ©

Getting There & Away

For most major destinations, you'll need to backtrack to Madrid.

From Toledo's **bus station** (**Avenida de Castilla La Mancha**), buses depart for Madrid roughly every half-hour (from €5.25, one hour), some direct, some via villages. There are also services to Albacete (€15, 2¾ hours) and Cuenca (€12.80, 2¼ hours).

From the pretty **train station** (**902 24 02 02; Paseo de la Rosa**) high-speed AVE services run every hour or so to Madrid (€10.60, 30 minutes).

Getting Around

BUS Buses (€1.40) run between Plaza de Zocodover and the bus station (bus 5) and train station (buses 61 and 62). Bus 12 does a circuit within the Old Town.

CAR Driving in the Old Town is a nightmare. There are underground carparks throughout the area and several large free carparks at the base of the Old Town. Zones blocked off by bollards can be accessed if you have a hotel reservation..

Ávila

POP 59,010 / ELEV 1130M

Ávila's old city, surrounded by imposing city walls comprising eight monumental gates, 88 watchtowers and more than 2500 turrets, is one of the best-preserved medieval bastions in all Spain. In winter, when an icy wind whistles in off the plains, the old city huddles behind the high stone walls as if seeking protection from the harsh Castilian climate. At night, when the walls are illuminated to magical effect, you'll wonder if you've stumbled into a fairy tale. Within the walls, Ávila can appear caught in a time warp. It's a deeply religious city that, for centuries, has drawn pilgrims to the cult of Santa Teresa de Ávila, with many churches, convents and high-walled palaces. As such, Ávila is the essence of Castilla, the epitome of old Spain.

Sights

MURALLAS Walls

(adult/child €4/2.50; 10am-8pm Tue-Sun)

Ávila's splendid 12th-century walls rank among the world's best-preserved medieval defensive perimeters. Raised to a height of 12m between the 11th and 12th centuries, the walls stretch for 2.5km atop the remains of earlier Roman and

Muslim battlements. They have been much restored and modified, with various Gothic and Renaissance touches, and even some Roman stones re-used in the construction.

Two sections of the walls can be climbed – a 300m stretch that can be accessed from just inside the **Puerta del Alcázar**, and a longer 1300m stretch that runs the length of the old city's northern perimeter, in the process connecting the two access points at **Puerta de los Leales** (10am-8pm Tue-Sun for both) and **Puerta del Puente Adaja**; it's possible to climb down (but not up) from the latter stretch at Puerta del Carmen.

FREE CONVENTO DE SANTA TERESA Museum

(8.45am-1.30pm & 3.30-9pm Tue-Sun) Built in 1636 over the saint's birthplace, this is the epicentre of the cult surrounding Teresa. There are three attractions in one here: the church (built around the room where the saint was born), a relics room and museum. Inside the main church, to the left of the main altar as you enter, the room where Teresa was born in 1515 is now a chapel smothered in gold and lorded over by a baroque altar by Gregorio Fernández; it features a statue of the saint. An adjoining relics room is crammed with Teresa relics, some of which, such as her ring finger (complete with ring), border on the macabre; that didn't stop Franco from keeping it by his bedside throughout his rule. There's also a basement museum dedicated to the saint, accessible from Calle Aizpuru.

CATEDRAL Cathedral

(Plaza de la Catedral; admission €4; 10am-7.30pm Mon-Fri, 10am-8pm Sat, noon-6.30pm Sun) Ávila's 12th-century cathedral is at once a house of worship and an ingenious fortress: its stout granite apse forms the central bulwark in the heavily fortified eastern wall of the old city. Although the main facade hints at the cathedral's 12th-century, Romanesque origins, the church was finished 400 years later in a predominantly Gothic style, making it the first Gothic church in Spain.

Who was Santa Teresa?

Teresa de Cepeda y Ahumada, probably the most important woman in the history of the Spanish Catholic Church, was born in Ávila on 28 March 1515, one of 10 children of a merchant family. Raised by Augustinian nuns after her mother's death, she joined the Carmelite order at age 20. After her early, undistinguished years as a nun, she was shaken by a vision of hell in 1560, which crystallised her true vocation: she would reform the Carmelites.

In stark contrast to the opulence of the church in 16th-century Spain, her reforms called for the church to return to its roots, taking on the suffering and simple lifestyle of Jesus Christ. The Carmelites demanded the strictest of piety, went *descalzadas* (barefoot), lived in extremely basic conditions and even employed flagellation to atone for their sins. Not surprisingly, all this proved extremely unpopular with the mainstream Catholic Church.

With the help of many supporters, Teresa founded convents of the Carmelitas Descalzas (Shoeless Carmelites) all over Spain. She also co-opted San Juan de la Cruz (St John of the Cross) to undertake a similar reform in the masculine order, a task that earned him several stints of incarceration. Santa Teresa's writings were first published in 1588 and proved enormously popular, perhaps partly for their earthy style. She died in 1582 in Alba de Tormes, where she is buried. She was canonised by Pope Gregory XV in 1622.

MONASTERIO DE LA ENCARNACIÓN Monastery
(Calle de la Encarnación; admission €2; 9.30am-1.30pm & 3.30-6pm Mon-Fri, 10am-1pm & 4-6pm Sat & Sun) North of the city walls, this Renaissance monastery is where Santa Teresa took on the monastic life and lived for 27 years. There are three main rooms open to the public. The most interesting is the third (up the stairs where the saint is said to have had a vision of the baby Jesus), where you'll find relics such as the piece of wood used by Teresa as a pillow and the chair upon which St John of the Cross made his confessions. To reach here, head north from Plaza de Fuente el Sol, via Calle de la Encarnación, for approximately 500m.

Sleeping

HOTEL EL RASTRO Historic Hotel €
(920 35 22 25; www.elrastroavila.com; Calle Cepedas; s/d €35/55;) This superb choice occupies a former 16th-century palace with original natural stone, exposed brickwork and a warm earth-toned colour scheme exuding a calm understated elegance. Each room has a different form, but most have high ceilings and plenty of space. Rooms 205 to 209 are more modern – avoid these to really soak up the atmosphere.

HOTEL LAS LEYENDAS Historic Hotel €€
(920 35 20 42; www.lasleyendas.es; Calle de Francisco Gallego 3; s/d €56/79;) Occupying the house of 16th-century Ávila nobility, this intimate hotel overflows with period touches wedded to modern amenities. Some rooms have views out across the plains, others look onto an internal garden. Some rooms have original wooden beams, exposed brick and stonework, others are more modern with muted tones.

Eating

HOSTERÍA LAS CANCELAS Castilian €€
(920 21 22 49; www.lascancelas.com; Calle de la Cruz Vieja 6; mains €16-25; Feb-Dec) This courtyard restaurant occupies a delightful interior patio dating back to the 15th century; across the road, the summer-only terrace occupies part of a former cathedral courtyard. Renowned for being a mainstay of Ávila cuisine, traditional meals are prepared with a salutary attention to detail; the *solomillo con salsa al ron y nueces* (sirloin in a rum and walnut sauce) is a rare deviation from tradition.

LA BRUJA Contemporary Castilian €€
(920 35 24 96; www.la-bruja.es; Paseo del Rastro 1; menú del día €14.50, mains €15-23) In the shadow of the old city walls, 'The Witch' combines a beautifully adapted 16th-century space with creative tapas that have won a host of gastronomic awards and meat and fish mainstays.

MESÓN DEL RASTRO Castilian €€
(www.elrastroavila.com; Plaza del Rastro 1; menú del día €13, mains €9-22; Thu-Sat, lunch only Sun-Wed) The dark-wood beamed interior announces immediately that this is a bastion of robust Castilian cooking and has been since 1881. Expect delicious mainstays such as *judías del barco de Ávila* and *cordero asado*, mercifully light salads and, regrettably, the occasional coach tour.

Drinking

LA BODEGUITA DE SAN SEGUNDO Wine Bar
(www.vinoavila.com; Calle de San Segundo 19; 11am-midnight Thu-Tue) Situated in the 16th-century Casa de la Misericordia, this superb wine bar is standing-room only most nights and more tranquil in the quieter afternoon hours. Its wine list is renowned throughout Spain with over 1000 wines to choose from, with tapas-sized servings of cheeses and cured meats the perfect accompaniment.

Information

Centro de Recepción de Visitantes (920 35 40 00, ext 790; www.avilaturismo.com; Avenida de Madrid 39; 9am-8pm) Municipal tourist office.

Regional Tourist Office (☎920 21 13 87; www.turismocastillayleon.com; Casa de las Carnicerías, Calle de San Segundo 17; ⏰9am-8pm)

Getting There & Away

BUS Frequent services to Segovia (€5, one hour), Salamanca (€6.08, 1½ hours) and Madrid (€8.06, 1½ hours); a couple of daily buses also head for the main towns in the Sierra de Gredos.

CAR & MOTORCYCLE From Madrid the driving time is around one hour; the toll costs €8.

TRAIN There are services to Madrid (from €6.80, 1¼ to two hours), Salamanca (from €8.55,1¼ hours, eight daily) and León (from €24.80, three hours, three daily).

Salamanca

POP 153,470

Whether floodlit by night or bathed in the light of sunset, there's something magical about Salamanca. This is a city of rare beauty, awash with golden sandstone overlaid with ochre-tinted Latin inscriptions, showcasing a virtuosity of plateresque and Renaissance styles. The monumental sights are many, and the exceptional Plaza Mayor (stunningly illuminated at night) an unforgettable highlight. This is also Castile's liveliest city; home to a massive Spanish and international student population that throngs the streets at night and provides the city with so much vitality.

Sights & Activities

UNIVERSIDAD CIVIL Historic Building

(Calle de los Libreros; adult/child €4/2, Mon morning free; ⏰9.30am-1.30pm & 4-6.30pm Mon-Fri, 10am-1.30pm Sun) The visual feast of the entrance facade to Salamanca's university is a tapestry in sandstone, bursting with images of mythical heroes, religious scenes and coats of arms. It's dominated in the centre by busts of Fernando and Isabel.

Founded initially as the Estudio Generál in 1218, the university came into being in 1254 and reached the peak of its renown in the 15th and 16th centuries. Behind the facade, the highlight of an otherwise modest collection of rooms lies upstairs: the extraordinary **university library**, the oldest university library in Europe. With some 2800 manuscripts gathering dust, it's a real cemetery of forgotten books.

Among the small lecture rooms arranged around the courtyard downstairs, the **Aula de Fray Luis de León** was named after the celebrated 16th-century theologian and writer whose statue adorns the Patio de las Escuelas Menores outside. It conserves the original benches and lectern from Fray Luis' day. Arrested by the Inquisition for having translated the Song of

Frog-Spotting

Arguably a lot more interesting than trainspotting (and you don't have to drink tea from a thermos flask), a compulsory task facing all visitors to Salamanca is to search out the frog sculpted into the facade of the Universidad Civil. Once pointed out, it's easily enough seen, but the uninitiated can spend considerable time searching. Why bother? Well, they say that those who detect it without help can be assured of good luck and even marriage within a year. Some hopeful students see a guaranteed examination's victory in it. If you believe all this, stop reading now: if you need help, look at the busts of Fernando and Isabel. From there, turn your gaze to the largest column on the extreme right of the front. Slightly above the level of the busts is a series of skulls, atop the leftmost of which sits our little amphibious friend (or what's left of his eroded self).

DIEGO VELO/GETTY IMAGES ©

Don't Miss Plaza Mayor

Built between 1729 and 1755, Salamanca's exceptional grand square is widely considered to be Spain's most beautiful central plaza. The square is particularly memorable at night when illuminated (until midnight) to magical effect. Designed by Alberto Churriguera, it's a remarkably harmonious and controlled baroque display. The medallions placed around the square bear the busts of famous figures. Look for the controversial inclusion of Franco in the northeast corner – it looks different from the others, being moulded in a special easy-to-clean plastic to counter its regular subjection to vandalism.

Solomon into Spanish, the sardonic theologian returned to his class after five years in jail and resumed lecturing with the words, 'As I was saying yesterday…'. It was here, too, that the famous Spanish philosopher and essayist, Miguel de Unamuno, claimed the Nationalist rising was 'necessary to save Western Civilization', and was saved from the fury of the crowd by Franco's wife.

The **Escalera de la Universidad** (University Staircase) that connects the two floors has symbols carved into the balustrade, seemingly of giant insects having a frolic with several bishops – to decode them was seen as symbolic of the quest for knowledge.

FREE **CATEDRAL NUEVA** Cathedral
(Plaza de Anaya; 9am-8pm) The tower of the late-Gothic Catedral Nueva lords over the centre of Salamanca, its compelling *churrigueresco* (ornate style of baroque) dome visible from almost every angle. The interior is similarly impressive, with elaborate choir stalls, main chapel and retrochoir all courtesy of the prolific José Churriguera. The ceilings are also exceptional. It is, however, the magnificent Renaissance doorways, particularly the **Puerta del Nacimiento** on the western face, that stand out as one of several miracles worked in the city's native sandstone. The **Puerta de Ramos**, facing

Plaza de Anaya, contains an encore to the 'frog spotting' challenge on the university facade. Look for the little astronaut and ice-cream cone chiselled into the portal by stonemasons during restorations.

CATEDRAL VIEJA Cathedral
(Plaza de Anaya; admission €4.75; 10am-7.30pm) The Catedral Nueva's largely Romanesque predecessor, the Catedral Vieja is adorned with an exquisite 15th-century **altarpiece**, with 53 panels depicting scenes from the lives of Christ and Mary, topped by a representation of the Final Judgment – it's one of the most beautiful Renaissance altarpieces outside Italy. The entrance is inside the Catedral Nueva.

Tours

Both the Municipal Tourist Office and Regional Tourist Office (p236) organise multilingual guided tours of the city. These depart at noon daily and cost €6 (daytime) to €7 (night tours). The duration is roughly 1½ hours but you must reserve in advance. They're conducted in Spanish, but you may also be able to arrange tours in English and French.

Sleeping

MICROTEL PLACENTINOS Boutique Hotel **€€**
(923 28 15 31; www.microtelplacentinos.com; Calle de Placentinos 9; s/d incl breakfast Sun-Thu €56/72, Fri & Sat €86/99;) One of Salamanca's most charming boutique hotels, Microtel Placentinos is tucked away on a quiet street and has rooms with exposed stone walls and wooden beams. The service is faultless, and the overall atmosphere is one of intimacy and discretion. All rooms have a hydromassage shower or tub and there's a summer-only outside whirpool spa.

HOSTAL CONCEJO Hostal **€**
(923 21 47 37; www.hconcejo.com; Plaza de la Libertad 1; s/d €45/60; P) A cut above the average *hostal*, the stylish Concejo has polished-wood floors, tasteful furnishings, light-filled rooms and a superb central location. Try and snag one of the corner rooms (like number 104) with its traditional glassed-in balcony, complete with a table, chairs and people-watching views.

Eating

LA COCINA DE TOÑO Tapas **€€**
(www.lacocinadetoño.es; Calle Gran Via 20; menú del día €17, tapas €1.30-3.80, mains €6.90-23; lunch & dinner Tue-Sat, lunch Sun) We're yet to hear a bad word about this place and its loyal following owes everything to its creative *pinchos* (snacks) and half-servings of dishes such as escalope of foie gras with roast apple and passionfruit gelatin. The restaurant serves more traditional fare as befits the decor, but the bar is one of Salamanca's gastronomic stars.

EL PECADO Modern Spanish **€€**
(923 26 65 58; www.elpecadorestaurante.es; Plaza de Poeta Iglesias 12; menú del día €15, mains €15-33) A trendy place that regularly attracts Spanish celebrities (eg Pedro Almodóvar and Ferran Adrià), El Pecado (The Sin) has an intimate dining room and a quirky, creative menu; it's a reasonably priced place to sample high-quality, innovative Spanish cooking. The hallmarks are fresh tastes, intriguing combinations and dishes that regularly change according to

Salamanca Card

If you plan on visiting most of Salamanca's attractions, consider the Salamanca Card (www.salamancacard.com), which entitles you to free entry to most museums, an MP3 audioguide to the city, and discounts at some restaurants, hotels and shops. It can be purchased online or from both tourist offices, and costs €16/22 for 24/48 hours.

what's fresh at the market that day. Reservations recommended.

MESÓN LAS CONCHAS Castilian **€€**
(Rúa Mayor 16; menú del día €12, mains €10-21; noon-midnight) Enjoy a choice of outdoor tables (in summer), an atmospheric bar or the upstairs, wood-beamed dining area. The bar caters mainly to locals who know their *embutidos* (cured meats). For sit-down meals, there's a good mix of roasts, *platos combinados* and *raciones* (full-plate-size tapas serving). It serves a couple of cured meat platters (€17 to €20) that can be good to share. If you're craving fish, the oven-baked turbot is delicious.

Information

Municipal Tourist Office (923 21 83 42; www.turismodesalamanca.com; Plaza Mayor 14; 9am-2pm & 4.30-8pm Mon-Fri, 10am-8pm Sat, 10am-2pm Sun)

Regional Tourist Office (923 26 85 71; www.turismocastillayleon.com; Casa de las Conchas, Rúa Mayor; 9am-8pm)

Getting There & Away

The bus and train stations are a 10- and 15-minute walk northwest and northeast, respectively, of the Plaza Mayor.

BUS There are buses to the following destinations: Madrid (regular/express €12.88/20.30, three to 2½ hours, hourly), Ávila (€6.08, 1½ hours, one to four daily), León (€13.70, three hours, two daily) and Segovia (€11.08, 2½ hours, two daily).

TRAIN Regular departures to Madrid's Chamartín station (€19.85, 2½ hours).

Best Views of Town

For *the* shot of Segovia to impress the folks back home, head out of town due north (towards Cuéllar) for around 2km. The view of the city unfolds in all its movie-style magic, with the aqueduct taking a star role – as well it should. Other fine views are to be had from the Convento de los Carmelitas Descalzos and from the car park next to the Alcázar.

Getting Around

Bus 4 runs past the bus station and around the old-city perimeter to Calle Gran Vía. From the train station, the best bet is bus 1, which heads into the centre along Calle de Azafranal. Going the other way, it can be picked up at the Mercado Central.

Segovia

POP 55,220 / ELEV 1002M

Unesco World Heritage–listed Segovia has always had a whiff of legend about it, not least in the myths that Segovia was founded by Hercules or by the son of Noah. It may also have something to do with the fact that nowhere else in Spain has such a stunning monument to Roman grandeur (the soaring aqueduct) survived in the heart of a vibrant modern city. Or maybe it's because art really has imitated life Segovia-style – Walt Disney is said to have modelled Sleeping Beauty's castle in California's Disneyland on Segovia's Alcázar.

Whatever it is, the effect is stunning: a city of warm terracotta and sandstone hues set amid the rolling hills of Castilla and against the backdrop of the Sierra de Guadarrama.

Sights

ACUEDUCTO Roman Aqueduct
Segovia's most recognisable symbol is El Acueducto (Roman Aqueduct), an 894m-long engineering wonder that looks like an enormous comb plunged into Segovia.

First raised here by the Romans in the 1st century AD, the aqueduct was built with not a drop of mortar to hold the more than 20,000 uneven granite blocks together. It's made up of 163 arches and, at its highest point in Plaza del Azoguejo, rises 28m high.

It was most probably built around AD 50 as part of a complex system of aqueducts and underground canals that brought water from the mountains more than 15km away. By some accounts, it once reached as far as the Alcázar. The aqueduct's pristine condition is attributable to a major restoration project in the 1990s. For a different perspective, climb the stairs next to the aqueduct that begin behind the tourist office.

ALCÁZAR Castle

(www.alcazardesegovia.com; Plaza de la Reina Victoria Eugenia; adult/child €4/3, tower €2, EU citizens free 3rd Tue of month; 10am-7pm Apr-Sep) Rapunzel towers, turrets topped with slate witches' hats and a deep moat at its base make the Alcázar a prototype fairy-tale castle.

Fortified since Roman days, the site takes its name from the Arabic *al-qasr* (fortress). It was rebuilt and expanded in the 13th and 14th centuries, but the whole lot burned down in 1862.

What you see today is an evocative, over-the-top reconstruction of the original. Highlights include the **Sala de las Piñas**, with its ceiling of 392 pineapple-shaped 'stalactites', and the **Sala de Reyes**, featuring a three-dimensional frieze of 52 sculptures of kings who fought during the Reconquista.

The views from the summit of the Torre de Juan II are truly exceptional and put the Old Town's hilltop location into full context.

IGLESIA DE VERA CRUZ Church

(Carretera de Zamarramala; admission €1.75; 10.30am-1.30pm & 4-7pm Tue-Sun, closed Nov) This 12-sided church is the most interesting of Segovia's churches, and one of the best-preserved of its kind in Europe.

Built in the early 13th century by the Knights Templar and based on Jerusalem's Church of the Holy Sepulchre, it once housed a piece of the Vera Cruz (True Cross), now in the nearby village church of Zamarramala (on view only at Easter).

If You Like... Castles

While Segovia's Disneyesque Alcázar may get all the attention, lonely hilltop castles are something of a regional specialty. Our favourites include the following:

1 **CASTILLO DE PEDRAZA**
(Pedraza de la Sierra; admission €5; 11am-2pm & 5-8pm Wed-Sun) An unusually intact outer wall northeast of Segovia.

2 **COCA CASTLE**
(Coca; guided tours €2.50; tours 10am-1.30pm & 4.30-7pm Mon-Fri, 11am-1pm & 4-7pm Sat & Sun) An all-brick, virtuouso piece of Gothic-Mudéjar architecture 50km northwest of Segovia.

3 **CASTILLO TEMPLARIO**
(Ponferrada; adult/concession €4/2; 10am-2pm & 4.30-8.30pm Tue-Sun) A fortress-monastery built by the Knights Templar in the 13th century west of León.

4 **CASTILLO DE PEÑAFIEL**
(Museo Provincial del Vino; Peñafiel; admission castle €3, incl museum €6, audioguides €2; 11am-2.30pm & 4.30-8.30pm Tue-Sun)

5 **CASTILLO DE TURÉGANO**
A unique 15th-century castle-church complex 30km north of Segovia.

6 **GORMAZ**
10th-century, Muslim-era fortress with 21 towers 14km south of El Burgo de Osma.

CATEDRAL Cathedral

(Plaza Mayor; adult/concession €3/2; 9.30am-6.30pm) Started in 1525 after its Romanesque predecessor had burned to the ground in the War of the Communities, Segovia's cathedral is a final, powerful expression of Gothic architecture in Spain that took almost 200 years to complete. The austere three-nave interior is anchored by an imposing choir stall and enlivened by 20-odd chapels.

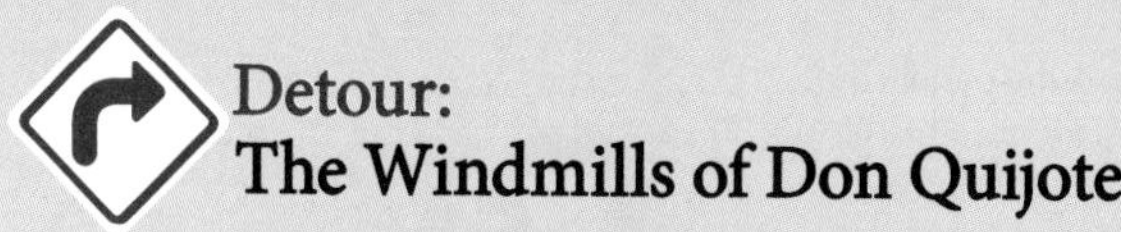

Detour: The Windmills of Don Quijote

Part of the charm of a visit to central Spain is the chance to track down the real-life locations in which Miguel de Cervantes placed his hero, Don Quijote. These days it requires less puzzling over maps as, to celebrate the fourth centenary of the tale in 2007, the 250km route of Don Quijote was created with sign posts that direct you along paths, cattle ways and historic routes throughout the region.

Of all the places and sights you can ponder along the way the *molinos de vientos* (windmills) are the most obvious, for it was these 'monstrous giants' that so haunted El Quijote and with which he tried to battle. Although Consuegra's are the most attractive, those that are specifically mentioned in Cervantes novel are the windmills of **Campo de Criptana** and **Mota del Cuervo**. Other highlights on the trail include the castle of **Belmonte** and **El Toboso**, where the knight discovered the lovely Dulcinea.

Sleeping

HOSPEDERÍA LA GRAN CASA MUDÉJAR Historic Hotel **€€**
(**921 46 62 50; www.lacasamudejar.com; Calle de Isabel la Católica 8; r €90;**) Spread over two buildings, this place has been magnificently renovated, blending genuine, 15th-century Mudéjar-carved wooden ceilings in some rooms with modern amenities. In the newer wing, the rooms on the top floors have fine mountain views out over the rooftops of Segovia's old Jewish quarter. Adding to the appeal, there's a small spa and the hotel's El Fogón Sefardi restaurant comes highly recommended.

HOTEL ALCÁZAR Boutique Hotel **€€€**
(**921 43 85 68; www.alcazar-hotel.com; Calle de San Marcos 5; s/d incl breakfast €135/163;**) Sitting by the riverbank in the valley beneath the Alcázar, this charming, tranquil little hotel has lavish rooms beautifully styled to suit those who love old-world luxury.

Eating

RESTAURANTE EL FOGÓN SEFARDÍ Sephardic **€€**
(**921 46 62 50; www.lacasamudejar.com; Calle de Isabel la Católica 8; meals €30-40**) Located within the Hospedería La Gran Casa Mudéjar, this is one of the most original places in town. Sephardic cuisine is served either on the intimate patio or in the splendid dining hall with original, 15th-century Mudéjar flourishes.

CASA DUQUE Grill **€€**
(**921 46 24 87; www.restauranteduque.es; Calle de Cervantes 12; menús del día €21-40, meals €25-35**) *Cochinillo asado* (roast suckling pig) has been served here since the 1890s. For the uninitiated, try the *menú segoviano* (€30), which includes *cochinillo*, or the *menú gastronómico* (€43.50).

MESÓN DE CÁNDIDO Grill **€€**
(**921 42 81 03; www.mesondecandido.es; Plaza del Azoguejo 5; meals €30-40**) Set in a delightful 18th-century building in the shadow of the aqueduct, Mesón de Cándido is famous throughout Spain for its *cochinillo asado* and the more unusual roast boar with apples.

Information

Centro de Recepción de Visitantes (Tourist Office; www.turismodesegovia.com; Plaza del Azoguejo 1; 10am-7pm Sun-Fri, 10am-8pm Sat) Segovia's main tourist office has plenty of information and also runs guided tours, departing daily at 11.15am for a minimum of four people.

Regional Tourist Office (www.segoviaturismo.es; Plaza Mayor 10; ⌚9am-8pm Sun-Thu, 9am-9pm Fri & Sat)

Getting There & Away

BUS The bus station is just off Paseo de Ezequiel González, near Avenida de Fernández Ladreda. Buses run half-hourly to Segovia from Madrid's Paseo de la Florida bus stop (€6.70, 1½ hours). Buses depart to Ávila (€5, one hour, five daily) and Salamanca (€11.08, 2½ hours, two daily).

CAR & MOTORCYCLE Of the two main roads down to the AP6, which links Madrid and Galicia, the N603 is the prettier. The alternative N110 cuts southwest across to Ávila and northeast to the main Madrid–Burgos highway.The nearest underground car park to the historic centre is in Plaza de la Artillería near the aqueduct.

TRAIN There are two options by train: up to nine normal trains run daily from Madrid to Segovia (€6.75 one way, two hours), leaving you at the main train station 2.5km from the aqueduct. The faster option is the high-speed Avant (one way €10.60, 28 minutes), which deposits you at the newer Segovia-Guiomar station, 5km from the aqueduct.

Getting Around

Bus 9 does a circuit through the Old Town, bus 8 goes to Segovia train station and bus 11 goes to Segovia-Guiomar station. All services cost €0.90 and leave from just outside the aqueduct.

Seville & Andalucía's Hill Towns

A parched region fertile with culture, a conquered land that went on to conquer, a fiercely traditional place that has accepted rapid modernisation; Seville and western Andalucía has multiple faces. Here, in the cradle of quintessential Spain, the questions are often as intriguing as the answers. Who first concocted flamenco? How did tapas become a national obsession? Could Cádiz be Europe's oldest settlement? Are those really Christopher Columbus' bones inside Seville cathedral? Putting together the missing pieces of the puzzle is what makes travel in western Andalucía the glorious adventure it is, a never-ending mystery trail that will deposit you in places where you can peel off the checkered history in dusty layers: vivacious Seville, sleepy Grazalema, rugged Ronda; places that lodge in your memory like collected souvenirs, luring you back.

Flamenco, Seville

Catedral (p284), Cádiz

Seville & Andalucía's Hill Towns
PORTUGAL
Peñarroya-
Pueblonuevo
Río Guadiato
CÓRDOBA
Parque
Natural Sierra de
Hornachuelos
Córdoba
Aracena
Parque Natural
Sierra de Aracena
y Picos de Aroche
Cazalla de
la Sierra
Constantina
Río Huéznar
Nerva
Río Tinto
Río Odiel
Valverde
del Camino
Río Guadiana
Lora
del Río
Palma
del Río
Pradollano
Carmona
Río Corbones
Écija
Aguilar de
la Frontera
Bollullos Par
del Condado
Seville
Alcalá de Guadaira
ANDALUCÍA
Puente Genil
Huelva
Ayamonte
Lepe
Moguer
Almonte
Isla
Cristina
Punta
Umbria
Río Guadalquivir
Río Guadaira
Dos
Hermanas
Marchena
El Arahal
Osuna
Parque
Nacional
de Doñana
Los Palacios
y Villafranca
Utrera
Morón de la
Frontera
Lucio de
los Ansares
Lucio del
Membrillo
Lebrija
Villamartín
Olvera
Embalse
del Conde del
Guadalhorce
Sanlúcar de Barrameda
Chipiona
El Puerto de
Santa María
Rota
Arcos de la
Frontera
Embalse de
Bornos
Parque Natural
Sierra de
Grazalema
MÁLAGA
Álora
Ronda
Jerez de la
Frontera
Ubrique
Parque
Natural Sierra
de las Nieves
Cártama
Coín
Bahía de Cádiz
Cádiz
Puerto
Real
Medina
Sidonia
Río Guadiaro
Río Genal
San Pedro de
Alcántara
Mijas
Marbella
San
Fernando
Embalse de
Barbate
Estepona
Parque
Natural Los
Alcornocales
Vejer de la
Frontera
Costa del Sol
Barbate
La Línea de
la Concepción
ATLANTIC OCEAN
Algeciras
Gibraltar
Tarifa
Strait of Gibraltar
Tangier
MOROCCO
1 Flamenco and tapas, Seville
2 Córdoba
3 Jerez de la Frontera
4 Seville Cathedral
5 Seville's Alcázar
6 Cádiz
7 Arcos de la Frontera
0 50 km
0 25 miles

Seville & Andalucía's Hill Towns Highlights

1 Seville's Tapas & Flamenco

If you want to experience the essence of Spain, Seville (p254) is the place to do it. Its architecture – a sublime mix of Islamic splendour and Catholic extravagance – and festivals are quintessentially Spanish. But Seville is known above all for its obsession with tapas and as the possible birthplace of flamenco, where the genre still sends shivers down your spine.

Need to Know

BEST PHOTO OP From the top of Seville's cathedral **BEST FLAMENCO FESTIVAL** Bienal de Flamenco **SURVIVAL TIP** When eating tapas, just take one or two at each bar

Seville Don't Miss List

BY TONI VICHEZ, OWNER OF EXTRAVERDE (P261) TAPAS BAR.

1 NEIGHBOURHOOD TAPAS

To appoint one street as the best for tapas is difficult, because in Seville most downtown streets are lined with tapas bars. However, I could highlight two main areas. The first is the neighborhood of Santa Cruz, where you can find traditional Sevillan cuisine. The second, La Alameda de Hercules, is a more innovative and cool area.

2 SEVILLE CULINARY SPECIALITIES

Cuisine in Seville has been greatly influenced by the city's history, culture, and surrounding environment. Examples include the fried fish, marinades and salted meats. The result: dishes like spinach with chickpeas (with its obvious Arab heritage), Iberian ham from the Sierra de Huelva, and oranges.

3 PURCHASING OLIVE OIL

The tip for buying a good extra virgin olive oil is to choose an olive oil of a superior category. Its label must carry a statement, visible by law, saying: 'Extra Virgin Olive Oil'. Olive oil branded like this will have been made using only the best olives and produced in a traditional way.

4 FLAMENCO BARRIOS

You can find good flamenco in any neighborhood of Seville. However, there are two neighborhoods which have the greatest number of *tablaos* (flamenco clubs). The neighborhood of Santa Cruz, despite being touristy, has good quality and interesting clubs, while Triana is more popular and has deeper roots in the tradition.

5 BEST FLAMENCO CLUBS

In the Barrio de Santa Cruz, one of the more upscale *tablaos* which respects the tradition of flamenco is Casa de la Memoria de Al-Andalus (p264). It has the best young artists of Seville and the performances take place in the courtyard of a palatial house of Jewish origin. In this neighborhood, I also recommend visiting the Museo del Baile Flamenco (p258), an interactive museum where you can see, hear and touch flamenco.

Córdoba – Crossroad of Civilisations

Córdoba's (p266) diverse and surprising fingerprints to the past are not always what they seem. Yes, there are reminders of a tolerant past when three religions co-existed. But the reality of Córdoba as a symbol of historical coexistence is far more complicated. Discovering if this Córdoba was myth or reality is a fascinating journey.

Below & Bottom Right: La Mezquita; Top Right: *Judería* (p267)

Need to Know

BEST TIME TO VISIT Mid-April to mid-June **CÓRDOBA'S ROMAN TEMPLE** On the corner of Calle de Claudio Marcelo and Calle de los Capitulares

2

Local Knowledge

Córdoba Don't Miss List

BY SEBASTIÁN DE LA OBRA, EMINENT LOCAL HISTORIAN

1 LA MEZQUITA DE CÓRDOBA

Córdoba's Mezquita (p270) is one of the most prestigious buildings in Arab-Islamic culture. The interior is indescribably beautiful – a labyrinth of bicoloured columns with horseshoe arches, a forest of palm trees rendered in stone and brickwork that is most beautiful in the mihrab.

2 LA SINAGOGA DE CÓRDOBA

Built in 1315, Córdoba's synagogue (p267) is richly decorated with Mudéjar art and fragments of the Psalms in Hebrew; women worshipped upstairs, men downstairs. After Jewish people were expelled from Spain, the synagogue served as a school, hermitage, hospital and even a brotherhood of shoemakers, but is now one of the few remaining signposts to Spain's Jewish heritage.

3 TEMPLO ROMANO DE CÓRDOBA

Away from the heart of tourist Córdoba, the city's spectacular Roman temple is a reminder that Córdoba's fame predates Al-Andalus. Córdoba was the capital of Hispania Ulterior (and later Córdoba Bética), and in the 3rd century was considered the cultural and economic powerhouse of Roman Iberia. The ruins wonderfully evoke this period.

4 CHURCHES OF THE FERNANDO PERIOD

In the 14th century, churches were built in all the city's neighbourhoods and today provide the focal point for a beautiful route through the city. Thirteen of the original fourteen churches survive and all share common architectural features – three naves with an apse, rose windows, stone walls and Mozarabic windows. My favourites are the Capilla de San Bartolomé and the Iglesia de Santa Marina.

5 CASA DE SEFARAD

This privately run museum and cultural space occupies a beautiful 14th-century house and serves as a centre for recovering the heritage and historical memory of Spain's Jewish community. It's home to one of the most prestigious libraries in Andalucía, and also hosts concerts of Sephardic and other Andalucian music.

Jerez de la Frontera

The home of sherry and prancing, dancing horses. The true heart of firey, authentic flamenco and the proud owner of magnificent Christian and Islamic monuments, Jerez de la Frontera (p274) is strangely overlooked by many visitors to the region, but if you want a real, unfiltered immersion into all things classically Andalucian then Jerez de la Frontera is really the only place to be. Feria del Caballo (Horse Fair; p43), Jerez de la Frontera

3

4

Seville Cathedral

It's widely stated that when the architects of the cathedral (p260) started building their house of worship, they said 'We are going to build a church so large, future generations will think we were mad'. They were wrong. Future generations, overawed by the scale and sheer majesty of this Gothic masterpiece, actually thought they were geniuses.

VISIONS OF OUR LAND/GETTY IMAGES ©

5 Seville's Alcázar

Seville's sublime and romantic Alcázar (p254) is the building every other building in Seville wants to be. The highlights of this Moorish masterpiece are the stunning Palacio de Don Pedro at the heart of which stands the Patio of the Maidens and the palace gardens – the perfect example of the Islamic belief that Paradise is a garden. Salón de Embajadores, Seville Alcázar

CAROLINE VON TUEMPLING/GETTY IMAGES ©

6 Cádiz

Ask any Spaniard for their favourite Spanish city, and the chances are that many will say Cádiz (p284), usually accompanied by a broad smile. Renowned for its sense of fun, especially during Carnaval, famous for its fantastic food, and celebrated as a stunning city with numerous high-above-the-rooftops vantage points from which to survey it, Cádiz is one of our favourite Andalucian cities, too.

7 Arcos de la Frontera

One of Andalucía's signature images, Arcos de la Frontera (p271) ranks among Andalucía's most beautiful *pueblos blancos* (white villages). Stretched out along a ridge like a string of pearls, surveying the plains from its clifftop perch, Arcos combines small-town Andalucian charm with architecture that will live long in the memory.

Seville & Andalucía's Hill Towns' Best...

Tapas Bars

- **Vinería San Telmo, Seville** (p261) We've tried them all and we think this is the best tapas bar in Seville.
- **Los Coloniales, Seville** (p261) Quality tapas lined up like catwalk models.
- **El Aljibe, Cádiz** (p285) The super cool tapas here are almost enough reason alone to visit Cádiz.
- **Taberna San Miguel El Pisto, Córdoba** (p269) Brimming with local character and delicious tapas.

Rural Bliss

- **Grazalema** (p280) Few *pueblos blancos* are as generically perfect as this one.
- **Zahara de la Sierra** (p281) Set around a vertiginous crag and humming with Moorish mystery.
- **El Rocío** (p285) Overlooking flamingo pink marshes and dominated by a shimmering white church.
- **Parque Natural Sierre de Aracena y Picos de Aroche** (p280) The beautiful peaks and villages of this national park are tonic to city dwellers' congested souls.

Journeys Back in Time

- **Itálica** (p264)A 2nd-century Roman town with a massive amphitheatre.
- **Medina Azahara** (p267) The ghosts of Moorish al-Andalus live on in this abandoned city.
- **Cádiz** (p284) Towns don't come with much more history than this one.
- **Cordoba** (p266) The perfect melding of Islamic and Christian houses of worship.

Party Time

- **Feria de Abril** (April) Andalucía's biggest *feria* is a joyful celebration of the arrival of spring.
- **Semana Santa** (Easter) Large, life-size *pasos* (sculptures representing events from Christ's Passion) are paraded through Seville.
- **Bienal de Flamenco** (September) You'll love Spain's biggest flamenco festival, held in Seville every second year.
- **Romeria del Rocio** (Pentecost) Thousands of pilgrims pay their respects to the Virgin.
- **Carnaval** (February or March) Dress up for Spain's answer to Rio.

Left: Semana Santa, Carmona (p265); **Above:** Zahara de la Sierra (p281)

Need to Know

ADVANCE PLANNING

- **Three months before** Book your hotel for Seville's Feria de Abril or Carnaval in Cádiz.
- **Two weeks before** Reserve your high-speed AVE ticket (www.renfe.es) from Madrid to Seville.

RESOURCES

- **Andalucía Te Quiere** (www.andalucia.org) Terrific tourist office site for the entire region.
- **Andalucia.com** (www.andalucia.com) Excellent privately run site on Andalucía.
- **La Guía de Flamenco** (www.guiaflama.com) The best source of upcoming flamenco concerts.
- **Centro Andaluz de Flamenco** (www.centroandaluzdeflamenco.es) Another good resource for flamenco performances.

GETTING AROUND

- **Air** International airports with intra-Spain connections in Seville and Jerez de la Frontera.
- **Train** Renfe has good north-south connections, fewer from east to west.
- **Bus** Wherever trains don't reach.
- **Road** Excellent network of roads.

BE FOREWARNED

- Public transport between and around the *pueblos blancos* is skeletal at best; to make life easy hire a car.

Seville & Andalucía's Hill Towns Itineraries

Filled with unforgettable sights, sounds and experiences, western Andalucía is classic Spain. This vast region could fill many weeks of travel but it's still possible to get a feel for this bewitching region in a short time.

3 DAYS

CÁDIZ TO RONDA

The White Towns

Atlantic waves crash against sea walls and narrow streets echo to the sound of crawing gulls and frying fish. Ah, the romance of **(1) Cádiz**, where this tour begins. Looming moodily atop a rocky hill an hour southeast of Cádiz is **(2) Vejer de la Frontera**. With a cool labyrinth of twisting streets heavy in the scent of the exotic and some fabulous nearby beaches, Vejer might well end up being your favourite white hill town. Squiggle your way northeast along country roads into increasingly wild terrain until you hit gorgeous **(3) Grazalema**; a village of spotless white-wash houses topped in a wig of red-tiled roofs and surrounded by the pillar-like rocks of the Sierra de Grazalema. A short but breathtaking drive away is miniscule **(4) Zahara de la Sierra** which positively hums in Moorish mystery and contains all the elements of a classic white town. From here it's a stunning drive to **(5) Ronda**, the largest and liveliest of the white towns and a place famous for its gorge-spanning bridge.

Top Left: Vejer de la Frontera (p278); **Top Right:** Glass of sherry at Bodegas González Byass (p275), Jerez de la Frontera

5 DAYS

SEVILLE TO CÓRDOBA

Flamenco & Sherry

Flamenco was born in western Andalucía, and it's in the intimate tiled courtyards of **(1) Seville**, the genre's reputed birthplace, where you can still hear flamenco in its purest form. With hundreds of tapas bars nearby and monuments to visit, Seville deserves at least two days. An hour south of Seville by regular train, or just off the AP4, (**2) Jerez de la Frontera** shares many of the same passions – it's a hotbed of authentic flamenco (ask at the Centro Andaluz de Flamenco for the latest performances), fantastic places to eat, and is famous for its Andalucian horses. Jerez also has world-renowned sherry bodegas, most of which run tours. A short distance away, the burning white hill-town of **(3) Arcos de la Frontera** is one of the signature images of sultry southern Spain and is the *pueblo blanco* (white village) par excellence. If time allows drive through pretty hills and golden fields of crops northeast to **(4) Córdoba**. This isn't a city renowned for its flamenco scene (though there is still some action) but it excels at art of another kind: flower sprinkled, white-wash patios and a melding of Islamic and Christian architectural styles.

Discover Seville & Andalucía's Hill Towns

At a Glance

- **Seville** (p254) Home to all things Andalucian.
- **Córdoba** (p266) The Mezquita and a fine Jewish quarter.
- **White hill towns** (p271) Green hills, long views and searing whitewashed villages.
- **Cádiz province** (p284) The coastal city of Cádiz and hill towns in the north.

Feria de Abril (p43), Seville
JUERGEN RICHTER/GETTY IMAGES ©

SEVILLE

POP 703,000

Some cities have looks. Others have personality. The *sevillanos* – lucky devils – get both, courtesy of their flamboyant, charismatic, ever-evolving Andalucian metropolis founded, according to mythology, 3000-years ago by the Greek God Hercules. Doused in never-ending sunlight, Seville's beauty is relatively easy to uncover; watch pretty girls in polka-dot dresses ride in carriages to the Feria de Abril. Its soul is a darker and more complex force. Flamenco was partially born here in the dusty taverns of Triana, and greedy conquistadores once roamed the sinuous streets of El Arenal counting their colonial gold. Tugged by the pull of both forces, it is Seville's capriciousness that leaves the heaviest impression. Come here in April and watch as haunting **Semana Santa (www.semana-santa.org)** metamorphoses into the cacophony of spring fair and you'll wonder whether Bizet's Carmen wasn't more real than imagined.

Sights

ALCÁZAR Castle

(adult/child €7.50/free; 9.30am-7pm Apr-Sep, to 6pm Oct-Mar) If heaven really *does* exist, then let's hope it looks a little bit like the inside of Seville's Alcázar. Built primarily in the 1300s during the so-called 'dark ages' in Europe, the architecture is anything but dark. Indeed, compared to our modern-day shopping malls and throw-away apartment blocks, it could be argued that the Alcázar marked one of history's architectural high points. Unesco agreed, making it a World Heritage Site in 1987.

From the ticket office inside the **Puerta del León** (Lion Gate) you'll emerge into the **Patio del León** (Lion Patio), which was the garrison yard of the original Al-Muwarak palace. Just off here is the **Sala de la Justicia** (Hall of Justice), with beautiful Mudéjar plaster work and an *artesonado* (ceiling of interlaced beams with decorative insertions). It leads on to the pretty **Patio del Yeso**, which is part of the 12th-century Almohad palace reconstructed in the 19th century.

Posterity owes Pedro I a big thank you for creating the **Palacio de Don Pedro** (also called the Palacio Mudéjar), the single most stunning architectural feature in Seville.

At the heart of the palace is the wonderful **Patio de las Doncellas** (Patio of the Maidens), surrounded by beautiful arches, plasterwork and tiling. The sunken garden in the centre was uncovered by archaeologists in 2004 from beneath a 16th-century marble covering.

The **Cámara Regia** (King's Quarters), on the northern side of the patio, has stunningly beautiful ceilings and wonderful plaster- and tile-work. Its rear room was probably the monarch's summer bedroom.

From here you can move west into the little **Patio de las Muñecas** (Patio of the Dolls), the heart of the palace's private quarters, featuring delicate Granada-style decoration. Indeed, plasterwork was actually brought here from the Alhambra in the 19th century when the mezzanine and top gallery were added for Queen Isabel II.

The spectacular **Salón de Embajadores** (Hall of Ambassadors), at the western end of the Patio de las Doncellas, was the throne room of Pedro I's palace. The room's fabulous wooden dome of multiple star patterns, symbolising the universe, was added in 1427.

On the western side of the Salón de Embajadores, the beautiful Arco de Pavones, named after its peacock motifs, leads into the **Salón del Techo de Felipe II**, with a Renaissance ceiling (1589–91).

The **Salones de Carlos V** are reached via a staircase at the southeastern corner of the Patio de las Doncellas; these are the much-remodelled rooms of Alfonso X's 13th-century Gothic palace. The rooms are now named after the 16th-century

Metropol Parasol

Some call him the Ferran Adrià of modern architecture, and it's true, German architect Jurgen Mayer H possesses a strange kind of artistic genius. Who else would have dreamt of constructing a 'flying waffle' in the middle of one of Sevillés most traditional shopping squares? Smarting with the audacity of a modern-day Eiffel Tower, the opinion-dividing **Metropol Parasol** (Plaza de la Encarnación), which opened in March 2011 in the Plaza de la Encarnación, claims to be the largest wooden building in the world. Its undulating honeycombed roof is held up by five giant mushroom-like pillars earning it the local nickname *Las Setas de la Encarnación*. Six years in the making, the construction covers a former dead zone in Seville's central district once filled with an ugly car park. Roman ruins discovered during the building's conception have been cleverly incorporated into the foundations in the **Museo Antiquarium** (Plaza de la Encarnación; admission €2; ⌚11am-2pm & 3-8pm) while upstairs on level 2 you can pay €1.20 to stroll along a surreal panoramic walkway with killer city views.

Seville

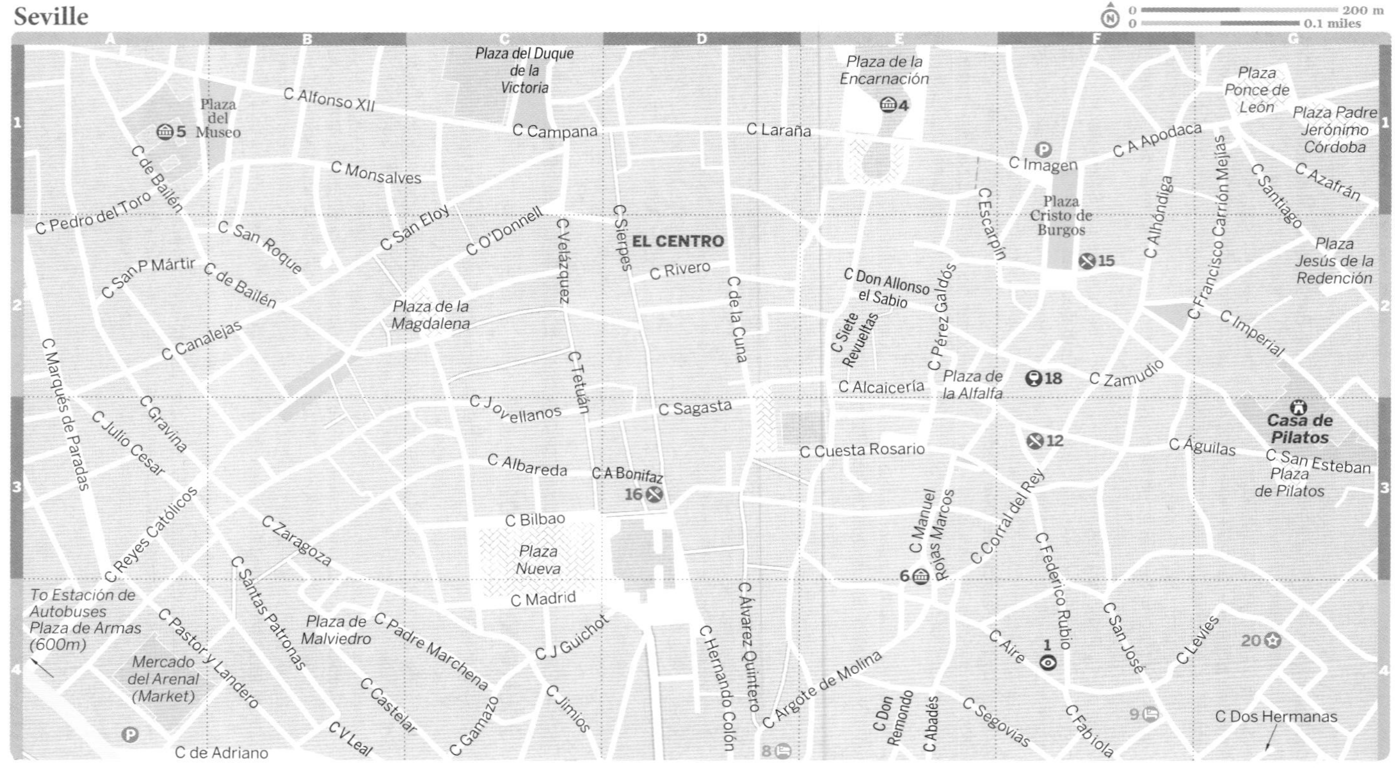
0 200 m
0 0.1 miles
A
B
C
D
E
F
G
1
2
3
4
Plaza del Duque de la Victoria
Plaza de la Encarnación
4
Plaza Ponce de León
Plaza Padre Jerónimo Córdoba
Plaza del Museo
5
C Alfonso XII
C Campana
C Laraña
C A Apodaca
C Imagen
C Monsalves
C de Bailén
C Pedro del Toro
C San Roque
C San Eloy
C O'Donnell
C Velázquez
C Sierpes
EL CENTRO
C Rivero
C Escarpín
Plaza Cristo de Burgos
C Alhóndiga
C Francisco Carrión Mejías
C Santiago
C Azafrán
Plaza Jesús de la Redención
15
C San P Mártir
C de Bailén
Plaza de la Magdalena
C de la Cuna
C Don Allonso el Sabio
C Pérez Galdós
C Siete Revueltas
C Imperial
C Canalejas
C Marqués de Paradas
C Tetuán
C Alcaicería
Plaza de la Alfalfa
18
C Zamudio
Casa de Pilatos
C Gravina
C Julio Cesar
C Jovellanos
C Sagasta
C Cuesta Rosario
12
C Águilas
C San Esteban
Plaza de Pilatos
C Albareda
C A Bonifaz
16
C Reyes Católicos
C Zaragoza
C Bilbao
Plaza Nueva
C Manuel Rojas Marcos
C Corral del Rey
C Federico Rubio
6
C Madrid
C Santas Patronas
To Estación de Autobuses Plaza de Armas (600m)
C Pastor y Landero
Plaza de Malviedro
C Padre Marchena
C J Guichot
C Hernando Colón
C Álvarez Quintero
C Aire
1
C San José
C Levíes
20
Mercado del Arenal (Market)
C Castelar
C Jimios
C Argote de Molina
C Don Remondo
C Abadés
C Segovias
C Fabiola
9
C Dos Hermanas
C V Leal
C Gamazo
C de Adriano
8

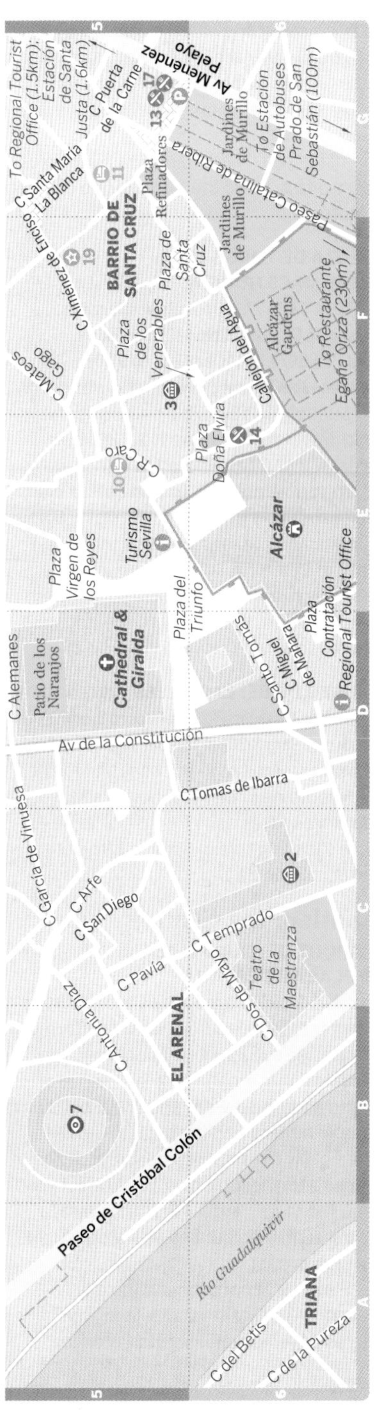

Seville

Top Sights

- Alcázar E6
- Casa de Pilatos G3
- Cathedral & Giralda D5

Sights

- 1 Baños Árabes F4
- 2 Hospital de la Caridad C6
- 3 Hospital de los Venerables Sacerdotes F5
- Metropol Parasol .... (see 4)
- 4 Museo Antiquarium E1
- 5 Museo de Bellas Artes A1
- 6 Museo del Baile Flamenco E3
- 7 Plaza de Toros de la Real Maestranza B5

Sleeping

- 8 EME Catedral Hotel D4
- 9 Hotel Amadeus F4
- 10 Hotel Casa 1800 .... E5
- 11 Un Patio en Santa Cruz G5

Eating

- 12 Bar Alfalfa F3
- 13 Catalina G5
- 14 Extraverde E6
- 15 Los Coloniales F2
- 16 Robles Laredo D3
- 17 Vinería San Telmo G5

Drinking

- Baños Árabes Tetería .... (see 1)
- 18 El Garlochi F2

Entertainment

- 19 Casa de la Memoria de Al-Andalus F5
- 20 La Carbonería G4

Spanish king Carlos I, using his title as Holy Roman Emperor, Charles V.

From the Salones de Carlos V you can go out into the Alcázar's large and sleepy gardens. Immediately in front of the building is a series of small linked gardens, some with pools and fountains. From one, the **Jardín de las Danzas** (Garden of the Dances), a passage runs beneath the Salones de Carlos V to the **Baños de Doña María de Padilla** (María de Padilla Baths).

Barrio de Santa Cruz

Seville's medieval *judería* (Jewish quarter), east of the cathedral and Alcázar, is today a tangle of atmospheric, winding streets and lovely plant-decked plazas perfumed with orange blossom.

HOSPITAL DE LOS VENERABLES SACERDOTES Art Gallery
(**☎954 56 26 96; Plaza de los Venerables 8; adult/child €4.75/2.40, Sun afternoon free; ⏰10am-2pm & 4-8pm**) Once a residence for ageing priests, this 17th-century baroque mansion guards what is perhaps Seville's most typical *sevillano* patio – intimate, plant embellished and spirit-reviving. The building's other highlights are its 17th-century church with rich religious murals, and the celebrated painting *Santa Rufina* by Diego Velázquez, procured for a hefty €12.5 million by the onsite Centro Velázquez foundation in 2007.

El Centro

MUSEO DEL BAILE FLAMENCO Museum
(**www.museoflamenco.com; Calle Manuel Rojas Marcos 3; adult/child €10/6; ⏰9.30am-7pm**) The brainchild of Sevillana flamenco dancer Cristina Hoyos, this museum spread over three floors of an 18th-century palace makes a noble effort to showcase the mysterious art, although at €10 a pop it is more than a little overpriced. Exhibits include sketches, paintings, photos of erstwhile (and contemporary) flamenco greats, plus a collection of dresses and shawls.

CASA DE PILATOS Palace, Museum
(**☎954 22 52 98; www.fundacionmedinaceli.org; Plaza de Pilatos; admission ground fl only €5, whole house €8; ⏰9am-7pm Apr-Oct, to 6pm Nov-Mar**) The haunting Casa de Pilatos, which is still occupied by the ducal Medinaceli family, is one of the city's most glorious mansions. It's a mixture of Mudéjar, Gothic and Renaissance styles, with some beautiful tile work and *artesonado*.

El Arenal

HOSPITAL DE LA CARIDAD Art Gallery
(**Calle Temprado 3; admission €5; ⏰9.30am-1pm & 3.30-7pm Mon-Sat, 9am-12.30pm Sun**) The Hospital de la Caridad, a block east of the river, is an art gallery that was once a hospice for the elderly founded by Miguel de Mañara, by legend a notorious libertine who changed his ways after seeing a vision of his own funeral procession.

Inside you'll find marvellous examples of *sevillano* art of the Siglo de Oro (Golden Century).

PLAZA DE TOROS DE LA REAL MAESTRANZA Bullring, Museum
(**☎954 22 45 77; www.realmaestranza.es; Paseo de Cristóbal Colón 12; tours adult/child €6.50/2.50; ⏰half-hourly 9.30am-8pm, 9.30am-3pm bullfight days**) In the world of bullfighting, Seville's bullring is the Old Trafford and Camp Nou. In other words, if you're selected to fight here then you've made it. In addition to being regarded as a building of almost religious significance to fans, it's also the oldest ring in Spain (building began in 1758). Slightly robotic guided visits, in English and Spanish, take you into the ring and its museum.

MUSEO DE BELLAS ARTES Art Gallery
(**Fine Arts Museum; Plaza del Museo 9; admission €1.50; ⏰9am-8.30pm Tue-Sat, to 2.30pm Sun & holidays**) Housed in the beautiful former Convento de la Merced, Seville's Museo de Bellas Artes does full justice to Seville's leading role in Spain's 17th-century artistic Siglo de Oro.

South of the Centre

PARQUE DE MARÍA LUISA & PLAZA DE ESPAÑA Park
(**⏰8am-10pm**) A large area south of the former tobacco factory was transformed for Seville's 1929 international fair, the Exposición Iberoamericana, when architects adorned it with fantastical buildings, many of them harking back to Seville's past glory or imitating the native styles of Spain's former colonies. In its midst you'll find the large Parque de María Luisa, a living expression of Seville's Moorish and Christian past.

Plaza de España, one of the city's favourite relaxation spots, faces the park across Avenida de Isabel la Católica.

Tours

SEVILLA WALKING TOURS Walking Tour
(📞902 15 82 26; www.sevillawalkingtours.com; per person €12) Walk around the city like a *sevillano* in the know.

Sleeping

Barrio de Santa Cruz

HOTEL CASA 1800 Luxury Hotel **€€€**
(📞954 56 18 00; www.hotelcasa1800sevilla.com; Calle Rodrigo Caro 6; d €145-198; ❄@📶) Straight in at number one as Seville's favourite hotel is this newly revived Santa Cruz jewel where the word *casa* (house) is taken seriously. This really is your home away from home (albeit a posh one!), with charming staff catering for your every need. Historic highlights include a sweet afternoon tea buffet, plus a quartet of penthouse garden suites with Giralda views.

UN PATIO EN SANTA CRUZ Hotel **€€**
(📞954 53 94 13; www.patiosantacruz.com; Calle Doncellas 15; s €65-85, d €65-125; ❄📶) Feeling more like an art gallery than a hotel, the Patio has starched white walls coated in loud works of art, and strange sculptures and preserved plants. The rooms are immensely comfortable, staff are friendly and there's a cool rooftop terrace with mosaic Moroccan tables.

HOTEL AMADEUS Hotel **€€**
(📞954 50 14 43; www.hotelamadeussevilla.com; Calle Farnesio 6; s/d €85/95; P❄📶) Just when you thought you could never find hotels with pianos in the rooms anymore, along came Hotel Amadeus run by an engaging musical family in the old *judería,* where several of the astutely decorated rooms come complete with soundproofed walls and upright pianos, ensuring you don't miss out on your daily practice.

EME CATEDRAL HOTEL Luxury Hotel **€€€**
(📞954 56 00 00; www.emecatedralhotel.com; Calle de los Alemanes 27; d €187-348; ❄@📶🏊) Take 14 fine old Sevillan houses and knock them into one. Bring in a top designer and Spain's most decorated chef. Carve out a hamman, rooftop

Alcázar, Seville (p254)

ALLAN BAXTER/GETTY IMAGES ©

MICHELE FALZONE/GETTY IMAGES ©

Don't Miss Cathedral & Giralda

After Seville fell to the Christians in 1248 the mosque was used as a church until 1402. Then, in view of its decaying state, the church authorities decided to knock it down and start again. Let's 'construct a church so large, future generations will think we were mad', they decided (or so legend has it). The result is a cathedral measuring 126m long and 83m wide.

Inside the **Puerta de los Príncipes** (Door of the Princes) stands the monumental tomb of Christopher Columbus (Cristóbal Colón in Spanish) containing what were long believed to be the great explorer's bones, brought here from Cuba in 1898.

East of the choir is the **Capilla Mayor** (Main Chapel). Its Gothic retable is the jewel of the cathedral and reckoned to be the biggest altarpiece in the world. Begun by Flemish sculptor Pieter Dancart in 1482 and finished by others in 1564, this sea of gilt and polychromed wood holds over 1000 carved biblical figures.

In the northeastern corner of the cathedral you'll find the passage for the climb up to the belfry of the **Giralda**. The decorative brick tower which stands 104m tall was the minaret of the mosque, constructed between 1184 and 1198 at the height of Almohad power. At the very top is **El Giraldillo**, a 16th-century bronze weathervane representing 'faith' that has become a symbol of Seville.

NEED TO KNOW

adult/child €8/free; ⌚11am-5.30pm Mon-Sat, 2.30-6.30pm Sun Sep-Jun, 9.30am-4.30pm Mon-Sat, 2.30-6.30pm Sun Jul & Aug

pool, four restaurants and slick, striking rooms with red colour accents. Then stick it all nose-to-nose with the largest Gothic cathedral in the world.

The result: EME Catedral Hotel, the city's most talked about new accommodation where ancient Seville has been fused with something a bit more cutting edge.

Eating

Barrio de Santa Cruz

VINERÍA SAN TELMO Tapas, Fusion **€€**
(☎954 41 06 00; www.vineriasantelmo.com; Paseo Catalina de Ribera 4; tapas €3.50, media raciones €10) San Telmo invented the *rascocielo* (skyscraper) tapa, an 'Empire State' of tomatoes, aubergine, goat's cheese and smoked salmon. If this and other creative nougats such as foie gras with quails eggs and lychees, or exquisitely cooked bricks of tuna don't make you drool with expectation, then you're probably dead.

CATALINA Tapas **€€**
(Paseo Catalina de Ribera 4; raciones €10) If your view of tapas is 'glorified bar snacks'; then your ideas could be blown out of the water here with a creative mix of just about every ingredient known to Iberian cooking. Start with the cheese, aubergine and paprika special.

RESTAURANTE EGAÑA ORIZA Contemporary Spanish **€€€**
(off Map p256 www.restauranteoriza.com; Calle San Fernando 41; mains €22-32; ⌚closed Sat lunch & Sun) Basque is a byword for fine-dining these days, so it's not surprising that Basque-run Egaña Oriza is regarded as one of the city's stand-out restaurants.

EXTRAVERDE Tapas **€**
(www.extraverde.es; Plaza de Doña Elvira 8; tapas €2.50-4; ⌚10.30am-11.30pm) Recently arrived on the Santa Cruz scene, Extraverde is a unique bar-shop specialising in Andalucian products such as olive oil, cheese and wine. You can taste free samples standing up, or sit down inside and order full tapas serves.

El Centro

LOS COLONIALES Contemporary Andalucian **€€**
(www.tabernacoloniales.es; cnr Calle Dormitorio & Plaza Cristo de Burgos; tapas €2.50, raciones €10-12) The quiet ones are always the best. It might not look like much from the outside but, take it on trust, Los Coloniales is something very special. The quality plates line up like models on a catwalk: *chorizo a la Asturiana*, a divine spicy sausage in an onion sauce served on a bed of lightly fried potato; aubergines in honey; and pork tenderloin *al whiskey*.

ROBLES LAREDO Contemporary Spanish **€€**
(www.casa-robles.com; Plaza de San Francisco; raciones €9-12; 👪) This small Italianite cafe-restaurant is fairly dwarfed by its two huge chandeliers and a vast collection of delicate desserts displayed in glass cases. The tapas are equally refined. Try the foie gras, beefburgers with truffle sauce, or oysters and whitebait.

BAR ALFALFA Tapas **€**
(cnr Calles Alfalfa & Candilejo; tapas €3) It's amazing how many people, hams, wine bottles and other knick-knacks you can stuff into such a small space. No matter, order through the window when the going gets crowded. You won't forget the tomato-tinged magnificence of the Italy-meets-Iberia *salmorejo* bruschetta.

Drinking

BAÑOS ÁRABES TETERÍA Teahouse
(Calle Aire 15) Seville's no Granada when it comes to exotically infused teahouses, though exceptions should be made for this cushioned comfort zone encased in the pin-dropping tranquility of the **Baños Árabes** **(☎955 01 00 25; www.airedesevilla.com; Calle Aire 15; admission from €20; ⌚every 2hr from 10am-midnight)** in Santa Cruz. With no on-site shisha pipes or yodeling singers, the atmosphere is generated by the edgy art and murmuring intellectuals discussing Almodóvar movies.

EL GARLOCHI Bar
(Calle Boteros 4) Dedicated entirely to the iconography, smells and sounds of Semana Santa, the ubercamp El Garlochi is a true marvel. A cloud of church incense hits you as you walk up the stairs, and the faces of baby Jesus and the Virgin welcome you into the velvet-walled bar, decked out with more Virgins and Jesuses.

Seville Cathedral

What To Look For

'We're going to construct a church so large future generations will think we were mad,' declared the inspired architects of Seville in 1402 at the beginning of one of the most grandiose building projects in medieval history. Just over a century later their madness was triumphantly confirmed.

To avoid getting lost, orient yourself by the main highlights. Directly inside the southern (main) entrance is the grand **mausoleum of Christopher Columbus** 1. Turn right here and head into the south-eastern corner to uncover some major art treasures: a Goya in the Sacristía de los Cálices, a Zurbarán in the **Sacristía Mayor** 2, and Murillo's shining Immaculada in the Sala Capitular. Skirt the cathedral's eastern wall taking a look inside the **Capilla Real** 3 with its important royal tombs. By now it's impossible to avoid the lure of **Capilla Mayor** 4 with its fantastical altarpiece. Hidden over in the northwest corner is the **Capilla de San Antonio** 5 with a legendary Murillo. That huge doorway almost in front of you is rarely opened **Puerta de la Asunción** 6. Make for the **Giralda** 7 next, stealing admiring looks at the high, vaulted ceiling on the way. After looking down on the cathedral's immense footprint, descend and depart via the **Patio de los Naranjos** 8.

TOP TIPS

Queue-dodge Reserve tickets online at www.servicaixa.com for an extra €1 up to six weeks in advance.

Pace yourself Don't visit the Alcazar and Cathedral on the same day. There is far too much to take in.

Viewpoints Take time to admire the cathedral from the outside. It's particularly stunning at night from the Plaza Virgen de los Reyes, and from across the river in Triana.

ONTHEROAD/ALAMY ©

Capilla Mayor
Behold! The cathedral's main focal point contains its greatest treasure, a magnificent gold-plated altarpiece depicting various scenes in the life of Christ. It constitutes the life's work of one man, Flemish artist Pieter Dancart.

Patio de los Naranjos
Inhale the perfume of 60 Sevillan orange trees in a cool patio bordered by fortress-like walls – a surviving remnant of the original 12th-century mosque. Exit is gained via the horseshoe-shaped Puerta del Perdón.

Puerta del Perdón

5

Iglesia del Sagrario

Puerta del Bautismo

6

Puerta de la Asunción
Located on the western side of the cathedral and also known as the Puerta Mayor, these huge, rarely opened doors are pushed back during Semana Santa to allow solemn processions of Catholic *hermanadades* (brotherhoods) to pass through.

ADB TRAVEL/ALAMY ©

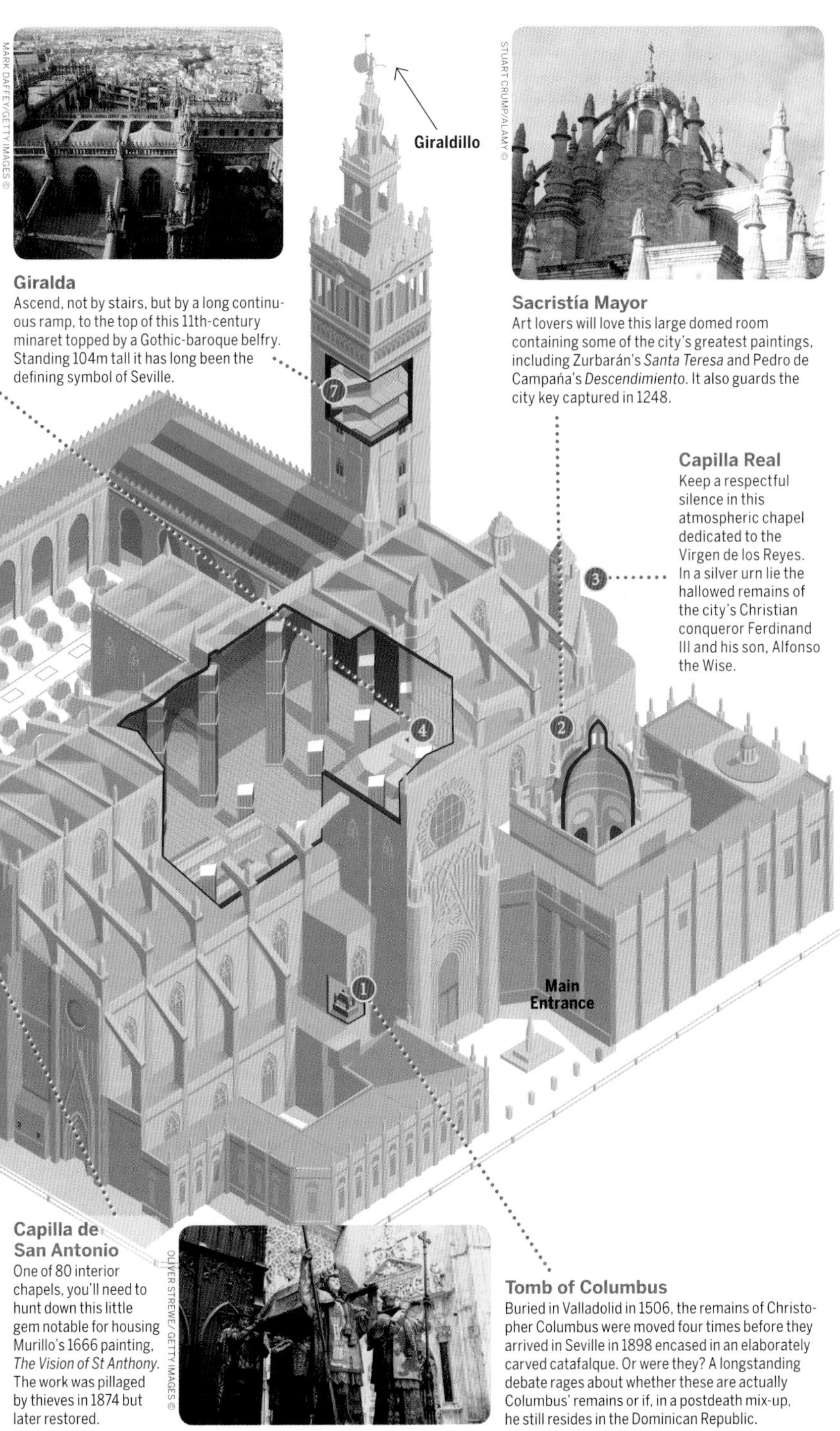

MARK DAFFEY/GETTY IMAGES ©
Giraldillo
STUART CRUMP/ALAMY ©
Giralda
Ascend, not by stairs, but by a long continuous ramp, to the top of this 11th-century minaret topped by a Gothic-baroque belfry. Standing 104m tall it has long been the defining symbol of Seville.
Sacristía Mayor
Art lovers will love this large domed room containing some of the city's greatest paintings, including Zurbarán's *Santa Teresa* and Pedro de Campaña's *Descendimiento*. It also guards the city key captured in 1248.
Capilla Real
Keep a respectful silence in this atmospheric chapel dedicated to the Virgen de los Reyes. In a silver urn lie the hallowed remains of the city's Christian conqueror Ferdinand III and his son, Alfonso the Wise.
7
3
4
2
1
Main Entrance
Capilla de San Antonio
One of 80 interior chapels, you'll need to hunt down this little gem notable for housing Murillo's 1666 painting, *The Vision of St Anthony*. The work was pillaged by thieves in 1874 but later restored.
OLIVER STREWE/ GETTY IMAGES ©
Tomb of Columbus
Buried in Valladolid in 1506, the remains of Christopher Columbus were moved four times before they arrived in Seville in 1898 encased in an elaborately carved catafalque. Or were they? A longstanding debate rages about whether these are actually Columbus' remains or if, in a postdeath mix-up, he still resides in the Dominican Republic.

Detour: Itálica

Situated in the suburban settlement of Santiponce, 8km northwest of Seville, **Itálica** (**955 62 22 66; www.juntadeandalucia.es/cultura/italica; Avenida de Extremadura 2; admission €1.50; 8.30am-9pm Tue-Sat, 9am-3pm Sun & holidays Apr-Sep, 9am-6.30pm Tue-Sat, 10am-4pm Sun & holidays Oct-Mar**) was the first Roman town in Spain. Founded in 206 BC, it was also the birthplace and home of the 2nd-century-AD Roman emperors Trajan and Hadrian. The partly reconstructed ruins include one of the biggest of all the Roman amphitheatres, broad paved streets, ruins of several houses with beautiful mosaics, and a theatre.

Buses run to Santiponce (€1.30, 40 minutes) from Seville's Plaza de Armas bus station, at least twice an hour from 6.35am to 11pm Monday to Friday, and a little less often at weekends. They stop right outside the Itálica entrance.

Entertainment

CASA DE LA MEMORIA DE AL-ANDALUS Flamenco

(**954 56 06 70; www.casadelamemoria.es; Calle Ximénez de Enciso 28; tickets €15; 9pm**) This *tablao* in Santa Cruz is without doubt the most intimate and authentic nightly flamenco show outside the Museo del Baile Flamenco, offering a wide variety of *palos* (flamenco styles) in a courtyard of shifting shadows and overhanging plants. Space is limited, so reserve tickets in advance.

FREE **LA CARBONERÍA** Flamenco

(**Calle Levíes 18; admission free; 8pm-4am**) During the day there is no indication that this happening place is anything but a garage. But come 8pm this converted coal yard in the Barrio de Santa Cruz reveals two large bars, and nightly live flamenco (11pm and midnight) for no extra charge.

CASA ANSELMA Flamenco

(**Calle Pagés del Corro 49; midnight-late Mon-Sat**) If you can squeeze in past the foreboding form of Anselma (a celebrated flamenco dancer) at the door, you'll quickly realise that anything can happen in here. Casa Anselma (there's no sign, just a doorway embellished with azulejos tiles) is the antithesis of a tourist flamenco *tablao*, with cheek-to-jowl crowds, thick cigarette smoke, zero amplification and spontaneous outbreaks of dexterous dancing.

Anselma is in Triana on the corner of Calle Alfarería, about 200m from the western side of the Puente de Isabel.

Information

Tourist Information

There are regional tourist offices at Avenida de la Constitución 21 (**9am-7pm Mon-Fri, 10am-2pm & 3-7pm Sat, 10am-2pm Sun, closed holidays**) and Estación Santa Justa (**954 53 76 26; 9am-8pm Mon-Fri, 10am-2pm Sat & Sun, closed holidays**)

Turismo Sevilla (**www.turismosevilla.org; Plaza del Triunfo 1; 10.30am-7pm Mon-Fri**) Information on all Sevilla province.

Getting There & Away

Air

Seville's Aeropuerto San Pablo has a fair range of international and domestic flights. Iberia (www.iberia.com) flies direct to Barcelona, Madrid and half a dozen other Spanish cities, as well as to London and Paris. Air Europa and Vueling (p367) fly to Barcelona. Vueling also covers Paris, and Amsterdam to Seville.

Bus

Seville has two bus stations. Buses to/from the north of Sevilla province, Huelva province, Portugal, and most other parts of Spain including Madrid, use the main Estación de Autobuses

Plaza de Armas **(Avenida del Cristo de la Expiración)**. Other buses – primarily those running inside Andalucia (except Huelva) – use the Estación de Autobuses Prado de San Sebastián **(Plaza San Sebastián)**. Buses from here run roughly hourly to Cádiz, Córdoba, Granada, Jerez de la Frontera, Málaga and Madrid.

Train

Seville's Estación Santa Justa **(☎902 43 23 43; Avenida Kansas City)** is 1.5km northeast of the centre. Trains go to/from Madrid (€83.30, 2½ hours, 20 daily), Cádiz (€13.25, 1 hour 45 minutes, 15 daily), Córdoba (€33.20, 42 minutes, 30 daily), Huelva (€10.05, 1½ hours, three daily), Granada (€24.80, three hours, four daily) and Málaga (€38.70, two hours, 11 daily).

Getting Around

To/From the Airport

The airport is 7km east of the city centre on the A4 Córdoba road. Los Amarillos **(www.losamarillos.es)** runs buses between the airport and Avenida del Cid near the San Sebastián bus station (€2.40; every 15 minutes, 5.45am-12.45am; less frequent on Sundays). A taxi costs about €22.

Car & Motorcycle

Hotels with parking usually charge you €12 to €18 a day for the privilege – no cheaper than some public car parks but at least your vehicle will be close at hand. Parking Paseo de Colón **(cnr Paseo de Cristóbal Colón & Calle Adriano; per hr up to 10hr €1.20, 10-24hr €13.50)** is a relatively inexpensive underground car park.

Carmona

POP 27,950 / ELEV 250 M

Perched on a low hill overlooking a wonderful *vega* (valley) that sizzles in the summer heat, dotted with old palaces and impressive monuments, Carmona comes as an unexpected highlight of western Andalucía.

Sights

The tourist office in the **Puerta de Sevilla**, the impressive fortified main gate of the old town, sells tickets (adults/students and seniors €2/1) for the gate's interesting upper levels.

The **Puerta de Córdoba (Calle de Dolores Quintanilla; admission €2; ⏰tours min 8 people**

Flower-decked street in Triana, Seville

You can look down into a dozen family tombs, hewn from the rock.

If You Like… Small Town Life

If you like Carmona's lazy small town feel (and you will) cruise on by these places for a similar experience:

1 **ÉCIJA**
A stack of Gothic-Mudéjar palaces and churches and a genuine insight into small town Andalucian life.

2 **OSUNA**
Sleepy and unassuming Osuna has a stash of beautifully preserved Baroque mansions.

3 **CAZALLA DE LA SIERRA**
Attractive white hill town with pleasant walks in the woods and some great places to stay.

4 **LA RÁBIDA, PALOS DE LA FRONTERA AND MOGUER**
Three little townships that together helped send Columbus to America.

5 **NIEBLA**
Encircled by ochre red walls and home to a grotesquely fascinating museum of torture.

11.30am, 12.30pm & 1.30pm Tue, Sat & Sun), in Calle Dolores Quintanilla at the end of the street passing the Iglesia Priorial de Santa María, is an original Roman gate in marvellous repair, framing the fertile Seville countryside that unfolds like a precious, faded rug. South of here is the stark, ruined **Alcázar** (adult/child €2/1, Mon free; 10am-6pm Mon-Sat, 10am-3pm Sun & holidays), an Almohad fort that Pedro I turned into a country palace.

FREE ROMAN NECROPOLIS Cemetery, Ruins
(954 14 08 11; Avenida de Jorge Bonsor; 9am-2pm Tue-Sat 15 Jun–14 Sep, to 5pm Tue-Fri, closed holidays & 1 Jul–31 Aug) Just over 1km southwest of the Puerta de Sevilla is Carmona's impressive Roman Necropolis.

Sleeping & Eating

PARADOR ALCÁZAR DEL REY DON PEDRO Historic Hotel €€€
(954 14 10 10; www.parador.es; Calle Alcázar; r €160-171) Carmona's luxuriously equipped *parador* (state-owned historic hotel) feels even more luxurious for the ruined Alcázar in its grounds. The beautiful dining room (*menú del día* – daily set menu – €32) overlooks a jaw-dropping (and unexpected) view of the surrounding Vega roasting under the Sevillian sun.

CASA CURRO MONTOYA Tapas €€
(Calle Santa María de Gracia 13; tapas €2.50; closed Tue) This friendly, family-run joint opposite the Convento de Santa Clara occupies a narrow hall littered with memorabilia. Long-cultivated family traditions find expression in such items as fresh tuna in a luscious onion sauce, foie gras–stuffed eggplant and fried *pizcotas* (small sardine-like fish).

Information

Tourist office (www.turismo.carmona.org; Alcázar de la Puerta de Sevilla; 10am-6pm Mon-Sat, 10am-3pm Sun & holidays) This helpful tourist office is inside the Puerta de Sevilla.

Getting There & Away

Monday to Friday, Casal runs hourly buses to Seville from the stop on Paseo del Estatuto, on weekends less often. Two or three buses a day go to Córdoba via Écija from the car park next to the Puerta de Sevilla.

CÓRDOBA

POP 328,000 / ELEV 110M

Picture a city 500,000 strong, embellished with fine architecture and fuelled by a prosperous and diverse economy. Picture universities and libraries filled

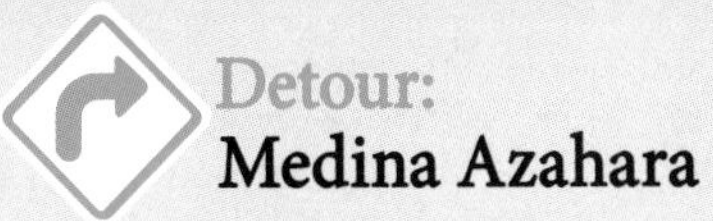

Detour: Medina Azahara

Even in the cicada-shrill heat and stillness of a summer afternoon, the **Medina Azahara** (Medina Azahara; ☎957 32 91 30; Carretera Palma del Río; admission €1.50; ⌚10am-8.30pm Tue-Sat May–mid-Sep, 10am-6.30pm Tue-Sat mid-Sep–Apr, 10am-2pm Sun year-round) whispers of the power and vision of its founder, Abd ar-Rahman III. The self-proclaimed caliph began the construction of a magnificent new capital 8km west of Córdoba around 936, and took up full residence around 945. Medina Azahara was a resounding declaration of his status, a magnificent trapping of power.

The new capital was very short-lived; between 1010 and 1013, during the caliphate's collapse it was wrecked by Berber soldiers. Today, less than a tenth has been excavated, and only about a quarter of that is open to visitors.

A new **museum** on the foundation of one of the excavated buildings blends seamlessly with its surroundings and traces the history of the city, with beautifully displayed pieces taken from the site and some amazing interactive displays.

Medina Azahara is signposted on Avenida de Medina Azahara, which leads west out of Córdoba onto the A431. A taxi costs €37 for the return trip, with one hour to view the site, or you can book a three-hour coach tour for €6.50 to €10 through many Córdoba hotels.

with erudite artists and wise philosophers. Picture an Islamic caliphate more advanced and civilised than anything else the world had ever known. Picture Córdoba c AD 975.

OK, so this slightly grainy image may be over 1000 years old now, but enough of ancient Córdoba remains to place it in the contemporary top three drawcards of Andalucía. The centrepiece is the gigantic Mezquita, an architectural anomaly and one of the only places in the world where you can worship Mass in a mosque. Surrounding it is an intricate web of winding streets, geranium-sprouting flower boxes and cool intimate patios that are at their most beguiling in late spring.

Sights & Activities

JUDERÍA Historic Neighbourhood

Jews were among the most dynamic and prominent citizens of Islamic Córdoba. The medieval *judería*, extending northwest from the Mezquita almost to Avenida del Gran Capitán, is today a maze of narrow streets and whitewashed buildings with flowery window boxes.

The beautiful little 14th-century **Sinagoga** (Calle de los Judíos 20; admission €0.30; ⌚9.30am-2pm & 3.30-5.30pm Tue-Sat, 9.30am-1.30pm Sun & holidays) is one of only three surviving medieval synagogues in Spain and the only one in Andalucía.

In the heart of the *judería*, and once connected by an underground tunnel to the Sinagoga, is the 14th-century **Casa de Sefarad** (www.casadesefarad.es; Calle Judíos; admission €4; ⌚10am-6pm Mon-Sat, 11am-2pm Sun). Opened in 2008 on the corner of Calles de los Judíos and Averroes, this small, beautiful museum is devoted to reviving interest in the Sephardic-Judaic-Spanish tradition.

ALCÁZAR DE LOS REYES CRISTIANOS Castle

(Castle of the Christian Monarchs; Campo Santo de Los Mártires; admission €4, Fri free; ⌚10am-2pm & 5.30-7.30pm Tue-Sat, 9.30am-2.30pm Sun & holidays) Built by Alfonso XI in the 14th century on the remains of Roman and

Córdoba

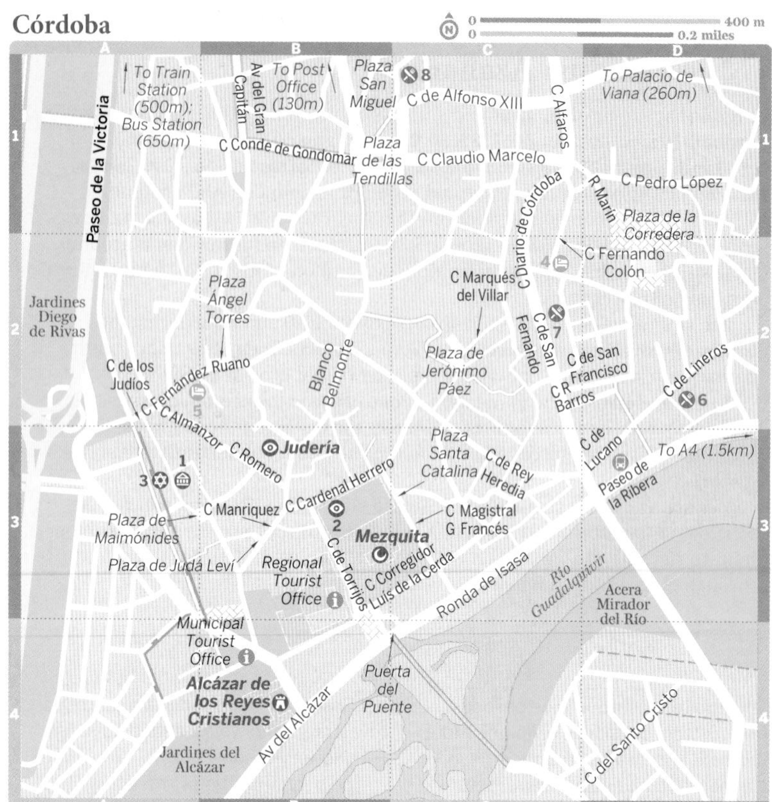

Córdoba

Top Sights

Alcázar de los Reyes Cristianos	B4
Judería	B3
Mezquita	B3

Sights

1 Casa de Sefarad	A3
2 Puerta del Perdón	B3
3 Sinagoga	A3

Sleeping

4 Casa de los Azulejos	C2
5 Hospedería Alma Andalusí	A2

Eating

6 Bodegas Campos	D2
7 La Boca	C2
8 Taberna San Miguel El Pisto	C1

Arab predecessors, the castle began life as a palace. Its terraced gardens – full of fish ponds, fountains, orange trees, flowers and topiary – are a pleasure to stroll and a joy to behold from the tower.

PALACIO DE VIANA Museum

(www.palaciodeviana.com; Plaza de Don Gome 2; admission whole house/patios only €6/3; 10am-7pm Tue-Fri, 10am-3pm Sat & Sun Sep-Jun, 9am-3pm Tue-Sun Jul & Aug) This stunning renaissance palace is set around 12 beautiful patios that are a genuine pleasure to visit in the spring. Occupied by the Marqueses de Viana until a few decades ago, the 6500 sq m building is packed with art and antiques.

Sleeping

PARADOR NACIONAL ARRUZAFA Historic Hotel **€€€**
(☎957 27 59 00; www.parador.es; Avenida de la Arruzafa ; r €161; P ❄ ☎ ≋) This parador is 3km north of the city centre, fabulously situated on the site of Abd ar-Rahman I's summer palace. It's a modern affair set amid lush gardens where Europe's first palm trees were planted.

HOSPEDERÍA ALMA ANDALUSÍ Boutique Hotel **€€**
(☎957 76 08 88; www.almaandalusi.com; Calle Fernández Ruano 5; s/d €45/100; ❄ ☎) The builders of this guesthouse in a quiet section of the Judería have brilliantly converted an ancient structure into a stylish modern establishment while keeping the rates down. Thoughtfully chosen furnishings, polished wood floors and solid colors make for a comfortable base.

CASA DE LOS AZULEJOS Hotel **€€**
(☎957 47 00 00; www.casadelosazulejos.com; Calle Fernando Colón 5; s/d incl breakfast from €85/107; ❄ @ ☎) Mexican and Andalusian styles converge in this stylish hotel, where the patio is all banana trees, ferns and potted palms bathed in sunlight. Colonial-style rooms feature tall antique doors, massive beds, walls in lilac and sky blues, and floors adorned with the beautiful old *azulejos* (tiles) that give the place its name.

Eating

TABERNA SAN MIGUEL EL PISTO Tapas **€**
(Plaza San Miguel 1; tapas €3, media raciones €5-10; ⏲closed Sun & Aug) Brimming with local character, El Pisto is one of Córdoba's best *tabernas,* both in terms of atmosphere and food. Traditional tapas and *media-raciones* are done perfectly, and inexpensive Moriles wine is ready in jugs on the bar. Be sure to try the namesake item, a sort of ratatouille topped with a fried egg.

BODEGAS CAMPOS Andalucian **€€**
(☎957 49 75 00; www.bodegascampos.com; Calle de Lineros 32; tapas €5, mains €13-21) One of Córdoba's most atmospheric and famous wine cellar/restaurants, this sprawling hall features dozens of rooms and patios, with oak barrels signed by local and international celebrities stacked up alongside. The bodega produces its own house Montilla, and the restaurant, frequented by swankily dressed *cordobeses,* serves up a delicious array of meals.

LA BOCA International, Fusion **€€**
(☎957 47 61 40; www.restaurantelaboca.com; Calle San Fernando 39; mains €11-15; ⏲closed Mon dinner & Tue) Trendy for a reason, this cutting-edge eatery whips up exciting global variations on traditional ingredients, then presents them in eye-catching ways: Iberian pork on a bed of thai noodles? Zuheros cheese garnished with sun-dried tomatoes? Why not?

Córdoba for Children

When you and the kids just don't want to look at old stones a moment longer, it's time to head a little way out of town and leave the past behind. Just southwest of Córdoba's city centre and adjoining the **Zoo and Wildlife Centre** (Avenida de Linneo; adult/child €4/2; ⏲10am-7pm Tue-Sun Apr & May, to 8pm Jun-Aug, to 7pm Sep), historic buildings morph into brightly coloured climbing equipment. Welcome to **La Ciudad de los Niños** (☎663 035709; laciudaddelosninos@educasur.es; Avenida Menéndez Pidal; admission free; ⏲10am-2pm & 7-11pm Jun–mid-Sep), Córdoba's City for Kids. A calendar of special events aimed at four- to 12-year-olds runs throughout the summer – check the website for details, or ask at the regional tourist office. Buses 2 and 5 (heading to Hospital Reina Sofia) from the city centre stop here.

KARL BLACKWELL/GETTY IMAGES ©

Don't Miss Mezquita

Founded in 785, Córdoba's gigantic mosque is a wonderful architectural hybrid with delicate horseshoe arches making this unlike anywhere else in Spain. The main entrance is the **Puerta del Perdón**, a 14th-century Mudéjar gateway; the ticket office is immediately inside.

Once inside, you can see straight ahead to the mihrab, the prayer niche in the mosque's qibla (the wall indicating the direction of Mecca). The first 12 transverse aisles inside the entrance, a forest of pillars and arches, comprise the original 8th-century mosque.

In the centre of the building is the Christian cathedral. Just past the cathedral's western end, the approach to the mihrab begins, marked by heavier, more elaborate arches. Immediately in front of the mihrab is the **maksura**, the royal prayer enclosure, with its intricately interwoven arches and lavishly decorated domes created by Caliph Al-Hakam II in the 960s. The decoration of the **mihrab portal** incorporates 1600kg of gold mosaic cubes, a gift from the Christian emperoro of Byzantium, Nicephoras II Phocas.

NEED TO KNOW

Mosque; ☎957 47 05 12; www.mezquitadecordoba.org; Calle Cardenal Herrero; adult/child €8/4, 8.30-10am Mon-Sat free ; ⏰10am-7pm Mon-Sat, 8.30-10am & 2-7pm Sun Mar-Oct, 8.30am-6pm Mon-Sat, 8.30-10am & 2-6pm Sun Nov-Feb

Information

Municipal tourist office (**☎902 20 17 74; www.turismodecordoba.org; ⏰9am-2pm & 5-7pm**) Opposite the Alcázar de los Reyes Cristianos.

Regional tourist office (**Calle de Torrijos 10; ⏰9am-7.30pm Mon-Fri, 9.30am-3pm Sat, Sun & holidays**) Inside the Palacio Episcopal.

Getting There & Away

Bus

The bus station is behind the train station. Each bus company has its own terminal. ALSA (**www.alsa.es**) runs services to Seville (€10.36, 1¾ hours, six daily), Granada (€12.52, 2½ hours, seven daily), Málaga (€12.75, 2¾ hours, five daily), and Baeza (€10, three hours, one daily). Secorbus (902 22 92 92; www.socibus.es) operates buses to Madrid (€15.80, 4½ hours, six daily).

Train

Córdoba's train station (957 40 02 02; Glorieta de las Tres Culturas) is on the high-speed AVE line between Madrid and Seville. Rail destinations include Seville (€11 to €33, 40 to 90 minutes, 23 or more daily), Madrid (€53 to €68, 1¾ to 6¼ hours, 23 or more daily), Málaga (€22 to €45, 45 minutes to 2½ hours, 16 daily), Barcelona (€138, 4½ hours, four daily). For Granada, change at Bobadilla.

WHITE HILL TOWNS

Arcos de la Frontera

POP 31,500 / ELEV 185M

Choosing your favourite *pueblo blanco* is like choosing your favourite Beatles album – they're all so damned good, it's hard to make a definitive decision. Pressured for an answer, many people single out Arcos, a larger-than-average white town thrillingly sited on a high, unassailable ridge with sheer precipices plummeting away on both sides. With the Sierra de Grazalema as a distant backdrop, Arcos possesses all the classic white-town calling cards: spectacular location, soporific old town, fancy *parador*, and volatile frontier history.

Sights

PLAZA DEL CABILDO Square

The old town captures multiple historical eras evoking the ebb and flow of the once-disputed Christian-Moorish frontier. Plaza del Cabildo is the centre of this quarter. Close your eyes to the modern car park and focus instead on the fine surrounding buildings (all old) and a vertiginous **mirador** (lookout) with views over Río Guadalete. The 11th-century **Castillo de los Duques** is firmly closed to the public, but its outer walls frame classic Arcos views. On the plaza's northern side is the Gothic-cum-baroque **Basíllica-Parroquia de Santa María** sporting beautiful stone choir stalls and Isabelline ceiling tracery. On the eastern side, the **Parador Casa del Corregidor** hotel is a reconstruction of a 16th-century magistrate's house.

Sleeping

PARADOR CASA DEL CORREGIDOR Historic Hotel **€€€**

(956 70 05 00; www.parador.es; Plaza del Cabildo, Arcos de la Frontera; r from €155;) This rebuilt 16th-century magistrate's residence combines typical parador luxury with another magnificent cliffside setting. Eight of the 24 rooms have balconies with sweeping cliff-top views.

HOTEL REAL DE VEAS Hotel **€€**

(956 71 73 70; www.hotelrealdeveas.com; Calle Corredera 12; s/d incl breakfast €55/70) A superb option inside a lovingly restored building. The dozen or so rooms are arranged around a glass-covered patio and are cool and comfortable. It's one of the few places that has easy car access.

Eating

BAR LA CÁRCEL Tapas **€€**

(956 70 04 10; Calle Deán Espinosa 18; tapas & montaditos €2.50, raciones €8-12; 8am-noon Mon, to late Tue-Sun) A *cárcel* (prison) in name only, this place offers no nonsense tapas (bank on fajitas, or aubergine with goat's cheese and honey) with ice-cold *cañas* of beer for customers who sit at beer barrels doubling up as tables. It's friendly and authentic.

Information

The tourist office (956 70 22 64; Calle Cuesta de Belén 5; 10am-2.30pm & 5.30-8pm Mon-Fri, 10.30am-1.30pm & 5-7pm Sat, 10.30am-1.30pm Sun) is on the old town's main square.

Getting There & Away

From the bus station (956 70 49 77), Los Amarillos (www.losamarillos.es) and/or Comes

Mezquita

Timeline

AD 600 Foundation of the Christian Visigothic church of St Vincent on the site of the present Mezquita.

AD 785 Salvaging Visigoth and Roman ruins, Emir Abd ar-Rahman I converts the Mezquita into a mosque.

AD 822-5 Mosque enlarged in reign of Abd ar-Rahman II.

AD 912-961 A new minaret is ordered by Abd ar-Rahman III.

AD 961-6 Mosque enlarged by Al-Hakam II who also enriches the **mihrab** 1.

AD 987 Mosque enlarged for the last time by Al-Mansur Ibn Abi Aamir. With the addition of the Patio de los **Naranjos** 2, the building reaches its current dimensions.

1236 Mosque reconverted into a Christian church after Córdoba is recaptured by Ferdinand III of Castile.

1271 Instead of destroying the mosque, the overawed Christians elect to modify it. Alfonso X orders the construction of the **Capilla de Villaviciosa** 3 and **Capilla Real** 4.

1300s Original minaret is replaced by the baroque **Torre del Alminar** 5.

1520s A Renaissance-style cathedral nave is added by Charles V. 'I have destroyed something unique to the world,' he laments on seeing the finished work.

2004 Spanish Muslims petition to be able to worship in the Mezquita again. The Vatican doesn't consent.

TOP TIPS

Among the oranges The Patio de los Naranjos can be enjoyed free of charge at any time

Early birds Entry to the rest of the Mezquita is offered free every morning except Sunday between 8.30am and 10am

Quiet time Group visits are prohibited before 10am, meaning the building is quieter and more atmospheric in the early morning

Capilla de Villaviciosa
Sift through the building's numerous chapels till you find this gem, an early Christian modification added in 1277 which fused existing Moorish features with Gothic arches and pillars. It served as the Capilla Mayor until the 1520s.

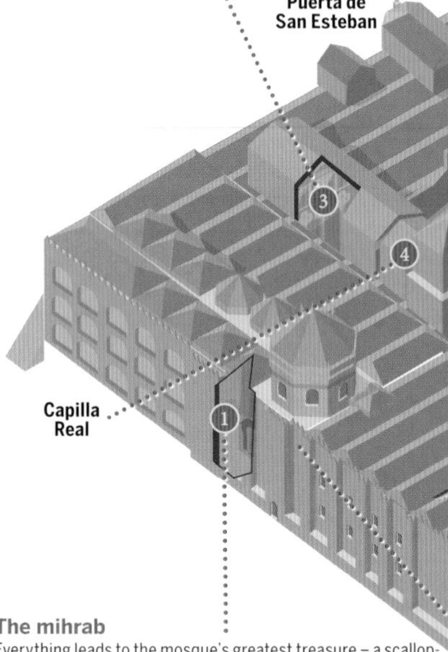

The mihrab
Everything leads to the mosque's greatest treasure – a scallop-shell-shaped prayer niche facing Mecca that was added in the 10th century. Cast your eyes over the gold mosaic cubes crafted by imported Byzantium sculptors.

B.O'KANE/ALAMY ©

The cathedral choir
Few ignore the impressive *coro* (choir): a late-Christian addition dating from the 1750s. Once you've admired the skilfully carved mahogany choir stalls depicting scenes from the Bible, look up at the impressive baroque ceiling.

RUTH TOMLINSON / GETTY IMAGES ©

5

Torre del Alminar
This is the Mezquita's cheapest sight because you don't have to pay to see it. Rising 93m and viewable from much of the city, the baroque-style bell tower was built over the mosque's original minaret.

KARL BLACKWELL / GETTY IMAGES ©

The Mezquita arches
No, you're not hallucinating. The Mezquita's most defining characteristic is its unique terracotta-and-white striped arches that support 856 pillars salvaged from Roman and Visigoth ruins. Glimpsed through the dull light they're at once spooky and striking.

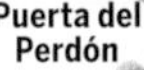
Puerta del Perdón

2

Patio de los Naranjos
Abandon architectural preconceptions all ye who enter here. The ablutions area of the former mosque is a shady courtyard embellished with orange trees that acts as the Mezquita's main entry point.

Capilla Mayor
A Christian monument inside an Islamic mosque sounds beautifully ironic, yet here it is: a Gothic church commissioned by Charles V in the 16th century and planted in the middle of the world's third largest mosque.

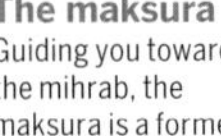

The maksura
Guiding you towards the mihrab, the maksura is a former royal enclosure where the caliphs and their retinues prayed. Its lavish, elaborate arches were designed to draw the eye of worshippers towards the mihrab and Mecca.

PAUL KINGSLEY/ALAMY ©

DWB/IMAGEBROKER ©

Right: Jerez de la Frontera's annual Feria del Caballo (Horse Fair; p43); **Below:** Flamenco dress shop, Seville

(www.tgcomes.es) have daily buses (fewer on weekends) to Cádiz (€5.11, one hour, eight daily) and Jerez de la Frontera (€2.64, 45 minutes, 19 daily), Málaga (€16.85, 3½ hours, two daily) and Ronda (€8.75, two hours, two daily).

Jerez de la Frontera

POP 211,000

Stand down all other claimants. Jerez, as most savvy Spain-o-philes know, *is* Andalucía. It just doesn't broadcast the fact in the way that Seville and Granada do. As a result, few people plan their trip around a visit here, preferring instead to jump-cut to the glories of the Giralda and the Alhambra. If only they knew. Jerez is the capital of *andaluz* horse culture, stop one on the famed sherry triangle and – cue the protestations from Cádiz and Seville – the cradle of Spanish flamenco. The *bulería*, Jerez's jokey, tongue-in-cheek antidote to Seville's tragic *soleá*, was first concocted in the legendary Roma *barrios* of Santiago and San Miguel. If you really want to unveil the eternal riddle that is Andalucía, start here.

Sights & Activities

ALCÁZAR Fortress

(☎956 14 99 55; Alameda Vieja; admission incl/excl camera obscura €5.40/3; ⏰10am-7.30pm Mon-Sat, to 2.30pm Sun May–mid-Sep, 10am-5.30pm Mon-Sat, to 2.30pm Sun mid-Sep–Apr) Jerez's muscular yet refined 11th- or 12th-century fortress is one of the best preserved Almohad-era (1140s–1212) relics left in Andalucía.

You'll enter the Alcázar via the **Patio de Armas**. On the left is the beautiful *mezquita* (mosque), which was converted to a chapel by Alfonso X in 1264. Beyond the Patio de Armas, the lovely gardens re-create the ambience of Islamic times with their geometrical plant beds and tinkling fountains, while the domed **Baños**

Árabes (Arab Baths) with their shafts of light are another highlight.

CATEDRAL DE SAN SALVADOR Cathedral
(Plaza de la Encarnación; admission €5; 10.30am-6.30pm Mon-Sat, 12.30-3.30pm Sun) Echoes of Seville colour Jerez's wonderful cathedral, a surprisingly harmonious mix of baroque, neoclassical and gothic styles.

REAL ESCUELA ANDALUZA DEL ARTE ECUESTRE Equestrian Show
(956 31 80 08; www.realescuela.org; Avenida Duque de Abrantes; training sessions adult/child €10/6, exhibición adult/child €19/12 ; training sessions 11am-1pm Mon, Wed & Fri Sep-Jul, Mon & Wed Aug, noon Tue & Thu Sep-Jul, exhibición noon Tue, Thu & Fri Aug) The famed Royal Andalucian School of Equestrian Art trains horses and riders in equestrian skills, and you can watch them going through their paces in **training sessions** and visit the **Horse Carriage Museum**, which includes an 18th-century Binder Hunting Break.

Sherry Bodegas

Jerez is home to around 20 bodegas (cellars) and most are open to visitors, but they're scattered around town and many of them require you to call ahead. The tourist office has up-to-date information.

BODEGAS GONZÁLEZ BYASS Winery
(Bodegas Tio Pepe; 956 35 70 16; www.bodegastiopepe.com; Calle Manuel María González 12; tour €11, with tapas €16; tours in English & Spanish hourly 11am-6pm Mon-Sat, to 2pm Sun Oct-Apr) Six or seven tours each are given daily in English and Spanish, and a few in German and French.

BODEGAS TRADICIÓN Winery
(956 16 86 28; www.bodegastradicion.com; Plaza Cordobeses 3; tours €18; 9am-6.30pm Mon-Fri, 10am-2pm Sat Mar-Jun, 8am-3pm Sat Jul & Aug) An interesting bodega, not only for its extra-aged sherries (20 or more years old), but because it houses the Colección Joaquín Rivera, a private

Jerez de la Frontera

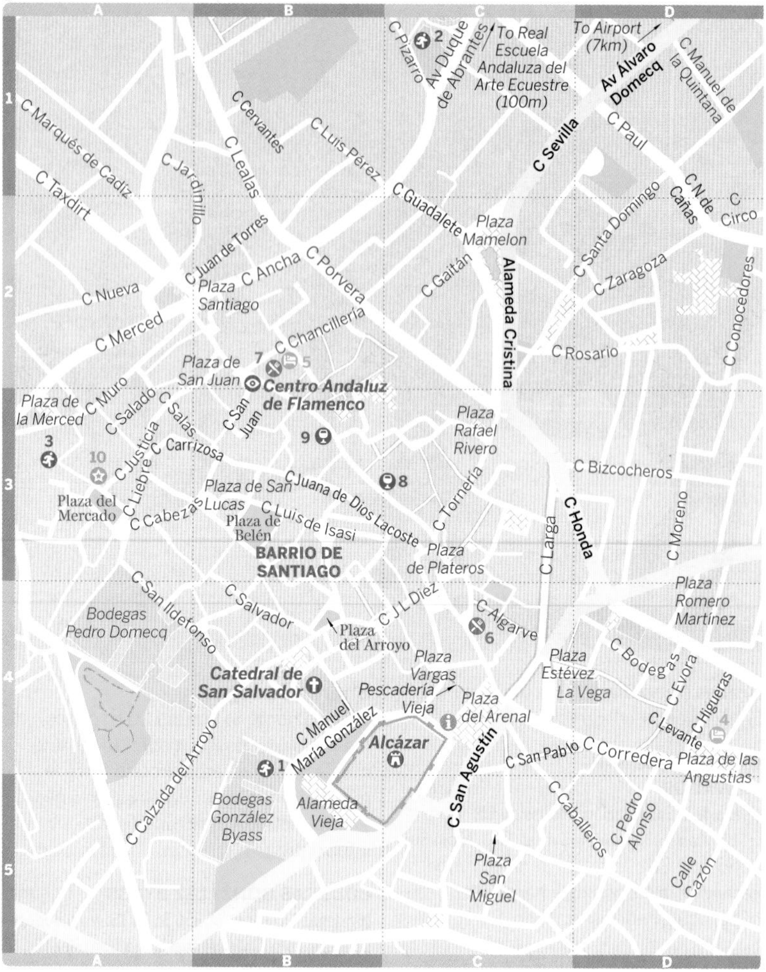

A B C D
1 2 3 4 5
C Pizarro
Av Duque de Abrantes
To Real Escuela Andaluza del Arte Ecuestre (100m)
To Airport (7km)
Av Álvaro Domecq
C Manuel de la Quintana
C Marqués de Cádiz
C Cervantes
C Luis Pérez
C Jardinillo
C Lealas
C Taxdirt
C Sevilla
C Paul
C Guadalete
C Santa Domingo
C N de Cañas
C Circo
Plaza Mamelon
C Juan de Torres
C Ancha
C Porvera
C Gaitán
Alameda Cristina
C Zaragoza
C Nueva
Plaza Santiago
C Conocedores
C Merced
C Chancillería
C Rosario
Plaza de San Juan
Centro Andaluz de Flamenco
Plaza de la Merced
C Muro
C Salado
C Salas
C San Juan
Plaza Rafael Rivero
C Justicia
C Carrizosa
C Bizcocheros
C Liebre
Plaza de San Lucas
C Juana de Dios Lacoste
C Tornería
Plaza del Mercado
C Cabezas
Plaza de Belén
C Luis de Isasi
C Honda
C Larga
C Moreno
BARRIO DE SANTIAGO
Plaza de Plateros
C San Ildefonso
C Salvador
C J L Diez
Plaza Romero Martínez
Bodegas Pedro Domecq
Plaza del Arroyo
C Algarve
Plaza Vargas
Plaza Estévez
C Bodegas
C Evora
Catedral de San Salvador
Pescadería Vieja
La Vega
Plaza del Arenal
C Higueras
C Manuel María González
Alcázar
C San Agustín
C Levante
C San Pablo
C Corredera
Plaza de las Angustias
C Calzada del Arroyo
Bodegas González Byass
Alameda Vieja
C Caballeros
C Pedro Alonso
Plaza San Miguel
Calle Cazón

Spanish art collection that includes important works by Goya, Velázquez and Zurbarán.

BODEGAS SANDEMAN Winery

(956 15 17 11; www.sandeman.com; Calle Pizarro 10; tour in English €7, with tasting €14; tours hourly 11.30am-2.30pm Mon, Wed & Fri, 10.30am & hourly noon-3pm Tue & Thu, 11am, 1pm & 2pm Sat) Has three or four tours each in English, Spanish and German, one in French.

Sleeping

HOTEL CASA GRANDE Hotel **€€**

(956 34 50 70; www.casagrande.com.es; Plaza de las Angustias 3, Jerez de la Frontera; r €85-105, ste €115-125; P ❄ @) This brilliant hotel occupies a carefully restored 1920s mansion. Rooms are spread over three floors and set around a patio, or beside the roof terrace, which has views of Jerez's roof line.

HOTEL CHANCILLERIA Hotel €€
(956 30 10 38; www.hotelchancilleria.com; Calle Chancilleria 21, Jerez de la Frontera; s €55-140, d €80-180;) Opened in January 2008, this stunning renovation of two 17th-century homes is a discreet temple to good taste. There are many highlights: African art, an original 17th-century wall, a lovely garden, stylish and spacious rooms, a delightful roof terrace and one of Jerez's best restaurants, Sabores.

Jerez de la Frontera

Top Sights
- Alcázar C4
- Catedral de San Salvador B4
- Centro Andaluz de Flamenco B2

Activities, Courses & Tours
- 1 Bodegas González Byass B4
- 2 Bodegas Sandeman C1
- 3 Bodegas Tradición A3

Sleeping
- 4 Hotel Casa Grande D4
- 5 Hotel Chancilleria B2

Eating
- 6 Cruz Blanca C4
- 7 Sabores B2

Drinking
- 8 Damajuana C3
- 9 El Arriate B3

Entertainment
- 10 El Lagá Tio Parrilla A3

Eating

SABORES Contemporary Andalucian €€
(956 32 98 35; www.restaurantesabores.es; Chancillera 21; mains from €12) When scrambled eggs go gourmet, you know you're onto something special. In actual fact, the eggs are flambéed with cured ham, but whatever the method, the results are delicious. You can back it up with dishes such as beef cheek or creative fish, all presented like modern art on your plate.

CRUZ BLANCA Tapas €
(www.lacruzblanca.com; Plaza de la Yerva; tapas €1.80-3) The Cruz whips up good seafood, egg, meat and salad offerings and has tables on a quiet little plaza. The marinated fish in a pesto-inflected sauce could steal the crown for Jerez's best meal.

Entertainment

EL LAGÁ TIO PARRILLA Flamenco
(Plaza del Mercado; show & 2 drinks €25; 10.30pm Mon-Sat) A high quota of Roma

Jerez's Flamenco Scene

Explorations of Jerez's flamenco scene ought to start at the **Centro Andaluz de Flamenco** (Andalusian Flamenco Centre; 856 81 41 32; www.centroandaluzdeflamenco.es; Plaza de San Juan 1; 9am-2pm Mon-Fri), Spain's only bona fide flamenco library where you can pick up information on clubs, performances and singing/dance/guitar lessons. From here you can stroll down **Calle Francos** and visit legendary flamenco bars such as **Damajuana** (www.damajuanacafebar.com; Calle Francos 18; 4.30pm-3am Tue-Sun) and **El Arriate** (Calle Francos 41) where singers and dancers still congregate. To the north, in the Santiago quarter, you'll find dozens of small private clubs or *peñas*, all known for their accessibility and intimacy; entrance is normally free if you buy a drink at the bar. The *peña* scene is particularly fertile during the February flamenco festival, which is arguably Andalucía's finest.

(both performers and clientele) ensures that this place wins most plaudits for its regular flamenco *tablaos*. Gutsy shows rarely end without rousing renditions of that old Jerez stalwart – the *bulería*.

Information

Municipal tourist office (956 33 88 74; www.turismojerez.com; Plaza del Arenal; 9am-3pm & 5-7pm Mon-Fri, 9.30am-2.30pm Sat & Sun)

Provincial tourist office (Airport; 8.15am-2pm & 5-6.30pm Mon-Fri)

Getting There & Around

Air

Jerez airport (956 15 00 00; www.aena.es) the only one serving Cádiz province, is 7km northeast of town on the NIV. Over a dozen airlines fly into Jerez from elsewhere in Europe including: Ryanair from Barcelona and London-Stansted (seasonal), Air-Berlin from Mallorca and Düsseldorf (seasonal), and Iberia daily to/from Madrid. Taxis from the airport start at €14. The local airport buses M050 and M051 (€1, 30 minutes) run 12 times daily Monday to Friday and six times daily on weekends. From Jerez this service continues to El Puerto de Santa María and Cádiz.

Bus

The **bus station** (956 33 96 66; Plaza de la Estación) is 1.3km southeast of the centre. Destinations include Seville (€7.50, 1¼ hours, 11 or more daily), Cádiz (€1.72, one hour, nine or more daily), Arcos de la Frontera (€2.64, 45 minutes,13 daily), and Ronda (€11.50, three hours, three daily).

Train

Jerez **train station** (956 34 23 19; Plaza de la Estación) is right beside the bus station. Regular trains go to Cádiz (€5, 40 minutes, 15 daily), and 10 or more to Seville (€9.15, 1¼ hours, 15 daily).

Vejer de la Frontera

POP 12,800 / ELEV 190M

Vejer – the jaw drops, the eyes blink, the eloquent adjectives dry up. Looming moodily atop a rocky hill above the busy N340, 50km south of Cádiz, this placid, yet compact white town is something very special. Yes, there's a cool labyrinth of twisting streets, some serendipitous viewpoints, and a ruined castle. But, Vejer possesses something else – soulfulness, an air of mystery, an imperceptible touch of *duende* (spirit).

Sights

FREE **CASTLE** Castle

(Calle del Castillo; approx 10am-9pm Jun-Sep) Vejer's much-reworked castle has great views from its battlements.

Sleeping & Eating

V... Boutique Hotel **€€€**
(☎956 45 17 57; www.hotelv-vejer.com; Calle Rosario 11-13, Vejer de la Frontera; d €139-199; ❄ @) V...(that's V for Vejer not V for five, and, yes, the three dots are part of the name) is one of Andalucía's most exquisite creations, an old world boutique hotel where trendy modern design features (bath tubs in the middle of the room) mix with antique artifacts (antique doors).

HOTEL LA CASA DEL CALIFA Hotel **€€**
(☎956 44 77 30; www.lacasadelcalifa.com; Plaza de España 16, Vejer de la Frontera; s/d incl breakfast €73/86; ❄ @) Rambling over several floors, this gorgeous hotel oozes character. Rooms are peaceful and very comfortable, with Islamic decorative touches. Downstairs there's a superb Middle Eastern restaurant, **El Jardín del Califa** (mains €8-16; ✍).

LA VERA CRUZ Contemporary Andalucian **€€**
(☎956 45 16 83; www.restaurantelaveracruz.es; Calle Shelly 1; mains €12-18; ⏰lunch Tue-sun, dinner Thu-Sat) Situated in an old convent with slightly limited opening hours, the 'True Cross' specialises in gourmet tapas such as cold anchovy lasagna and glazed ribs with wasabi puree.

Information

Buses stop beside the **tourist office** (☎956 45 17 36; Avenida Los Remedios 2; ⏰10am-2pm daily, 6-8pm Mon-Sat approx May-Oct), about 500m below the town centre. Also here is a convenient large, free car park.

Getting There & Away

Comes (☎902 19 92 08; www.tgcomes.es) buses leave from Avenida Los Remedios. Buses run to Cádiz (one hour) five or six times a day. Buses for Tarifa (45 minutes, 10 daily), Algeciras (1¼ hours, 10 daily), Jerez de la Frontera (1½ hours, two daily), Málaga (2¾ hours, two daily) and Seville (2¼ hours, four daily) stop at La Barca de Vejer,

Vejer de la Frontera

XAVI GOMEZ/GETTY IMAGES ©

If You Like... The Outdoors

If you like the Sierra de Grazalema and its combination of wilderness areas and possibilities for getting active, we also recommend the following:

1 **PARQUE NACIONAL SIERRA NEVADA** The highest mountains in mainland Spain, as well as gorgeous green valleys lined with walking trails; in Granada province.

2 **PARQUE NATURAL DE LAS SIERRAS DE CAZORLA, SEGURA Y LAS VILLAS** Stunning, rugged mountain ranges with high plains and deep, forested valleys and one of the best places in Spain for spotting wildlife; in eastern Jaén province.

3 **PARQUE NATURAL SIERRA DE ARACENA Y PICOS DE AROCHE** Lovely, rolling hill country of northern Huelva province, with fortress-like villages and fine walking.

4 **LA AXARQUÍA** Wild landscapes, orchards and deep valleys with quiet walking trails; in Málaga province.

5 **LAGUNA DE FUENTE DE PIEDRA** Hosts up to 20,000 pairs of the spectacular greater flamingo from January or February until August; close to Antequera in Málaga province.

on the N340 at the bottom of the hill. It's a steep 20-minute walk up to town from here or an equally steep €6 in a taxi.

Parque Natural Sierra de Grazalema & Around

Of all Andalucía's protected areas, Parque Natural Sierra de Grazalema is the most accessible and best set up for lung-stretching sorties into the countryside. Though not as lofty as the Sierra Nevada, the park's rugged pillarlike peaks nonetheless rise abruptly off the plains northeast of Cádiz, revealing precipitous gorges, wild orchids and hefty rainfall (stand aside Galicia and Cantabria, this is the wettest part of Spain, logging an average 2000 millimetres annually). Grazalema is also fine walking country (the best months are May, June, September and October).

The **Centro de Visitantes** (☎956 72 70 29; Avenida de la Diputación; ⏰10am-2pm & 6-8pm Mon-Sat, 9am-2pm Sun), with limited displays and information, is situated in the village of El Bosque, 20km east of Grazalema village.

Grazalema

POP 2200 / ELEV 825M

A true mountain 'white town', Grazalema looks like it has been dropped from a passing spaceship onto the steep rocky slopes of its eponymous mountain range. Few *pueblos blancos* are as generically perfect as this one, with its spotless whitewashed houses sporting rust-tiled roofs and wrought-iron window bars.

Activities

You're in walking country, so make the most of it. Good hiking info can be procured at the tourist office. Four of the park's best hikes (including the 12.5km El Pinsapar walk through Spain's best-preserved fir woodland) traverse restricted areas and must be booked ahead at the **visitor centre** (☎956 72 70 29; Calle Federico García Lorca 1; ⏰10am-2pm & 5-7pm Mon-Sat, 9am-2pm Sun) in El Bosque.

Eating

RESTAURANTE EL TORREÓN Andalucian **€€**

(www.restauranteeltorreongrazalema.com; mains €8-12) This friendly mountain restaurant is where you can take a break from the Cádiz fish monopoly with local chorizo, spinach, soups and the menu speciality, partridge. There's pasta for kids.

Information

The village centre is the pretty Plaza de España, overlooked by the 18th-century Iglesia de la Aurora. Here you'll find the tourist office (☎956

13 20 73; 10am-2pm & 4-9pm), with a shop selling local products.

Zahara de la Sierra

POP 1500 / ELEV 550M

Rugged Zahara, set around a vertiginous crag at the foot of the Sierra de Grazalema, hums with Moorish mystery. These days Zahara encapsulates all of the best elements of a classic white town and is popular as a result. Come during the afternoon siesta, however, and you can still hear a pin drop.

Getting There & Around

Los Amarillos (**902 21 03 17; www.losamarillos.es**) and **Comes** (**902 19 92 08; www.tgcomes.es**) run daily buses from Jerez de la Frontera via Arcos de la Frontera to Olvera (€8.22, 2 hours 15 minutes, three daily) and Setenil de las Bodegas (€8.88, 2½ hours, three daily). Two of these buses carry onto Málaga (€11.04, 2 hours 15 minutes).

Los Amarillos runs twice daily buses either way between Zahara de la Sierra and Ronda (€3, one hour). Grazalema has buses to/from Ronda (€2.63, 45 minutes, twice daily); El Bosque (€2.35, 30 mins, one daily), where you can change for Arcos; and Ubrique/Benaocaz (€2.13, 40 minutes, two daily).

Ronda

POP 37,000 / ELEV 744M

Perched on an inland plateau riven by the 100m fissure of El Tajo gorge, Ronda is Málaga province's most spectacular town. It has a superbly dramatic location, and owes its name ('surrounded' by mountains), to the encircling Serranía de Ronda.

Sights & Activities

LA CIUDAD Neighbourhood

Straddling the dramatic gorge and the Río Guadalevín (Deep River) is Ronda's most recognisable sight, the towering **Puente Nuevo**, best viewed from the **Camino de los Molinos**, which runs along the bottom of the gorge. The bridge separates the old and new towns.

The old town is surrounded by massive fortress walls pierced by two ancient gates: the Islamic Puerta de Almocábar which, in the 13th century, was the main gateway to the castle; and

Grazalema

the 16th-century Puerta de Carlos V. Inside, the Islamic layout remains intact, and its maze of narrow streets now takes its character from the Renaissance mansions of powerful families whose predecessors accompanied Fernando el Católico in the taking of the city in 1485.

PLAZA DE TOROS Bullring
(Calle Virgen de la Paz; admission €5; 10am-8pm) Ronda's Plaza de Toros is a mecca for bullfighting aficionados.

The on-site Museo Taurino is crammed with memorabilia such as blood-spattered costumes worn by Pedro Romero and 1990s star Jesulín de Ubrique.

Sleeping

HOTEL ALAVERA DE LOS BAÑOS Hotel **€€**
(952 87 91 43; www.alaveradelosbanos.com; Hoyo San Miguel, Ronda; s/d incl breakfast €70/95;) Taking its cue from the Arab baths next door, the Alavera de los Baños continues the Hispano-Islamic theme throughout, with oriental decor and tasty North African-inspired cuisine using predominantly organic foods.

JARDÍN DE LA MURALLA Historic Hotel **€€**
(952 87 27 64; www.jardindelamuralla.com; Calle Espiritu Santo 13, Ronda; s/d incl breakfast €80/91; @) José María has ensured that his historic family home retains plenty of evocative atmosphere with antiques, chandeliers, ancestral portraits and wonderful claw foot bathtubs.

Eating

BODEGA SAN FRANCISCO Tapas **€**
(www.bodegasanfrancisco.com; Calle Ruedo Alameda; raciones €6-10) With three dining rooms and tables spilling out onto the narrow pedestrian street, this may well be Ronda's top tapas bar. The menu is

Left & Below: Elevated views around Ronda
LEFT: LUIS CASTANEDA INC./GETTY IMAGES ©; BELOW: JOHN & LISA MERRILL/GETTY IMAGES ©

vast and should suit the fussiest of families, even vegetarians with nine-plus salad choices.

RESTAURANTE TRAGABUCHES Contemporary Spanish **€€€**
(**952 19 02 91; www.tragabuches.com; Calle José Aparício 1; menus €59-87; 1.30-3.30pm & 8-10.30pm Tue-Sat)** Ronda's best and most famous restaurant is a 180-degree turn away from the ubiquitous 'rustic' look and cuisine. Michelin-starred in 1998, Tragabuches is modern and sleek with an innovative menu to match.

Information

Muncipal tourist office (**www.turismoderonda.es; Paseo de Blas Infante; 10am-7.30pm Mon-Fri, 10.15am-2pm & 3.30-6.30pm Sat, Sun & holidays)**

Regional tourist office (**www.andalucia.org; Plaza de España 1; 9am-7.30pm Mon-Fri May-Sep, to 6pm Oct-Apr, 10am-2pm Sat year-round)**

Getting There & Away

Bus

The bus station is at Plaza Concepción García Redondo 2. **Comes** (**www.tgcomes.es**) has buses to Arcos de la Frontera (€8.75, two hours, two daily), Jerez de la Frontera (€11.50, three hours, three daily) and Cádiz (€15, two hours, three daily). **Los Amarillos** (**www.losamarillos.es**) goes to Seville via Algodonales, Grazalema, and to Málaga via Ardales.

Train

Ronda's **train station** (**952 87 16 73; Avenida de Andalucía**) is on the line between Bobadilla and Algeciras. Trains run to Algeciras via Gaucín and Jimena de la Frontera. This train ride is incredibly scenic and worth taking just for the views. Other trains depart for Málaga, Córdoba, Madrid, and Granada via Antequera. For Seville, change at Bobadilla or Antequera.

CÁDIZ

POP 125,000

You could write several weighty university theses about Cádiz and still fall a mile short of nailing its essence. Old age accounts for much of the complexity. Cádiz is generally considered to be the oldest continuously inhabited settlement in Europe. Now well into its fourth millennium, the ancient centre is as romantic as it is mysterious, an ocean settlement surrounded almost entirely by water, where Atlantic waves crash against eroded sea walls, municipal beaches stretch for miles, and narrow streets echo with the sounds of cawing gulls and frying fish. Come here for the seafood, surfing, and the cache of intriguing churches and museums that inflict little, if any, damage on your wallet. More importantly, come here for the *gaditanos* (residents of Cádiz), an upfront and gregarious populace who have made *alegrías* (upbeat flamenco songs) into an eloquent art form.

Sights & Activities

PLAZA SAN JUAN DE DIOS Square

Broad Plaza San Juan de Dios is lined with cafes and is dominated by the imposing neoclassical **ayuntamiento** built around 1800. Between here and the cathedral is the Barrio del Pópulo, the kernel of medieval Cádiz and a focus of the city's ongoing sprucing-up program. At the nearby **Roman Theatre** (Campo del Sur; 10am-2.30pm & 5-7pm Wed-Mon) you can walk along a gallery beneath the tiers of seating.

CATEDRAL Church

(Plaza de la Catedral; adult/student €5/3, free 7-8pm Tue-Fri, 11am-1pm Sun; 10am-6.30pm Mon-Sat, 1.30-6.30pm Sun) Cádiz's yellow-domed cathedral is an impressively proportioned baroque-neoclassical construction, but by Spanish standards very sober in its decoration.

MUSEO DE CÁDIZ Museum

(Plaza de Mina; admission €1.50; 2.30-8.30pm Tue, 9am-8.30pm Wed-Sat, 9.30am-2.30pm Sun)

Beach promenade, Cádiz

Detour: Parque Nacional de Doñana

Spain's most celebrated and in many ways most important wildlife refuge, the Doñana National Park, created in 1969, is one of Europe's last remaining great wetlands. Covering 542 sq km in the southeast of Huelva province and neighbouring Seville province, this World Heritage site is a vital refuge for such endangered species as the Spanish imperial eagle. It offers a unique combination of ecosystems and a place of haunting beauty that is well worth the effort of getting to. To visit the national park you must take a tour from the Centro de Visitantes El Acebuche on the western side of the park, or from El Rocío at the park's northwestern corner, or from Sanlúcar de Barrameda at its southeastern corner.

The village of **El Rocío** overlooks a section of the Doñana marismas at the park's northwestern corner. The village's sandy streets bear as many hoofprints as tyre marks, and they are lined with rows of verandahed buildings that are empty most of the time. But this is no ghost town: most of the houses belong to the 90-odd *hermandades* (brotherhoods) of pilgrim-revellers and their families, who converge on El Rocío every year in the extraordinary Romería del Rocío.

The Museo de Cádiz, on one of Cádiz's leafiest squares, is the best museum in the province.

PLAYA DE LA VICTORIA Beach

This lovely, wide strip of fine Atlantic sand stretches about 4km along the peninsula from its beginning at the Puertas de Tierra.

Sleeping

HOTEL ARGANTONIO Hotel €€

(☎956 21 16 40; www.hotelargantonio.com; Calle Argantonio 3; s/d incl breakfast €90/107; ❄@📶) The stand-out features here are the hand-painted doors, beautifully tiled floors that adorn both bedrooms and bathrooms, and the intricate Moorish arch in the lobby. The hotel has three themes: the first floor is mudejar, the second floor is colonial, and the third floor is a mix.

HOTEL PATAGONIA SUR Hotel €€

(☎856 17 46 47; www.hotelpatagoniasur.es; Calle Cobos 11; d €80-130; ❄@📶) The newest establishment in Cádiz's old town, this sleek gem opened in 2009 and offers clean-lined modernity just steps from the 18th century cathedral. Bonuses include its sun-filled attic rooms on the fifth floor with cathedral views and a glass-fronted minimalist cafeteria at street level.

Eating

Cádiz's hallowed seafood street is Calle Virgen de la Palma in the Viña quarter. Good un-fancy restaurants are legion here. Try **El Faro** (www.elfarodecadiz.com; Calle San Félix 15; mains €15-25), decorated with pretty ceramics, or the even grittier **Taberna El Albero** (Cnr Calles San Félix & Virgen de la Palma).

EL ALJIBE Tapas €€

(www.pablogrosso.com; Calle Plocia 25; tapas €2-3.50, mains €10-15) Refined restaurant upstairs and supercool tapas bar downstairs, El Aljibe on its own is almost reason enough to come to Cádiz. The cuisine developed by *gaditano* chef Pablo Grosso is a delicious combination of the traditional and the adventurous – goat's cheese on nut bread with blueberry sauce, courgette and prawn lasagna.... you get the drift?

Cádiz

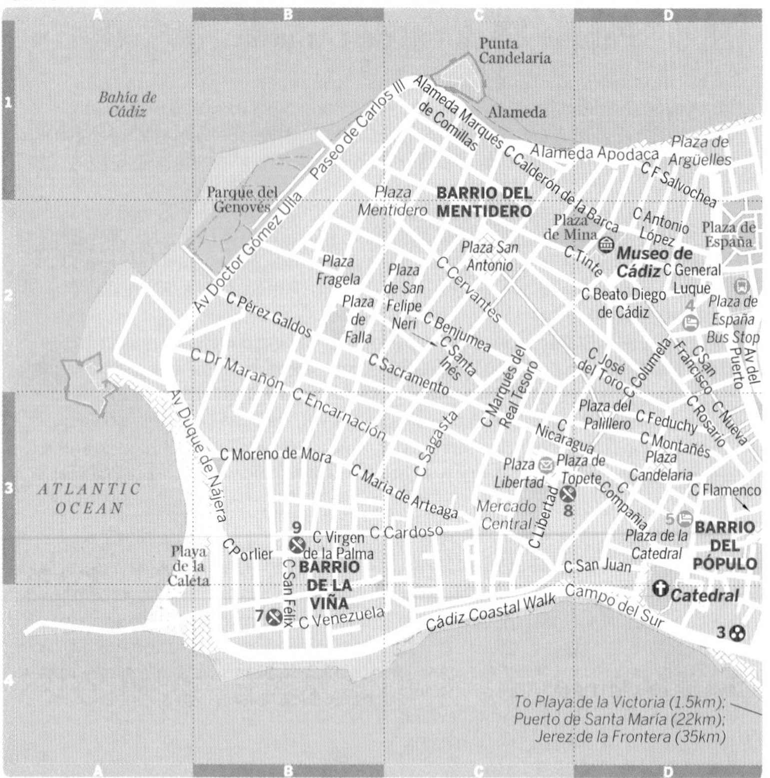

Cádiz

Top Sights

Catedral ... D4
Museo de Cádiz ... D2

Sights

1 Ayuntamiento ... E3
2 Plaza San Juan de Dios ... E3
3 Roman Theatre ... D4

Sleeping

4 Hotel Argantonio ... D2
5 Hotel Patagonia Sur ... D3

Eating

6 El Aljibe ... E3
7 El Faro ... B4
8 Freiduría Las Flores ... C3
9 Taberna El Albero ... B3

Entertainment

10 Peña Flamenca La Perla ... E4

FREIDURÍA LAS FLORES Seafood **€**

(**☎956 22 61 12; Plaza de Topete 4; seafood per 250g €3-8**) Cádiz's addiction to fried fish finds wonderful expression here. If it comes from the sea, chances are that it's been fried and served in Las Flores as either a tapa, *ración* (meal-sized serving of tapas) or *media-ración* (half a *ración*), or served in an improvised paper cup, fish-and-chips style. You order by weight (250g is the usual order).

Entertainment

FREE PEÑA FLAMENCA LA PERLA Flamenco

(956 25 91 01; www.laperladecadiz.es; Calle Carlos Ollero; admission free) The paint-peeled Peña La Perla set romantically next to the crashing Atlantic surf hosts flamenco nights at 10pm most Fridays, more so in spring and summer. Right beside the ocean just off Calle Concepción Arenal in the Barrio de Santa María, entry is free and the audience is stuffed with aficionados.

Information

Municipal tourist office (Paseo de Canalejas; 8.30am-6pm Mon-Fri, 9am-5pm Sat & Sun)

Regional tourist office (Avenida Ramón de Carranza; 9am-7.30pm Mon-Fri, 10am-2pm Sat, Sun & holidays)

Getting There & Around

Bus

Comes (956 80 70 59; www.tgcomes.es; Plaza de la Hispanidad) has regular departures from the **bus station** (956 80 70 59; Plaza Sevilla) to Arcos de la Frontera (€5.11, one hour), Granada (€32.80, 5½ hours), Jerez de la Frontera (€1.72, one hour), Málaga (€24.62, four hours), Ronda (€15, two hours), Seville (€8.68, one hour 45 minutes), Tarifa (€8.60, 1½ hours), and Vejer de la Frontera (€5.95, 1 hour 20 minutes). Buses M050 and M051, run by the **Consorcio de Transportes Bahía de Cádiz** (956 01 21 00; www.cmtbc.com), travel from Jerez de la Frontera airport to Cádiz's Comes bus station, via Jerez city and El Puerto de Santa María.

Car & Motorcycle

The AP4 motorway from Seville to Puerto Real on the eastern side of the Bahía de Cádiz carries a €5.50 toll. The toll-free A4 is slower.

There's a handily placed **underground car park** (Paseo de Canalejas; per 24hr €9) near the port area.

Train

From the **train station** (902 24 02 02), plenty of trains run daily to/from Jerez de la Frontera (€5, 40 minutes, 15 daily), Seville (€13.25, one hour 45 minutes, 15 daily) and Madrid (€72.20, 4½ hours, three daily). The high-speed AVE service from Madrid should operate to Cádiz by 2013.

Granada & Andalucía's South Coast

Granada is a meeting point of worlds. On the one hand it's a city as Spanish as any other, with the requisite tapas bars and carefree, liberal attitude. But this is also a city largely born of Islam. Its old quarter looks, tastes and smells of the exotica of North Africa, while its palaces and gardens recall a bygone age of Moorish magnificence.

The feeling of two cultures colliding continues in the green valleys of Las Alpujarras, where whitewashed villages with a distinctly Moroccan look sit like early spring snowfall on the lush slopes. Head to the coast, though, and everything changes. This is the land of the infamous Costa del Sol, with its mega resorts and dirty dancing, although even here cultural and geographic gems can be found, such as the art galleries of Málaga, charming Nerja and the crystal clear waters off Cabo de Gata.

Beach at Nerja (p318)

Granada & Andalucía's South Coast

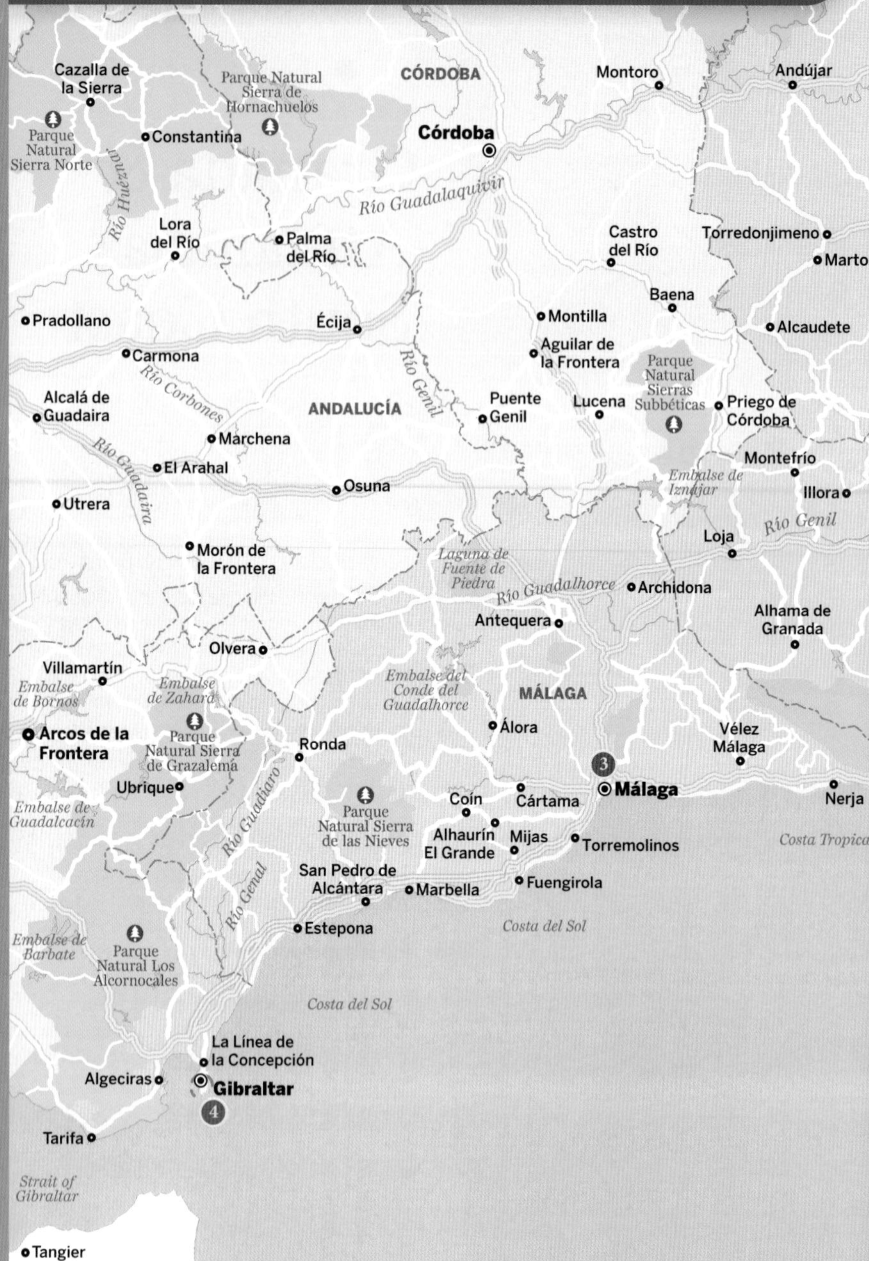

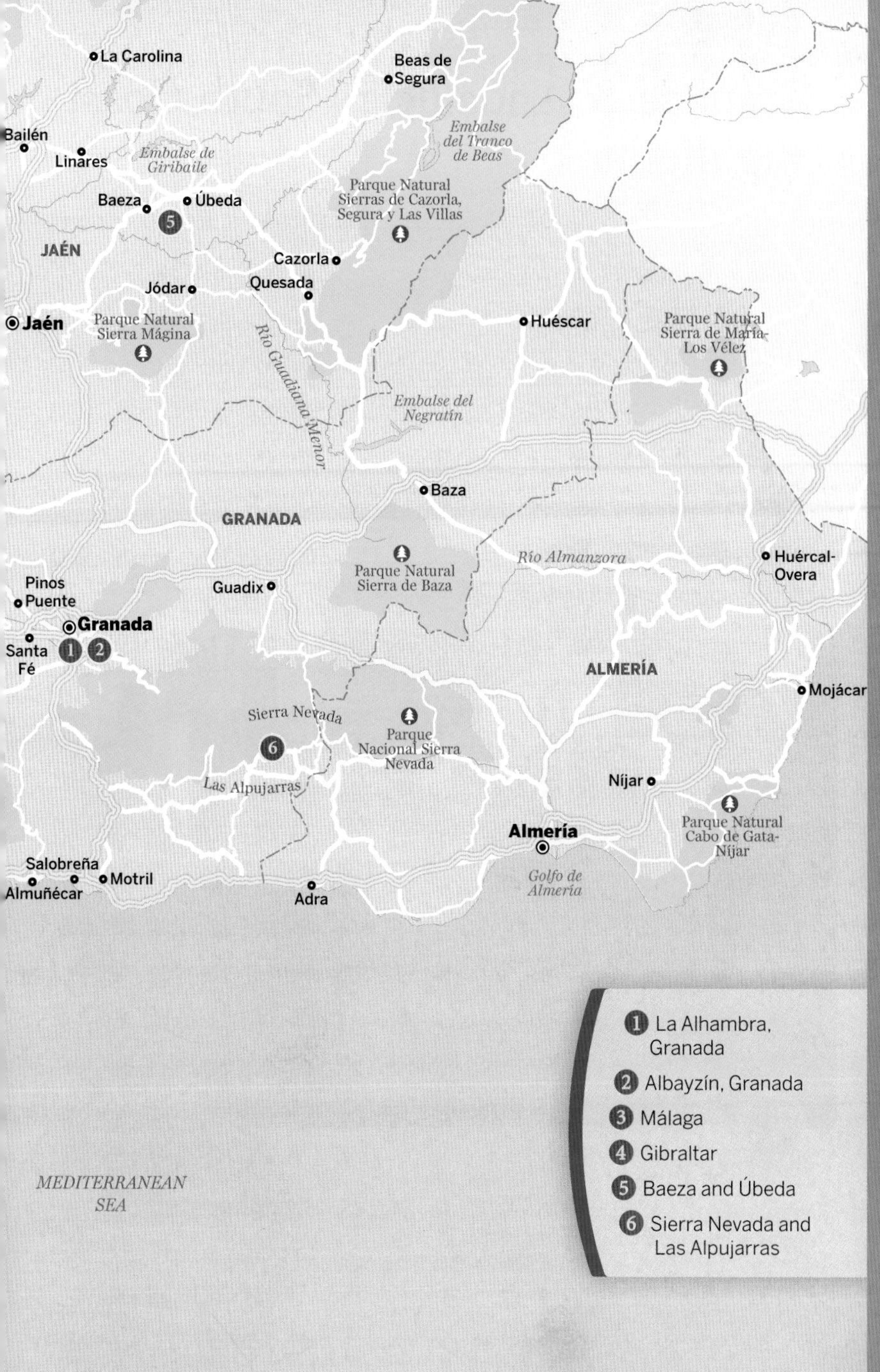

La Carolina
Beas de Segura
Bailén
Linares
Embalse de Giribaile
Embalse del Tranco de Beas
Parque Natural Sierras de Cazorla, Segura y Las Villas
Baeza
Úbeda
5
JAÉN
Cazorla
Jódar
Quesada
Jaén
Parque Natural Sierra Mágina
Río Guadiana Menor
Huéscar
Parque Natural Sierra de María-Los Vélez
Embalse del Negratín
Baza
GRANADA
Río Almanzora
Huércal-Overa
Pinos Puente
Guadix
Parque Natural Sierra de Baza
Granada
Santa Fé
1
2
ALMERÍA
Mojácar
Sierra Nevada
6
Parque Nacional Sierra Nevada
Las Alpujarras
Níjar
Almería
Parque Natural Cabo de Gata-Níjar
Golfo de Almería
Salobreña
Motril
Almuñécar
Adra
MEDITERRANEAN SEA
1 La Alhambra, Granada
2 Albayzín, Granada
3 Málaga
4 Gibraltar
5 Baeza and Úbeda
6 Sierra Nevada and Las Alpujarras
0 50 km
0 25 miles

Granada & Andalucía's South Coast Highlights

1

La Alhambra

The Alhambra (p304) is exceptional: the only medieval palace of its type and cultural significance to have survived anywhere in the world. This shining example of the conservation and restoration of heritage buildings displays a harmonious relationship between architecture, the landscape and its refined aesthetic. Top Right: Gardens of Alhambra; Bottom Right: Palacios Nazaríes

Need to Know

ADMISSION €12
TOP TIP Of the 6600 daily tickets issued, just 2000 are available at the gate, so book ahead or get there by 7am **See the author's review on p301**

Local Knowledge

La Alhambra Don't Miss List

BY MARÍA DEL MAR VILLAFRANCA, DIRECTOR OF PATRONATO DE LA ALAMBRA Y GENERALIFE

1 FACADE OF THE PALACIO DE COMARES

Unlike many visitors, take the time to contemplate this iconic and perfectly proportioned facade. So many of the Alhambra's signature decorative forms are on display here, including *epigrafía* (inscriptions and calligraphy), *lacerías* (interlocking wooden lengths to form geometric patterns), *atauriques* (stylised plant motifs) in plaster and ceramics, and a magnificent wooden *dosel* (canopy) to round it all off.

2 PATIO DE ARRAYANES

Visit here for the overall majesty, but what's special is the use of water, which is at once decorative and functional. It has the effect of making the porticos seem longer, adding a symbolic dimension and amplifying the sense of light, even as it gives the visitor the feeling that this is not just a garden but an oasis.

3 PATIO DE LOS LEONES

My favourite place from which to view this famous patio is from the Sala de Dos Hermanas (Hall of the Two Sisters) on the patio's northern side. This perspective reveals the glorious pinnacle of Nasrid architecture, blending the careful designs of Al-Andalus' most skilled artisans with the wider heritage of oriental art.

4 PEINADOR DE LA REINA

The 'Queen's Dressing Room' is like a bridge between the Islamic and Christian periods of the Alhambra. As such, it's an outstanding example of cultural synthesis, where the beautiful decorative art of the Renaissance occupies the heart of an earlier Nasrid tower. It also serves as one of the Alhambra's open windows with sweeping views out onto the world beyond the palace.

5 THE SPIRIT OF THE AGE

Two corners of the Alhambra in particular give a powerful sense of what it was like to live here. The base of the Torre de la Vela conserves that spirit perfectly, while the baths are unique in enabling you to understand the social, cultural and religious practices that gave meaning to life in Al-Andalus.

Granada's Albayzín

Cobblestone streets, mosques, palaces, and plazas tinkling with the sound of fountains. Getting lost in Granada's wonderful Albayzín (p300), or old quarter, is as close to a Moroccan dream as you can get this side of Africa. Don't miss the Colegiata del Salvador, a 16th-century church sitting atop the remains of a mosque. Its fusion of Islamic and Christian design perfectly sums up Granada's history.

2

3

Málaga

Much maligned Málaga (p308) is the birthplace of Picasso and so therefore it only seems right that it's quietly reinventing itself from mere transit hub for the huge nearby beach resorts to a fully fledged city of art and culture with some impressive art galleries. Throw in the odd Islamic era palace, a giant cathedral, and the ruins of a lofty castl and you get an altogether delightful, an totally Spanish, city. Plaza del Obispo, Málaga

INGOLF POMPE/GETTY IMAGES ©

Gibraltar

4

There's pubs and pies, apes and Union Jack flags, so bring your passport and some British Pound Sterling (you can actually use Euros) and head off for a surreal trip into a little England. We're willing to bet that fascinating Gibraltar (p314) is not at all what you expected to find in 'Spain'.

5

Baeza & Úbeda

Way out in the heart of the olive-ribbed countryside in the remote Jaén region, the twin towns of Baeza and Úbeda (p322) might be well off the standard tourist routes, but they reward the adventurous with a fabulous collection of Renaissance beauty that is almost unrivalled in Spain. The highlight is Úbeda's famous chapel, Sacra Capilla del Salvador. Baeza cathedral

6

Sierra Nevada & Las Alpujarras

The icy sentinels of mainland Spain's highest peaks lord it over Las Alpujarras (p319), a jumble of electric green valleys and scorching white, pocket-sized villages that represent some of the most breathtaking scenery in Spain. This is serious walking country, and the hiking trails here come as short and gentle or long and tough as you care to make them. Parque Nacional Sierra Nevada

Granada & Andalucía's South Coast's Best...

Old Towns

- **Albayzín, Granada** (p300) Nowhere else in Spain does the Moorish past feel so alive.
- **Tarifa** (p313) Twisting, whitewashed streets and views to Africa.
- **Baeza** (p322) A treasure trove of Renaissance architecture.
- **Úbeda** (p322) Spain's most impressive collection of Renaissance architecture.

Beaches

- **Tarifa** (p313) Windsurfing, whales and horse riding.
- **Cabo de Gata** (p323) Hidden coves without the crowds.
- **Zahara de los Atunes** (p314) An expanse of sand like the Spanish coast used to be.
- **Los Caños de Meca** (p314) Long, laid-back beaches around the Cabo de Trafalgar.

Museums

- **Museo Picasso, Málaga** (p309) Stunning collection of Picasso's works in the city of his birth.
- **Museo Carmen Thyssen, Málaga** (p310) Impressive collection of 19th-century Spanish art.
- **Museo Ralli, Marbella** (p317) Superb private art gallery.
- **Gibraltar Museum** (p314) Discover the Rock's British history.

Places To Connect With Nature

- **Sierra Nevada** (p319) Andalucía's most spectacular natural area.
- **Las Alpujarras** (p319) Berber-style villages and snaking valleys.
- **Cabo de Gata** (p323) Semi-desert landscapes and near pristine beaches.
- **Straits of Gibraltar** (p314) Watch whales and dolphins swim between Europe and Africa.

Left: Bubión (p320), Las Alpujarras; **Above:** Cabo de Gata

Need to Know

ADVANCE PLANNING

- **One month before** Reserve your entry ticket for the Alhambra.
- **Three weeks before** If it's summertime, reserve your beachfront hotel.

RESOURCES

- **Andalucía Te Quiere** (www.andalucia.org) Terrific tourist office site for the entire region.
- **Andalucia.com** (www.andalucia.com) Excellent privately run site on Andalucía.
- **Visit Granada** (www.granadatur.com) Official tourist board website for Granada.

GETTING AROUND

- **Air** International airports with intra-Spain connections in Málaga, Granada and Almería.
- **Train** Renfe has good north-south connections, fewer from east to west.
- **Bus** Wherever trains don't reach.
- **Road** Excellent network of roads.

BE FOREWARNED

- The Alhambra has 6600 daily tickets, but just 2000 are available at the gate.

Granada & Andalucía's South Coast Itineraries

The contrasting classics of Andalucía are found on these two itineraries, from the Islamic perfect of Granada's Alhambra to beach resorts via mountain retreats and a truly bizarre slice of 1950's Britain.

3 DAYS

GRANADA TO CAPILEIRA

Al-Andalus Heartland

Any attempt to catch a glimpse of Islamic Al-Andalus just has to begin in **(1) Granada**, which served as the capital of Islamic Spain long after the rest of the country had fallen to the Christian Reconquista. Having had centuries to perfect their distinctive architectural style, Granada's Islamic rulers created the Alhambra, quite possibly one of the most exquisite collections of buildings on earth. You could spend a day in the Alhambra alone, and the Albayzín (Granada's historical and present-day heartbeat), the Capilla Real and the city's wonderful tapas culture deserve another day at least. Getting much more rural but retaining the Moorish vibe are the snow drop villages of Las Alpujarras. Start by heading to **(2) Pampaneira** before moving on to explore **(3) Bubión** with its interesting folk museum and finishing in little old **(4) Capileira**. As you explore these slope-hugging villages you'll be watched constantly by the mighty mass of the snow-streaked Sierra Nevada mountains.

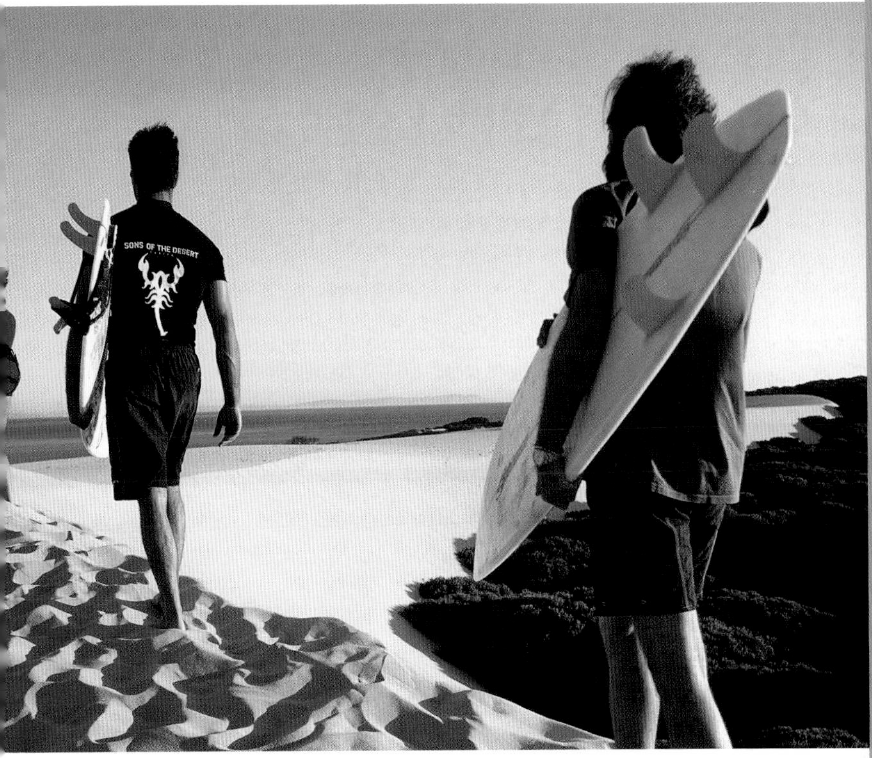

5 DAYS

GRANADA TO TARIFA

Cruising the Costa

In **(1) Granada** sun-bleached streets and splashes of green are overlaid with a sense of having one foot in modern Spain and another planted firmly in the scented alleyways of a Moroccan Medina. And overlooking it all is the sublime Alhambra. Head southwest to **(2) Málaga**, in which, with its rich history, a party-hard population and Picasso as its favourite son it's hard not to find something to like. You're now firmly on the Costa del Sol, a place with a reputation for low budget mass tourism and some serious tack. This may well be the case in places but come to **(3) Marbella** and you may well find yourself rubbing shoulders with a glitzy starlet or a high roller in a multi-million Euro yacht. **(4) Gibraltar** has been British longer than the United States has been American, but even knowing that it comes as a surprise to discover a place that can appear more classically 'British' than Britain. Follow the coast west and you'll come to **(5) Tarifa**, whose ancient core of sea salt, Moorish white houses contrasts beautifully with the town's modern focus on all things surfy.

Surfers at Tarifa beach (p313)
DIEGO LEZAMA/GETTY IMAGES ©

Discover Granada & Andalucía's South Coast

At a Glance

- **Granada** (p300) The city of Granada and the wonderful Alhambra.
- **Málaga** (p308) An art-infused beachside city.
- **Andalucía's South Coast** (p313) Includes the Costa del Sol, Gibraltar and the Costa de la Luz.
- **Sierra Nevada** (p319) Mainland Spain's highest mountains and detours to Cabo de Gata.

Albayzín and the Mirador San Nicolás, Granada
ALFREDO MAIQUEZ/GETTY IMAGES ©

GRANADA

POP 258,000 / ELEV 685M

Boabdil the Moor wasn't the last departing traveller to shed a farewell tear for Granada, a city of sun-bleached streets and parched earth interspersed with soothing splashes of green, including the woods and gardens that embellish the Alhambra. For those who dig deeper, Granada hides a more elusive allure. This is a place to put down your guidebook and let your intuition lead the way – through mysterious labyrinthine streets and shady Moroccan *teterías* (teahouses).

Sights & Activities

ALBAYZÍN Historic Neighbourhood
(Map p302) On the hill facing the Alhambra across the Darro valley, Granada's old Muslim quarter, the Albayzín, is an open-air museum in which you can lose yourself for a whole morning. The cobblestone streets are lined with gorgeous *cármenes* (large mansions with walled gardens, from the Arabic *karm* for garden).

Plaza del Salvador, near the top of the Albayzín, is dominated by the **Colegiata del Salvador**, a 16th-century church on the site of the Albayzín's main mosque. The mosque's horseshoe-arched patio, cool and peaceful, survives at its western end.

The **Arco de las Pesas**, off Plaza Larga, is an impressive gateway in the Albayzín's 11th-century defensive wall. If you follow Callejón de San Cecilio from here you'll end up at the **Mirador San Nicolás**, the Albayzín's premier (and perennially crowded) lookout, with unbeatable views of the Alhambra and Sierra Nevada.

Just east of Mirador San Nicolás, off Cuesta de las Cabras, the Albayzín's first new mosque in 500 years, the **Mezquita Mayor de Granada**, has been built to serve modern Granada's growing Muslim population.

Another well-placed lookout is the **Placeta de San Miguel Bajo**, with its lively cafe-restaurants. Close to this square off Callejón del Gallo and down a short lane is the 15th-century **Palacio de Dar-al-Horra**, a romantically dishevelled mini-Alhambra that was home to the mother of Boabdil, Granada's last Muslim ruler.

Downhill from Placeta de San Miguel Bajo you'll find the lovely **Alminar de San José** (San José Minaret; Map p302; Calle San José) in Calle San José, a minaret that survives from an 11th-century mosque.

CATEDRAL Cathedral

(Map p302; ☎958 22 29 59; admission €3.50; 10.45am-1.30pm & 4-8pm Mon-Sat, 4-8pm Sun, to 7pm daily Nov-Mar) Granada's cavernous cathedral was commissioned by the Catholic monarchs, but construction began only after Isabel's death, and didn't finish until 1704. The result is a mishmash of styles: baroque outside, by the 17th-century master Alonso Cano, and Renaissance inside, where the Spanish pioneer in this style, Diego de Siloé, directed operations to construct huge piers, white as meringue, a black-and-white tile floor and the gilded and painted chapel.

CAPILLA REAL Historic Building

(Map p302; www.capillareal.granada.com; Calle Oficios; admission €3.50; 10.30am-1.30pm & 4-7.30pm Mon-Sat, 11am-1.30pm & 4-7pm Sun Apr-Oct) The Royal Chapel adjoins Granada's cathedral and is an outstanding Christian building. Catholic monarchs Isabel and Fernando commissioned this elaborate Isabeline-Gothic-style mausoleum.

MONASTERIO DE SAN JERÓNIMO Monastery

(Map p302; Calle Rector López Argüeta 9; admission €3.50; 10am-2.30pm & 4-7.30pm) One

Alhambra Admission

Some areas of the Alhambra can be visited at any time without a ticket, but the highlight areas can be entered only with a ticket. Up to 6600 tickets are available for each day. About one third of these are sold at the ticket office on the day, but they sell out early and you need to start queuing by 7am to be reasonably sure of getting one. It's highly advisable to book in advance (€1 extra per ticket). You can book up to three months ahead in two ways:

Alhambra Advance Booking (☎for international calls 0034 934 92 37 50, for national calls 902 88 80 01; www.alhambra-tickets.es; 8am-9pm)

Servicaixa (www.servicaixa.com) Online booking in Spanish and English. You can also buy tickets in advance from Servicaixa cash machines, but only in the Alhambra grounds.

For internet or phone bookings you need a Visa card, MasterCard or Eurocard. You'll receive a reference number, which you must show, along with your passport, national identity card or credit card, at the Alhambra ticket office when you pick up the ticket on the day of your visit.

Buses 30 and 32 (€1.10) both run between Plaza Nueva and the Alhambra ticket office every five to nine minutes from 7.15am to 11pm, or it's an easy and pleasant walk up the Cuesta de Gomérez from Plaza Nueva.

Granada

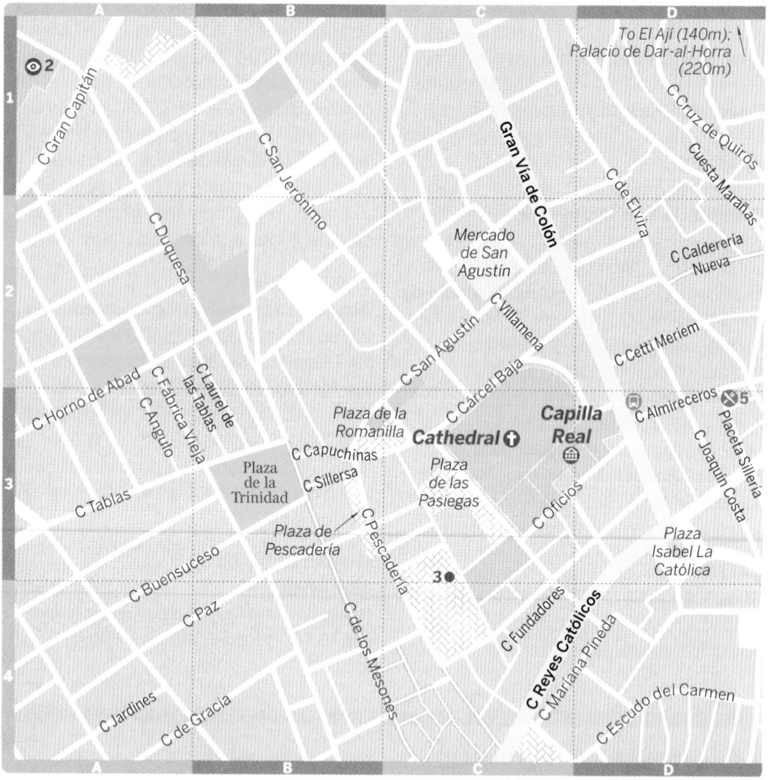

To El Ají (140m); Palacio de Dar-al-Horra (220m)
C Gran Capitán
C San Jerónimo
Gran Vía de Colón
C Cruz de Quirós
Cuesta Marañas
C de Elvira
C Duquesa
Mercado de San Agustín
C Caldereria Nueva
C Villamena
C San Agustín
C Cetti Meriem
C Horno de Abad
C Fábrica Vieja
C Angulo
C Laurel de las Tablas
C Cárcel Baja
Plaza de la Romanilla
Capilla Real
Cathedral
C Almireceros
Placeta Sillería
C Joaquín Costa
C Capuchinas
Plaza de la Trinidad
C Sillersa
Plaza de las Pasiegas
C Tablas
C Oficios
Plaza de Pescadería
C Pescadería
Plaza Isabel La Católica
C Buensuceso
C Paz
C de los Mesones
C Fundadores
C Reyes Católicos
C Mariana Pineda
C Jardines
C de Gracia
C Escudo del Carmen

of the most stunning Catholic buildings in Granada is a little out of the centre. At the 16th-century Monasterio de San Jerónimo, where nuns still sing vespers, every surface of the church has been painted – the stained glass literally pales in comparison.

MONASTERIO DE LA CARTUJA Monastery
(Paseo de la Cartuja; admission €3.50; ⌚10am-1pm & 4-8pm Mon-Sat, 10am-noon Sun) Built between the 16th and 18th centuries by the Carthusian monks themselves, this 16th-century monastery has an imposing sand-coloured stone exterior. But it is the lavish baroque monastery church that people come to see, especially the *sagrario* (sanctuary) behind the main altar, a confection of red, black, white and grey-blue marble, columns with golden capitals, profuse sculpture and a beautiful frescoed cupola.

Tours

CICERONE CULTURA Y OCIO Walking Tour
(Map p302; ☎650 541669; www.ciceronegranada.com; tour €15) Informative walking tours of central Granada and the Albayzín leave daily from Plaza Bib-Rambla, at 10.30am, or 11am in winter.

ALHAMBRA NIGHT TOUR Cultural Tour
(☎902 44 12 21; www.alhambra-patronato.es; adult/child under 12yr €13/free; ⌚10-11.30pm Tue-Sat) The Palacios Nazaríes are romantically lit in the evening. You won't

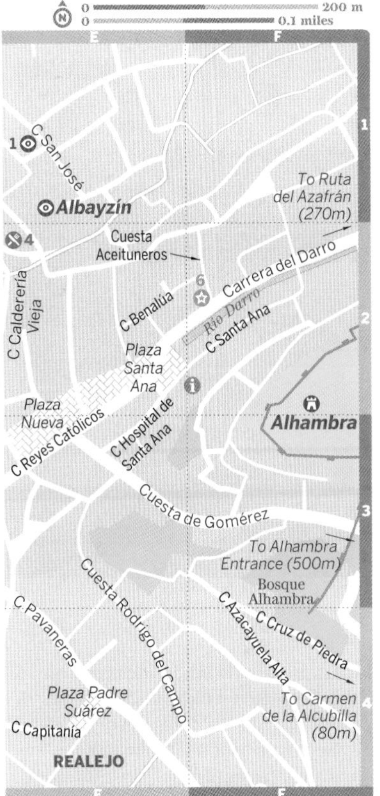

Granada

Top Sights
- Albayzín ... E1
- Alhambra ... F2
- Capilla Real ... C3
- Cathedral ... C3

Sights
1. Alminar de San José ... E1
2. Monasterio de San Jerónimo ... A1

Activities, Courses & Tours

3. Cicerone Cultura y Ocio ... C3

Eating

4. Arrayanes ... E2
5. Bodegas Castañeda ... D3

Entertainment

6. Le Chien Andalou ... F2

get to see as much as on a day visit, but you won't have to deal with the same crowds either.

Sleeping

CASA MORISCA HOTEL Historic Hotel €€
(☎958 22 11 00; www.hotelcasamorisca.com; Cuesta de la Victoria 9; d €118-148; ❄ @ 📶) This late-15th-century mansion perfectly captures the spirit of the Albayzín. A heavy wooden door shuts out city noise, and rooms are soothing, with lofty ceilings, fluffy white beds and flat-weave rugs over brick floors. The least expensive ones look only onto the central patio with its fountain – cosily authentic, but potentially claustrophobic for some.

CARMEN DE LA ALCUBILLA Historic Hotel €€
(☎958 21 55 51; www.alcubilladelcaracol.com; Calle del Aire Alta 12; s/d €100/120; ❄ @ 📶) This exquisitely decorated place is located on the slopes of the Alhambra. Rooms are washed in pale pastel colours contrasting with cool cream and antiques. There are fabulous views and a pretty terraced garden.

Eating

RUTA DEL AZAFRÁN Fusion €€
(www.rutadelazafran.es; Paseo del Padre Manjón 1; mains €13-20) One of the few high-concept restaurants in Granada, this sleek spot with its steely modern interior has an eclectic menu which ranges from Asian-inspired tempuras to broccoli-based pesto, lamb couscous and roasted pork.

BODEGAS CASTAÑEDA Bar €€
(Map p302; Calle Almireceros; tapas €2-3, raciónes €6-8) An institution among locals and tourists alike, this buzzing bar doles out hearty portions of food (try a hot or cold *tabla*, or platter; a half order, €6, is ample for two) and dispenses drinks from big casks mounted in the walls. The best choice is a lively, herbaceous *vermut*

ROBERTO A SANCHEZ/GETTY IMAGES ©

Don't Miss Alhambra

The sheer red walls of the Alhambra rise from woods of cypress and elm. Inside is one of the more splendid sights of Europe, a network of lavishly decorated palaces and irrigated gardens, a World Heritage Site and the subject of scores of legends and fantasies.

The central palace complex, the **Palacio Nazaríes**, is the pinnacle of the Alhambra's design. Enter through the 14th-century **Mexuar**, perhaps an antechamber for those awaiting audiences with the emir. Look up here and elsewhere to appreciate the geometrically carved wood ceilings. From the Mexuar, you'll pass into the **Patio del Cuarto Dorado**.

Rooms likely used for lounging and sleeping look onto the rectangular pool, and traces of cobalt blue paint cling to the walls at the north end. Originally, all the walls were lavishly coloured; the paint on the stucco-trimmed walls in the adjacent **Sala de la Barca** resembled flocked wallpaper. Adjacent is the **Patio de los Leones** (Courtyard of the Lions), built by Muhammad V in the second half of the 14th century.

On the patio's north side, doors once covered the entrance to the **Sala de Dos Hermanas** (Hall of Two Sisters). The dizzying ceiling is a muqarnas dome with some 5000 tiny cells. At the far end, the **Mirador de Lindaraja** looks out onto the garden below. The terraced gardens and reflecting pool were created in the early 20th century. At the west end of the grounds are the remnants of the palace-fortress **Alcazaba**. The **Torre de la Vela** (Watchtower) is where the cross and banners of the Reconquista were raised in January 1492.

The **Generalife** is a soothing arrangement of pathways, patios, pools, fountains, tall trees and, in season, flowers of every imaginable hue. At the north end is the emirs' **summer palace**, a whitewashed structure on the hillside facing the Alhambra. Palacio Nazaríes

NEED TO KNOW

Map p302; ☎902 44 12 21; www.alhambra-tickets.es; adult/under 8yr €13/free, Generalife €6; ⏰8.30am-8pm Apr-Oct, to 6pm Nov-Mar, night visits 10-11.30pm Tue-Sat Mar-Oct, 8-9.30pm Fri & Sat Nov-Feb (vermouth) topped with soda. Don't confuse this place with Antigua Bodega Castañeda around the corner, which is not as enticing.

ARRAYANES Moroccan **€€**
(Map p302; 958 22 84 01; www.rest-arrayanes.com; Cuesta Marañas 4; mains €8-15; from 8pm;) The best Moroccan food in a city that is well known for its Moorish throwbacks? Recline on lavish patterned seating, try the rich, fruity tagine casseroles and make your decision.

EL AJÍ Modern Spanish **€€**
(Plaza San Miguel Bajo 9; mains €12-20;) Up in the Albayzín, this chic but cosy neighbourhood restaurant is no bigger than a shoebox but serves from breakfast right through to the evening. Chatty staff at the tiny marble bar can point out some of the highlights of the creative menu (such as prawns with tequila and honey).

Entertainment

PEÑA DE LA PLATERÍA Flamenco
(Placeta de Toqueros 7) Buried in the Albayzín warren, Peña La Platería claims to be the oldest flamenco aficionados' club in Spain. It's a private affair, though, and not always open to nonmembers. Performances are usually Thursday and Saturday at 10.30pm – look presentable, and speak a little Spanish at the door, if you can.

LE CHIEN ANDALOU Flamenco
(Map p302; www.lechienandalou.com; Carrera del Darro 7; admission €8; shows 9pm) This is one of Granada's most atmospheric venues to enjoy some vigorous castanet-clicking flamenco with a varied and professional line up of musicians and dancers throughout the week.

Information

Tourist Information

There are regional tourist offices in Plaza Nueva (**tel, info 958 22 10 22; Calle Santa Ana 1; 9am-7pm Mon-Sat, 10am-2pm Sun & holidays)** and the Alhambra (**902 88 80 01; www.alhambra -tickets.es)**.

Municipal Tourist Office **(www.granadatur.com; Calle Almona del Campillo, 2; 9am-7pm Mon-Fri, to 6pm Sat, 10am-2pm Sun)** Sleek, efficient centre opposite the city's Parque Federico García Lorca.

Provincial Tourist Office **(www.turismodegranada.org; Plaza de Mariana Pineda 10; 9am-10pm Mon-Fri, 10am-7pm Sat)** Helpful staff with information on the whole Granada region; a short walk east of Puerta Real.

Getting There & Away

Air

Iberia (**902 40 05 00; www.iberia.com)** flies daily to/from Madrid from Aeropuerto Federico García Lorca **(www.aena.es)** 17km west of the city. There are also flights to Barcelona and the Canary Islands, and seasonally to Paris.

Bus

Granada's bus station is 3km northwest of the city centre. Take city bus 3 to the centre or a taxi for €7. Alsa **(www.alsa.es)** handles buses in the province and across the region, plus a night bus direct to Madrid's Barajas airport (€24.50, six hours). Other destinations include Córdoba (€13.50, 2¾ hours direct, eight daily),Seville (€20.50, three hours direct, 10 daily), Málaga (€10.50, 1½ hours direct,18 daily) and Las Alpujarras.

Train

The train station (**958 24 02 02; Avenida de Andaluces)** is 1.5km west of the centre, off Avenida de la Constitución. Four trains run daily to/from Seville (€23.85, three hours) and Almería (€16.50, 2¼ hours) via Guadix, and six daily to/from Antequera (€20.50, 1½ hours). Three go to Ronda (€15, three hours) and Algeciras (€25, 4½ hours). For Málaga (€16.50, 2½ hours) or Córdoba (€35.50, 2½ hours) take an Algeciras train and change at Bobadilla. One or two trains go to each of Madrid (€68, four to five hours), Valencia (€52.50, 7½ to eight hours) and Barcelona (€58, 12 hours).

Alhambra

Timeline

900 The first reference to *al-qala'at al-hamra* (red castle) atop Granada's Sabika Hill.

1237 Founder of the Nasrid dynasty, Muhammad I, moves his court to Granada. Threatened by belligerent Christian armies he builds a new defensive fort, the **Alcazaba** 1.

1302-09 Designed as a summer palace-cum-country estate for Granada's foppish rulers, the bucolic **Generalife** 2 is begun by Muhammad III.

1333-54 Yusuf I initiates the construction of the **Palacio Nazaríes** 3, still considered the highpoint of Islamic culture in Europe.

1350-60 Up goes the **Palacio de Comares** 4, taking Nasrid lavishness to a whole new level.

1362-91 The second coming of Muhammad V ushers in even greater architectural brilliance exemplified by the construction of the **Patio de los Leones** 5.

1527 The Christians add the **Palacio de Carlos V** 6. Inspired Renaissance palace or incongruous crime against the Moorish art? You decide.

1829 The languishing, half-forgotten Alhambra is 'rediscovered' by American writer Washington Irving during a protracted sleep-over.

1954 The Generalife gardens are extended southwards to accommodate an outdoor theatre.

TOP TIPS

Queue-dodger Reserve tickets in advance online at www.alhambra-tickets.es

Money-saver You can visit the general areas of the palace free of charge any time by entering through the Puerta de Justica

Stay over Two fine hotels are encased in the grounds: Parador de Granada (expensive) and Hotel América (more economical)

MICHAEL TAYLOR / GETTY IMAGES ©

Sala de la Barca

Throw your head back in the anteroom to the Comares Palace where the gilded ceiling is shaped like an upturned boat. Destroyed by fire in the 1890s, it has been painstakingly restored.

Palacio de Carlos V

It's easy to miss the stylistic merits of this Renaissance palace added in 1527. Check out the ground floor Museo de la Alhambra with artefacts directly related to the palace's history.

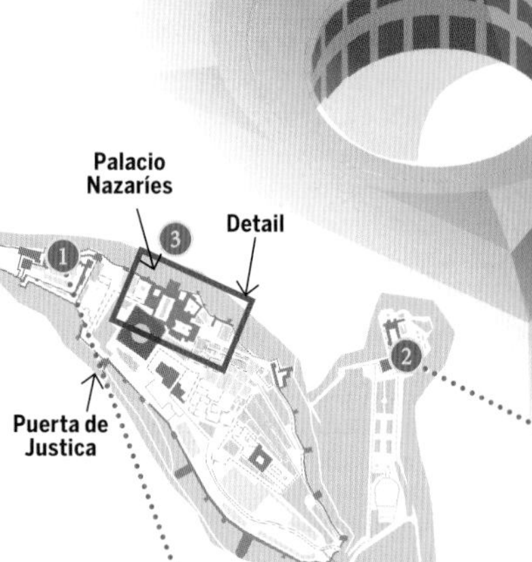

Alcazaba

Find time to explore the towers of the original citadel, the most important of which – the Torre de la Vela – takes you, via a winding staircase, to the Alhambra's best viewpoint.

DAVID TOMLINSON / GETTY IMAGES ©

JOHN ELK III / GETTY IMAGES ©

DAVID TOMLINSON / GETTY IMAGES ©

JOHN ELK III / GETTY IMAGES ©

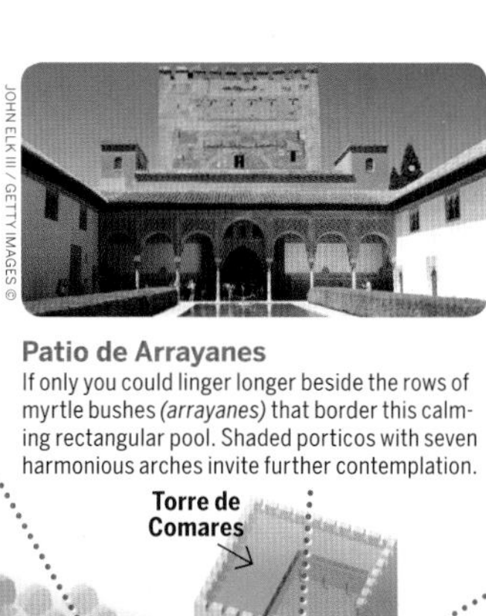

Patio de Arrayanes

If only you could linger longer beside the rows of myrtle bushes *(arrayanes)* that border this calming rectangular pool. Shaded porticos with seven harmonious arches invite further contemplation.

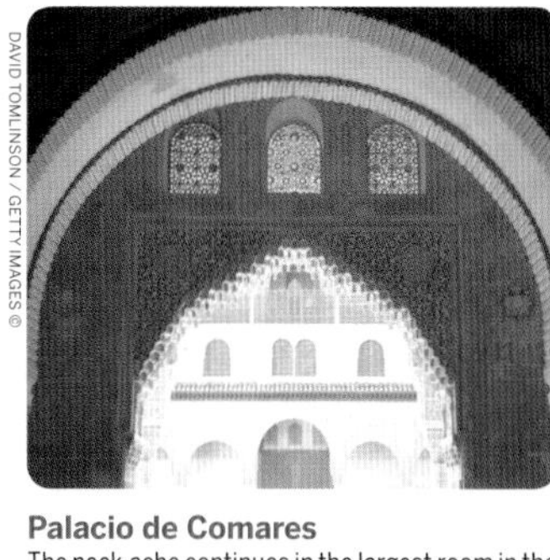

Palacio de Comares

The neck-ache continues in the largest room in the Comares Palace renowned for its rich geometric ceiling. A negotiating room for the emirs, the Salón de los Embajadores is a masterpiece of Moorish design.

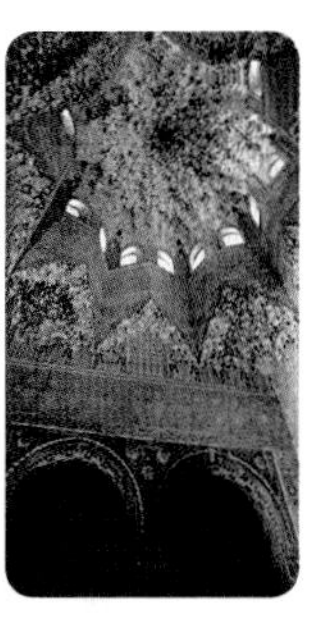

Sala de Dos Hermanas

Focus on the *dos hermanas* – two marble slabs either side of the fountain – before enjoying the intricate cupola embellished with 5000 tiny moulded stalactites. Poetic calligraphy decorates the walls.

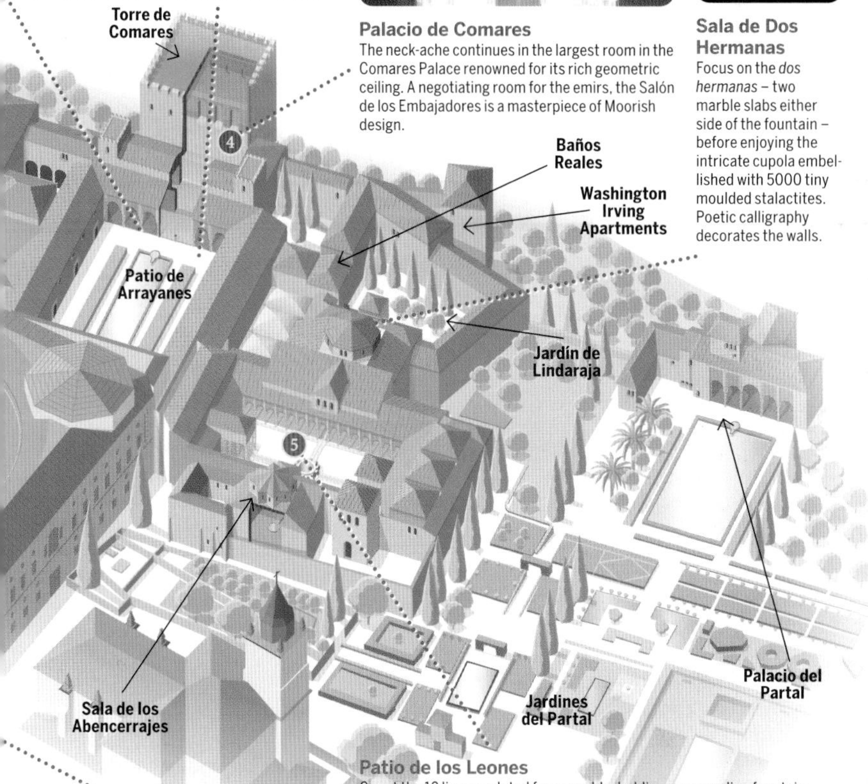

Torre de Comares
4
Baños Reales
Washington Irving Apartments
Patio de Arrayanes
Jardín de Lindaraja
5
Sala de los Abencerrajes
Jardines del Partal
Palacio del Partal

Patio de los Leones

Count the 12 lions sculpted from marble, holding up a gurgling fountain. Then pan back and take in the delicate columns and arches built to signify an Islamic vision of paradise.

Generalife

A coda to most people's visits, the 'architect's garden' is no afterthought. While Nasrid in origin, the horticulture is relatively new: the pools and arcades were added in the early 20th century.

SAMUEL MAGAL / GETTY IMAGES ©

JOHN ELK III / GETTY IMAGES ©

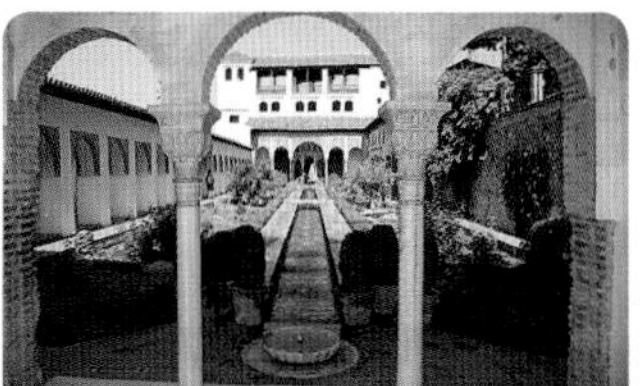

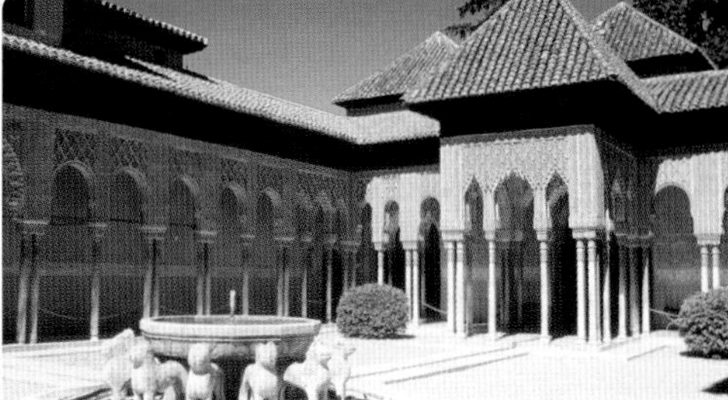

Right: Málaga cathedral; **Below:** Local produce from southern Spain
BELOW: NNIE GRIFFITHS BELT/GETTY IMAGES ©; RIGHT: KIM SCHANDORFF/GETTY IMAGES ©

Getting Around

To/From the Airport

The airport is 17km west of the city on the A92. Autocares J González (www.autocaresjosegonzalez.com) runs buses between the airport and a stop near the Palacio de Congresos (€3, five daily), with a stop in the city centre on Gran Vía de Colón, where a schedule is posted opposite the cathedral, and at the entrance to the bus station. A taxi costs €18 to €22 depending on traffic conditions and pick-up point.

Car & Motorcycle

Vehicle access to the Plaza Nueva area is restricted by red lights and little black posts known as *pilonas*, which block certain streets during certain times of the day. If you are going to stay at a hotel near Plaza Nueva, press the button next to your hotel's name beside the *pilonas* to contact reception, which will be able to lower the *pilonas* for you.

Central underground public car parks include Parking San Agustín **(Calle San Agustín; per hr/day €1.75/20)**, Parking Neptuno **(Calle Neptuno)** and Parking Plaza Puerta Real **(Acera del Darro; per hr/day €1.45/17)**. Free parking is available at the Alhambra car parks.

MÁLAGA

POP 558,000

The Costa del Sol can seem wholly soulless until you decamp to Málaga, an unmistakably Spanish metropolis curiously ignored by the lion's share of the 11 million tourists who land annually at Pablo Ruíz Picasso International Airport before getting carted off to the golf courses and beaches of 'Torrie' and Fuengirola. Their loss could be your gain. Stubborn and stalwart, Málaga's history is as rich as its parks are green, while its feisty populace challenges *sevillanos* as 24-hour party people.

Sights & Activities

MUSEO PICASSO MÁLAGA Museum

(Map p310; ☎902 44 33 77; www.museopicassomalaga.org; Calle San Agustín 8; permanent/temporary collection €6/4.50, combined ticket €8; ⌚10am-8pm Tue-Thu & Sun, to 9pm Fri & Sat) The Museo Picasso has an enviable collection of 204 works, 155 donated and 49 loaned to the museum by Christine Ruiz-Picasso (wife of Paul, Picasso's eldest son) and Bernard Ruiz-Picasso (his grandson), and includes some wonderful paintings of the family, including the heartfelt *Paulo con gorro blanco* (Paulo with a white cap), a portrait of Picasso's eldest son painted in the 1920s.

CATHEDRAL Cathedral

(Map p310; ☎952 21 59 17; Calle Molina Lario; cathedral & museum €3.50; ⌚10am-6pm Mon-Sat, closed holidays) Málaga's cathedral was started in the 16th century and building continued for some 200 years. From the start, the project was plagued by overambition, and the original proposal for a new cathedral had to be shelved. Instead, a series of architects (five in total) set about transforming the original mosque – of this, only the **Patio de los Naranjos** survives, a small courtyard of fragrant orange trees where the ablutions fountain used to be.

ALCAZABA Castle

(Map p310; Calle Alcazabilla; admission €2.10, incl Castillo de Gibralfaro €3.40; ⌚9.30am-8pm Tue-Sun Apr-Oct) No time to visit Granada's Alhambra? Then Málaga's Alcazaba can provide a taster.

Extensively restored, this palace-fortress dates from the 11th century Moorish period and the caliphal horseshoe arches, courtyards and bubbling fountains are evocative of this influential period in Málaga's history.

CASTILLO DE GIBRALFARO Castle

(admission €2.10; ⌚9am-9pm Apr-Sep, to 6pm Oct-Mar) One remnant of Málaga's Islamic past is the craggy ramparts of

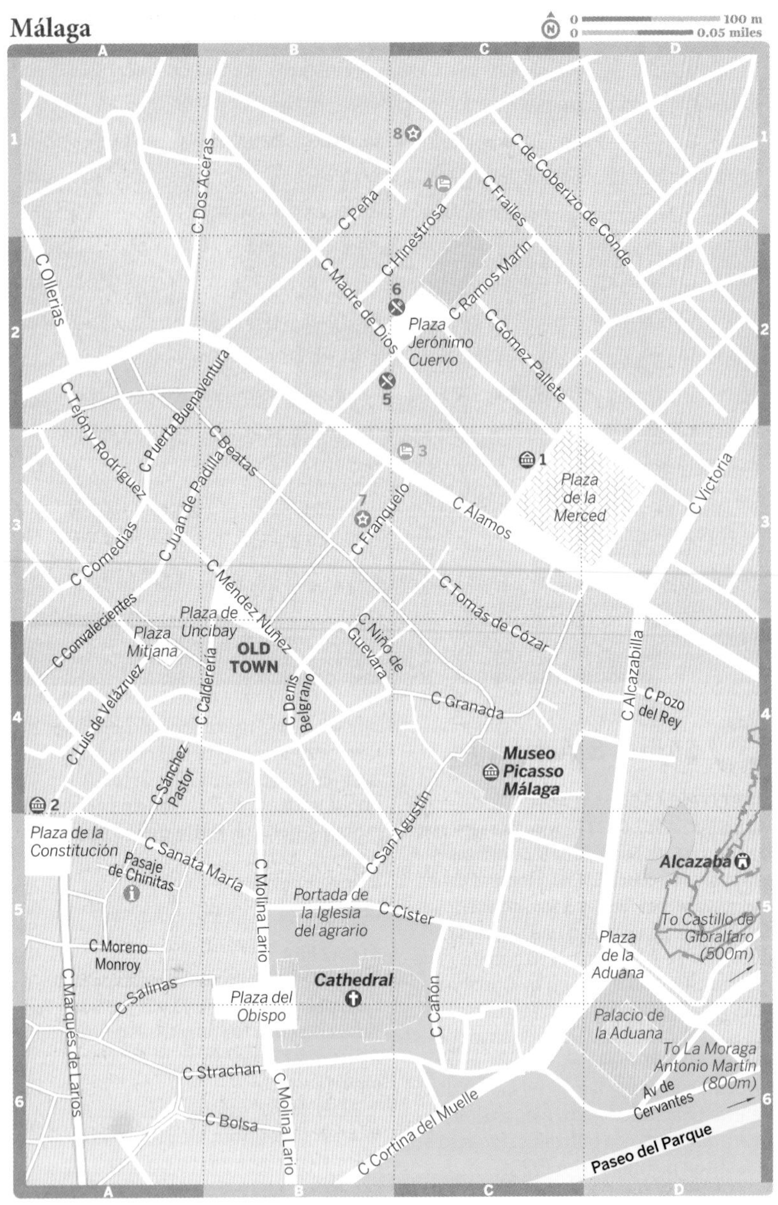

the Castillo de Gibralfaro, spectacularly located high on the hill overlooking the city. Built by Abd ar-Rahman I, the 8th-century Cordoban emir, and later rebuilt in the 14th century when Málaga was the main port for the emirate of Granada, the castle originally acted as a lighthouse and military barracks.

MUSEO CARMEN THYSSEN Museum

(Map p310; www.carmenthyssenmalaga.org; Calle Compañia 10; adult/child €6/free; ⌚10am-8pm

Málaga

Top Sights

- Alcazaba D5
- Cathedral B5
- Museo Picasso Málaga C4

Sights

1 Casa Natal de Picasso C3
2 Museo Carmen Thyssen A4

Sleeping

3 El Hotel del Pintor C3
4 El Riad Andaluz C1

Eating

5 Tapeo de Cervantes B2
6 Vino Mio C2

Entertainment

7 Amargo B3
8 Kelipe C1

Tue-Sun) One of the city's latest museums opened in 2011 in an aesthetically renovated 16th-century palace in the heart of the city's historic centre, the former old Moorish quarter of Málaga. The extensive collection concentrates on 19th-century Spanish and Andalucían art and includes paintings by some of the country's most exceptional painters, including Joaquín Sorolla y Bastida, Ignacio Zuloaga and Francisco de Zurbarán.

CASA NATAL DE PICASSO Museum
(Map p310; Plaza de la Merced 15; admission €1; 9.30am-8pm) For an intimate insight into Picasso's childhood, head to the house where he was born in 1881, which now acts as a study foundation. The house has a replica 19th-century artist's studio and small quarterly exhibitions of Picasso's work.

Sleeping

EL RIAD ANDALUZ Guesthouse **€€**
(Map p310; 952 21 36 40; www.elriadandaluz.com; Calle Hinestrosa 24; s/d €70/86;) This French-run guesthouse, near the Teatro Cervantes, has eight rooms set around the kind of atmospheric patio that's known as a *riad* in Morocco. The decoration is Moroccan but each room is different, including colourful tiled bathrooms.

EL HOTEL DEL PINTOR Hotel **€€**
(Map p310; 952 06 09 81; www.hoteldelpintor.com; Calle Álamos 27; r from €75;) The red, black and white colour scheme of this friendly small hotel echoes the abstract artwork of *malagueño* artist Pepe Bornov, whose paintings are on permanent display throughout the public areas and rooms.

Eating

VINO MIO International **€€**
(Map p310; www.restaurantevino.mio.com; Plaza Jeronimo Cuervo 2; mains €10-15) This Dutch-owned restaurant has a diverse and interesting menu that includes dishes like kangaroo steaks, vegetable stir fries, duck breast with sweet chilli, pasta, and several innovative salads. Tasty international tapas, like hummus and Roquefort croquettes, are also available to tantalise the tastebuds.

LA MORAGA ANTONIO MARTÍN Contemporary Andalucían **€€€**
(952 22 41 53; www.lamoraga.com; Plaza Malagueta 4; tapas from €5, mains from €20) This is Michelin-star chef Dani Garcia's second Málaga-based La Moraga (the first is on Calle Fresca in the centre). The concept is based on traditional tapas given the nouvelle treatment – like cherry *gazpacho* garnished with fresh cheese, anchovies and basil; king prawns wrapped in fried basil leaves; and mini-burgers created from oxtail. The dining spaces have a cool contemporary look and overlook the beach.

TAPEO DE CERVANTES Tapas **€**
(Map p310; www.eltapeodecervantes.com; Calle Cárcer 8; tapas €4-6; Tue-Sun) This place has caught on big time which, given its squeeze-in space, can mean a wait. Choose from traditional or more innovative tapas and *raciónes* (large tapas servings)

with delicious combinations and stylish presentation. Think polenta with oyster mushrooms, chorizo and melted cheese or the more conventional *tortilla* (potato omelette), spiked with a veg or two.

Entertainment

Málaga's substantial flamenco heritage has its nexus to the northwest of Plaza de la Merced. Venues here include **Kelipe** (Map p310; 692 82 98 85; www.kelipe.net; Calle Pena 11), a flamenco centre which puts on *muy puro* performances Thursday to Saturday at 9.30pm; entry of €15 includes one drink and tapa – reserve ahead. **Amargo** (Map p310; Calle R Franquillo 3) offers Friday and Saturday night gigs.

Information

Regional Tourist Office (www.andalucia.org; Pasaje de Chinitas 4; 9am-7.30pm Mon-Fri, 10am-7pm Sat, 10am-2pm Sun) There is another branch at the airport; these cover the whole of Málaga and all of Andalucía.

Getting There & Away

Air

Málaga's Pablo Picasso Airport (www.aena.es), the main international gateway to Andalucía, is 9km southwest of the city centre and underwent a considerable expansion in 2010. It is a major hub in southern Spain serving top global carriers, as well as budget airlines.

Bus

Málaga's bus station (952 35 00 61; www.estabus.emtsam.es; Paseo de los Tilos) is just 1km southwest of the city centre. Frequent buses travel along the coasts, and others go to Seville (€30, 2½ hours, six daily), Granada (€10.50, 1½ to two hours, 18 daily), Córdoba (€13.50, 3½ hours, four daily), Antequera (€5, one hour, 13 daily) and Ronda (€9.50, 2½ hours, nine or more daily). Five buses also run daily to Madrid Airport (€36, five hours), and a few go up Spain's Mediterranean coast.

Car

Numerous local and international agencies (including Avis and Hertz) have desks at the airport.

Tarifa

Train

The Málaga-Renfe train station is near the bus station. Destinations include: Córdoba (€25.90, 2½ hours, 18 daily), Seville (€18.35, 2¾ hours, 11 daily) and Madrid (€87, 2½ hours, 10 daily). Note that for Córdoba and Seville the daily schedule includes faster trains at roughly double the cost.

 Getting Around

To/From the Airport

BUS Bus 75 to the city centre (€1.20, 20 minutes) leaves from outside the arrivals hall every 20 minutes from 7am to midnight. The bus to the airport leaves from the western end of Paseo del Parque, and from outside the bus and train stations, about every half-hour from 6.30am to 11.30pm.

TAXI A taxi from the airport to the city centre costs around €16.

TRAIN Trains run every 20 minutes from 6.50am to 11.54pm to the Málaga-Renfe Station and the Málaga-Centro station beside the Río Guadalmedina. Departures from the city to the airport are every 20 minutes from 5.30am to 10.30pm.

ANDALUCÍA'S SOUTH COAST

Tarifa

POP 17,900

Tarifa's tip-of-Spain location has given it a different climate and a different personality to the rest of Andalucía. Stiff Atlantic winds draw in surfers, windsurfers and kitesurfers who, in turn, lend this ancient, yet deceptively small settlement a laidback internationalist image that is noticeably (some would say, refreshingly) at odds with the commercialism of the nearby Costa del Sol.

Sights

OLD TOWN Old Town

A wander round the old town's narrow streets, which are of mainly Islamic origin, is an appetiser for Morocco. The Mudéjar **Puerta de Jerez** was built after the Reconquista. Look in at the small but action-packed **market (Calle Colón)** before wending your way to the mainly 15th-century **Iglesia de San Mateo (Calle Sancho IV El Bravo; 9am-1pm & 5.30-8.30pm)**. South of the church, the **Mirador El Estrecho**, atop part of the castle walls, has spectacular views across to Africa, located only 14km away.

Whale-Watching

The waters off Tarifa are one of the best places in Europe to see whales and dolphins as they swim between the Atlantic and the Mediterranean between April and October; sightings of some description are almost guaranteed between these months. Of the dozens of whale-watching outfits not-for-profit **FIRMM (956 62 70 08; www.firmm.org; Calle Pedro Cortés 4; Mar-Oct)** is a good bet, not least because its primary purpose is to study the whales, record data and encourage environmentally sensitive tours.

Sleeping & Eating

LA CASA DE LA FAVORITA Hotel, Apartment €€

(690 180253; www.lacasadelafavorita.com; Plaza de San Hiscio 4, Tarifa; d €60-125;) A quick internet search will reveal that La Favorita has become a lot of people's favourite recently. It must be something to do with creamy furnishings, the surgical indoor cleanliness, the kitchenettes in every room, the small library, the roof terrace, and the dynamic colorful art.

MANDRÁGORA Moroccan, Arabic €€

(956 68 12 91; Calle Independencia 3; mains €12-18; from 8pm Mon-Sat) Behind Iglesia de San Mateo, this intimate place serves Andalusian-Arabic food and does so

If You Like… Beaches

If you like the beaches around Tarifa, you'll also appreciate the long stretches of white sand northwest along the Costa de la Luz:

1 ZAHARA DE LOS ATUNES
Twelve kilometres of uninterrupted sand and very little development next to the beach.

2 BOLONIA
A beautiful bay, a long beach, views of Africa, and Baelo Claudia, the most complete Roman town yet uncovered in Spain.

3 LOS CAÑOS DE MECA
A bohemian village with fine beaches around the Cabo de Trafalgar, which marks the site of the famous eponymous battle in 1805.

4 EL PALMAR
Almost 5km of sand with few buildings and beloved by surfers from October to May and less active beach-lovers the rest of the year.

terrifically well. It's hard to know where to start, but the options for mains include lamb with plums and almonds, prawns with *ñora* (Andalusian sweet pepper) sauce, or monkfish in a wild mushroom and sea urchin sauce.

Information

Tourist office (**956 68 09 93; www.aytotarifa.com; Paseo de la Alameda; 10am-2pm daily, 6-8pm Mon-Fri Jun-Sep**) Near the top end of the palm-lined Paseo de la Alameda.

Getting There & Around

Comes (**956 68 40 38; www.tgcomes.es; Calle Batalla del Salado 13**) operates buses from the small open lot near the petrol station at the north end of Calle Batalla del Salado. It has regular departures to Cádiz, Jerez de la Frontera, La Línea de La Concepción (for Gibraltar), Málaga, Seville and Zahara de los Atunes.

Gibraltar

POP 30,000

Red pillar boxes, fish-and-chip shops, bobbies on the beat, and creaky seaside hotels with 1970s furnishings; Gibraltar – as British writer Laurie Lee once opined – is a piece of Portsmouth sliced off and towed 500 miles south. As with many colonial outposts, 'The Rock', as it's invariably known, tends to overstate its underlying Britishness, a bonus for lovers of pub grub and afternoon tea, but a confusing double-take for modern Brits who thought that their country had moved on since the days of stuffy naval prints and Lord Nelson memorabilia. Stuck strategically at the jaws of Europe and Africa, Gibraltar's Palladian architecture and camera-hogging Barbary apes make an interesting break from the tapas bars and white towns of Cádiz province. Playing an admirable supporting role is its swashbuckling local history; lest we forget, the Rock has been British longer than the United States has been American.

Sights

Pedestrianised Main St has a typically British appearance (including pubs, imperial statues and familiar British shops), though you'll catch Spanish inflections in the shuttered windows, narrow winding side streets and bilingual locals who have a tendency to start their sentences in English and finish them in Spanish.

GIBRALTAR MUSEUM Museum
(**Bomb House Lane; adult/child £2/1; 10am-6pm Mon-Fri, to 2pm Sat**) Gibraltar's history, from Neanderthal to medieval to the infamous 18th century siege, is swashbuckling to say the least and it quickly unfolds in this fine museum – comprising a labyrinth of rooms large and small.

UPPER ROCK NATURE RESERVE Nature Reserve
(**adult/child incl attractions £10/5, vehicle £2, pedestrian excl attractions £0.50; 9am-6.15pm,**

last entry 5.45pm) Most of the upper parts of the Rock (but not the main lookouts) come within the Upper Rock Nature Reserve; entry tickets include admission to St Michael's Cave, the Apes' Den, the Great Siege Tunnels, the Moorish castle, Military Heritage Centre, the 100-tonne supergun and the 'Gibraltar: A City Under Siege' exhibition. The upper Rock is home to 600 plant species and is the perfect vantage point for observing the migrations of birds between Europe and Africa.

The Rock's most famous inhabitants are the tailless Barbary macaques. Some of the 200 apes hang around the top cable-car station, while others are found at the **Apes' Den** (near the middle cable-car station) and the Great Siege Tunnels.

Sleeping

BRISTOL HOTEL Hotel **€€**

(☎20 07 68 00; www.bristolhotel.gi; 10 Cathedral Sq; s/d/tr £63/81/93; P ❄ 📶 🏊) Veterans of bucket-and-spade British seaside holidays can wax nostalgic at the stuck-in-the-70s Bristol with its creaking floorboards, red patterned carpets and Hi-de-Hi reception staff.

Eating

Goodbye tapas, hello fish and chips. Gibraltar's food is unashamedly British. The staples are pub grub, beer and sandwiches, chippies and stodgy desserts. Grand Casemates Square has a profusion of cooler, more modern Euro-cafes, though the newest movers and shakers (including some good ethnic places) can be found in Marina Bay's spanking new Ocean Village.

BISTRO MADELEINE Cafe, Bistro **€**

(256 Main St; cakes from £3; ⏲9am-11pm; 📶 🚭) If you've just polished off steak-and-ale pie in the local pub, come here for your dessert, a refined, smoke-free bistro where *Illy* coffee is served with big chunks of British-inspired cakes.

ROYAL CALPE Pub **€€**

(176 Main St; mains £8-12) If halfway through your quintessential Gibraltar pub crawl, you get an unstoppable urge for heavily

Bolonia, Costa de la Luz

BEN WELSH/GETTY IMAGES ©

If You Like... Outdoor Activities

With its close to perfect climate and huge array of landscapes Andalucía is tailor-made for energy burning outdoor activities. If this sounds like you we think you'll like the following:

1 **WINDSURFING/KITESURFING**
Tarifa, Los Caños de Meca

2 **BIRDWATCHING**
Parque Nacional de Doñana

3 **HIKING**
Parque Nacional Sierra Nevada

4 **DIVING**
Tarifa

5 **WHALE-WATCHING**
Gibraltar & Tarifa

crusted meat pies, fish and chips, and a pint of Caffrey's *without* the cigarette smoke (yes, you can still smoke inside Gibraltar pubs), roll into the Royal Calpe whose non-smoking rear conservatory is popular with young mothers, health freaks and the nicotine-patch brigade.

Information

Electricity

Electric current is the same as in Britain: 220V or 240V, with plugs of three flat pins. You'll thus need an adaptor to use your Spanish plug lead, available for £3 to £4 from numerous electronics shops in Main St.

Money

The currencies are the Gibraltar pound (£) and pound sterling, which are interchangeable. You can spend euros (except in payphones and post offices), but conversion rates are poor. Change unspent Gibraltar currency before leaving.

Banks are generally open from 9am to 3.30pm weekdays; there are several on Main St.

Telephone

To dial Gibraltar from Spain, you now precede the five-digit local number with the code 00350; from other countries, dial the international access code, then the Gibraltar country code 350 and local number. To phone Spain from Gibraltar, just dial the nine-digit Spanish number.

Tourist Information

Gibraltar has several helpful tourist offices, with information booths at the Airport (tel, info 73026; Airport; Mon-Fri, mornings only) and Customs House (tel, info 200 50762; 9:00am-4:30pm Mon-Fri, 10am-1pm Sat)

Tourist office (Grand Casemates Sq; 9am-5.30pm Mon-Fri, 10am-3pm Sat, to 1pm Sun & holidays) Several information desks provide all the information you'll need about Gibraltar, with plenty of pleasant cafes in the same square where you can read through it all at leisure.

Visas

To enter Gibraltar, you need a passport or EU national identity card. EU, USA, Canadian, Australian, New Zealand and South African passport-holders are among those who do not need visas for Gibraltar. For further information contact Gibraltar's Immigration Department (20072500; Joshua Hassan House; 9am-12.45pm Mon-Fri).

Getting There & Away

Air

Easyjet (www.easyjet.com) flies daily to/from London-Gatwick and three times a week from Liverpool, while Monarch Airlines (www.flymonarch.com) flies daily to/from London-Luton and Manchester. British Airways (www.ba.com) flies seven times a week from London-Heathrow.

Bus

There are no regular buses to Gibraltar, but La Línea de la Concepción bus station is only a five-minute walk from the border.

Car & Motorcycle

Snaking vehicle queues at the 24-hour border and congested traffic in Gibraltar often make it easier to park in La Línea and walk across the border. To take a car into Gibraltar (free) you need an insurance certificate, registration document, nationality plate and driving licence.

Getting Around

Bus 5 goes from the border into town (and back) every 15 minutes on weekdays, and every 30 minutes on weekends. The fare is £1. Buses 1, 2, 3 and 4 cover the rest of Gibraltar and are free of charge.

All of Gibraltar can be covered on foot, if you're energetic. You can also ascend to the upper Rock, weather permitting, by the cable car **(Red Sands Rd; adult/child return £8/4.50, incl entry to Nature Reserve £16/12.50; every few min 9.30am-8pm Mon-Sat, last cable up, 7.15pm, last cable down 7.45pm, to 5pm Oct-Apr)**. For the Apes' Den, disembark at the middle station.

Marbella

POP 136,000

Marbella is the Costa del Sol's classiest, and most expensive, resort. This inherent wealth glitters most brightly along the Golden Mile, a tiara of star-studded clubs, restaurants and hotels which stretches from Marbella to Puerto Banús, the flashiest marina on the Costa del Sol, where black-tinted Mercs slide along a quayside of luxury yachts.

Sights & Activities

FREE MUSEO RALLI Museum
(Urbanización Coral Beach; 10am-2pm Tue-Sat) This superb private art museum exhibits paintings by primarily Latin American and European artists in bright, well-lit galleries. Part of a non-profit foundation, exhibits include sculptures by Henry Moore and Salvador Dali, and vibrant contemporary paintings by Argentinian surrealist painter Alicia Carletti and Cuban Wilfredo Lam, plus works by Joan Miró, Chagall and Chirico.

MUSEO DEL GRABADO ESPAÑOL Museum
(Calle Hospital Bazán; admission €2.50; 10am-2pm & 5.30-8.30pm) This small art museum in the old town includes works by some of the great masters, including Picasso, Joan Miró and Salvador Dali, among other, primarily Spanish painters.

Sleeping & Eating

CLAUDE Boutique Hotel **€€€**
(952 90 08 40; www.hotelclaudemarbella.com; Calle San Francisco 5; s/d €225/250;) Situated in the quieter upper part of town, this sumptuous hotel is housed in a 17th-century mansion of some historical significance – it was the former summer

Puerto Banús, Marbella
KEN WELSH/GETTY IMAGES ©

Cueva de Nerja

DANITA DELIMONT/GETTY IMAGES ©

home of Napoleon's third wife. The decor successfully marries contemporary flourishes with the original architecture, while claw foot tubs and crystal chandeliers add to the classic historical feel.

CALIMA Modern European **€€€**
(952 76 42 52; www.restaurantecalima.es; Hotel Melia Don Pepé, Calle Jose Melia; mains €22-28; 7-10pm Tue-Fri, 7.30-10pm & 1.30-3pm Sat) Michelin star chef Dani Garcia cut his culinary teeth at Ronda's famous Tragabuches restaurant and has carried on to acquire considerable fame here, as well as at his chain of smart tapas bars: La Moraga. Dishes are based on contrasts and have tantalising names like 'egg without an egg' and litchis and roses popcorn.

Information

Tourist office (www.marbella.es; Plaza de los Naranjos 1; 9.30am-9pm Mon-Fri) Has plenty of leaflets and a good town map.

Getting There & Around

Buses to Fuengirola (€3.20, one hour), Puerto Banús (€1.50, 20 minutes) and Estepona (€2.80, one hour) leave about every 30 minutes from Avenida Ricardo Soriano. Other services use the bus station (952 76 44 00; Avenida Trapiche), 1.2km north of Plaza de los Naranjos. Bus 7 (€1.10) runs between the bus station and the central Fuengirola/Estepona bus stop (Avenida Ricardo Soriano); returning to the bus station, take bus 2 from Avenida Ramón y Cajal.

Marbella's streets are notoriously traffic-clogged. Fortunately there are a number of pay car parks where you can take refuge on arrival.

Nerja

POP 22,000

Nerja, 56km east of Málaga, is where the Costa del Sol becomes a little easier on the eye, with more precipitous topography and prettier vistas allowing a peek into the Spain that once was.

The town's pièce de résistance, right in the centre, is the spectacular **Balcón de Europa**, a palm-shaded walkway that protrudes out into the ocean. The new **Museo de Nerja** (Plaza de España; adult/child €6/3, incl Cueva de Nerja €12.50/6.50; 10am-2pm & 4-6.30pm Tue-Sun) traces Nerja's history from cave dwellers to tourist boom and acts as an ideal prelude to a visit to the enormous **Cueva de Nerja** (see boxed text, right) 3km north of town.

Sleeping & Eating

HOTEL CARABEO Hotel **€€**
(☎952 52 54 44; www.hotelcarabeo.com; Calle Carabeo 34, Nerja; d/ste incl breakfast €85/180; ❄@📶🏊) Full of stylish antiques, this small, family-run, seafront hotel is set above manicured terraced gardens. There's also a good restaurant and the pool is on a terrace overlooking the sea.

OLIVA Modern European **€€**
(☎952 52 14 29; www.restauranteoliva.com; Calle Pintada 7; mains €15-19) Think single orchids, a drum and bass soundtrack and a charcoal grey-and-green colour scheme. In short, this place has class. The menu is reassuringly brief and changes regularly according to what is fresh in season; typical dishes are grilled scallops in a beetroot sauce and sea bass with wasabi, soy and ginger.

Information

Municipal tourist office (☎952 52 15 31; www.nerja.org; Puerta del Mar; ⏰10am-2pm & 6-10pm Jul–mid-Sep, 10am-2pm & 5-8pm mid-Sep–Jun) Has plenty of useful leaflets.

Getting There & Away

From the N340 near the top of Calle Pintada, **Alsa** (www.alsa.es) runs regular buses to/from Málaga (€4.15, 1¾ hours, 23 daily) and Marbella (€9.50, 1¼ hours, one daily). There are also buses to Almería and Granada.

SIERRA NEVADA & LAS ALPUJARRAS

True to their name, Spain's highest mountains rise like icy sentinels behind the city of Granada, culminating in the rugged summit of Mulhacén (3479m), mainland Spain's highest peak. The upper reaches of the range form the 862-sq-km Parque Nacional Sierra Nevada, Spain's biggest national park, with a rare high-altitude environment that is home to about 2100 of Spain's 7000 plant species. Andalucía's largest ibex population (about 5000) is here too. The mountains and Las Alpujarras valleys comprise one of the most spectacular areas in Spain, and the area offers wonderful opportunities for walking, horse riding, climbing, mountain biking and, in winter, good skiing and snowboarding.

Below the southern flank of the Sierra Nevada lies the 70km-long jumble of valleys known as Las Alpujarras. Arid hillsides split by deep ravines alternate with oasis-like white villages set beside rapid streams and surrounded by gardens, orchards and woodlands.

Cueva de Nerja

Nerja's big tourist attraction is the **Cueva de Nerja** (www.cuevadenerja.es; adult/child €8.50/4.50, incl Museo de Nerja €12.50/6.50; ⏰10am-2pm & 4-7.30pm), just off the N340, 3km east of town on the slopes of the Sierra Almijara. The enormous 4km-long cave complex, hollowed out by water around five million years ago and once inhabited by Stone Age hunters, is a theatrical wonderland of extraordinary rock formations, subtle shifting colours and stalactites and stalagmites. Large-scale performances, including ballet and flamenco, are staged here throughout the summer. About 14 buses run daily from Málaga and Nerja, except Sunday. The whole site is very well organised for large-scale tourism and has a huge restaurant and car park.

Pampaneira, Bubión & Capileira

POP 1270 / ELEV 1200-1440M

These small villages clinging to the side of the deep Barranco de Poqueira valley, 14km to 20km northeast of Órgiva, are three of the prettiest, most dramatically sited (and most touristy) in Las Alpujarras. Capileira is the best base for walks.

Sights & Activities

All three villages have solid 16th-century Mudéjar churches. They also have small weaving workshops, descendants of a textile tradition that goes back to Islamic times, and plentiful craft shops. In Bubión, get a marvellous glimpse of bygone Alpujarras life at the excellent little folk museum, **Casa Alpujarreña** (Calle Real; admission €2; 11am-2pm Sun-Thu, 11am-2pm & 5-7pm Sat & holidays), beside the church.

Eight walking trails, ranging from 4km to 23km (two to eight hours), are marked out in the beautiful Barranco de Poqueira with little colour-coded posts. Their starting points can be hard to find, but they are marked and described on Editorial Alpina's Sierra Nevada, La Alpujarra map. **Nevadensis** (958 76 31 27; www.nevadensis.com), at the information office in Pampaneira, offers hikes and treks, 4WD trips, horse riding, mountain biking, climbing and canyoning, all with knowledgeable guides.

Sleeping & Eating

Pampaneira

Opened in 2010, **Estrella de las Nieves** (958 76 39 81; www.estrelladelasnieves.com; Calle Huerto 21; s/d €60/70; P), just above the town, has airy, light and modern rooms with terraces overlooking the rooftops and mountains. **Restaurante Casa Diego** (Plaza de la

Left: Nerja (p318); **Below:** Capileira

LEFT: KEN WELSH/GETTY IMAGES ©; BELOW: BRUNO ABARCA/GETTY IMAGES ©

Libertad 3; menú €9, mains €6.50-13.50), across from the church, has a pleasant upstairs terrace and serves local trout and ham.

Capileira

Hostal Atalaya (958 76 30 25; www.hostalatalaya.com; Calle Perchel 3; d without/with view €30/35) is a good budget option, while **Finca Los Llanos** (958 76 30 71; www.hotelfincalosllanos.com; Carretera de Sierra Nevada; s/d €54/76;) has tasteful rooms, a pool and a good restaurant. It's also an official Sierra Nevada information point. **Bar El Tilo** (Plaza Calvario; raciones €8), Capileira's village tavern enjoys prime position on a lovely whitewashed square with a terrace. Raciones such as *albóndigas* (meatballs in a tomato sauce) are enormous. **El Corral del Castaño** (Plaza del Calvario 16; menú €10, mains €8.50-14) has an Italian menu and does a local take on gastronomic dishes.

Information

Punto de Información Parque Nacional de Sierra Nevada (www.nevadensis.com; Plaza de la Libertad; 10am-2pm & 4-6pm Tue-Sat, to 3pm Sun & Mon, Oct-March) Plenty of information about Las Alpujarras and Sierra Nevada; outdoor gear, maps and books for sale. Located in Pampaneira.

Servicio de Interpretación de Altos Cumbres (958 76 34 86, 671 56 44 06; picapileira@oapn.mma.es; about 9am-2pm & 4.30-7.30pm) By the main road in Capileira; information mainly about the national park, but also on Las Alpujarras.

Getting There & Away

Alsa (958 18 54 80) runs three daily buses from Granada to Pampaneira (€6, two hours), Bubión (€6.50, 2¼ hours) and Capileira (€6.50, 2½ hours).

Baeza & Úbeda

If the Jaén region is known for anything (apart from olives) it's the twin towns of Baeza (ba-eh-thah) and Úbeda (oo-be-dah), two shining examples of Renaissance beauty. Smaller Baeza has a richness of architecture that defies the notion that there is little of architectural interest in Andalucía apart from Moorish buildings. Here a handful of wealthy, fractious families, made rich by the wool trade, left a staggering catalogue of perfectly preserved Renaissance churches and civic buildings.

Baeza's most extraordinary palace, the **Palacio de Jabalquinto** (Plaza de Santa Cruz; admission free; ⌚9am-2pm Mon-Fri), was probably built in the early 16th century for one of the Benavides clan. It has a spectacularly flamboyant facade with pyramidal stone studs typical of Isabeline Gothic style, and a patio with Renaissance marble columns, two-tiered arches and an elegant fountain. The **Antigua Universidad** (Old University; Calle del Beato Juan de Ávila; ⌚10am-2pm & 4-7pm Wed-Sun) was founded in 1538 and became a fount of progressive ideas that generally conflicted with Baeza's conservative dominant families, often causing scuffles between the highbrows and the well-heeled. Baeza's eclectic **cathedral** (Plaza de Santa María; donations welcome; ⌚10.30am-1pm & 4-6pm Oct-Mar, 10.30am-1pm & 5-7pm Apr-Sep) is chiefly in 16th-century Renaissance style, with an interior designed by Andrés de Vandelvira and Jerónimo del Prado.

Úbeda is a slightly different proposition to its little sister, Baeza. Exposed to the cultural influences of the Italian Renaissance and benefiting from the wealth and privilege of the powerful Molina family, the city turned out what are now considered to be some of the purest examples of Renaissance architecture in Spain.

The purity of Renaissance lines is best expressed in the famous chapel, **Sacra Capilla del Salvador** (Plaza Vázquez de Molina; adult/child €3/1.50; ⌚10am-2pm

Baeza

QUADRIGA IMAGES/GETTY IMAGES ©

Detour: Cabo de Gata

If you can find anyone old enough to remember the Costa del Sol before the bulldozers arrived they'd probably say it looked a bit like Cabo de Gata. Some of Spain's most beautiful and least crowded beaches are strung between the grand cliffs and capes east of Almería city, where dark volcanic hills tumble into a sparkling turquoise sea. Though Cabo de Gata is not undiscovered, it still has a wild, elemental feel and its scattered fishing villages (remember them?) remain low-key. You can walk along, or not far from, the coast right round from Retamar in the northwest to Agua Amarga in the northeast (61km); but beware – the sun can be intense and there's often little shade.

Parque Natural de Cabo de Gata-Níjar covers Cabo de Gata's 60km coast plus a slice of hinterland. The park's main information centre is the **Centro de Interpretación Las Amoladeras** (950 16 04 35; 10am-2pm & 5.30-9pm mid-Jul–mid-Sep, to 3pm Tue-Sun mid-Sep–mid-Jul), about 2.5km west of Ruescas.

& 4-7.30pm Mon-Sat, 11.15am-2pm & 5-8pm Sun); the first of many works executed in Úbeda by celebrated architect Andrés de Vandelvira. The classic portal is topped by a carving of the transfiguration of Christ, flanked by statues of St Peter and St Paul. The underside of the arch is an orgy of classical sculpture, executed by French sculptor Esteban Jamete, depicting the Greek gods – a Renaissance touch that would have been inconceivable a few decades earlier.

Spain In Focus

Gaudí's La Pedrera (p75), Barcelona

Spain Today

“It's almost impossible these days to have a conversation in Spain that doesn't make reference to la crisis”

belief systems
(% of population)

Roman Catholic

Other (mostly Islam)

if Spain were 100 people

74 would speak Castilian Spanish
17 would speak Catalan
7 would speak Galician
2 would speak Basque

population per sq km

Spain

USA

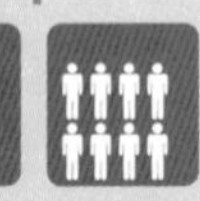

United Kingdom

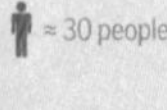

≈ 30 people

Spain's *indignados* protest in Madrid's Plaza de la Puerta del Sol

Economic Crisis

It can be difficult to remember, but Spain was, not so long ago, the envy of Europe. Its economy was booming and the whole country seemed brimful of optimism. Then things fell apart. In 2008, unemployment stood at around 6%. Four years later, one out of every four Spaniards (over 5.5 million people) can't find work. Old-timers you speak to can't remember a time this bad, with businesses closing their doors forever, including many that weathered civil war and dictatorship through the decades. Elections in November 2011 replaced a left-of-centre government that waited a painfully long time to recognise that a crisis was looming, with a right-of-centre one promoting a deep austerity drive that threatens the generous welfare state on which Spaniards have come to depend – strangling the life out of the economy, say some; taking much-needed remedial action to correct years of spending beyond our means, counter others. Where did

PEDRO ARMESTRE/STRINGER/GETTY IMAGES ©

it all go wrong? Spain's economy was heavily reliant on construction and tourism, two industries that are exceptionally susceptible to economic downturns. Spain's property market also spiralled out of control for far too long – prices rose exponentially, prompting banks to hand out money to those who simply couldn't afford to pay it back. What began in 2008 shows no signs of abating, and it's almost impossible these days to have a conversation in Spain that doesn't make reference to *la crisis*.

Spain's Young

If Spain's economic numbers make for depressing reading, those relating to the country's younger generation can seem catastrophic. Almost one out of every two young Spaniards is out of work, and there is talk of an entire generation being lost to the economic downturn. The disparity between salaries – the *mileuristas* (those earning no more than €1000 a month) became a cause célèbre in the Spanish media – and still-high house prices means that Spaniards are taking ever longer to move out of home. For the first time in decades, younger Spaniards are leaving the country in search of opportunity in greater numbers than there are immigrants wanting to come to Spain.

Reclaiming the Streets

And yet, many of Spain's young and restless have refused to play the role of victims. On 15 May 2011, the *indignados* (those who are indignant) took over the iconic Plaza de la Puerta del Sol in the centre of Madrid in a peaceful sit-in protest. The protests, which drew Spaniards from all walks of life, were driven by a dissatisfaction with mainstream politics, and a desire to overturn some of the more unfair aspects of Spanish economic life; among these is the requirement that homeowners whose homes are repossesed by banks must continue to pay their mortgage (ie the bank gets the house *and* the money). While it was business as usual during the elections in November 2011, which swept the conservative Popular Party to power, the *indignados'* public meetings and prominent media presence continue, prompting many to hope that a new kind of politics may have been born. With the economy in free fall and with Spain's government forced to seek a massive bailout for its banking industry from the EU, protesters returned to the streets of Madrid and other Spanish cities in growing numbers in 2012. Heavy government crackdowns on protesters only served to heighten the sense of crisis.

History

Segovia's Roman *acueducto* (p236)

CARHOVE PHOTOGRAPHY/GETTY IMAGE

Spanish history reads like a thriller. The story begins with the great empires of antiquity, then moves on to one of the most enlightened civilisations ever to have ruled on European soil, before the rise of Christendom and its powerful kings and queens transformed Spain forever. Jump forward to the turbulent 20th century and you find a nation convulsed by a fratricidal war, whereafter the country disappeared into the long shadows cast by Francisco Franco for four decades. But there's a happy ending: Spain has emerged phoenix-like from dictatorship to become one of Europe's most dynamic and modern countries.

The Phoenicians

To the Ancient Greeks and Romans, the dramatic limestone ridge at Gibraltar, together with Jebel Musa in Morocco, were the Pillars of Hercules and represented the limits of the known world. But the Phoenicians, who came before them, knew differently. From their base on what is now the southern coast of Lebanon, the seafaring Phoenicians were

8th century BC

The Phoenicians found Cádiz, which is Europe's oldest continuously inhabited city.

the first of the ancient civilisations to rule the Mediterranean. Not restricted by the narrow Straits of Gibraltar, they continued on along the Atlantic coast and, in the 8th century BC, established the port of Gadir, the site of modern Cádiz in southwestern Andalucía. Around 700 BC the colonists introduced iron-making technology and the Phoenician-influenced culture that developed was very likely the fabled Tartessos, mythologised by later Greek, Roman and biblical writers as a place of unimaginable wealth. Sadly, no traces remain.

The Celtic North

Around the same time as the Phoenicians brought iron technology to the south, the Celts (originally from Central Europe) brought it – and beer-making – to the north when they crossed the Pyrenees. In contrast to the dark-featured Iberians, the Celts were fair. Celts and Iberians who merged on the *meseta* (plateau; the high tableland of central Spain) are known as Celtiberians. Celts and Celtiberians typically lived in sizable hill-fort towns called *castros*.

Greeks and Romans

In the 7th century BC, Greek traders arrived along the Mediterranean coast and brought with them several things now considered quintessentially Spanish – the olive tree, the grapevine and the donkey – along with writing, coins, the potter's wheel and poultry. But the Romans, who ruled Hispania (as Roman Iberia was known) for 600 years until the 5th century AD, would go on to leave a far more lasting impression. By AD 50, most of Hispania had adopted the Roman way of life.

Rome gave the country a road system, aqueducts, temples, theatres, amphitheatres and bathhouses, but they began the process of deforestation as they culled the extensive forests that in their time covered half the *meseta* (plateau). Even more than these, their cultural impact was profound. They brought Christianity to Spain, planted olive trees on a massive scale, introduced olive oil production and may even have invented *jamón* (cured ham). The basis of most of the languages still spoken here – Castilian, Catalan, Galician and Portuguese – are versions of the vernacular Latin spoken by Roman legionaries and colonists, filtered through 2000 years of linguistic mutation. The Roman era also saw the arrival of Jewish people in Spain, who were to play a big part in Spanish life for over 1000 years.

218 BC
Roman legions arrive in Spain, initiating the 600-year Roman occupation of Iberia.

711
Muslims invade Iberia from North Africa, overrunning all but Asturias within a few years.

10th century
The Cordoban Caliphate reaches its zenith and the city is home to nearly half a million people.

Islamic Spain

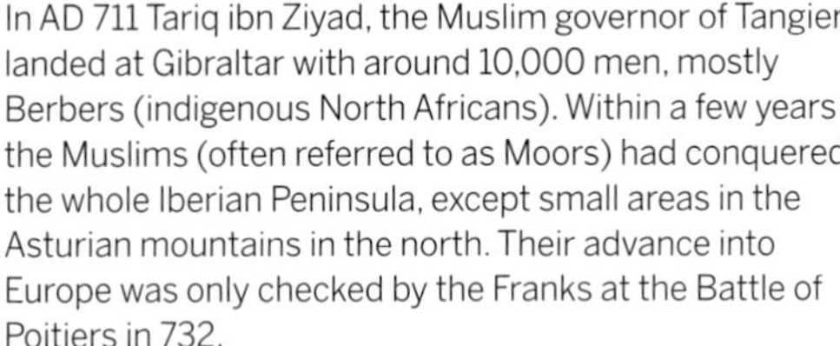

In AD 711 Tariq ibn Ziyad, the Muslim governor of Tangier, landed at Gibraltar with around 10,000 men, mostly Berbers (indigenous North Africans). Within a few years the Muslims (often referred to as Moors) had conquered the whole Iberian Peninsula, except small areas in the Asturian mountains in the north. Their advance into Europe was only checked by the Franks at the Battle of Poitiers in 732.

The name given to Muslim territory on the peninsula was Al-Andalus. Political power and cultural developments centred initially on Córdoba (756-1031), then Seville (c 1040-1248) and lastly Granada (1248-1492). It was during the 10th and early 11th centuries, under the independent Caliphate of Córdoba, that Al-Andalus reached the height of its power and lustre, and became famous for enlightened scholarship (it was through Al-Andalus that much of the learning of ancient Greece was transmitted to Christian Europe) and religious tolerance. Al-Andalus also developed an extraordinary architectural legacy and developed the Hispano-Roman agricultural base by improving irrigation and introducing new fruits and crops, many of which are still widely grown today. Even in language the Muslims left strong traces and Spanish still contains many words of Arabic origin.

The Best... Roman Ruins

1 Itálica (p264)

2 Tarragona (p108)

3 Segovia (p236)

4 Bolonia (p314)

The Spanish Inquisition

An ecclesiastical tribunal set up by Fernando and Isabel in 1478, the Spanish Inquisition in Al-Andalus focused first on *conversos* (Jews converted to Christianity), accusing many of continuing to practise Judaism in secret. In April 1492, Isabel and Fernando expelled all Jews who refused Christian baptism. Up to 100,000 converted, but some 200,000 (the first Sephardic Jews) fled into exile. The Inquisitors also carried out forced mass baptisms of Muslims, burnt Islamic books and banned the Arabic language. In 1500, Muslims were ordered to convert to Christianity or leave. Those who converted *(moriscos)* were later expelled between 1609 and 1614.

1218
The University of Salamanca is founded by Alfonso IX, King of León, making it the oldest university in the country.

1236
Córdoba falls to Fernando III of Castilla, with Seville following 12 years later.

1478
Isabel and Fernando, the Reyes Católicos (Catholic Monarchs) establish the Spanish Inquisition.

The Christian Reconquista

The Christian Reconquest of Iberia began in about 722 at Covadonga, Asturias, and ended with the fall of Granada in 1492. It was a stuttering affair, conducted by Christian kingdoms that were as often at war with each other as with the Muslims. An essential ingredient in the Reconquista was the cult of Santiago (St James), one of the 12 apostles. In 813 the saint's supposed tomb was discovered in Galicia. The city of Santiago de Compostela grew here, to become the third-most popular medieval Christian pilgrimage goal after Rome and Jerusalem. Santiago became the inspiration and special protector of soldiers in the Reconquista, earning the sobriquet Matamoros (Moor-slayer).

By 757, Christians occupied nearly a quarter of the Iberian Peninsula, although progress thereafter was slow. The year 1212, when the combined Christian armies routed a large Muslim force at Las Navas de Tolosa in Andalucía, marked the beginning of the end for Islamic Al-Andalus. The royal wedding of Isabel (of Castilla) and Fernando (of Aragón) in 1469 united two of the most powerful Christian kingdoms, enabling the armies of the Reconquista to make a final push. On 2 January 1492, Isabel and Fernando entered Granada. The surrender terms were fairly generous to Boabdil,

Procession celebrating the Christian Reconquista

1492
Isabel and Fernando capture Granada and the Reconquista is complete. They expel 200,000 Jews who refused baptism.

1556-98
The reign of Felipe II marks the zenith of Spanish power.

1702-13
The War of the Spanish Succession sees Spain lose Gibraltar and the Low Countries.

Why Madrid?

When Felipe II chose Madrid as Spain's capital in 1561, it was hardly the most obvious choice. Madrid (population 30,000) was much smaller and less powerful than Toledo and Seville (each with more than 80,000 people) or Valladolid, the capital of choice for Isabel and Fernando. Unlike other cities, however, Madrid was described by one king as 'very noble and very loyal': Felipe II chose the path of least resistance. Another reason was the location: 'a city fulfilling the function of a heart located in the middle of the body,' as Felipe II was heard to say.

the last emir, who was given the Alpujarras valleys south of Granada and 30,000 gold coins. The remaining Muslims were promised respect for their religion, culture and property, but this promise was quickly discarded.

The Golden Age of Empire

Isabel and Fernando were never going to be content with Spain alone. In April 1492, *Los Reyes Católicos* (the Catholic Monarchs) granted the Genoese sailor Christopher Columbus (Cristóbal Colón to Spaniards) funds for his long-desired voyage across the Atlantic in search of a new trade route to the Orient. Columbus set off from the Andalucian port of Palos de la Frontera on 3 August 1492, with three small ships and 120 men. After a near mutiny as the crew despaired of sighting land, they finally arrived on the island of Guanahaní, in the Bahamas, and went on to find Cuba and Hispaniola. Columbus returned to a hero's reception from the Catholic Monarchs in Barcelona, eight months after his departure.

Brilliant but ruthless conquistadors followed Columbus' trail, seizing vast tracts of the American mainland for Spain. By 1600 Spain controlled Florida, all the biggest Caribbean islands, nearly all of present-day Mexico and Central America, and a large strip of South America. The new colonies sent huge cargoes of silver, gold and other riches back to Spain. Seville enjoyed a monopoly on this trade and grew into one of Europe's richest cities.

Two Spains

Spain was united for the first time in almost eight centuries after Fernando annexed Navarra in 1512, and in 1519 Carlos I (Fernando's grandson) succeeded to the Habsburg lands in Austria and was elected Holy Roman Emperor (as Charles V). He

1805

Nelson's British ships defeat a Spanish-French fleet at the Battle of Trafalgar. Right: 19th-century depiction of the Battle of Trafalgar

DEA PICTURE LIBRARY/GETTY IMAGES ©

1808-13

Carlos IV abdicates and French occupation begins, with Napoleon's brother, Joseph, on the throne.

ruled all of Spain, the Low Countries, Austria, several Italian states, parts of France and Germany, and the expanding Spanish colonies in the Americas. But the storm clouds were brewing. Colonial riches lined the pockets of a series of backward-looking monarchs, a wealthy, highly conservative Church, and idle nobility. Although some of this wealth was used to foster a golden age of art, little was done to improve the lot of ordinary Spaniards and food shortages were rife.

Spain's overseas possessions were ebbing away, but problems at home were even more pressing. In 1812 a national Cortes (parliament) meeting at Cádiz drew up a new liberal constitution for Spain, prompting a backlash from conservatives (the Church, the nobility and others who preferred the earlier status quo) and liberals (who wanted vaguely democratic reforms). Over the next century, Spain alternated between federal republic and monarchy, a liberal-conservative schism that saw the country lurch from one crisis to the next. By the 1930s, Spain was teetering on the brink of war.

The Best... Civil War Reads

1 *For Whom the Bell Tolls*, Ernest Hemingway

2 *Homage to Catalonia*, George Orwell

3 *Blood of Spain*, Ronald Fraser

4 *The Spanish Civil War*, Hugh Thomas

5 *The Spanish Civil War: A Very Short Introduction*, Helen Graham

6 *Soldiers of Salamis*, Javier Cercas

The Spanish Civil War

On 17 July 1936, the Spanish army garrison in Melilla, North Africa, rose up against the left-wing government, followed the next day by garrisons on the mainland. The leaders of the plot were five generals, among them Francisco Franco, who on 19 July flew from the Canary Islands to Morocco to take charge of his legionnaires. The civil war had begun.

Wherever the blame lies, the civil war split communities, families and friends, killed an estimated 350,000 Spaniards (some writers put the number as high as 500,000), and caused untold damage and misery. Both sides (Franco's Nationalists and the left-wing Republicans) committed atrocious massacres and reprisals, and employed death squads to eliminate opponents. On 26 April 1937, German planes bombed the Basque town of Guernica (called Gernika in Basque), causing terrible casualties. The USSR withdrew from the war in September 1938, and in January 1939 the Nationalists took Barcelona unopposed. The Republican government and hundreds of thousands of supporters fled to France and, on 28 March 1939, Franco's forces entered Madrid.

1872-74

The Second Carlist War begins and the First Republic, a federal union of 17 states, collapses.

1898

Spain loses Cuba, Puerto Rico, Guam and the Philippines, its last remaining colonies.

1923-30

General Miguel Primo de Rivera launches a coup and establishes himself as dictator.

Franco's Spain

Francisco Franco would go on to rule Spain with an iron fist for almost four decades until his death in 1975. An estimated 100,000 people were killed or died in prison after the war. The hundreds of thousands imprisoned included many intellectuals and teachers; others fled abroad, depriving Spain of a generation of scientists, artists, writers, educators and more. The army provided many government ministers and enjoyed a most generous budget. Catholic supremacy was fully restored, with secondary schools entrusted to the Jesuits, divorce made illegal and church weddings compulsory.

During WWII Franco flirted with Hitler (although Spain watched the war from the sidelines), but Spain was desperately poor to the extent that the 1940s are known as *los años de hambre* (years of hunger). Despite small-scale rebel activity, ongoing repression and international isolation (Spain was not admitted to the UN until 1955), an economic boom began in 1959 and would last through much of the 1960s. The recovery was funded in part by US aid, and remittances from more than a million Spaniards working abroad, but above all by tourism, which was developed initially along Andalucía's Costa del Sol and Catalonia's Costa Brava. By 1965 the number of tourists arriving in Spain was 14 million a year.

Artist's impression of a street battle in Madrid, 1936

1936
The Spanish Civil War begins when General Francisco Franco's rebels rise up against the elected government.

1939
Franco enters Madrid after 350,000 people die during the Civil War; his dictatorship begins.

1959
ETA is founded with the aim of gaining Basque independence.

But with the jails still full of political prisoners and Spain's restive regions straining under Franco's brutal policies, labour unrest grew and discontent began to rumble in the universities and even in the army and Church. The Basque-nationalist terrorist group Euskadi Ta Askatasuna (ETA; Basque Homeland and Freedom) also appeared in 1959. In the midst of it all, Franco chose as his successor Prince Juan Carlos. In 1969 Juan Carlos swore loyalty to Franco and the Movimiento Nacional, Spain's fascist and only legal political party. Franco died on 20 November 1975.

The International Brigades

The International Brigades never numbered more than 20,000 and couldn't turn the tide against the better armed and organised Nationalist forces. Nazi Germany and Fascist Italy supported the Nationalists with planes, weapons and men (75,000 from Italy and 17,000 from Germany), turning the war into a testing ground for WWII. The Republicans had some Soviet planes, tanks, artillery and advisers, but the rest of the international community refused to become involved (apart from 25,000 French, who fought on the Republican side).

Spain's Democratic Transition

Juan Carlos I, aged 37, took the throne two days after Franco died. The new king's links with the dictator inspired little confidence in a Spain now clamouring for democracy, but Juan Carlos had kept his cards close to his chest and can take most of the credit for the successful transition to democracy that followed. He appointed Adolfo Suárez, a 43-year-old former Franco apparatchik with film-star looks. To general surprise, Suárez got the Francoist-filled Cortes to approve a new, two-chamber parliamentary system, and in early 1977 political parties, trade unions and strikes were all legalised and the Movimiento Nacional was abolished. After elections in 1977, a centrist government led by Suárez granted a general amnesty for acts committed in the civil war and under the Franco dictatorship. In 1978 the Cortes passed a new constitution making Spain a parliamentary monarchy with no official religion and granting a large measure of devolution to Spain's regions.

At a social level, Spaniards embraced democracy with all the zeal of an ex-convent schoolgirl. Contraceptives, homosexuality and divorce were legalised, and the Madrid party and arts scene known as *la movida* formed the epicentre of a newly unleashed hedonism that still looms large in Spanish life. Despite challenges such as the brutal campaign by ETA, which killed hundreds in the 1980s, and an unsuccessful

1975

Franco dies after ruling Spain for 37 years. King Juan Carlos I succeeds him.

1977

Spaniards vote in the first free elections since the 1930s, cementing Spain's return to democracy.

1986

Spain joins the European Community (now the EU), having joined NATO in 1982.

ETA – A Snapshot

The first underground cells of ETA appeared in 1959 at the height of Franco's repression. ETA's founders called for independence, but their primary goal was the promotion of the outlawed Basque language, Euskera. In 1967 the old guard of leaders was ousted during an internal crisis over strategy, and a younger, more militant leadership emerged. On 7 June 1968, ETA killed a Spanish civil guardsman near San Sebastián. After several short lived ceasefires, in October 2011 ETA announced a 'definitive cessation of its armed activity'. According to the Spanish government, more than 800 people have been killed by ETA terrorism in the decades since they were formed, two-thirds of these in the Basque region.

coup attempt by renegade Civil Guards in 1981, Spain's democratic, semi-federal constitution and multiparty system have proved at once robust and durable.

Spain Grows up

The 1980s in particular saw Spain pass a succession of milestones along the road to becoming a mature European democracy. That they took these steps so quickly and so successfully after four decades of fascism is one of modern Europe's most remarkable stories.

In 1982 the left-of-centre Partido Socialista Obrero Español (PSOE; Spanish Socialist Worker Party) was elected to power, led by a charismatic young lawyer from Seville, Felipe González. During its 14 years in power, the PSOE brought Spain into mainstream Europe, joining the European Community (now the EU) in 1986. They also oversaw the rise of the Spanish middle class, established a national health system and improved public education, and Spain's women streamed into higher education and jobs, although unemployment was the highest in Europe. But the PSOE finally became mired in scandal and, in the 1996 elections, the centre-right Partido Popular (PP; People's Party), led by José María Aznar, swept the PSOE from power.

Upon coming to power, José María Aznar promised to make politics dull, and he did, but he also presided over eight years of solid economic progress. Spain's economy grew annually by an average of 3.4%, and unemployment fell from 23% (1996) to 8% (2006). Not surprisingly, the PP won the 2000 election as well, with an absolute parliamentary majority. Aznar's popularity began to wane thanks to his strong support for the US-led invasion of Iraq in 2003 (which was deeply unpopular in Spain) and his decision to send Spanish troops to the conflict.

1996
The centre-right Partido Popular (PP), led by José María Aznar, wins national elections.

2004 (11 March)
Islamic terrorists bomb four commuter trains in Madrid killing 191 people.

JAVIER SORIANO/STAFF/GETTY IMAGES ©

Zapatero's Spain

As the 2004 general election approached, Aznar handed the PP reins to Mariano Rajoy. He was pitted against the PSOE's José Luis Rodríguez Zapatero, who had successfully managed to distance himself from his party's less than pristine past. The PP looked headed for victory, but early on Thursday 11 March 2004, three days before the general election, bombs exploded on four crowded commuter trains in and near Madrid, killing 191 people and injuring 1800; eleven million people poured onto Spain's streets in demonstrations of peace and solidarity the following day. As the evidence mounted that the bombing was the work of Islamic extremists, the government continued to maintain that ETA was responsible, prompting accusations that the PP was attempting to mislead the public (by blaming the bombings on ETA) and thereby escape a backlash for its support for the war in Iraq. Three days after the bombing, the PSOE won the election. Subsequent court cases have established that the bombings were carried out by a local group of North Africans settled in Spain.

Spain's new PSOE government hit the ground running. The Zapatero government quickly pulled Spanish troops out of Iraq. It also legalised gay marriage, made divorce easier, took religion out of the compulsory school curriculum, gave dissatisfied Catalonia an expanded autonomy charter, and declared an amnesty for illegal immigrants. In March 2006, ETA, which wants an independent state covering the Spanish and French Basque Country and Navarra, declared a 'permanent ceasefire', but resumed violence nine months later with a bomb that killed two people at Madrid airport. Zapatero then called off any moves towards dialogue. A year later, parliament also passed the 'Historical Memory Law' designed to officially honour the Republican victims of the civil war and the Franco dictatorship.

The PSOE government won another four years at elections in 2008, but with a vastly reduced majority. However, the early signs of economic crisis quickly contributed to the sense of a government under siege. Zapatero's delay in acknowledging the crisis sealed the government's fate, and it was defeated by the PP, led by Prime Minister Mariano Rajoy, in late 2011. With the highest unemployment in the Eurozone and an economy in freefall, the new government faces a daunting task.

The Best... Best History Museums

1 Museo & Cueva de Altamira (p155), Santillana del Mar

2 Museu Nacional Arqueològic de Tarragona (p109), Tarragona

3 Euskal Museoa (p149), Bilbao

4 Museu d'História de Barcelona (p65)

5 Museo del Teatro de Caesaraugusta (p121), Zaragoza

2004 (14 March)

PSOE, led by José Luis Rodríguez Zapatero, wins a surprise election victory.

Left: José Luis Rodríguez Zapatero

2004-06

Zapatero introduces a raft of social reforms and withdraws Spanish troops from Iraq.

2011

The Popular Party sweeps to power. Spain is gripped by its worst recession in 50 years.

Family Travel

Spanish bars and restaurants are child-friendly places

MICHAEL BLANN/GETTY IMAGES

Spain is a great place to bring your kids, not least because children are made to feel welcome just about everywhere. Children are such an integral part of Spanish life that you'll see families together in the most unlikely places, such as bars. At fiestas it's common to see even tiny ones toddling the streets at 2am or 3am. Visiting kids like this idea, too - but can't always cope with it quite so readily.

Accompanied children are welcome at all kinds of accommodation, as well as in many cafes, bars and restaurants. Before you baulk at taking your kids into a bar, remember that Spanish bars are as much hubs of social life as they are places to drink, and with smoking in bars now illegal they've suddenly become even more child-friendly places.

Food and children are two of the great loves for Spaniards and they make for a happy combination in most restaurants. If highchairs aren't available, staff will improvise and you shouldn't be made to feel uncomfortable as your children run amok. As for the food itself, children's menus may be scarce, but Spanish fare is rarely spicy and kids tend to like it. Toddlers are usually fed straight from their parents' plate. When kids get hungry between meals it's easy to zip into the nearest *tasca* (tapas bar) and get them a snack and there are also sweet shops every few blocks.

For more general information on travelling with children, pick up a copy of Lonely Planet's *Travel with Children* or visit the websites www.travelwithyourkids.com and www.familytravelnetwork.com.

The Best... Attractions for Children

1 Cosmocaixa (p69), Barcelona

2 Casa de Campo (p211), Madrid

3 Whale watching, (p313) Tarifa

4 Alcázar (p237), Segovia

Sights & Activities

Many child-focused attractions (such as zoos and amusement parks) are often inconveniently located on the outskirts of cities, but most cities and larger towns have swimming pools and plentiful playgrounds. There are also some fabulous parks, including Park Güell in Barcelona and Parque del Buen Retiro in Madrid. Football-addicted youngsters will probably want to visit either FC Barcelona's Camp Nou or Real Madrid's Santiago Bernabéu. Interactive museums are another sure winner, while there's always the obvious appeal of beaches (and all the seaside activities), or the fishy lure of aquariums (seek out Oceanogràfic in Valencia or L'Aquàrium in Barcelona).

Some of Spain's best attractions for children are the CosmoCaixa in Barcelona, Casa de Campo in Madrid, whale watching in Tarifa and the Alcázar in Segovia.

Wherever you find yourself, your first stop should be the local tourist office where staff can point you in the direction of family-friendly activities.

Need to Know

Change facilities Extremely rare in bars and restaurants

Cots Available in midrange and top-end hotels, but reserve in advance

Health High health-care standards

Highchairs Many restaurants have at least one

Nappies (diapers) Widely available

Strollers Bring your own

Transport Trains are fine; car-hire companies (but not taxis) have car seats

Flamenco

Flamenco performance, Cádiz

PAUL BERNHARDT/GETTY IMAGES ©

Flamenco, Spain's soul-stirring gift to the world of music, provides the ever-present soundtrack to Spanish life. The passion of the genre is accessible to anyone who has heard its melancholy strains in the background at a crowded Spanish bar or during an uplifting live performance. At the same time, flamenco can seem like an impenetrable world of knowledgeable yet taciturn initiates. Where these two worlds converge is in that rare yet famous, almost mystical, moment known as duende (spirit), when a performer sends shivers down your spine.

No one is quite sure where flamenco came from, although it probably owes its origins to a mosaic of ancient sources. Songs brought to Spain by the *gitanos* (Roma people) were almost certainly part of the mix, wedded to the music and verses of medieval Muslim Andalucía. Some historians argue that the Byzantine chant used in Visigothic churches prior to the Muslim arrival also played its part.

Wherever it came from, flamenco first took recognisable form in the late-18th and early 19th centuries among *gitanos* in the lower Guadalquivir Valley in western Andalucía. Suitably, for a place considered the cradle of the genre, the Seville-Jerez de la Frontera-Cádiz axis is still considered flamenco's heartland and it's here, purists believe, that you must go for the most authentic flamenco experience. Early flamenco was *cante jondo* (deep song), an anguished form of expression for a people on the margins of society. *Jondura* (depth) is still the essence of flamenco.

Modern Flamenco Legends

All flamenco performers aspire to the fame enjoyed by Manuel Torre (1878–1933); Torre's singing, legend has it, could drive people to rip their shirts open and upturn tables. One man who undoubtedly achieved this aim was El Camarón de la Isla (whose real name was José Monge Cruz) from San Fernando near Cádiz. El Camarón's incredible vocal and emotional range and his wayward lifestyle made him a legend well before his tragically early death in 1992 at the age of 42. As his great guitar accompanist Paco de Lucía observed, 'Camarón's cracked voice could evoke, on its own, the desperation of a people'.

Paco de Lucía, born in Algeciras in 1947, is the doyen of flamenco guitarists, with a virtuosity few can match. He is also almost single-handedly responsible for transforming the guitar, formerly the junior partner of the flamenco trinity, into an instrument of solo expression far beyond traditional limits. Such is his skill that de Lucía can sound like two or three people playing together and, for many in the flamenco world, he is the personification of *duende*.

The Best... Flamenco Festivals

1 Bienal de Flamenco (p44), Seville (September)

2 Festival de Jerez, Jerez de la Frontera (February–March)

3 Festival Internacional de la Guitarra (p44), Córdoba (June–July)

4 Festival Flamenco, Madrid (February)

5 Suma Flamenca, Madrid (May)

New Flamenco

Flamenco is enjoying something of a golden age, but part of its appeal lies in a new generation of artists broadening flamenco's horizons. In the 1970s musicians began mixing flamenco with jazz, rock, blues, rap and other genres. At the forefront of the transformation was Enrique Morente (b 1942), referred to by one Madrid paper as 'the last bohemian' and a cult figure who enjoys rare popularity among both purists and the new generation of flamenco aficionados. While careful

Flamenco Resources

Flama (www.guiaflama.com) Good for upcoming live concerts.

Duende (Jason Webster) Chronicles the author's gripping search for the true flamenco spirit.

Camarón (Director Jaime Chávarri; 2005) A terrific biopic of flamenco legend El Camarón de la Isla.

Bodas de Sangre (1981) and **Flamenco** (1995) These two Carlos Saura films are flamenco classics; the former is a film version of Federico García Lorca's dramatic play of the same name.

not to alienate flamenco purists, Morente, through his numerous collaborations across genres, helped lay the foundations for Nuevo Flamenco (New Flamenco) and Fusion.

Other genres that have made their way into the repertoire of Nuevo Flamenco include rock (Kiko Veneno and Raimundo Amador), jazz and blues (Pata Negra), Latin and African rhythms (Ketama and Diego El Cigala), reggae, Asian and dance rhythms (Ojos de Brujo), and electronica (Chambao). When it comes to dance, Joaquín Cortés fuses flamenco with contemporary dance, ballet and jazz, accompanied by music at rock-concert amplification.s

Seeing Flamenco

If you're eager to catch some live flamenco while in Spain, Seville has the widest number of regular, high-quality shows, followed by Jerez de la Frontera, Granada and Madrid.

Aside from widely advertised concerts held in large-scale arenas, the best places for live performances are usually *peñas:* clubs where flamenco fans band together. The atmosphere in such places is authentic and at times very intimate, and is proof that the best flamenco feeds off an audience that knows their flamenco. Most Andalucian towns in particular have dozens of *peñas* and most tourist offices have a list.

The other option is to attend a performance at a *tablao* (flamenco venue), which hosts regular shows put on for largely undiscriminating tourist audiences, usually with high prices and dinner included. The quality of the flamenco in *tablaos* can be top-notch, even if the atmosphere lacks the gritty authenticity of the *peñas*.

Flamenco guitarist, Seville
KARL BLACKWELL/GETTY IMAGES ©

Master Painters

Family of Charles I by Goya, Museo del Prado, Madrid

PETER BARRITT/ALAMY ©

Spain's artistic tradition is arguably Europe's most distinguished, and its big names read like a roll-call of Western art history's elite. Although many Spanish artists deserve the term of 'master', we have restricted ourselves to Spain's Big Four. The story begins with Diego Rodríguez de Silva Velázquez and Francisco José de Goya y Lucientes, and 'ends' with two of the towering artistic figures of the 20th century: Pablo Picasso and Salvador Dalí.

Velázquez

No painter has come to symbolise Spain's golden age of the arts in the 17th century quite like Diego Rodríguez de Silva Velázquez (1599–1660). Born in Seville, Velázquez moved to Madrid as court painter and composed scenes (landscapes, royal portraits, religious subjects, snapshots of everyday life) that owe their vitality not only to his photographic eye for light and contrast but also to a compulsive interest in the humanity of his subjects, so that they seem to breathe on the canvas. His masterpieces include *Las Meninas* (Maids of Honour) and *La Rendición de Breda* (The Surrender of Breda), both on view in the Museo del Prado.

Goya

Born into a modest provincial family in the village of Fuendetodos in Aragón, Francisco José de Goya y Lucientes (1746–1828) began

The Best... Forgotten Art Galleries

1 Fundació Joan Miró (p82), Barcelona

2 Museo de Bellas Artes (p127), Valencia

3 Museo de Bellas Artes (p258), Seville

4 Museo de Bellas Artes (p148), Bilbao

designing for Madrid's Real Fábrica de Tapices (Royal Tapestry Workshop) in Madrid in 1776, but illness in 1792 left him deaf; many critics speculate that his condition was largely responsible for his wild, often merciless style that would become increasingly unshackled from convention. By 1799, Goya was appointed Carlos IV's court painter.

In the last years of the 18th century he painted enigmatic masterpieces such as *La Maja Vestida* (The Young Lady Dressed) and *La Maja Desnuda* (The Young Lady Undressed). The arrival of the French and war in 1808 had a profound impact on Goya. Unforgiving portrayals of the brutality of war are *El Dos de Mayo* (The Second of May) and, more dramatically, *El Tres de Mayo* (The Third of May).

After he retired to the Quinta del Sordo (Deaf Man's House) in Madrid, he created his nightmarish *Pinturas Negras* (Black Paintings), which now hang in the Museo del Prado. The *Saturno Devorando a Su Hijo (Saturn Devouring His Son)* captures the essence of Goya's genius and *La Romería de San Isidro* and *El Akelarre (El gran cabrón)* are profoundly unsettling.

Pablo Picasso

Considered by many to be the finest and most influential artist of the 20th century, Pablo Ruiz Picasso (1881–1973) stormed onto the Spanish artistic scene like a thunderclap. Born in Málaga in Andalucía, he moved with his family when still a child to Barcelona. Although he later studied in Madrid's staid Real Academia de Bellas Artes de San Fernando, it was amid the avant-garde freedom of Barcelona's Modernisme that Picasso the artist was formed.

Although best known for his weird and wonderful cubist paintings, Picasso's oeuvre spans an extraordinary breadth of styles as his work underwent repeated revolutions, passing from one creative phase to another. The best place to get an overview is Málaga's Museo Picasso.

His early style began, rather gloomily, with what is known as his Blue Period, then moved on through the brighter Pink Period; Barcelona's Museu Picasso offers an excellent collection of Picasso's early, pre-Cubist years. In 1907 Picasso painted *Les Demoiselles d'Avignon,* which was strongly influenced by the stylised masks and wood carvings of Africa, and from there it was a small step to the cubist style (which involved taking objects apart and analysing their shapes), which he pioneered. By the mid-1920s he was even dabbling in surrealism. His most famous painting is *Guernica*.

Picasso's Guernica

In the first year of the Civil War, Picasso was commissioned by the Republican government of Madrid to do the painting for the Paris Exposition Universelle in 1937. As news filtered out about the bombing of Gernika (Guernica) on 26 April 1937 in the Basque Country (by Hitler's Legión Condor, at the request of Franco), Picasso committed his anger to canvas; it was a poignant memorial to the first use of airborne military hardware to devastating effect. You can see *Guernica* in Madrid's Centro de Arte Reina Sofía (p200).

Salvador Dalí

Vying with Pablo Picasso for the title of Spain's most original artist is Salvador Dalí. He did spend time in Madrid, where he decided that the eminent professors of Madrid's Real Academia de Bellas Artes de San Fernando were not fit to judge him, and thereafter spent four years romping through the city with poet Federico García Lorca and future film director Luis Buñuel.

But Dalí belongs above all to Catalonia. He was born in Figueres, home now to the Teatre-Museu Dalí, which is one of Spain's most memorable museums thanks to its elevation of art to a form of theatre, which seems such an apt legacy for such a charismatic figure. Dalí spent much of his adult life in Port Lligat, near Cadaques, and left his mark on the Castell de Púbol, near Girona.

Dalí was a larger-than-life figure, but he was also unrelentingly brilliant. He started off by dabbling in cubism, but became more readily identified with the surrealists. His 'hand-painted dream photographs', as he called them, are virtuoso executions brimming with fine detail and nightmare images dragged up from a feverish and Freud-fed imagination.

Las Meninas by Velázquez, Museo del Prado, Madrid

Spanish Architecture

Detail of the Mezquita (p270), Córdoba

OLIVER STREW/GETTY IMAGES ©

Spain's architecture tells the story of the country's past. It is an epic tale that recalls the glories of Al-Andalus and of the sublime Romanesque, Gothic, Renaissance and baroque movements of Christian Spain, before detouring into the Modernisme of Antoni Gaudí and his Catalan cohorts. But Spanish architecture's secret has always been one of constant revolution, and therein lies the story of the country's creative future.

Islamic Spain

Islamic Al-Andalus was, for much of its nearly 800-year history, one of the most civilised places on earth and its architects were worthy contributors to this ideal. In 756, a mere 45 years after Islamic armies first swept across the Strait of Gibraltar and at a time when Islamic rulers controlled three-quarters of Spain, Abd ar-Rahman I founded Córdoba's Mezquita. More than Spain's oldest surviving Islamic building of significance, the Mezquita was (and is) the epitome of Islamic architecture's grace and pleasing unity of form.

Hundreds of years later, with Islamic sovereignty restricted to Granada's Nasrid emirate, the Alhambra (from the Arabic *al-qala'at al-hamra,* meaning 'red castle'), came to symbolise the last-days decadence of Islamic rule. The only surviving large medieval Islamic palace complex in the world, the Alhambra is at once a palace city and a fortress, with 2km of walls and 23 towers. Within the Alhambra's walls were seven separate palaces, along with mosques, garrisons, houses, offices, baths, a summer residence (the Generalife) and exquisite gardens, but scale is only one element of the Alhambra's charm: the Nasrid architects also refined existing decorative techniques to new peaks of delicacy, elegance and harmony.

Between these two landmarks lie centuries of compelling history, but together the Mezquita and Alhambra give expression to the enduring characteristics of Al-Andalus: enlightened Islam, the opulence of Islamic rule, the imperative to defend against enemies at the gates, and the importance of gardens as a manifestation of earthly paradise. Other significant places where these elements remain include the Alcázar and Giralda in Seville, the Aljafería in Zaragoza, the Alcázar in Jerez de la Frontera, and the Alcazaba and Castillo de Gibralfaro in Málaga.

Romanesque & Gothic

As the Reconquista gathered momentum, Spanish architects in Christian-controlled territories turned not to the Middle East but to Europe for inspiration. From the 11th century, churches and monasteries in the Romanesque style mushroomed in the north. Many of the finest extant examples are in Catalonia, especially in Girona, the monastery in El Port de la Selva and in the Pyrenean Vall de Boí.

A more elaborate Gothic style, characterised by the use of flying buttresses and other technical innovations, replaced the Romanesque; three of Spain's most important Gothic cathedrals – Burgos, León and Toledo – were all begun in the 13th century. After an interlude known as Isabelline style, pure Gothic returned in the 16th century, perhaps best exemplified by Salamanca's Catedral Nueva and the cathedral in Segovia.

Renaissance & Baroque

The Renaissance in architecture was an Italian-originated return to classical ideals of harmony and proportion, dominated by columns and shapes such as the square, circle and triangle. Many Renaissance buildings feature elegant interior courtyards lined by two tiers of wide, rounded arcades. To visit Salamanca is to receive a concentrated dose of the most splendid work of plateresque (an early form of Renaissance) style. The university facade, especially, is a virtuoso piece, featuring busts, medallions and a complex

Mudéjar Architecture

After the Christian Reconquista, the term Mudéjar (from Arabic *mudayan*, meaning domesticated) was given to Muslims who stayed on in areas conquered by the Christians and it came into use as an architectural label. Hallmarks of Mudéjar style include geometric decorative designs, often embellished with tiles, and elaborately carved timber ceilings. *Artesonado* is the word used to describe ceilings with interlaced beams leaving regular spaces for decorative insertions. Another unmistakable Mudéjar feature is the preponderance of brick: castles, churches and mansions all over the country were built of this material. Teruel has an especially rich concentration of Mudéjar architecture.

floral design. Another fine example of the plateresque is the Capilla de Reyes Nuevos in Toledo's Catedral.

The heady frills of baroque are a Spanish speciality, although Cádiz's cathedral is one of only a few almost-complete baroque buildings. Baroque reached new heights of opulence with the Sagrario in Granada's Monasterio de La Cartuja and the Transparente in Toledo's cathedral. Seville is jammed with gems, while the facade superimposed over the Romanesque original in the cathedral of Santiago de Compostela is notable.

The Best... Modern Temples to Spanish Architecture

1 Ciudad de las Artes y las Ciencias (p128), Valencia

2 Museo Guggenheim (p153), Bilbao

3 Torre Agbar (p75), Barcelona

4 Barajas Airport Terminal 4, Madrid

Modernista Madness

At the end of the 19th century, Catalonia was the powerhouse of the country. Into this optimistic time stepped a group of architects known as the Modernistas. Leading the way was Antoni Gaudí (1852-1926), who sprinkled Barcelona with exotic creations such as his immense, and still unfinished, La Sagrada Família, along with Casa Batlló and La Pedrera.

Gaudí was by no means the only Catalan Modernista master to leave his mark on Barcelona. Lluís Domènech i Montaner (1850-1923), for example, was behind the stunning Palau de la Música Catalana and the Hospital de la Santa Creu i de Sant Pau.

Contemporary Creations

More recently, international experts have been buzzing about the energy and creativity surrounding Spanish architecture, and Spanish architects such as Santiago Calatrava (who transformed Valencia and built the Olympic stadium in Athens) are taking the world by storm.

Construction has slowed almost to a halt in Spain since the economic crash, but until recently architects from all over world were clamouring for contracts with Spanish municipal governments, whose programs for urban renewal were some of the most innovative in Europe, and who were funding an extraordinary explosion of architectural ambition (yes, there may be a connection between that largesse and the current state of the Spanish economy!).

Bullfighting

Matador meets his match in the Plaza de Toros

KRZYSZTOF DYDYNSKI/GETTY IMAGES ©

An epic drama of blood and sand or a cruel blood 'sport' that has no place in modern Spain? This most enduring and controversial of Spanish traditions is all this and more, at once compelling theatre and an ancient ritual that sees 40,000 bulls killed in around 17,000 fights every year in Spain. Perhaps it was best summed up by Ernest Hemingway – a bullfighting aficionado – who described it as a 'wonderful nightmare'.

The Basics

The matador (more often called the *torero* in Spanish) is the star of the team. Adorned in his glittering *traje de luces* (suit of lights), it is his fancy footwork, skill and bravery before the bull that has the crowd in raptures, or in rage, depending on his (or very occasionally her) performance. A complex series of events takes place in each clash, which can last from about 20 to 30 minutes (there are usually six fights in a programme). *Peones* (the matadors' 'footmen' whose job it is to test the strength of the bull) dart about with grand capes in front of the bull; horseback *picadores* (horsemen) drive lances into the bull's withers and *banderilleros* (flagmen) charge headlong at the bull in an attempt to stab its neck. Finally, the matador kills the bull.

If you do plan to attend a bullfight, it's important to understand what you're about to experience. The bull's back and neck are

repeatedly pierced by the lances, resulting in quite a lot of blood. The bull gradually becomes weakened through blood loss before the *torero* delivers the final sword thrust. If done properly, the bull dies instantly from this final thrust, albeit after bleeding some time from its other wounds. If the *coup de grace* is not delivered well, the animal dies a slow death. When this happens, the scene can be extremely disturbing.

When & Where

The bullfighting season begins in the first week of February with the fiestas of Valdemorillo and Ajalvir, near Madrid, to mark the feast day of San Blas. Elsewhere – especially in the two Castillas and Andalucía – *corridas* (bullfights) and *encierros* (running of the bulls through town), as in Pamplona, are part of town festivals. By October, you'd be hard-pressed to find a *corrida* anywhere in the country.

The Best... Bullrings

1 Plaza de Toros Monumental de Las Ventas (p220), Madrid

2 Plaza de Toros de la Real Maestranza (p258), Seville

3 Plaza de Toros (p282), Ronda

The Bullfighting Debate

The popular image of Spain would have us all believe that every Spaniard is a die-hard bullfighting fan, but this couldn't be any further from the truth. While bullfighting remains strong in some parts of the country, notably Andalucía, in other areas such as Galicia, Cantabria and other northern regions it's never really been a part of local culture. A recent poll found that just 17% of Spaniards under 25 had any interest in bullfighting, compared with 41% of those aged over 64. Similar polls suggest that three-quarters of Spaniards have no interest in the sport.

Today there's a large, growing antibullfighting movement in Spain. The government has banned children under 14 from attending bullfights, and state-run TV has stopped broadcasting live coverage of bullfights (although the TVE state-run channel does still broadcast *Tendido Cero*, a weekly magazine-style bullfighting program, and various private broadcasters continue to screen live fights). The bullfighting world was given a further blow when the Catalan government's ban on bullfighting officially became law on 1 January 2012. On the flip side, though, bullfighting does still have some fans in high places. In 2008 around €600 million of public money, including some from European funds, was given to the bullfight breeding industry, and King Juan Carlos is on record as saying: 'The day the EU bans bullfighting is the day Spain leaves the EU'.

That this is a debate at all in Spain owes a little to bullfighting's waning popularity and arguably more to the country's growing integration with the rest of Europe since Spain's return of democracy in the late 1970s. The fall in bullfighting's popularity has fostered some antibullfighting organisations, such as the Madrid-based Equanimal (www.equanimal.org). But the greatest impetus has come from groups beyond Spanish shores, such as the League Against Cruel Sports (www.leagueagainstcruelsports.org). For information on creative protests against bullfighting, see www.runningofthenudes.com.

The Spanish Kitchen

Seafood paella

DAVID SUTHERLAND/GETTY IMAGES ©

Spanish cuisine is all the rage around the world – and no wonder. Uniquely Spanish ways of eating (such as tapas), the enduring appeal of Spanish staples (including jamón, paella and olive oil) and the astonishing regional varieties partly explain the phenomenon. But sheer culinary excellence wedded to the new wave of innovation that has taken hold in the Basque Country, Catalonia and elsewhere have taken Spanish cuisine to a whole new level.

Eating Like a Local

Spanish cuisine is one of Europe's most accessible. But sometimes the first-time visitor can feel so overwhelmed about what to eat, when to eat it and how to order it that they head instead for the nearest tourist restaurant and consequently end up never really experiencing proper Spanish cuisine.

Spaniards are usually so utterly absorbed in having a good time that you're unlikely to stand out if you're unsure what to do. And, despite first impressions, knowing what to do is easy. For a start, take your time to look around at what other people are eating, and don't hesitate to point to someone else's plate when ordering – Spaniards do this all the time. Another important weapon in your armoury is to repeat that well-worn Spanish mantra when entering a bar: '*¿Cuál es la especialidad de la casa?*' ('What's the house speciality?'). Most bars do most things well, but the chances are that locals come here for one or two dishes in particular. Even if you don't understand what the dish is, just go ahead and order it.

Ways of Eating

Most visitors complain not about the quality of Spanish food but about its timing. Outside of the regular business hours, many bars serve tapas throughout the day. *Bocadillos* (bread rolls with filling) are another convenient option. Once you do find a bar or restaurant that's open when you're hungry, the typical *carta* (menu) begins with starters such as *ensaladas* (salads), *sopas* (soups) and *entremeses* (hors d'oeuvres). If you can't face a full menu, the *plato combinado* is a meat-and-three-veg dish.

The Art of Eating Tapas

Too many travellers miss out on the joys of tapas because, unless you speak Spanish, the art of ordering can seem one of the dark arts of Spanish etiquette. Fear not – it's not as difficult as it first appears.

In the Basque Country, Zaragoza and many bars in Madrid, Barcelona and elsewhere, it couldn't be easier. With so many tapas varieties lined up along the bar, you either take a small plate and help yourself, or point to the morsel you want. It's customary to keep track of what you eat. Otherwise, many places have a list of tapas, either on the menu or posted up behind the bar. If you can't choose, ask for *la especialidad de la casa* (the house speciality) and it's hard to go wrong. Another way of ordering tapas is to order *raciones* (literally 'rations'; large tapas servings) or *media raciones* (half-rations; smaller tapas servings). These plates and half-plates of a particular dish are a good way to go if you particularly like something and want a little bit more than a single piece. Remember, however, that after a couple of *raciones* you'll almost certainly be full. In some bars you'll also get a small (free) *tapa* when you buy a drink – but this is very much the exception to the rule.

The Laws Of Spanish Cooking

The laws of traditional Spanish cooking are deceptively simple: take the freshest ingredients and interfere with them as little as possible.

If simplicity is the cornerstone of Spanish cooking, it's the innovation and nouvelle cuisine emerging from Spanish kitchens that has truly taken the world by storm. Celebrity chefs such as Ferran Adrià and Mari Arzak have developed their own culinary

Menú del Día

To cap prices at lunchtime Monday to Friday, order the *menú del día*, a three-course set menu that includes water, bread and a drink (usually €10 and up). You'll be given a menu with five or six starters, the same number of mains, and a handful of desserts – choose one from each category. Few working Spaniards have time to go home for lunch and taking a packed lunch is just not the done thing. The *menú del día* allows them to eat home-style food without breaking the bank.

laboratories, experimenting with all that's new, but always with a base rooted in traditional Spanish cuisine.

Icons of the Spanish Kitchen

The list of signature Spanish dishes and ingredients, not to mention their regional variations, could fill encyclopedias. But if we had to choose just three culinary icons, they would be olive oil, *jamón* and paella.

The Best... Cooking Courses & Tours

1 Adventurous Appetites, Madrid (p204)

2 Cook and Taste, Barcelona (p82)

3 San Sebastián Food (p158), San Sebastián

4 Sabores de San Sebastián (p158), San Sebastián

Olive Oil

Andalucía is the olive oil capital of the world. There are over 100 million olive trees in Andalucía and a remarkable 20% of the world's olive oil originates in Jaén Province. *Aceite de oliva* (olive oil) will appear in just about every dish you order while in Spain – it's a standard base for cooking, is used to dress all manner of salads, and breakfast for many Spaniards includes toasted bread drizzled with olive oil and rubbed with tomato and garlic.

Jamón

Spaniards are devoted to their cured meats (such as chorizo, *salchichón* and *lomo*), but *jamón* (ham) is Spain's true culinary constant and one of the few things that unites the country. The best *jamón* comes from Andalucía (especially around Jabugo in Huelva Province), around Salamanca, and Aragón.

Jamón serrano (which accounts for approximately 90% of cured ham in Spain) refers to *jamón* made from white-coated pigs introduced to Spain in the 1950s. *Jamón ibérico* – the more expensive and the elite of Spanish hams – comes from a black-coated pig indigenous to the Iberian Peninsula and a descendant of the wild boar.

Paella

Easily Spain's best-known culinary export, paella well deserves its fame. The base of a good paella always includes short-grain rice, garlic, parsley, olive oil and saffron. The best rice is the *bomba* variety, which opens out accordion fashion when cooked, allowing for maximum absorption while remaining firm. Paella should be cooked in a large shallow pan to enable maximum contact with the bottom of the pan where most of the flavour resides. The main paella staples are *paella valenciana* (from Valencia, where paella has its roots), which is cooked with chicken, white beans and sometimes rabbit, and the more widespread *paella de mariscos* (seafood paella), which should be bursting with shellfish. In most restaurants, ordering a paella requires a minimum of two people.

For all paella's fame, a *really* good paella can be surprisingly hard to come by in Spanish restaurants. This is partly because saffron is extremely expensive, prompting many restaurants to cut corners by using yellow dye number 2. It's also because many restaurants play on the fact that every second foreign visitor to Spain will order a paella while in the country, but few will have any idea about what a good paella should taste like. Spaniards are much more discerning when it comes to their national dish, so check out the clientele before sitting down.

Practical Information

Throughout this book, the order of restaurant listings follows the author's preference, and the following price ranges refer to a standard main dish:

€ less than €10

€€ from €10 to €20

€€€ more than €20

Restaurant hours in Spain are lunch from 1pm to 4pm, and dinner from 8.30pm to midnight or later.

Spanish Wine

Spaniards invariably accompany their meal with a Spanish wine.

Probably the most common premium red table wine you'll encounter will be from La Rioja, in the north. Its wine is smooth and fruity, seldom as dry as its supposed French counterpart; look for the 'DOC Rioja' classification on the label and you'll find a good wine.

Not far behind are the wine-producing regions of Ribera del Duero in Castilla y León, Navarra, the Somontano wines of Aragón, and the Valdepeñas region of southern Castilla-la Mancha. The latter is famous for the quantity, rather than quality, of wine it produces, but is generally well priced and remains popular. For white wines, the Ribeiro wines of Galicia are well regarded.

Regional Variations

The Basque Country and Catalonia are Spain's undoubted culinary superstars. Elsewhere, Andalucía, Aragón, Galicia and much of the Spanish interior are considered the bastions of traditional cuisine, while Madrid has risen above the mediocrity of its home-grown culinary traditions to be the place where you can get the best of regional specialities from around Spain.

In the Spanish interior, meats are a much-loved mainstay. Above all else, these include *cochinillo asado* (roast suckling pig) in Segovia, *cordero asado* (roast lamb) in most of Castilla y León, and the steaks of Ávila, inland Andalucía or the Basque Country. Around the coast, there are few creatures from the sea that Spaniards don't eat, from the Atlantic seafood of Galicia (*pulpo gallego,* or spicy boiled octopus, is the most famous dish) to the fried fish of Andalucía, and the seafood-based rice dishes of Catalonia or the Balearic Islands.

Survival Guide

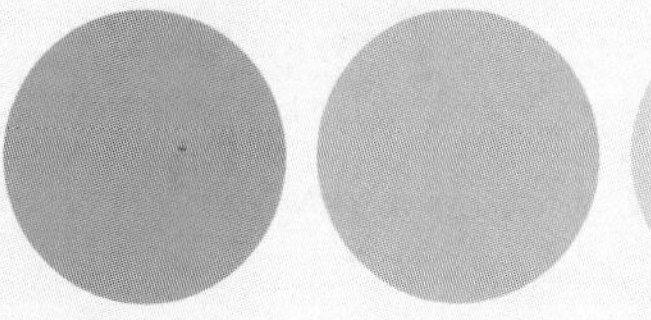

Picos de Europa (p173)

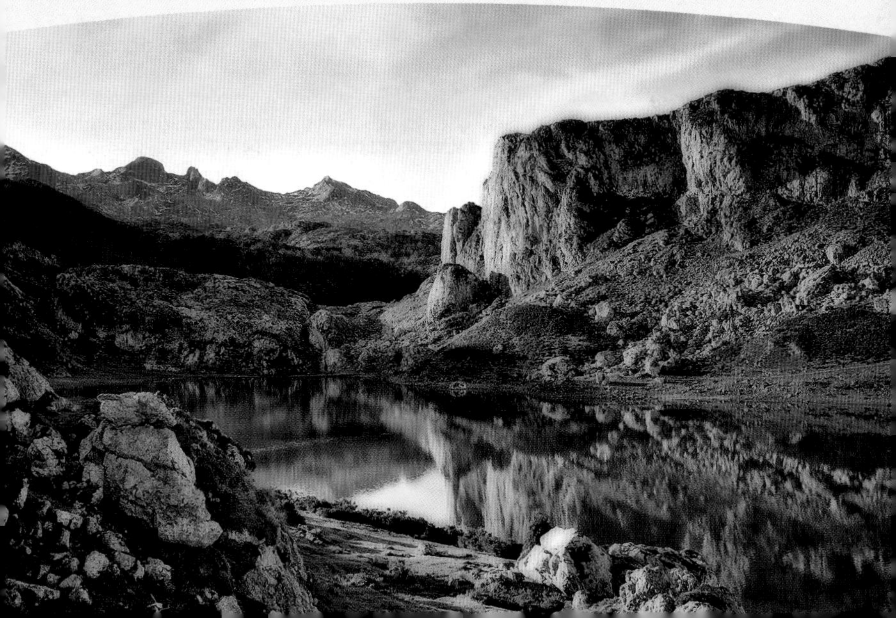

Directory

Accommodation

Spain's accommodation is generally of a high standard, from small, family-run *hostales* to the old-world opulence of *paradores*.

Officially, places to stay are classified into *hoteles* (hotels; one to five stars), *hostales* (one to three stars) and *pensiones* (basically small private hostales, often family businesses in rambling apartments; one or two stars). These are the categories used by the annual *Guía Oficial de Hoteles*, sold in bookshops, which lists almost every such establishment in Spain, except for one-star *pensiones*, with approximate prices.

Checkout time in most establishments is generally noon.

RESERVATIONS

Although there's usually no need to book ahead for a room in the low or shoulder seasons, booking ahead is generally a good idea, if for no other reason than to avoid a wearisome search for a room. Most places will ask for a credit-card number or will hold the room for you until 6pm unless you let them know that you'll be arriving later.

SEASONS

Prices throughout this guidebook are high-season maximums. You may be pleasantly surprised if you travel at other times. What constitutes low or high season depends on where and when. Most of the year is high season in Barcelona or Madrid, especially during trade fairs that you're unlikely to be aware of. August can be dead in the cities, but high season along the coast. Winter is high season in the ski resorts of the Pyrenees. Finding a place to stay without booking ahead in July and August along the Mediterranean Coast can be difficult. Weekends are high season for boutique hotels and *casas rurales* (rural homes), but low season for business hotels (which often offer generous specials then) in Madrid and Barcelona. Always check out hotel websites for discounts.

ACCOMMODATION TYPES

APARTMENTS, VILLAS

Throughout Spain you can rent self-catering apartments and houses from one night upwards. Villas and houses are widely available on the main holiday coasts and in popular country areas.

A simple one-bedroom apartment in a coastal resort for two or three people might cost as little as €30 per night, although more often you'll be looking at nearly twice that much, and prices jump even further in high season. More luxurious options with a swimming pool might come in at anything between €200 and €400 for four people.

Rural tourism has become immensely popular, with accommodation available in many new and often charming *casas rurales*. These are usually comfortably renovated village houses or farmhouses with a handful of rooms. They often go by other names, such as *cases de pagès* in Catalonia, *casas de aldea* in Asturias, *posadas* and *casonas* in Cantabria and so on. Some just provide rooms, while others offer meals or self-catering accommodation.

Accommodation Price Ranges

Throughout this guidebook, the order of accommodation listings is by author preference, and each place to stay is accompanied by one of the following symbols (the price relates to a double room with private bathroom):

€	less than €65
€€	from €65 to €140
€€€	more than €140

The price ranges for Madrid and Barcelona are inevitably higher:

€	less than €75
€€	from €75 to €200
€€€	more than €200

Lower-end prices typically hover around €30/50 for a single/double per night, but classy boutique establishments can easily charge €100 or more for a double.

Agencies include the following:

Apartments-Spain (www.apartments-spain.com)

Atlas Rural (www.atlasrural.com)

Casas Cantabricas (www.casas.co.uk)

Cases Rurals de Catalunya (www.casesrurals.com)

Escapada Rural (www.escapadarural.com)

Fincas 4 You (www.fincas4you.com)

Guías Casas Rurales (www.guiascasasrurales.com)

Holiday Serviced Apartments (www.holidayapartments.co.uk)

Owners Direct (www.ownersdirect.co.uk)

Ruralka (www.ruralka.com)

Rustic Rent (www.rusticrent.com)

Rusticae (www.rusticae.es)

Secret Destinations (www.secretdestinations.com)

Secret Places (www.secretplaces.com)

Top Rural (www.toprural.com)

Traum Ferienwohnungen (www.traum-ferienwohnungen.de)

Book Your Stay Online

For more accommodation reviews by Lonely Planet authors, check out http://hotels.lonelyplanet.com. You'll find independent reviews, as well as recommendations on the best places to stay. Best of all, you can book online.

Villas 4 You (www.villas4you.co.uk)

Vintage (http://vintagetravel.co.uk)

PENSIONES

Away from youth hostels and so on, a *pensión* is usually about the cheapest place to stay. Some cheap establishments forget to provide soap, toilet paper or towels. Don't hesitate to ask for these necessities.

HOSTALES

Hostales are a small step up again from *pensiones*. In both cases the better ones can be bright and spotless, with rooms boasting full en-suite bathroom – *baño privado*, most often with a shower *(ducha)* rather than bathtub – and usually a TV, air-conditioning and/or heating.

HOTELS

The remainder of establishments call themselves *hoteles* and run the gamut of quality, from straightforward roadside places, bland but clean, through to charming boutique gems and on to superluxurious hotels. Even in the cheapest hotels, rooms are likely to have an attached bathroom and there will probably be a restaurant.

Among the more tempting hotels for those with a little fiscal room to manoeuvre are the 90 or so **Paradores** (☎ in Spain 902 547 979; www.parador.es), a state-funded chain of hotels in often stunning locations, among them towering castles and former medieval convents. Similarly, you can find beautiful hotels in restored country homes and old city mansions, and these are not always particularly expensive. A raft of cutting-edge, hip design hotels with cool staff and a New York feel can be found in the big cities and major resort areas. At the top end you may pay more for a room with a view – especially sea views or with a *balcón* (balcony) – and will often have the option of a suite.

Business Hours

Standard opening hours are for high season only and tend to decrease outside that time.

Banks 8.30am-2pm Mon-Fri; some also open 4-7pm Thu and 9am-1pm Sat

Central post offices 8.30am-9.30pm Mon-Fri, 8.30am-2pm Sat

Nightclubs midnight or 1am to 5am or 6am

Restaurants lunch 1-4pm, dinner 8.30pm-midnight or later

Shops 10am-2pm & 4.30-7.30pm or 5-8pm; big supermarkets and

Climate

Barcelona

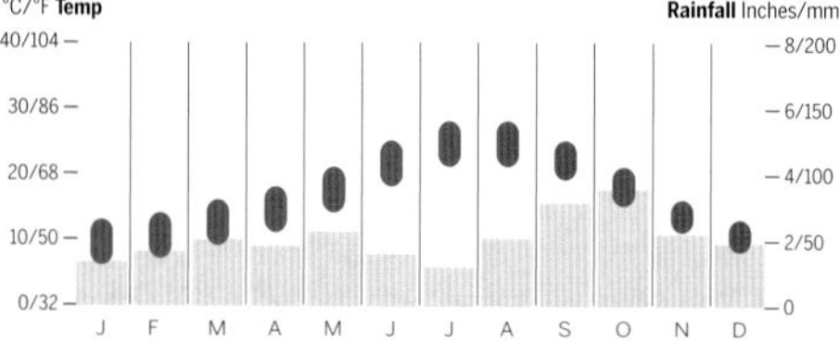

Madrid

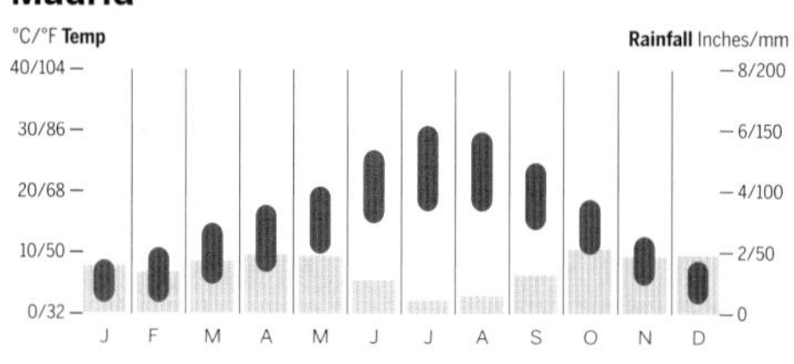

Seville

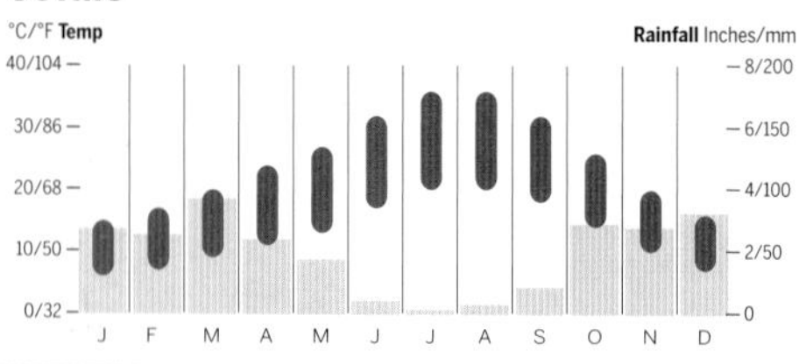

department stores generally open 10am-10pm Mon-Sat

Customs Regulations

Duty-free allowances for travellers entering Spain from outside the EU include 2L of wine (or 1L of wine and 1L of spirits), and 200 cigarettes or 50 cigars or 250g of tobacco.

Discount Cards

At museums, never hesitate to ask if there are discounts for students, young people, children, families or seniors.

Senior Cards Reduced prices for people over 60, 63 or 65 (depending on the place) at various museums and attractions (sometimes restricted to EU citizens only) and occasionally on transport.

Student Cards Discounts (usually half the normal fee) for students. You will need some kind of identification (eg an International Student Identity Card; www.isic.org) to prove student status. Not accepted everywhere.

Youth Card Travel, sights and youth hostel discounts with the Euro under 26 card (www.euro26.org), known as Carnet Joven in Spain. The International Youth Travel Card (IYTC; www.istc.org) offers similar benefits.

Electricity

Electrical plugs in Spain can also be round, but will always have two round pins. The bottom graphic is for Gibraltar.

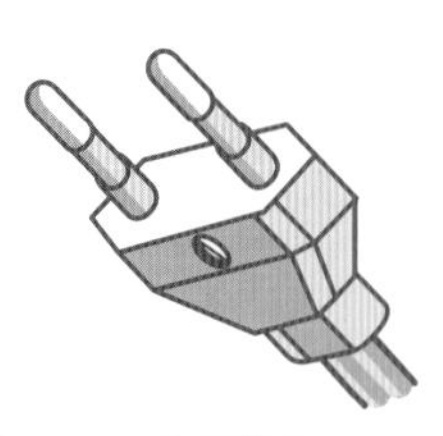

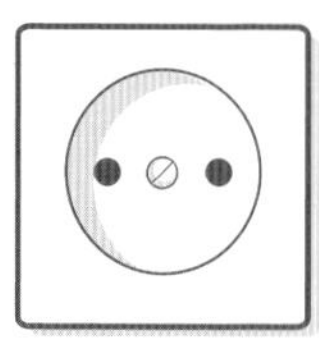

230V/50Hz

240V/50Hz

Gay & Lesbian Travellers

Homosexuality is legal in Spain and the age of consent is 13, as it is for heterosexuals. In 2005 the Socialist president, José Luis Rodríguez Zapatero, gave the country's conservative Catholic foundations a shake with the legalisation of same-sex marriages in Spain.

Lesbians and gay men generally keep a fairly low profile, but are quite open in the cities. Madrid, Barcelona, Sitges, Torremolinos and Ibiza have particularly lively scenes. Sitges is a major destination on the international gay party circuit; gays take a leading role in the wild **Carnaval** (www.sitges.com/carnaval) there in February/March. There are also gay parades, marches and events in several cities on and around the last Saturday in June, when Madrid's **gay and lesbian pride march** (www.orgullogay.org) takes place.

Health

Spain has an excellent health-care system.

AVAILABILITY AND COST OF HEALTH CARE

If you need an ambulance, call ☎061. For emergency treatment, go straight to the *urgencias* (casualty) section of the nearest hospital.

Farmacias offer valuable advice and sell over-the-counter medication. In Spain, a system of *farmacias de guardia* (duty pharmacies) operates so that each district has one open all the time. When a pharmacy is closed, it posts the name of the nearest open one on the door.

Medical costs are lower in Spain than many other European countries, but can still mount quickly if you are uninsured. Costs if you attend casualty range from nothing (in some regions) to around €80.

ALTITUDE SICKNESS

If you're hiking at altitude, altitude sickness may be a risk. Lack of oxygen at high altitudes (over 2500m) affects most people to some extent. Symptoms of Acute Mountain Sickness (AMS) usually develop during the first 24 hours at altitude but may be delayed up to three weeks. Mild symptoms include headache, lethargy, dizziness, difficulty sleeping and loss of appetite. AMS may become more severe without warning and can be fatal. Severe symptoms include breathlessness, a dry, irritative cough (which may progress to the production of pink, frothy sputum), severe headache, lack of coordination and balance, confusion, irrational behaviour, vomiting, drowsiness and unconsciousness.

Treat mild symptoms by resting at the same altitude until recovery, usually for a day or two. Paracetamol or aspirin can be taken for headaches. If symptoms persist or become worse immediate descent is necessary; even 500m can help. Drug treatments should never be used to avoid descent or to enable further ascent.

HYPOTHERMIA

The weather in Spain's mountains can be extremely changeable at any time of year. Proper preparation will reduce the risks of getting hypothermia: always carry waterproof garments and warm layers, and inform others of your route.

Hypothermia starts with shivering, loss of judgment and clumsiness. Unless rewarming occurs, the sufferer deteriorates into apathy, confusion and coma. Prevent further heat loss by seeking shelter, warm dry clothing, hot sweet drinks and shared body warmth.

BITES & STINGS

Nasty insects to be wary of are the hairy reddish-brown caterpillars of the pine processionary moth (touching the caterpillars' hairs sets off a severely irritating allergic skin reaction), and some Spanish centipedes have a very nasty but nonfatal sting.

Jellyfish, which have stinging tentacles, are an increasing problem at beaches along the Mediterranean coastline.

The only venomous snake that is even relatively common in Spain is Lataste's viper. It has a triangular-shaped head, grows up to 75cm long, and is grey with a zigzag pattern. It lives in dry, rocky areas, away from humans. Its bite can be fatal and needs to be treated with a serum, which state clinics in major towns keep in stock.

WATER

Tap water is generally safe to drink in Spain. If you are in any doubt, ask *¿Es potable el agua*

Practicalities

- **Currency** Euro
- **Electric current** 230V, 50Hz; 240V, 50Hz (Gibraltar)
- **Smoking** Banned in all enclosed public spaces.
- **Weights & measures** Metric
- **Major newspapers** Centre-left *El País* (www.elpais.com); centre-right *El Mundo* (www.elmundo.es); right-wing *ABC* (www.abc.es). The widely available *International Herald Tribune* includes an eight-page supplement of articles from *El País* translated into English (www.elpais.com/misc/herald/herald.pdf).
- **Radio** Radio Nacional de España (RNE)'s Radio 1, with general interest and current affairs programs; Radio 5, with sport and entertainment; and Radio 3 (Radio d'Espop). Stations covering current affairs include the left-leaning Cadena Ser, or the right-wing COPE. The most popular commercial pop and rock stations are 40 Principales, Kiss FM, Cadena 100 and Onda Cero.
- **TV** Spain's state-run Televisión Española (TVE1 and La 2) or the independent commercial stations (Antena 3, Tele 5, Cuatro and La Sexta). Regional governments run local stations, such as Madrid's Telemadrid, Catalonia's TV-3 and Canal 33 (both in Catalan), Galicia's TVG, the Basque Country's ETB-1 and ETB-2, Valencia's Canal 9 and Andalucía's Canal Sur. Cable and satellite TV is becoming widespread.

(de grifo)? (Is the (tap) water drinkable?). Do not drink water from rivers or lakes as it may contain bacteria or viruses that can cause diarrhoea or vomiting.

Insurance

A travel-insurance policy to cover theft, loss, medical problems and cancellation or delays to your travel arrangements is a good idea. Paying for your ticket with a credit card can often provide limited travel-accident insurance and you may be able to reclaim the payment if the operator doesn't deliver.

Worldwide travel insurance is available at lonelyplanet.com/travel_services. You can buy, extend and claim online anytime – even if you're on the road.

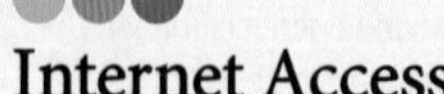

Internet Access

Wi-fi is increasingly available at most hotels and in some cafes, restaurants and airports; generally (but not always) free. Connection speed often varies from room to room in hotels, so always ask when you check in.

Good internet cafes that last the distance are increasingly hard to find; ask at the local tourist office. Prices per hour range from €1.50 to €3.

Legal Matters

In theory, you are supposed to have your national ID card or passport with you at all times. If asked for it by the police, you are supposed to be able to produce it on the spot. In practice it is rarely an issue and many people choose to leave passports in hotel safes.

The **Policía Local** or **Policía Municipal** operates at a local level and deals with such issues as traffic infringements and minor crime. The **Policía Nacional** (☎091) is the state police force, dealing with major crime and operating primarily in the cities. The military-linked **Guardia Civil** (created in the 19th century to deal with banditry) is largely responsible for highway patrols, borders, security, major crime and terrorism. Several regions have their own police forces, such as the **Mossos d'Esquadra** in Catalonia and the **Ertaintxa** in the Basque Country.

Money

The most convenient way to bring your money is in the form of a debit or credit card, with some extra cash for use in case of an emergency.

ATMS

Many credit and debit cards can be used for withdrawing money from *cajeros automáticos* (automatic teller machines) that display the relevant symbols such as Visa, MasterCard, Cirrus etc. Remember that there is usually a charge (around 1.5% to 2%) on ATM cash withdrawals abroad.

CASH

Most banks and building societies will exchange major foreign currencies and offer the best rates. Ask about commissions and take your passport.

CREDIT AND DEBIT CARDS

Can be used to pay for most purchases. You'll often be asked to show your passport or some other form of identification. Among the most widely accepted are Visa, MasterCard, American Express (Amex), Cirrus, Maestro, Plus, Diners Club and JCB. If your card is lost, stolen or swallowed by an ATM, you can call the following telephone numbers toll free to have an immediate stop put on its use: **Amex** (☎ 1800 528 2122, 91 572 03 03), **Diners Club** (☎ 902 401 112), **MasterCard** (☎ 900 971 231) and **Visa** (☎ 900 991 124).

MONEYCHANGERS

You can exchange both cash and travellers cheques at exchange offices – which are usually indicated by the word *cambio* (exchange). Generally they offer longer opening hours and quicker service than banks, but worse exchange rates and higher commissions.

TAXES AND REFUNDS

In Spain, value-added tax (VAT) is known as IVA (ee-ba; *impuesto sobre el valor añadido*). Visitors are entitled to a refund of the 18% IVA on purchases costing more than €90.16 from any shop if they are taking them out of the EU within three months. Ask the shop for a cash back (or similar) refund form showing the price and IVA paid for each item, and identifying the vendor and purchaser. Then present the refund form to the customs booth for IVA refunds at the airport, port or border from which you leave the EU.

TIPPING

Menu prices include a service charge. Most people leave some small change if they're satisfied: 5% is normally fine and 10% extremely generous. Porters will generally be happy with €1. Taxi drivers don't have to be tipped but a little rounding up won't go amiss.

TRAVELLERS CHEQUES

Can be changed (you'll often be charged a commission) at most banks and building societies. Visa, Amex and Travelex are widely accepted brands with (usually) efficient replacement policies. Get most of your cheques in fairly large denominations (the equivalent of €100 or more) to save on any per-cheque commission charges. It's vital to keep your initial receipt, and a record of your cheque numbers and the ones you have used, separate from the cheques themselves.

Public Holidays

The two main periods when Spaniards go on holiday are Semana Santa (the week leading up to Easter Sunday) and August. At these times accommodation in resorts can be scarce and transport heavily booked, but other places are often half-empty.

There are at least 14 official holidays a year – some observed nationwide, some locally. When a holiday falls close to a weekend, Spaniards like to make a *puente* (bridge), meaning they take the intervening day off too. Occasionally when some holidays fall close, they make an *acueducto* (aqueduct)! Here are the national holidays:

Año Nuevo (New Year's Day) 1 January

Viernes Santo (Good Friday) March/April

Fiesta del Trabajo (Labour Day) 1 May

La Asunción (Feast of the Assumption) 15 August

Fiesta Nacional de España (National Day) 12 October

La Inmaculada Concepción (Feast of the Immaculate Conception) 8 December

Navidad (Christmas) 25 December

Regional governments set five holidays and local councils two more. Common dates include the following:

Epifanía (Epiphany) or **Día de los Reyes Magos** (Three Kings' Day) 6 January

Jueves Santo (Good Thursday) March/April. Not observed in Catalonia and Valencia.

Corpus Christi June. This is the Thursday after the eighth Sunday after Easter Sunday.

Día de Santiago Apóstol (Feast of St James the Apostle) 25 July

Día de Todos los Santos (All Saints Day) 1 November

Día de la Constitución (Constitution Day) 6 December

Safe Travel

Most visitors to Spain never feel remotely threatened, but a sufficient number have unpleasant experiences to warrant an alert. The main thing to be wary of is petty theft (which may of course not seem so petty if your passport, cash, travellers cheques, credit card and camera go missing). What follows is intended as a strong warning rather than alarmism. In other words, be careful but don't be paranoid.

SCAMS

There must be 50 ways to lose your wallet. As a rule, talented petty thieves work in groups and capitalise on distraction. Tricks usually involve a team of two or more (sometimes one of them an attractive woman to distract male victims). While one attracts your attention, the other empties your pockets. More imaginative strikes include someone dropping a milk mixture on to the victim from a balcony. Immediately a concerned citizen comes up to help you brush off what you assume to be pigeon poo, and thus suitably occupied you don't notice the contents of your pockets slipping away.

Beware: not all thieves look like thieves. Watch out for an old classic: the ladies offering flowers for good luck. We don't know how they do it, but if you get too involved in a friendly chat with these people, your pockets almost always wind up empty.

On some highways, especially the AP7 from the French border to Barcelona, bands of delinquents occasionally operate. Beware of men trying to distract you in rest areas, and don't stop along the highway if people driving alongside indicate you have a problem with the car. While one inspects the rear of the car with you, his pals will empty your vehicle. Another gag has them puncturing tyres of cars stopped in rest areas, then following and 'helping' the victim when they stop to change the wheel. Hire cars and those with foreign plates are especially targeted. When you do call in at highway rest stops, try to park close to the buildings and leave nothing of value in view. If you do stop to change a tyre and find yourself getting unsolicited aid, make sure doors are all locked and don't allow yourself to be distracted.

Even parking your car can be fraught. In some towns fairly dodgy self-appointed parking attendants operate in central areas where you may want to park. They will direct you frantically to a spot. If possible, ignore them and find your own. If unavoidable, you may well want to pay them some token not to scratch or otherwise damage your vehicle after you've walked away. You definitely don't want to leave anything visible in the car (or open the boot [trunk] if you intend to leave luggage or anything else in it) under these circumstances.

THEFT

Theft is mostly a risk in tourist resorts, big cities and when you first arrive in a new city and may be off your guard. You are at your most vulnerable when dragging around luggage to or from your hotel. Barcelona, Madrid and Seville have the worst reputations for theft and, on very rare occasions, muggings.

Anything left lying on the beach can disappear in a flash when your back is turned. At night avoid dingy, empty city alleys and backstreets, or anywhere that just doesn't feel 100% safe.

Report thefts to the national police. You are unlikely to recover your goods but you need to make this formal *denuncia* for insurance purposes. To avoid endless queues at the *comisaría* (police station), you can make the report by phone (☎902 102 112) in various languages or on the web at www.policia.es (click on Denuncias). The following day you go to the station of your choice to pick up and sign the report, without queuing.

Telephone

The reasonably widespread blue payphones are easy to use for international and domestic calls. They accept coins, phonecards *(tarjetas telefónicas)* issued by the national phone company Telefónica and, in some cases, various credit cards. Calling from your computer using an internet-based service such as Skype is generally the cheapest option.

COLLECT CALLS

International collect calls *(una llamada a cobro revertido)* are simple. Dial ☎99 00 followed by the code for the country you're calling:

Australia 900 99 00 61

Canada 900 99 00 15

France 900 99 00 33

Germany 900 99 00 49

Ireland 900 99 03 53

Israel 900 99 09 72

New Zealand 900 99 00 64

UK for BT 900 99 00 44

USA for AT&T 900 99 00 11, for Sprint and various others 900 99 00 13

MOBILE PHONES

Spain uses GSM 900/1800, which is compatible with the rest of Europe and Australia but not with the North American GSM 1900 or the system used in Japan. From those countries, you will need to travel with a tri-band or quadric-band phone.

You can buy SIM cards and prepaid time in Spain for your mobile (cell) phone (provided you own a GSM, dual- or tri-band cellular phone). This only works if your national phone hasn't been code-blocked; check before leaving home. Only consider a full contract if you plan to live in Spain for a while.

All the Spanish mobile phone companies (Telefónica's MoviStar, Orange and Vodafone) offer *prepagado* (prepaid) accounts for mobiles. The SIM card costs from €50, which includes some prepaid phone time. Phone outlets are scattered across the country. You can then top up in their shops or by buying cards in outlets, such as tobacconists *(estancos)* and newsstands.

On 1 July 2010 the EU's new Roaming Regulation came into force. It reduced roaming charges and set in place measures designed to prevent travellers from running up massive bills. Check with your mobile provider for more information.

PHONE CODES

Mobile (cell) phone numbers start with 6. Numbers starting with 900 are national toll-free numbers, while those starting 901 to 905 come with varying costs. A common one is 902, which is a national standard rate number, but which can only be dialled from within Spain. In a similar category are numbers starting with 800, 803, 806 and 807.

- **International access code** 00
- **Spain country code** 34
- **Local area codes** None (these are incorporated into listed numbers)

PHONECARDS

Cut-rate prepaid phonecards can be good value for international calls. They can be bought from *estancos* (small grocery stores), *locutorios* (private call centres) and newsstands in the main cities and tourist resorts. If possible, try to compare rates. Many of the private operators offer better deals than those offered by Telefónica. *Locutorios* that specialise in cut-rate overseas calls have popped up all over the place in bigger cities.

USEFUL PHONE NUMBERS

Emergencies 112

English-speaking Spanish international operator 1008 (for calls within Europe) or 1005 (rest of the world).

International directory inquiries 11825 (A call to this number costs €2).

National directory inquiries 11818

Operator for calls within Spain 1009 (including for domestic reverse-charge [collect] calls).

Time

Time zone Same as most of Western Europe (GMT/UTC plus one hour during winter and GMT/UTC plus two hours during the daylight-saving period).

Daylight-saving From the last Sunday in March to the last Sunday in October.

UK, Ireland, Portugal & Canary Islands One hour behind mainland Spain.

Morocco Morocco is on GMT/UTC year-round. From the last Sunday in March to the last Sunday in October, subtract two hours from Spanish time to get Moroccan time; the rest of the year, subtract one hour.

USA Spanish time is USA Eastern Time plus six hours

and USA Pacific Time plus nine hours.

Australia During the Australian winter (Spanish summer), subtract eight hours from Australian Eastern Standard Time to get Spanish time; during the Australian summer, subtract 10 hours.

12- and 24-hour clock Although the 24-hour clock is used in most official situations, you'll find people generally use the 12-hour clock in everyday conversation.

Tourist Information

All cities and many smaller towns have an *oficina de turismo* or *oficina de información turística*. In the country's provincial capitals you will sometimes find more than one tourist office – one specialising in information on the city alone, the other carrying mostly provincial or regional information. National and natural parks also often have their own visitor centres offering useful information.

Turespaña (www.spain.info) is the country's national tourism body, and it operates branches around the world. Check the website for office locations.

Travellers with Disabilities

Spain is not overly accommodating for travellers with disabilities but some things are slowly changing. For example, disabled access to some museums, official buildings and hotels represent a change in local thinking. In major cities more is slowly being done to facilitate disabled access to public transport and taxis; in some cities, wheelchair-adapted taxis are called 'Eurotaxis'. Newly constructed hotels in most areas of Spain are required to have wheelchair-adapted rooms. With older places, you need to be a little wary of hotels who advertise themselves as being disabled-friendly, as this can mean as little as wide doors to rooms and bathrooms, or other token efforts.

ORGANISATIONS

Accessible Travel & Leisure (☎ 01452-729739; www.accessibletravel.co.uk) Claims to be the biggest UK travel agent dealing with travel for people with a disability and encourages independent travel.

Barcelona Turisme (☎ 93 428 52 27; www.barcelona-access.com) Website devoted to making Barcelona accessible for visitors with a disability.

Accessible Madrid (www.esmadrid.com) Madrid's tourist office website has some useful information (type 'Accessible' into their search box). You can download the free, generally outstanding 152-page Madrid Accessible Tourism Guide; it covers everything from sights, restaurants and transport to itineraries through the city. The site also allows you to download a list of wheelchair-accessible hotels, and a PDF called 'Lugares Accesibles', a list of wheelchair-friendly restaurants, shopping centres and museums.

ONCE (Organización Nacional de Ciegos Españoles; ☎ 91 577 37 56, 91 532 50 00; www.once.es; Calle de Prim 3, Madrid; M Chueca or Colón) The Spanish association for the blind. You may be able to get hold of guides in Braille to a handful of cities, including Madrid and Barcelona, although they're not published every year.

Society for Accessible Travel & Hospitality (SATH; ☎ 212-447-7284; www.sath.org; 347 Fifth Ave at 34th St, New York, USA; 9am-5pm; M34 to 5th Ave, M1 to 34th St, S 6 to 33rd St) Although largely concentrated on the USA (and based in New York), this organisation can provide general information.

Visas

Spain is one of 26 member countries of the Schengen Convention, under which 22 EU countries (all but Bulgaria, Cyprus, Ireland, Romania and the UK) plus Iceland, Norway, Liechtenstein and Switzerland have abolished checks at common borders.

The visa situation for entering Spain is as follows:

Citizens or residents of EU & Schengen countries No visa required.

Citizens or residents of Australia, Canada, Israel, Japan, New Zealand and the USA No visa required for tourist visits of up to 90 days.

Other countries Check with a Spanish embassy or consulate.

Transport

Getting There and Away

Spain is one of Europe's top holiday destinations and is well linked to other European countries by air, rail and road. Regular car ferries and hydrofoils run to and from Morocco, and there are ferry links to the UK, Italy, the Canary Islands and Algeria.

Flights, tours and rail tickets can be booked online at lonelyplanet.com/bookings.

ENTERING SPAIN

Immigration and customs checks (which usually only take place if you're arriving from outside the EU) normally involve a minimum of fuss, although there are exceptions.

Your vehicle could be searched on arrival from Andorra. Spanish customs look out for contraband duty-free products destined for illegal resale in Spain. The same generally goes on arrival from Morocco or the Spanish North African enclaves of Ceuta and Melilla. In this case the search is for controlled substances. Expect long delays at these borders, especially in summer.

PASSPORTS

Citizens of the 27 EU member states and Switzerland can travel to Spain with their national identity card alone. If such countries do not issue ID cards – as in the UK – travellers must carry a full valid passport. All other nationalities must have a full valid passport.

By law you are supposed to carry your passport or ID card with you in Spain at all times.

 AIR

There are direct flights to Spain from most European countries, as well as North America, South America, Africa, the Middle East and Asia. Those coming from Australasia will usually have to make at least one change of flight.

High season in Spain generally means Christmas, New Year, Easter and roughly June to September. This varies depending on the specific destination. You may find reasonably priced flights to Madrid available in August because it is stinking hot and everyone else has fled to the mountains or the sea. As a general rule, November to March is when airfares to Spain are likely to be at their lowest, and the intervening months can be considered shoulder periods.

AIRPORTS AND AIRLINES

All of Spain's airports share the user-friendly website and flight information telephone number of **Aena** (☎ 902 404 704; www.aena.es), the national airports authority. To find more information on each airport, choose English and click on the drop-down menu of airports. Each airport's page has details on practical information (including parking and public transport) and a full list of (and links to) airlines using that airport. They also have current flight information.

Madrid's Aeropuerto de Barajas is Spain's busiest (and Europe's fourth- or fifth-busiest, depending on the year) airport. Other major airports include Barcelona's Aeroport del Prat and the airports of Palma de

Climate Change & Travel

Every form of transport that relies on carbon-based fuel generates CO_2, the main cause of human-induced climate change. Modern travel is dependent on aeroplanes, which might use less fuel per kilometre per person than most cars but travel much greater distances. The altitude at which aircraft emit gases (including CO_2) and particles also contributes to their climate change impact. Many websites offer 'carbon calculators' that allow people to estimate the carbon emissions generated by their journey and, for those who wish to do so, to offset the impact of the greenhouse gases emitted with contributions to portfolios of climate-friendly initiatives throughout the world. Lonely Planet offsets the carbon footprint of all staff and author travel.

Mallorca, Málaga, Alicante, Girona, Valencia, Ibiza, Seville and Bilbao. There are also airports at A Coruña, Almería, Asturias, Jerez de la Frontera, Murcia, Reus and Seville.

LAND

Spain shares land borders with France, Portugal and Andorra.

Apart from shorter cross-border services, **Eurolines** (www.eurolines.com) are the main operators of international bus services to Spain from most of Western Europe and Morocco.

In addition to the rail services connecting Spain with France and Portugal, there are direct trains between Zurich and Barcelona (via Bern, Geneva, Perpignan and Girona), and between Milan and Barcelona (via Turin, Perpignan and Girona). For these and other services, visit the website of Renfe (www.renfe.com), the Spanish national railway company.

FRANCE

Car and Motorcycle

The main road crossing into Spain from France is the highway that links up with Spain's AP7 tollway, which runs down to Barcelona and follows the Spanish coast south (with a branch, the AP2, going to Madrid via Zaragoza). A series of links cut across the Pyrenees from France and Andorra into Spain, as does a coastal route that runs from Biarritz in France into the Spanish Basque Country.

Train

The principal rail crossings into Spain pierce the Franco-Spanish frontier along the Mediterranean coast and via the Basque Country. Another minor rail route runs inland across the Pyrenees from Latour-de-Carol to Barcelona.

In addition to the options listed below, two or three TGV (high-speed) trains leave from Paris-Montparnasse for Irún, where you change to a normal train for the Basque Country and on towards Madrid. Up to three TGVs also put you on track to Barcelona (leaving from Paris Gare de Lyon), with a change of train at Montpellier or Narbonne. For more information on French rail services, check out the **SNCF** (www.voyages-sncf.com) website.

There are plans for a high-speed rail link between Madrid and Paris. In the meantime, these are the major cross-border services:

Paris-Austerlitz to Madrid-Chamartín (chair/sleeper class €157.20/172.60, 15 hours, one daily) *Trenhotel Francisco de Goya* runs via Les Aubrais, Blois, Poitiers, Vitoria, Burgos and Valladolid.

Paris-Austerlitz to Barcelona–Estacio de Franca (chair/sleeper class €173.60/203.40, 12 hours, one daily) *Trenhotel Joan Miró* runs via Les Aubrais, Limoges, Figueres and Girona.

Montpellier to Lorca (€105, 13 hours, daily) Talgo service along the Mediterranean coast via Girona, Barcelona, Tarragona and Valencia.

PORTUGAL

Car and Motorcycle

The A5 freeway linking Madrid with Badajoz crosses the Portuguese frontier and continues on to Lisbon, and there are many other road connections up and down the length of the Spain–Portugal border.

Train

From Portugal, the main line runs from Lisbon across Extremadura to Madrid.

Lisbon to Madrid (chair/sleeper class €63.20/91.40, 9¼ hours, one daily)

Lisbon to Irún (chair/sleeper class €73.80/103.50, 14½ hours, one daily)

SEA

Ferries run to mainland Spain regularly from the Canary Islands, Italy, North Africa (Algeria, Morocco and the Spanish enclaves of Ceuta and Melilla) and the UK. Most services are run by the Spanish national ferry company, **Acciona Trasmediterránea** (☎ 902 45 46 45; www.trasmediterranea.es). You can take vehicles on most routes.

A useful website for comparing routes and finding links to the relevant ferry companies is www.ferrylines.com.

Getting Around

Spain's network of train and bus services is one of the best in Europe and there aren't many places that can't be reached using one or the other. The tentacles of Spain's high-speed train network are expanding rapidly with every passing year, while domestic air services are plentiful over longer distances and on routes that are more complicated by land.

AIR

Spain has an extensive network of internal flights. These are operated by both Spanish airlines and a handful of low-cost international airlines which include the following:

Air Berlin (www.airberlin.com) Madrid to Valencia, Palma de Mallorca, Ibiza, Seville, Jerez de la Frontera, Alicante, Bilbao and Santiago de Compostela.

Air Europa (www.aireuropa.com) Madrid to Ibiza, Palma de Mallorca, Vigo and Santiago de Compostela.

EasyJet (www.easyjet.com) Madrid to Ibiza, Menorca, Asturias (Gijón) and Santiago de Compostela.

Iberia (www.iberia.es) Spain's national airline and its subsidiary, Iberia Regional-Air Nostrum, have an extensive domestic network.

Ryanair (www.ryanair.com) Numerous domestic Spanish routes.

Volotea (www.volotea.com) New budget airline that flies domestically and internationally.

Vueling (www.vueling.com) Spanish low-cost company with loads of domestic flights within Spain, especially from Barcelona.

CAR AND MOTORCYCLE

Every vehicle should display a nationality plate of its country of registration and you must always carry proof of ownership of a private vehicle. Third-party motor insurance is required throughout Europe. A warning triangle and a reflective jacket (to be used in case of breakdown) are compulsory.

DRIVING LICENCE

All EU member states' driving licences are fully recognised throughout Europe. Those with a non-EU licence are supposed to obtain a 12-month International Driving Permit (IDP) to accompany their national licence, which your national automobile association can issue, although in practice car rental companies and police rarely ask for one. People who have held residency in Spain for one

Road Distances (Km)

	Alicante	Badajoz	Barcelona	Bilbao	Córdoba	Granada	A Coruña	León	Madrid	Málaga	Oviedo	Pamplona	San Sebastián	Seville	Toledo	Valencia	Valladolid
Badajoz	696																
Barcelona	515	1022															
Bilbao	817	649	620														
Córdoba	525	272	908	795													
Granada	353	438	868	829	166												
A Coruña	1031	772	1118	644	995	1043											
León	755	496	784	359	733	761	334										
Madrid	422	401	621	395	400	434	609	333									
Málaga	482	436	997	939	187	129	1153	877	544								
Oviedo	873	614	902	304	851	885	340	118	451	995							
Pamplona	673	755	437	159	807	841	738	404	407	951	463						
San Sebastián	766	768	529	119	869	903	763	433	469	13	423	92					
Seville	609	217	1046	933	138	256	947	671	538	219	789	945	1007				
Toledo	411	368	692	466	320	397	675	392	71	507	510	478	540	458			
Valencia	166	716	349	633	545	519	961	685	352	648	803	501	594	697	372		
Valladolid	615	414	663	280	578	627	455	134	193	737	252	325	354	589	258	545	
Zaragoza	498	726	296	324	725	759	833	488	325	869	604	175	268	863	396	326	367

Beating Parking Fines

If you've parked in a street parking spot and return to find that a parking inspector has left you a parking ticket, don't despair. If you arrive back within a reasonable time after the ticket was issued (what constitutes a reasonable time varies from place to place, but it is rarely more than a couple of hours), don't go looking for the inspector, but instead head for the nearest parking machine. Most machines in most cities allow you to pay a small penalty (usually around €5) to cancel the fine (keep both pieces of paper just in case). If you're unable to work out what to do, ask a local for help.

year or more should apply for a Spanish driving licence.

FUEL AND SPARE PARTS

Petrol *(gasolina)* in Spain is pricey, but generally slightly cheaper than in its major EU neighbours (including France, Germany, Italy and the UK).

Petrol is about 10% cheaper in Gibraltar than in Spain and 15% cheaper in Andorra.

You can pay with major credit cards at most service stations.

HIRE

To rent a car in Spain you'll need to have a licence, be aged 21 or over and, for the major companies at least, have a credit or debit card. Smaller firms in areas where car hire is particularly common (such as the Balearic Islands) can sometimes live without this last requirement. Although those with a non-EU licence should also have an IDP, you will find that national licences from countries such as Australia, Canada, New Zealand and the USA are usually accepted without question.

Auto Europe (www.auto-europe.com) US-based clearing house for deals with major car rental agencies.

Autos Abroad (www.autosabroad.com) UK-based company offering deals from major car rental agencies.

Avis (☎ 902 18 08 54; www.avis.es)

Europcar (☎ 902 10 50 30; www.europcar.es)

Hertz (☎ 91 749 77 78; www.hertz.es)

Ideamerge (www.ideamerge.com) Renault's car-leasing plan, motor-home rental and much more.

National/Atesa (☎ 902 10 01 01; www.atesa.es)

Pepecar (☎ 807 41 42 43; www.pepecar.com) Local low-cost company, but beware of 'extras' that aren't quoted in initial prices.

INSURANCE

Third-party motor insurance is a minimum requirement in Spain and throughout Europe. Ask your insurer for a European Accident Statement form, which can simplify matters in the event of an accident. A European breakdown-assistance policy such as the AA Five Star Service or RAC Eurocover Motoring Assistance is a good investment.

Car-hire companies also provide this minimum insurance, but be careful to understand what your liabilities and excess are, and what waivers you are entitled to in case of accident or damage to the hire vehicle.

ROAD RULES

Blood-alcohol limit: 0.05%. Breath tests are common, and if found to be over the limit you can be judged, condemned, fined and deprived of your licence within 24 hours. Fines range up to around €600 for serious offences. Nonresident foreigners may be required to pay up on the spot (at 30% off the full fine). Pleading linguistic ignorance will not help – your traffic cop will produce a list of infringements and fines in as many languages as you like. If you don't pay, or don't have a Spanish resident to act as guarantor for you, your vehicle could be impounded.

Legal driving age for cars 18 years.

Legal driving age for motorcycles & scooters 16 (80cc and over) or 14 (50cc and under). A licence is required.

Motorcyclists Must use headlights at all times and wear a helmet if riding a bike of 125cc or more.

Overtaking Spanish truck drivers often have the courtesy to turn on their right indicator to show that the way ahead of them is clear for overtaking (and the left one if it is not and you are attempting this manoeuvre).

Roundabouts (traffic circles) Vehicles already in the circle have the right of way.

Side of the road Drive on the right.

Speed limits In built-up areas, 50km/h (and in some cases, such as inner-city Barcelona, 30km/h), which increases to 100km/h on major roads and up to 120km/h on *autovías* and *autopistas* (toll-free and tolled dual-lane highways, respectively). Cars towing caravans are restricted to a maximum speed of 80km/h.

LOCAL TRANSPORT

Most of the major cities have excellent local transport. Madrid and Barcelona have extensive bus and metro systems, and other major cities also benefit from generally efficient public transport. By European standards, prices are relatively cheap.

BUS

Cities and provincial capitals all have reasonable bus networks. You can buy single tickets (usually between €1 and €1.50) on the buses or at tobacconists, but in cities such as Madrid and Barcelona you are better off buying combined 10-trip tickets that allow the use of a combination of bus and metro, and which work out cheaper per ride. These can be purchased in any metro station and from some tobacconists and newspaper kiosks.

Regular buses run from about 6am to shortly before midnight and even as late as 2am. In the big cities a night bus service generally kicks in on a limited number of lines in the wee hours. In Madrid they are known as *búhos* (owls) and in Barcelona more prosaically as *nitbusos* (night buses).

METRO

Madrid has the country's most extensive metro network. Barcelona follows in second place with a reasonable system. Valencia, Bilbao and Seville also have limited but nonetheless useful metro systems. Tickets must be bought in metro stations (from counters or vending machines), or sometimes from *estancos* (tobacconists) or newspaper kiosks. Single tickets cost the same as for buses (around €1.50). The best value for visitors wanting to move around the major cities over a few days are the 10-trip tickets, known in Madrid as Metrobús (€12) and in Barcelona as T-10 (€9.25).

TAXI

You can find taxi ranks at train and bus stations, or you can telephone for radio taxis. In larger cities taxi ranks are also scattered about the centre, and taxis will stop if you hail them in the street – look for the green light and/or the *libre* sign on the passenger side of the windscreen. The bigger cities are well populated with taxis, although you might have to wait a bit longer on a Friday or Saturday night. No more than four people are allowed in a taxi.

Daytime flagfall (generally to 10pm) is, for example, €2.15 in Madrid, and up to €3.10 after 10pm and on weekends and holidays. You then pay €1 to €1.20 per kilometre depending on the time of day. There are airport and luggage surcharges. A cross-town ride in a major city will cost about €7 to €10 – absurdly cheap by European standards – while a taxi between the city centre and airport in either Madrid or Barcelona will cost €25 to €35 with luggage.

TRAM

Trams were stripped out of Spanish cities decades ago, but they're making a timid comeback in some. Barcelona has a couple of new suburban tram services in addition to its tourist Tramvia Blau run to Tibidabo. Valencia has some useful trams to the beach, while various limited lines also run in Seville, Bilbao, Murcia and, most recently, Zaragoza.

TRAIN

Renfe (☎ **902 24 34 02; www.renfe.com**) is the excellent national train system that runs most of the services in Spain. A handful of small private railway lines also operate.

You'll find *consignas* (left-luggage facilities) at all main train stations. They are usually open from about 6am to midnight and charge from €3 to €5 per day per piece of luggage.

Spain has several types of trains, and long-distance trains (*largo recorrido* or *Grandes Líneas*) in particular have a variety of names.

Alaris, Altaria, Alvia, Arco and Avant Long-distance intermediate-speed services.

Cercanías For short hops and services to outlying suburbs and satellite towns in Madrid, Barcelona and 11 other cities.

Euromed Similar to the AVE trains, they connect Barcelona with Valencia and Alicante.

Regionales Trains operating within one region, usually stopping all stations.

Talgo and Intercity Slower long-distance trains.

Tren de Alta Velocidad Española (AVE) High-speed trains that link Madrid with Albacete, Barcelona, Burgos, Córdoba, Cuenca, Huesca, Lerida, Málaga, Seville, Valencia, Valladolid and Zaragoza. There are also Barcelona–Seville and Barcelona–Málaga services. In coming years Madrid–Cádiz and Madrid–Bilbao should also come on line.

Trenhotel Overnight trains with sleeper berths.

CLASSES & COSTS

All long-distance trains have 2nd and 1st classes, known as *turista* and *preferente*, respectively. The latter is 20% to 40% more expensive.

Fares vary enormously depending on the service (faster trains cost considerably more) and, in the case of some high-speed services such as the AVE, on the time and day of travel. Tickets for AVE trains are by far the most expensive. A one-way trip in 2nd class from Madrid to Barcelona (on which route only AVE trains run) could cost as much as €139 (it could work out significantly cheaper if you book well in advance).

Children aged between four and 12 years are entitled to a 40% discount; those aged under four travel for free (except on high-speed trains, for which they pay the same as those aged four to 12). Buying a return ticket often gives you a 10% to 20% discount on the return trip. Students and people up to 25 years of age with a Euro<26 Card (Carnet Joven in Spain) are entitled to 20% to 25% off most ticket prices.

On overnight trips within Spain on *trenhoteles* it's worth paying extra for a *litera* (couchette; a sleeping berth in a six- or four-bed compartment) or, if available, single or double cabins in *preferente* or *gran clase* class. The cost depends on the class of accommodation, type of train and length of journey. The lines covered are Madrid–A Coruña, Barcelona–Córdoba–Seville, Barcelona–Madrid (and on to Lisbon) and Barcelona–Málaga, as well as international services to France.

A Memorable Northern Train Journey

The romantically inclined could opt for an opulent and slow-moving, old-time rail adventure in the colourful north of Spain.

Catch the **Transcantábrico** (www.transcantabrico.feve.es) for a journey on a picturesque narrow-gauge rail route, from Santiago de Compostela (by bus as far as O Ferrol) via Oviedo, Santander and Bilbao along the coast, and then a long inland stretch to finish in León. The eight-day trip costs up to €3900 per person (you can shave €150 off the price by booking more than six months in advance), and can also be done in reverse. There are just six or seven departures a year, which works out almost monthly from May to September. The package includes various visits along the way, including the Museo Guggenheim in Bilbao, the Museo de Altamira, Santillana del Mar, and the Covadonga lakes in the Picos de Europa. The food is as pleasurable for the palate as the sights are for the eyes, with some meals being eaten on board but most in various locations.

The trains don't travel at night, making sleeping aboard easy and providing the opportunity to stay out at night.

Language

Spanish pronunciation is not difficult as most of its sounds are also found in English. You can read our pronunciation guides below as if they were English and you'll be understood just fine. And if you pronounce 'th' in our guides with a lisp and 'kh' as a throaty sound, you'll even sound like a real Spanish person.

To enhance your trip with a phrasebook, visit **lonelyplanet.com**. Lonely Planet iPhone phrasebooks are available through the Apple App store.

BASICS

Hello.
Hola. — *o*·la

How are you?
¿Qué tal? — ke tal

I'm fine, thanks.
Bien, gracias. — byen *gra*·thyas

Excuse me. (to get attention)
Disculpe. — dees·*kool*·pe

Yes./No.
Sí./No. — see/no

Thank you.
Gracias. — *gra*·thyas

You're welcome./That's fine.
De nada. — de *na*·da

Goodbye. /See you later.
Adiós./Hasta luego. — a·*dyos*/*as*·ta *lwe*·go

Do you speak English?
¿Habla inglés? — *a*·bla een·*gles*

I don't understand.
No entiendo. — no en·*tyen*·do

How much is this?
¿Cuánto cuesta? — *kwan*·to *kwes*·ta

Can you reduce the price a little?
¿Podría bajar un poco el precio? — po·*dree*·a ba·*khar* oon *po*·ko el *pre*·thyo

ACCOMMODATION

I'd like to make a booking.
Quisiera reservar una habitación. — kee·*sye*·ra re·ser·*var* *oo*·na a·bee·ta·*thyon*

How much is it per night?
¿Cuánto cuesta por noche? — *kwan*·to *kwes*·ta por *no*·che

EATING & DRINKING

I'd like ..., please.
Quisiera ..., por favor. — kee·*sye*·ra ... por fa·*vor*

That was delicious!
¡Estaba buenísimo! — es·*ta*·ba bwe·*nee*·see·mo

Bring the bill/check, please.
La cuenta, por favor. — la *kwen*·ta por fa·*vor*

I'm allergic to ...
Soy alérgico/a al ... (m/f) — soy a·*ler*·khee·ko/a al ...

I don't eat ...
No como ... — no *ko*·mo ...

chicken	*pollo*	*po*·lyo
fish	*pescado*	pes·*ka*·do
meat	*carne*	*kar*·ne

EMERGENCIES

I'm ill.
Estoy enfermo/a. (m/f) — es·*toy* en·*fer*·mo/a

Help!
¡Socorro! — so·*ko*·ro

Call a doctor!
¡Llame a un médico! — *lya*·me a oon *me*·dee·ko

Call the police!
¡Llame a la policía! — *lya*·me a la po·lee·*thee*·a

DIRECTIONS

I'm looking for (a/an/the) ...
Estoy buscando ... — es·*toy* boos·*kan*·do ...

ATM	*un cajero automático*	oon ka·*khe*·ro ow·to·*ma*·tee·ko
bank	*el banco*	el *ban*·ko
... embassy	*la embajada de ...*	la em·ba·*kha*·da de ...
market	*el mercado*	el mer·*ka*·do
museum	*el museo*	el moo·*se*·o
restaurant	*un restaurante*	oon res·tow·*ran*·te
toilet	*los servicios*	los ser·*vee*·thyos
tourist office	*la oficina de turismo*	la o·fee·*thee*·na de too·*rees*·mo

Behind the Scenes

Our Readers

Many thanks to the travellers who used the last edition and wrote to us with helpful hints, useful advice and interesting anecdotes: Virginia Keizer, Terri Sofarelli.

Author Thanks

STUART BUTLER

First and foremost I must once again thank my wife Heather for all her love and support and my young son, Jake, for putting up with daddy being away so much – and to them both for their help in such devotion to researching the *pintxos* of San Sebastián and Bilbao. Thank you also to all my co-authors on this book's Big Brother, *Spain*, and also to Toni Vichez in Seville and Andrea Fitzjones. Finally, Gracias to all the tourist office staff, hotel and restaurant owners and everyone else who helped out with my chapters.

Acknowledgments

Climate map data adapted from Peel MC, Finlayson BL & McMahon TA (2007) 'Updated World Map of the Köppen-Geiger Climate Classificatio n', Hydrology and Earth System Sciences, 11, 1633-44.
Illustrations p78-81, p208-9, p262-3, p272-3 and p306-7 by Javier Zarracina.

Cover photographs: Front: Plaza de España facade, Seville, Andalucia, Christopher Groenhout/Getty Images ©; Back: Cadaqués, Costa Brava, Catalonia, Gerth Roland/Alamy ©

This Book

This 3rd edition of Lonely Planet's Discover Spain guidebook was written by Stuart Butler. The content was researched and written by Stuart along with Anthony Ham, Anna Kaminski, John Noble, Miles Roddis, Brendan Sainsbury, Regis St Louis and Andy Symington. This guidebook was commissioned in Lonely Planet's London office, and produced by the following:

Commissioning Editor Dora Whitaker
Coordinating Editors Samantha Forge, Lorna Parkes
Coordinating Cartographer Andy Rojas
Coordinating Layout Designer Katherine Marsh
Managing Editors Annelies Mertens, Angela Tinson
Managing Cartographers Alison Lyall, Anthony Phelan
Managing Layout Designers Chris Girdler, Jane Hart
Assisting Editor Kate Kiely
Cover Research Naomi Parker
Internal Image Research Claire Gibson
Language Content Branislava Vladisavljevic
Thanks to Sasha Baskett, Ryan Evans, Larissa Frost, Jouve India, Asha Ioculari, Trent Paton, Raphael Richards, Jessica Rose, Luna Soo, Gerard Walker

SEND US YOUR FEEDBACK

We love to hear from travellers – your comments keep us on our toes and help make our books better. Our well-travelled team reads every word on what you loved or loathed about this book. Although we cannot reply individually to postal submissions, we always guarantee that your feedback goes straight to the appropriate authors, in time for the next edition. Each person who sends us information is thanked in the next edition, the most useful submissions are rewarded with a selection of digital PDF chapters.

Visit **lonelyplanet.com/contact** to submit your updates and suggestions or to ask for help. Our award-winning website also features inspirational travel stories, news and discussions.

Note: We may edit, reproduce and incorporate your comments in Lonely Planet products such as guidebooks, websites and digital products, so let us know if you don't want your comments reproduced or your name acknowledged. For a copy of our privacy policy visit lonelyplanet.com/privacy.

Index

A

B

000 Map pages

000 Map pages

C

D

E

F

G

H

I

J

K

L

M

000 Map pages

N

O

P

Q

R

000 Map pages

S

T

U

V

W

Z

NOTES

How to Use This Book

These symbols will help you find the listings you want:

- Sights
- Beaches
- Activities
- Courses
- Tours
- Festivals & Events
- Sleeping
- Eating
- Drinking
- Entertainment
- Shopping
- Information/ Transport

These symbols give you the vital information for each listing:

- Telephone Numbers
- Opening Hours
- Parking
- Nonsmoking
- Air-Conditioning
- Internet Access
- Wi-Fi Access
- Swimming Pool
- Vegetarian Selection
- English-Language Menu
- Family-Friendly
- Pet-Friendly
- Bus
- Ferry
- Metro
- Subway
- Tram
- Train

Reviews are organised by author preference.

Look out for these icons:

FREE No payment required

A green or sustainable option

Our authors have nominated these places as demonstrating a strong commitment to sustainability – for example by supporting local communities and producers, operating in an environmentally friendly way, or supporting conservation projects.

Map Legend

Sights

- Beach
- Buddhist
- Castle
- Christian
- Hindu
- Islamic
- Jewish
- Monument
- Museum/Gallery
- Ruin
- Winery/Vineyard
- Zoo
- Other Sight

Activities, Courses & Tours

- Diving/Snorkelling
- Canoeing/Kayaking
- Skiing
- Surfing
- Swimming/Pool
- Walking
- Windsurfing
- Other Activity/ Course/Tour

Sleeping

- Sleeping
- Camping

Eating

- Eating

Drinking

- Drinking
- Cafe

Entertainment

- Entertainment

Shopping

- Shopping

Information

- Post Office
- Tourist Information

Transport

- Airport
- Border Crossing
- Bus
- Cable Car/ Funicular
- Cycling
- Ferry
- Monorail
- Parking
- S-Bahn
- Taxi
- Train/Railway
- Tram
- Tube Station
- U-Bahn
- Underground Train Station
- Other Transport

Routes

- Tollway
- Freeway
- Primary
- Secondary
- Tertiary
- Lane
- Unsealed Road
- Plaza/Mall
- Steps
- Tunnel
- Pedestrian Overpass
- Walking Tour
- Walking Tour Detour
- Path

Boundaries

- International
- State/Province
- Disputed
- Regional/Suburb
- Marine Park
- Cliff
- Wall

Population

- Capital (National)
- Capital (State/Province)
- City/Large Town
- Town/Village

Geographic

- Hut/Shelter
- Lighthouse
- Lookout
- Mountain/Volcano
- Oasis
- Park
- Pass
- Picnic Area
- Waterfall

Hydrography

- River/Creek
- Intermittent River
- Swamp/Mangrove
- Reef
- Canal
- Water
- Dry/Salt/ Intermittent Lake
- Glacier

Areas

- Beach/Desert
- Cemetery (Christian)
- Cemetery (Other)
- Park/Forest
- Sportsground
- Sight (Building)
- Top Sight (Building)

MILES RODDIS

Catalonia & Eastern Spain Miles and his wife, Ingrid, have lived for over 20 years in a shoebox-sized apartment in the Barrio del Carmen, Valencia's oldest and most vital quarter. He's the author or coauthor of more than 50 Lonely Planet guidebooks, including *Valencia & the Costa Blanca*, *Valencia Encounter*, *Walking in Spain*, *Canary Islands* and seven editions of *Spain*. He loves Fallas about twice a decade, and gets the hell out of town in intervening years.

BRENDAN SAINSBURY

Seville & Andalucía's Hill Towns, Granada & Andalucía's South Coast An expat Brit, now living near Vancouver, Canada, Brendan once worked in Andalucía as a guide leading cultural and hiking trips in the hills of Grazalema. He fell unashamedly for the region's romantic charms when he met his future wife in a small white village near Ronda in 2003. He's been back numerous times since, and has developed a special passion for flamenco guitar and the city of Granada. Brendan also writes for Lonely Planet on Cuba, Italy and Mexico.

REGIS ST LOUIS

Barcelona Regis first fell in love with Catalunya on a grand journey across Iberia in the late 1990s. Subsequent trips cemented his relationship with Barcelona, one of his favourite cities on the planet. Memorable outings from his most recent trip include morning runs in Barceloneta, evening concerts in the Ciutat Vella and feasting on perhaps the last calçots of the season. Regis is also the author of *Barcelona*, and he has contributed to dozens of other Lonely Planet titles. He lives in Brooklyn, New York.

Read more about Regis at:
lonelyplanet.com/members/regisstlouis

ANDY SYMINGTON

Madrid & Around Andy hails from Australia but has been living in Spain for over a decade, where, to shatter a couple of stereotypes of the country, he can frequently be found huddled in sub-zero temperatures watching the tragically poor local football team. He has authored and co-authored many Lonely Planet guidebooks and other publications on Spain and elsewhere; in his spare time he walks in the mountains, embarks on epic tapas trails, and co-bosses a rock bar.

Our Story

A beat-up old car, a few dollars in the pocket and a sense of adventure. In 1972 that's all Tony and Maureen Wheeler needed for the trip of a lifetime – across Europe and Asia overland to Australia. It took several months, and at the end – broke but inspired – they sat at their kitchen table writing and stapling together their first travel guide, *Across Asia on the Cheap*. Within a week they'd sold 1500 copies. Lonely Planet was born.

Today, Lonely Planet has offices in Melbourne, London, Oakland and Delhi, with more than 600 staff and writers. We share Tony's belief that 'a great guidebook should do three things: inform, educate and amuse'.

Our Writers

STUART BUTLER

Coordinating author, Camino de Santiago & Basque Spain, Catalonia & Eastern Spain Stuart's first childhood encounters with Spain, in Parque Nacional de Doñana and on family holidays along the north coast, left lasting impressions. When he was older he spent every summer on the Basque beaches until one day he found himself unable to tear himself away – he has been there ever since. His travels for Lonely Planet, and various surf magazines, have taken him beyond Spain to the shores of the Arctic, the deserts of Asia and the forests of Africa. His website is stuartbutlerjournalist.com.

Read more about Stuart at:
lonelyplanet.com/members/stuartbutler

ANTHONY HAM

Madrid & Around, Catalonia & Eastern Spain In 2001 Anthony fell in love with Madrid on his first visit to the city. Less than a year later, he arrived on a one-way ticket, with not a word of Spanish and not knowing a single person. Having recently passed the 10-year mark in Madrid, he still adores his adopted city as much as the first day he arrived. When he's not writing for Lonely Planet, Anthony writes about and photographs Spain, Africa and the Middle East for newspapers and magazines around the world.

ANNA KAMINSKI

Catalonia & Eastern Spain Anna's love affair with Spain began in 2001 during a summer Spanish course in Santander and continued, unabated, in spite of a nasty bout of salmonella. Over the last decade she has found herself returning every year, both for research and pleasure – be it to hike in the Pyrenees, kitesurf in Tarifa, or go tapas bar-hopping in San Sebastián, Granada and Madrid. Memorable moments from her most recent trip include almost running out of petrol on a lonely mountain road and visiting the former home of the late, great Dalí. Anna currently calls Barcelona home.

JOHN NOBLE

Camino de Santiago & Basque Spain John, originally from England's Ribble Valley, has lived in an Andalucian mountain village since 1995. In that time he has travelled lengthily all over Spain and helped write every edition of Lonely Planet's Spain and Andalucía guides. He loves returning to far-away parts of the country like Galicia and the north coast, with their completely different landscapes, climate, people and culture, and being reminded just how diverse Spain is.

Read more about John at:
lonelyplanet.com/members/ewoodrover

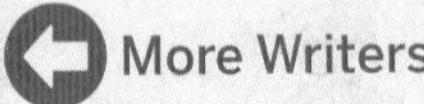

More Writers

Published by Lonely Planet Publications Pty Ltd
ABN 36 005 607 983
3rd edition – May 2013
ISBN 978 1 74220 573 1

10 9 8 7 6 5 4 3 2 1
Printed in China